Post-Cold War Russia and the Missed Opportunity for Global Stability

Sergey Aleksashenko

Post-Cold War Russia and the Missed Opportunity for Global Stability

The Faded Chance

Springer

Sergey Aleksashenko
New Eurasian Strategies Centre
London, UK

ISBN 978-3-032-01379-8 ISBN 978-3-032-01380-4 (eBook)
https://doi.org/10.1007/978-3-032-01380-4

This Springer imprint is published by the registered company Springer Nature Switzerland AG
The registered company address is: Gewerbestrasse 11, 6330 Cham, Switzerland

Introduction

The issue of aid to the Soviet Union, first of all, was one in which there was not a great deal of difference within the administration. Or, indeed, among most of the allies. In the course of '90 and, perhaps, into '91, Germany had given something like 15 billion dollars in aid to the Soviet Union - which disappeared, as far as we could figure out, without a trace… There was little thought about serious assistance before the Soviet Union - and subsequently Russia - adopted an economic program that assured that any money given would stick to the program - would be used for the intended purposes instead of just ending up in Switzerland. We never had that assurance. The absence of significant Western aid, which could have potentially catalyzed change, was a missed opportunity.

Brent Scowcroft
National Security Advisor to President George H W Bush[1]

On October 25, 1917, a coup d'état took place in Russia—armed detachments toppled the Provisional Government. The Bolshevik Party, led by Vladimir Lenin, seized most seats in the newly formed government. Two and a half months later, the Bolsheviks dispersed the Constituent Assembly, a Russian representative body created to determine the state structure after the fall of the monarchy. From that time onward, Russia began a grandiose socio-political experiment in state-building based on utopian principles of equality and collective ownership. Very soon, the declared state of workers and peasants was transformed into a rigid ideological dictatorship that existed for almost three-quarters of a century.

During this time, the state, which was named the Soviet Union or USSR in 1922, expelled much of its intellectual and governmental elite and repressed

[1] Miller Center. George H.W. Bush Presidency. Brent Scowcroft Oral History Part II.

tens of millions of its citizens; several million were executed, died in prisons, or were exiled.[2] Over the years, the Soviet Union initiated military operations on the territory of neighboring states at least a dozen times, aimed at seizing territory and/or changing political regimes. By the end of its existence, the Soviet Union spent more than ten percent of its national income on military purposes and possessed the largest arsenal of conventional and nuclear weapons, actively supplying arms to friendly regimes around the world. The Soviet Union created an economic system in which the countries of Eastern Europe were involved, and which was almost completely isolated from world trade and international financial relations, in which the state owned all production assets and set prices and wages at its discretion, and in which there was no competition and numerous monopolies.

From the mid-1960s onward, the Soviet economy's technological backwardness became increasingly apparent: while capable of producing devastating weapon systems, the Soviet Union was unable to produce basic consumer goods, and its agriculture could not produce enough food, forcing it to increase imports of grain and meat. Most large industrial enterprises were built with technology and equipment purchased abroad.

By the early 1980s, economic growth had virtually stopped, and the Soviet leadership, dominated by elderly politicians who remained in office until their deaths, could not grasp the scale of the problems that had arisen and identify their causes. The term "stagnation," which came to designate this period of Soviet history, defined the economic and political life in the country with grim accuracy. This economic stagnation was a source of frustration and a symbol of the country's lack of progress.

The situation began to change in 1985, when one of the next generation of politicians, 54-year-old Mikhail Gorbachev, came to the helm of the state. On the one hand, Gorbachev, who had risen rapidly to power, fully shared the communist ideology and dreamed of building a "bright future" in the Soviet Union. On the other hand, he, until the age of 47, had spent his entire life, except for his time at Moscow University, in Stavropol Krai, one of Russia's most fertile regions, and could see with his own eyes how inefficient the Soviet system was. This conflict—ideological blindness and the realization of the system's ineffectiveness—shadowed Gorbachev throughout his years in power.

---

[2] To date, there are no official statistics on political repression in Russia. Anatoly Vishnevsky, Russia's foremost demographer, estimates that between 35 and 40 million Soviet citizens were subjected to political repression, of whom between one and two million were shot, and between three and five million died in prisons and exile. "Remembering '37." Demoscope Weekly. December 10–31, 2007. Institute of Demography. Higher School of Economics, Moscow. https://www.demoscope.ru/weekly/2007/0313/s_map.php#1.

Once he became the first person in the state, he found that he needed ideas on his desk about what needed to be done or what could be done. However, there were no people around him who could offer him such ideas. He became convinced it was possible to build "socialism with a human face"—preserving communist ideals while dismantling barriers to growth, enshrining political rights in the constitution, and abandoning the arms race in favor of peaceful relations.

Internal conflict and the absence of a cohesive team able to devise a comprehensive plan to transform the country left Gorbachev's domestic reforms incoherent and inconsistent, often destroying elements of the old system without building the supporting framework of the new one.

The 67 years that passed from October 1917 to Gorbachev's arrival in the Kremlin are the span of nearly three human generations. By the mid-1980s, not only did no one in the country remember how a political or economic system other than the Soviet one could be built, but there were also no people who could at least roughly chart the course the country needed to follow to make it sustainable and prosperous.

The ideological pressure of the Communists in the USSR left no room for the creation of alternative political parties and for the emergence of political leaders capable of offering their principles and programs to society. The political process relied on colorful personalities who had no support from below. Any decisions were eventually made based on agreements and compromises between individual politicians and were presented to the population "on a silver platter." The population was only required to be politically active for large rallies held once every few months. The logic of the country's transformation was determined from above and was not a reaction to pressure from below.

The only idea that could be easily proposed and justified, which could quickly attract supporters and be the basis for the political process, was nationalism, which was rapidly gaining strength in all the union republics that made up the USSR and whose names necessarily contained an indication of the national identity of the population. The thesis "All problems are because of Moscow" was very simple, and, most importantly, it also contained a recipe for solving problems—independence.

The nationalist movement began to grow rapidly in the Baltic republics, which were finally annexed by the Soviet Union after World War II and where the memory of the possibility of "living differently" remained very strong. In mid-1990, it was dramatically accelerated by the election of Boris Yeltsin as leader of the Russian parliament, who, after the failure of an attempt to create a joint program of economic reforms (the "500 Days" program), began an intense power struggle with Gorbachev. The tug of war was rapidly undermining the country's economy and political structure.

In August 1991, the conservatives surrounding Gorbachev in the Soviet leadership attempted a coup d'état,[3] which failed largely due to Yeltsin's active position. The August putsch marked the end of the USSR—the Soviet system could not withstand the internal contradictions and collapsed under their weight. Legally, the Soviet Union existed for another four months. It seemed to many that the Soviet republics, having proclaimed their sovereignty and independence after the putsch, were trying to agree on a new configuration of the state, but it would be more precise to say that everyone was waiting to see who would make the first decisive step. Ukraine took this step by holding a referendum on December 1 and declaring its impossibility to continue being part of a single state.

On December 25, 1991, Gorbachev announced his resignation as President of the USSR, and the country ceased to exist. The Russian Federation became independent, declaring its desire to build a democratic, federative state that renounces the use of force in international relations.

Eight years later, on December 31, 1999, Vladimir Putin became acting President of Russia, holding supreme power in Russia in his hands ever since. In a quarter of a century, Putin has subjugated all branches of government, built a regime of personal dictatorship, destroyed political competition and freedom of speech, and turned the country into a de facto unitary state. The political regime Putin has built is far more brutal than the one that existed in the Soviet Union on the eve of Gorbachev's reforms: the number of political prisoners is in the hundreds, several thousand political activists have been forced to flee the country under threat of prosecution on invented charges, the country has re-established the most brutal political censorship, violation of which can result in years of imprisonment, and political opponents and civil activists are deprived of the right to a fair and just trial.

Just sixteen and a half years after the collapse of the Soviet Union, on August 8, 2008, the Russian army invaded neighboring Georgia. It established its control over South Ossetia, which proclaimed itself an independent state on the Kremlin's short leash. Another five and a half years later, in February–March 2014, the Russian Federation used its armed forces to annex the Ukrainian peninsula of Crimea, after which it initiated a separatist insurgency in eastern Ukraine that killed more than 14,000 people.

[3] The leaders of the August putsch were the Soviet vice president, the prime minister, the ministers of defense and internal affairs, the head of the KGB (political police), and the head of the defense department of the Communist Party Central Committee.

A further eight years later, on February 24, 2022, the Russian army carried out a full-scale invasion of Ukraine, occupying one-fifth of the neighboring country's territory. The war in Ukraine, which is ongoing as I write these lines, has claimed the lives of 200,000–250,000 people. Several hundred thousand soldiers on both sides have sustained disabling injuries; several million Ukrainian citizens have been displaced from their homes, and many have been forced to leave the country. The material damage to Ukraine runs into hundreds of billions of dollars.

The above evidence is sufficient to conclude that the Russian transformation attempt of the 1990s was a failure and that it resulted in a more violent and aggressive state. The questions—Why did this happen? What went wrong? Who is to blame?—are asked by many in Russia and abroad, but there are no answers that most people can agree on. The easiest thing to do is to use a soccer analogy and say: the coach wins, the team loses. This statement would be closest to the truth, but only some people are satisfied with this answer. Continuing with the soccer analogy—Which mistakes did the goalkeeper make? How many scoring chances did the forwards fail to capitalize on? How many times did the defenders concede in one-on-one battles?

In this book, I will continue my search for answers to these questions, which I began in "Battle for the Ruble," dedicated to the events of 1994–1998, and continued in "Counterrevolution," where I analyzed the changes that have taken place in Russia during the reign of Vladimir Putin. This time, I decided not only to focus on the period 1990–1995, which, in my opinion, largely shaped subsequent history but also to explore a narrower question: why the Western countries and primarily the United States did not come to Russia's aid and did not dare to involve it in their economic and political orbit, as happened with Germany and Japan after the end of World War II?

The similarity of the starting situation—1945 for Germany and Japan, 1991 for Russia—in the three countries is striking. Germany and Japan were defeated in World War II, capitulated to the Allies, and had to rebuild state structures; the essential requirement was the demilitarization of society, politics, and economy. The Soviet Union, unable to withstand the confrontation in the Cold War, ceased to exist, and the emerging Russian Federation had to build a state from scratch, promising to reduce military expenditures and abandon an aggressive foreign policy drastically. Most of the population had serious problems accessing food and essential goods. A whole range of negative emotions—disappointment, resentment, hatred, misunderstanding of the essence of what was happening—filled the public consciousness and transformed into a deep depression. Each of the three countries lost a significant part of its territory[4] and faced an influx of refugees/migrants from neighboring countries. Family and human ties were broken as millions of families were forced to leave their homes and seek a haven. The economies of each country had been heavily skewed toward war production. The cessation of armaments and ammunition production freed up large amounts of skilled labor and production capacity that had no use for them. The economies of each of the three countries were firmly integrated into local economic ties, being importers of raw materials and semi-finished products and exporters of processed products, and each of the three economies was shut out of such cooperation, which caused a sharp decline in production and living standards. The three economies lost export earnings and several years could not pay for necessary imports. Each country faced the threat of famine, which could only be overcome by massive foreign aid. Each country faced destabilization of the financial system and high inflation, which was very difficult to overcome in a devastated economy.

Each country was an open political adversary to the United States, the only difference being that Germany and Japan fought a hot war, while the Soviet Union fought a cold war, with numerous limited military confrontations between the opposing superpowers. After the defeat, each of the defeated countries expressed a willingness to build friendly relations with the United States, although the motivations for this decision varied.

In two cases, Germany and Japan, the transformation was successful: both countries received enormous aid from the US budget, which allowed them to rebuild their economic potential and create a foundation for rapid growth: in 1950, Western Germany's GNP exceeded its 1937 level[5]; a year later Japan's GNP exceeded its 1934–1936 level[6]. In the early 1950s, the economies of both countries surpassed their prewar levels of development; ten years after the end of the war, both countries became members of economic and political-military alliances created by the United States; and a couple of decades later, Japan and Germany became the largest economies in the world.

In the case of Russia, nothing similar happened. The country received little economic assistance from Western countries, and much of its accumulated industrial potential needed to be claimed and recovered. It took Russia 15 years to surpass the GDP level achieved during the Soviet era, and the Soviet level of industrial production was surpassed only 27 years after the collapse of

[4] Germany lost approximately 25% of its 1937 territory, Japan—18%, and Russia/USSR—23%.

[5] Hoffmann, W.G. und Muller, J.H. Das deutsche Volkseinkommen 1851-1957. Mohr, Tubingen, 1959. Statistical tables located at https://search.gesis.org/research_data/ZA8224.

[6] Warren S. Hunsberger. Japan. New Industrial Giant. American-Asian Educational Exchange, 1972, p. 74.

the USSR. Russia did not gain access to the World Trade Organization until 2012, by which time the place of its economy in the global division of labor was limited to the supply of raw materials and primary processed products, which accounted for three-quarters of exports. The Berlin Wall dividing Europe into East and West came down in 1989; five years later, the last Russian soldiers left their barracks in Germany, but a year after that, the United States decided to expand NATO which drew a new dividing line in Europe, dashing the hopes of Russian politicians for partnership and leading to the arrival of Yevgeny Primakov as Russian foreign minister of a politician who had never been sympathetic to the United States and opposed any efforts to build closer relations with that country. Why did this happen?

Why, having the "technology" of turning an adversary into an ally, the "technology" of restoring the economic potential of a country devastated by war, did American politicians not seize the chance? Why in 1995, just three years after the first presidential summit, did Russia and America move from the dream of building allied relations first to a pragmatic partnership, then to a competitive confrontation, and finally to a hybrid war, which turned out to be much closer to an open military conflict than the Cold War confrontation?

The easiest way to answer these questions is to say that unlike Germany and Japan, which were occupied and effectively deprived of state autonomy after the war, the occupying authorities made many decisions regarding state structure and economic policy. Russia was an independent state, and no one could impose their recommendations. Besides, not many Russian politicians wanted a partnership with America, few of them supported Yeltsin's pro-Western initiatives, and the military-industrial complex was strong enough in Russia to convince the Russian President that Russia had its geopolitical interests, which could be defended only by having strong armed forces and military potential sufficient to resist the West, whose only dream was the destruction of Russia. And many of these arguments would be valid.

We can also add that the denial of economic support for Gorbachev's reforms was because the Soviet leader never decided to give up state control of prices, without which it was impossible to build a market economy. Neither the Western leaders were sure that the money they could give to USSR/Russia would be used properly and not evaporate in the black hole. Indeed, Russia was inconsistent in its economic reforms, the parliament did not support Yeltsin's reform course, and how and why help someone who does not want to help himself? It can be remembered that the personnel policy of the Russian President was built on the desire to create conflicts and friction in his entourage, which made it easier to control the political process, and, in general,

Yeltsin did not want to see many strong reformers in his team. That is why he so easily parted with Yegor Gaidar, Boris Fedorov, Sergey Dubinin, and Alexander Shokhin, but constantly nominated anti-reformist representatives of "red directors" Oleg Lobov, Oleg Soskovets, Georgy Khizha, and Alexander Zaveriukha to the top of the government. And all this played a role in the fact that the Russian reforms turned out to be so protracted and painful.

But all of the above does not answer the question of why Clinton decided to expand NATO, even though the US military saw no threat from Russia and, on the contrary, said that they were able to build trusting professional relations with their Russian colleagues, and all analysts monitoring the situation in Russia unanimously said that this decision would sharply increase anti-American sentiment in the Russian political elite, where no one understands the benefits of this decision. Attempts to find someone in the Bush or Clinton administrations who could articulate the goals of US policy toward Russia and identify the tools that could help achieve them will be unsuccessful. Although State Department leaders knew the term "Marshall Plan," archival records reveal no substantive debates or objections to considering a comparable program for Russia. The above arguments say nothing about the reasons for the limited US budget assistance to Russia and other CIS countries in 1992–1995, which amounted to only $13.3 billion, of which about half was grain loans due for repayment in two years, and about 30% was so-called technical assistance, the recipients of which were US consultants. Similarly, the question remains unanswered as to why Russia did not receive a partial cancellation of its foreign debt from the G7 members, but, on the contrary, in the first years of reforms, it was demanded to make payments to service Soviet debts that exceeded the loans of international financial organizations.

The emerging conclusion is strikingly simple: Russia failed to receive Marshall-Plan-level support because no major actor believed it deserved one. Although the Soviet Union was gone and America proclaimed its victory in the Cold War, Russia was seen as an unstable country whose political future was uncertain and whose assistance risked reviving the Russian war machine. This view was openly shared by key figures in the Bush administration and persisted into the Clinton administration. Clinton was committed to building friendly relations with Russia when he came to the White House, and his personal relationship with Yeltsin was very warm, but he was much less interested in foreign policy than in the domestic situation. This led to the fact that he did not develop a vision of how to build relations with Russia, and most of his decisions and actions were situational, i.e., aimed at untangling numerous knots in the relations between the two countries.

Yegor Gaidar, the architect of the initial stage of Russian economic reforms, reflecting on the successes and failures of that time, said: "*I do not think that the leaders of the leading Western powers ignored the magnitude of the alternative they faced.*[7] *The main trouble, in my opinion, was that no leader was capable of playing an organizing, coordinating role like that played by G Truman and A* Marshall *in the post-war period in the reconstruction of Europe.*" While I fully agree with the second part of his assessment, I cannot support him in the first.

Reading numerous pages of archival documents, transcripts of negotiations, and memories of participants of the events, I have not found evidence that any of them put on the table an adequate assessment of the situation in the Russian economy, an analysis of the causes and recipes for a way out. When Michel Camdessus, head of the IMF, unexpectedly learned in the spring of 1992 that his organization was to take responsibility for supporting economic transformation in the post-Soviet space, he gave an estimate of the financial resources that might be required for the task—$150 billion over four years for twelve countries (not including the Baltics). Although the IMF had minimal knowledge of the economies of the post-Soviet countries (none of which were members by then), and this estimate was made over a few days and arguably could not stand up to critical analysis, the organization had a track record of financial stabilization in dozens of countries, including Eastern European countries that had begun their reforms earlier than Russia. Though the discussion on the IMF quota increases which could give the Fund extra-resources was launched, the Western leaders did not find it necessary to discuss the magnitude of Camdessus's request. Having failed to get support for its proposals, the IMF refused to consider Russia as a special case for the next couple of years, insisting on applying its standard programs, principles, and procedures.

The primary purpose of this book is not to name a culprit for the failure of Russian reforms and certainly not to assign this role to Western countries. History allows no what-ifs, and arguments about missed opportunities are nothing more than mind games. When a soccer match is lost, the team is to blame for the loss. But even a not-very-strong team with a not-very-good coach, after a lost game, makes sure that mistakes are analyzed to avoid repeating them in the next game. Real life is not a soccer championship; history never repeats itself, putting politicians in a unique situation each time. But just as in soccer, politicians must often look back at their predecessors when making decisions, remembering their successes and failures and scrutinizing their mistakes.

---

[7] Yegor Gaidar. Dni porazhenij i pobed. (*Days of defeats and victories.*) Moscow, Vagrius, 1996, p. 181.

Putin's unleashed war of aggression against Ukraine will eventually end. At some point, Putin will be out of political life forever and will not influence decision-making in Russia. It is possible that even after that, Russia will want to continue its hybrid war with the West, as the Cold War continued after Stalin's death, Khrushchev's ouster, Brezhnev's death, and Gorbachev's arrival. But undoubtedly, at some point, there will be people at the helm of power in Moscow for whom the scenario of normalization of relations with the West will be acceptable or even desirable—the long-term losses to Russia from the continuation of Putin's policy are too obvious, and their severity will only grow with time.

At that moment, history will give the West another chance to get out of the dangerous military and political confrontation in Europe, a chance to turn Russia from an adversary into an ally. I do not know when it will happen, but I know it will happen for sure. In order not to miss this chance, politicians and experts need to be ready to use the window of opportunity that has arisen—one that is closing much sooner than they would like.

The price of another missed chance may be much higher. We should carefully study the lessons of history to avoid repeating the mistakes made 30 years ago.

* * *

I want to thank those who helped me in my work and especially those who were willing to share some of their memories and emotions—Larry Summers, David Lipton, Dmitry Symes, Peter Aven, Alexander Shokhin, Alfred Koch, Teresa Ter-Minasyan, and John Odling-Smee. My work would have been much more difficult if not for the support of those people who helped me in my search for archival materials—Jason Kaplan and Kelly Hendren from the William J. Clinton Presidential Library, Buffy Hollis from the George H.W. Bush Presidential Library, Mark Levitt and Zoe Dickenson from the IMF Archives, and James Bufton, a former IMF Archives staff member. Communicating with the IMF's "Russian team" has always given me great pleasure, and even today, after many years, conversations with Yusuke Horiguchi and Dan Citrin bring up unexpected details that enrich my picture of the world. Special thanks go to my old friend Boris Lvin, Svetlana Savranskaya of the National Security Archive, Vadim Rozanov, and Suzy Lough who read the manuscript carefully for inaccuracies and to make important critical comments that sometimes made me see events more colorful. And finally, this book could not have happened without the support of my family, whose members not only created opportunities for me to work but also acted as critics (Artem), reviewers (Sergey Jr), literary editors (Katya), and a "moral support" group (Dasha, Alexey, Timur).

Technical Introduction

In working on the book, I relied on documents available in the archives, occasionally using personal recollections and stories told by participants in the events of those years. The primary sources of documents for me were the George H.W. Bush Presidential Library and William J. Clinton's—some of these documents are available on the Internet, and some can only be accessed by working in the archives. Very significant for understanding the situation and the problems faced by the actors during Clinton's presidency was the electronic archive of the US State Department, in which the publicist essays of Strobe Talbott, which he sent to Secretary of State Warren Christopher, deserve special attention. A certain array of documents is available in the electronic archives of the US Federal Reserve, the Wilson Center, and the Margaret Thatcher Foundation. Unfortunately, I was unable to travel to Russia and visit Russian archives while working on this book, which inevitably made my perspective somewhat skewed, but since the focus was on the actions of American politicians, I hope this is not a significant drawback.

In citing sources, I will follow the following principles: footnotes include the document's title, date, and storage place. The following abbreviations will be used:

GBPL&M—George H.W. Bush Presidential Library in College Station (Texas).

GB M&T—George H.W. Bush Presidential Library Electronic Archive of declassified transcripts of conversations and telephone conversations available online at https://bush41library.tamu.edu/archives/memcons-telcons.

WCPL&M—William J. Clinton Presidential Library in Little Rock, Arkansas.

CDL #XXXXXXXXXX—Electronic Archive of the William J. Clinton Presidential Library, located on the Internet at https://clinton.presidentiallibraries.us/items/show/101272. Here is available a huge array of declassified documents, working with which has a certain complexity—the documents are collected in thematic folders (a six-digit number indicates the internal number assigned to them in this archive), the logic of compilation and naming of which is not always well understood; the size of these folders can reach several hundred pages; and they do not contain a list of the documents stored inside.

US DoS—Virtual Reading Room Documents Search, located on the Internet at https://foia.state.gov/Search/Search.aspx. The footnote will include the number of each document assigned to it in this archive, which is as follows: Case F-2017-13804 Doc No C06698129.

NSA—National Security Archive located on the Internet at https://nsarchive.gwu.edu/.

Wilson Center—Wilson Center Virtual Archive, located online at https://digitalarchive.wilsoncenter.org/search.

MTF XXXXXXXXX—The Margaret Thatcher Foundation's Electronic Archive, located on the Internet at https://www.margaretthatcher.org/document/213783 (the six-digit number indicates the internal number assigned to them in this archive).

US DoT—Electronic Archive of the US Department of the Treasury (Press Releases of the United States Department of the Treasury), located on the Internet at https://fraser.stlouisfed.org/title/press-releases-united-states-department-treasury-6111; it collects official communications of the US Department of the Treasury and the text of official speeches of its leaders.

Miller Center—The American Presidents Oral Histories Project, maintained by the Miller Center at the University of Virginia, is located on the Internet at https://millercenter.org/the-presidency/presidential-oral-histories. It contains interviews with US politicians and officials who have been part of the inner circle of US presidents.

PPP—Public Papers of the Presidents of the United States, located on the Internet at https://www.archives.gov/federal-register/publications/presidential-papers.html.

Contents

1

From Enemy to Ally

German Miracle

From September 12 to 16, 1944, US President Franklin Roosevelt and British Prime Minister Winston Churchill met in Quebec City, Canada, for what became known as the Second Quebec Conference. There were still eight months to go before the end of the war in Europe, and although there was no doubt about the Allied victory, no one knew how difficult the final stage of the war would be. Therefore, unsurprisingly, a substantial amount of time was devoted to military topics. By this time, France had been almost wholly liberated, the Allied armies on the Western Front had reached the German border, and politicians realized that it was time to start preparing for postwar life—specifically, for the occupation and design of the Germany's future.

The hatred of the fascist regime, which unleashed the bloodiest war in European history, was combined with hatred of the German state, blamed for starting World War I, and spilled over into animosity toward everything German. The main political goal was simple: to make it so that Germany would not be able to threaten its neighbors and could not start another war. Should Germany remain on the map of Europe? And, if so, within what borders? And if not, what should emerge in its place?

Fragmented and Poor

The question of Germany's postwar future had been discussed by officials in Washington since 1942 and was the subject of debate at meetings of

S. Aleksashenko, *Post-Cold War Russia and the Missed Opportunity for Global Stability*,
https://doi.org/10.1007/978-3-032-01380-4_1

anti-Hitler coalition leaders in Casablanca and Tehran in January and November 1943. However, the main ideas that attracted attention were denazification and demilitarization of the country; economic reconstruction remained off the leaders' radar. A major breakthrough occurred in August 1944, when President Roosevelt announced that Germany would face a long period of occupation at the end of the war. The President's logic was to learn the lessons of World War I, when by offering an armistice and negotiating peace, Berlin evaded occupation, allowing it to prepare for and launch a new war.

Shortly thereafter, during lunch with President Roosevelt, his close friend and Treasury Secretary Henry Morgenthau floated a plan to partition and de-industrialize Germany, which Roosevelt endorsed. No written records of this meeting survived, but in his diary, Morgenthau recorded Roosevelt's passionate statement, "*You must either castrate the German people or threaten them in such a way that they simply cannot reproduce people who want to continue to live as they have lived in the past.*"[1]

After his trip to Europe, Morgenthau brought a plan for the postwar settlement of Germany and agreed in general terms with General Eisenhower, who commanded the Allied forces on the Western Front. This plan became known as the "Morgenthau Plan" and was presented to Roosevelt and Churchill for discussion in Quebec. The plan called for the liquidation of Germany as a single state created by Bismarck: large areas would be transferred to France (Alsace and the southern part of Rhineland-Palatinate), Poland (Silesia and most of East Prussia), the Soviet Union (Königsberg), while the Ruhr would come under international administration. The remaining territory was to be divided into two independent states—North and South Germany—and Austria's independence was to be restored. The main heavy industries were to be destroyed, and in the future, according to Morgenthau's plan, Germany was to become an underdeveloped country, barely able to feed its population.

At the Quebec meeting, the Morgenthau Plan was roundly criticized both by Churchill and his team and by much of Roosevelt's inner circle—experts warned a shrunken Germany could feed only 25 million people[2]—whereupon Roosevelt withdrew his support. A few days after the Quebec meeting ended, Morgenthau's plan leaked to reporters, and Roosevelt gave a clumsy justification: "*About this pastoral, agricultural Germany—it's just nonsense. I*

[1] August 19, 1944. John Morton Blum, ed., From the Morgenthau Diaries (Boston: Houghton Mifflin, 1959): vol. 4, 1387–1388.

[2] In early 1939, before the occupation of Bohemia and Moravia, Germany's population was about 80 million.

didn't approve of anything like that. I'm sure I didn't... I don't remember anything about it at all."[3]

However, the bureaucratic momentum generated by Morgenthau and Eisenhower continued unabated—the military, who were to play significant roles in the future occupation administration, favored the ideas of humiliation and revenge. On Eisenhower's orders, Morgenthau's report was printed in a thousand copies and distributed to the senior officers of the American army. The General stated that sending the document did not mean he supported it, but since no alternative ideas were offered to the military, Morgenthau's concept became firmly entrenched among them.

In February 1945, the Yalta Conference formalized the division of Germany into four zones of occupation and the establishment of a Control Commission with representatives of the four countries. The obvious leaders of the occupation forces in each zone were the military—the fear of armed resistance was in the air—who cared little about economic issues. The only economic subject discussed at Yalta was the question of reparations, which the Soviet Union, having suffered the most significant financial losses during the war, understandably insisted on.

Three weeks before his death, on March 23, 1945, President Roosevelt signed a "Memorandum Concerning American Policy Toward Germany."[4] The document stipulated that the Allies would strive to pursue a coordinated policy but prudently provided that, if agreement could not be reached, the commander of troops in the American zone would be entitled to make independent decisions within the memorandum's basic principles. The document prescribed a policy of demilitarization and decentralization of the economy, for which the heads of the occupation administration were given the right to impose restrictions on the operation of German companies "*to carry out programs of industrial disarmament and demilitarization, reparations and aid to liberated areas.*" In addition, they were to ensure that the standard of living in Germany did not exceed that of the countries it had attacked.

Two weeks after Franklin Roosevelt's death, on April 26, 1945, President Truman signed an updated and expanded version of the memorandum, which was titled "Directive to the Commander of the American Occupation Forces Concerning the Military Government of Germany" and gave Eisenhower full responsibility for postwar life in the American zone of occupation.[5]

[3] Michael Beschloss. The Conquerors: Roosevelt, Truman and the Destruction of Hitler's Germany, 1941–1945. New York: Simon & Schuster, 2002. p. 149.

[4] Foreign Relations of the United States (FRUS): Diplomatic Papers, 1945, vol. III, doc 343.

[5] FRUS: Diplomatic Papers, 1945, vol. III, doc 351.

The economic situation in Germany after the war's end in some elements strongly resembled that which would emerge almost half a century later after the collapse of the Soviet Union. West Germany's territory had shrunk by 52% compared to what it had been before the 1938 Anschluss of Austria. Germany lost more than 10% of its population, but the postwar displacement of Germans from Poland and Czechoslovakia increased the population in West Germany. Anglo-American bombing of Germany caused enormous damage to major German cities, where 40% of dwellings were destroyed,[6] but German industry suffered little damage from Allied air raids, and the overall production capacity exceeded prewar levels, though a substantial part of the industry that had produced war materiel became redundant in the postwar period. Economic ties with the countries of Europe built during recent decades[7] collapsed; European currencies became non-convertible, which was an essential obstacle to relaunching trade within Europe, and Germany's modest prewar exports to hard-currency America disappeared entirely.

New Challenges

In addition, friction and contradictions quickly arose between the recent allies on political and economic issues. The Soviet Union and France were interested in maximizing the reparations received, in the payment of which all four zones had to participate equally. A substantial part of the reparations in favor of the USSR was paid from the US and British occupation zones by supplying equipment from the so-called "reparation fund"—something that was considered excessive for the German economy, which was to be significantly reduced in size and ambition; at the same time, the Soviet Union conditioned the supply of coal and other raw materials, which were extracted in the eastern zone, by increasing the supply of equipment. Simultaneously, with the receipt of agreed reparations, the Soviets intensively dismantled many German factories without reporting the amount of equipment removed, which destroyed ties even between German companies. Each occupation command pursued its own monetary policy, flooding the economy with unbacked currency.

Hopes that the invisible hand of the market and liberal regulation would spark postwar recovery were soon dashed. On the contrary, the situation consistently deteriorated not only in Germany but also in other European countries. France began to introduce industry planning elements; in Great Britain,

---

[6] Ian Kershaw. To Hell and Back: Europe, 1914–1949. New York, Viking, 2015. pp. 470–471, 474.

[7] Before the war, three-quarters of German exports went to European countries.

the railroads, coal mines, and many heavy industry enterprises were nationalized. The weather aggravated the situation: the cold winter of 1945/46 was followed by a summer drought and an even colder winter of 1946/47. On 23 January 1947, heavy snowfalls began in Europe and lasted for several weeks.[8]

The difficult economic situation and the destruction of law enforcement structures, especially the police, led to an increase in crime and growing distrust in the ability of the occupation authorities to maintain order in the country and ensure economic recovery. Faith in the American way of life was visibly crumbling.

The Collapse of Pax Britannica

The United States' long-standing policy of isolationism was bearing fruit—the belief had taken firm hold among American politicians that normal life would return to Europe once it was first restored in Britain. The belief was that, although the global power of Pax Britannica was badly shaken after World War I, its resources would be sufficient to take charge of the European situation. This concept was strangely paired with the US anti-colonial policy, which was vividly manifested not only in the interval between the World Wars but also in the discussions of the leaders of the anti-war coalition countries at Tehran, Yalta, and Potsdam. While London used its colonial possessions to support the metropolis, including through holding the British pound zone, the United States demanded that Britain restore the convertibility of the pound as soon as possible, which, according to American experts, was to enable it to focus its efforts on Europe. However, on the one hand, the British economy had very limited ties with its neighbors on the continent so a reverse "domino effect" from US aid was unlikely; moreover, the loss of its empire stripped London of colonial revenues.

The US aid policy to Britain in the first postwar years was called "financial undermining of the empire." Immediately after the surrender of Germany, the US stopped deliveries of non-military goods and demanded that London pay in full for the stocks of goods that had been delivered to Britain but had not yet been distributed, as well as pay the cost of buildings and structures constructed by the American expeditionary forces in the country. The short delay in stopping Lend-Lease until victory and the war's end with Japan did little to relieve the ally, who was required to make immediate payments. London was required to give up tariff protection for the markets of countries within the

[8]Temperatures in the UK were below freezing for three weeks, paralyzing road and rail traffic.

empire's perimeter, which expanded export opportunities from the US but simultaneously reduced Britain's ability to maintain its export revenues. The loss of the merchant navy during the war increased the cost of exporting British goods and decreased revenues from the provision of transportation services, which were a significant part of the balance-of-payments revenues. By the outbreak of World War I, Britain's national debt was just over 25% of GDP; by 1923, it had ballooned to 180%, falling to 110% of GDP by 1940. By the end of the World War II, the Britain's public debt exceeded 240% of GDP.[9] According to John Maynard Keynes, the country had to increase its exports by unrealistic 75% over prewar levels to escape the debt crisis. For 1946–1947, London requested $6 billion in aid from Washington almost entirely in the form of grants. No one in the American capital was prepared for such generosity—the ally, whose economy had been crushed by the war, received a $3.75 billion loan and a $650 million loan to pay off Lend–Lease obligations.[10] London received another $1.25 billion in loans from Canada.[11]

But other European countries needed American financial support as well: from mid-1945 to the end of 1947, they received more than $6.5 billion in US grants and a further $8.5 billion in loans funded by the US budget.[12,13]

Soviet Expansion

Economic problems were overlaid with political issues—the Soviet Union was slowly but steadily "chewing up" the occupied countries of Eastern Europe, gradually ousting politicians who disagreed with Moscow and consolidating power in the hands of local communists. Communist influence was growing in Western European countries, where the poorly understood Soviet alternative appeared to many voters to be a plausible competitor to the American dream. In the 1945–46 elections, the Communists won 19% of the vote in Italy, 24% in Finland, and 26% in France. In June 1945, Stalin demanded that Turkey cede Kars and Ardahan to the Soviet Union. In early 1946, Soviet

[9] "Three Centuries of the National Debt." https://www.ukpublicspending.co.uk/debt_history

[10] William Adams Brown, Jr. and Redvers Opie. American Foreign Assistance. Washington DC, The Brookings Institution, 1953. p. 103.

[11] The UK made its last payments on these debts in 2006.

[12] William Adams Brown, Jr. and Redvers Opie. American Foreign Assistance. The Brookings Institution. Washington DC, 1953. p. 116.

[13] $15 billion at that time is just under $240 billion in 2024 prices if recalculated using the US Federal Reserve's inflation calculator (https://www.minneapolisfed.org/about-us/monetary-policy/inflation-calculator); measured in gold price ($35/oz. in 1945–1947, and $2206 in the end-2024) it exceeds $1.1 trillion.

soldiers who had been in Iran since 1942 blocked the path of Iranian military personnel the government had sent to suppress separatists in southern Azerbaijan, and the Kremlin declared its refusal to withdraw its troops from Iran within a pre-agreed time frame. In August 1946, the Kremlin's "wish list" was supplemented by a demand for Turkey to organize joint control over the Bosporus and Dardanelles straits. In early 1947, Syria, pushed by Moscow, lodged territorial claims against Turkey in the UN Security Council.

In the fall of 1946, having refused to take part in parliamentary elections and to recognize the results of the referendum on the preservation of the monarchy, the Greek Communists turned to the tactics of armed guerrilla struggle, receiving support from neighboring countries under communist control (Yugoslavia, Albania, Bulgaria). According to the decisions of the conference in Yalta, Greece was in the zone of influence of Great Britain, but the British troops stationed on the territory of the country did not really want to participate in the clarification of relations between local politicians. In addition, the financial situation in London was rapidly deteriorating, and in February 1947, the US Secretary of State received a "document of great importance" in which the British ambassador informed him of Britain's decision to withdraw its troops from Greece and to stop providing financial aid to the country, which amounted to $500 million a year.

Untimely Thoughts

By this time, George Kennan's "Long Telegram"[14] had been lying in the State Department for a whole year. It cannot be said that it lay unmoved—its contents were well known to American politicians and experts, who actively discussed Kennan's thoughts. However, although the telegram was Kennan's

[14] On February 22, 1946, US Charge d'Affaires in Moscow Kennan, who had worked in Moscow from 1933–1938 and returned there in 1944, dictated a 19-page telegram to the State Department outlining his views on the nature of the Soviet regime and the motives behind its foreign policy.

In Kennan's view, Stalin's belief in the inevitability of world revolution made the confrontation between the two systems inevitable. The Soviet Union's hope for success was based on taking advantage of the capitalist world's capabilities (financial and technological), actively expanding the sphere of influence of communist ideology, and encouraging clashes between capitalist countries as they led to the weakening of the enemy. "*The Soviet worldview is based on the idea that there is no compromise with rival states and that constructive activity can begin only when Communist power becomes dominant … we have a political force which fanatically believes that unchanging coexistence with the United States is impossible, that the destruction of the internal harmony of our society is desirable and obligatory, that our traditional way of life must be destroyed, the international prestige of our state must be.*" The telegram concludes with recommendations, the first of which became the basis for the containment policy applied by the United States to the Soviet Union during the Cold War. "*The Soviet power … does not follow rigidly established plans. It does not take unnecessary risks. Immune to the logic of reasoning, it is highly susceptible to the logic of force. For this reason it can easily retreat—which it usually does—any time it meets strong resistance.*"

response to Secretary of State James Byrnes' question about what US policy toward the Soviet Union should be, it came to Washington at the wrong time and to the wrong person.

James Byrnes was a unique American politician who, by July 1945, when President Truman appointed him as US Secretary of State a few days before the Potsdam Conference, had been a member of the House of Representatives for 14 years and a senator in the US Congress for 10 years, where he became one of the most influential senators and a friend of Harry Truman (then also a senator), a member of the US Supreme Court, and the head of the Office of Economic Stabilization and the Office of War Mobilization during the war years.[15] However, for all Byrnes' merits, his level of competence and understanding of foreign policy issues was extremely low, as was President Truman's—his predecessor, President Roosevelt, preferred to handle international affairs on his own, often informing State Department leaders of the results of negotiations after they were completed. As a senator, Harry Truman also had no foreign policy experience, and after his election as Vice President, he was not given access to international affairs. In addition, the last months of the war and the beginning of the occupation of Germany and Japan objectively led to a dramatic increase in the role of the Department of Defense and Generals Eisenhower and MacArthur, who were almost completely entrusted with managing the occupied countries.

At one time, James Byrnes did not like the work of the Supreme Court, so he asked President Roosevelt to release him 15 months after his appointment. He wanted the chair of the Secretary of State better, as it allowed him to realize his strengths, build relationships, and achieve compromise. However, numerous international trips, the rapidly changing situation in the world, and his unwillingness to rely on the State Department staff did not allow him to form a clear vision of the principles of American policy. Moreover, on a key issue—relations with the Soviet Union—his views diverged increasingly from the President's. While Harry Truman's views and positions were becoming increasingly hardline, Byrnes favored softer policies and concessions to the Kremlin. One such concession—the omission of Iran from the final documents of the Moscow Conference of Foreign Ministers (December 1945)—caused an extreme aggravation of the situation in that country and gave rise to the first intense confrontation between the two superpowers. In response to the USSR's refusal to withdraw its troops from Iran, President Truman sent

[15] After leaving the Truman administration (February 1947), Byrnes became the governor of South Carolina in 1950.

the most powerful American warship, the battleship Missouri, to Istanbul, demonstrating his unwillingness to strengthen Soviet positions in the region.

In addition, Byrnes—believing he now held all the levers of control over American foreign policy—stopped consulting the President before key meetings and at times failed even to brief him afterward.[16] For the blunt, straightforward Truman—whose schedule was increasingly dominated by foreign policy issues—this was unacceptable. The rupture occurred in January 1947, after Time magazine named Byrnes "Man of the Year," and President Truman requested him to submit a resignation letter.

By February 1946, when the Long Telegram appeared, Kennan had decided to end his diplomatic career: he had a clear sense that his thoughts and ideas did not form the basis of policy and did not attract any attention. He believed that Washington, failing to understand the nature of the Soviet regime and its intentions, unreasonably hoped for friendship and broad cooperation in the postwar world. His analytical essays attracted virtually no attention in the State Department. The Long Telegram was largely an accident—on February 9, Stalin gave a major speech in Moscow that did not attract the attention of Kennan, who was acting ambassador. He wrote briefly to the State Department that it was filled with banal theses and contained nothing of fundamental importance. However, this response did not satisfy his bosses at the European and East European departments. They drafted a short telegram to Moscow requesting an analysis of Soviet foreign policy and a forecast of the consequences of its implementation, which Secretary of State Byrnes signed. US Ambassador Harriman asked Kennan for a detailed response.[17]

Even when Kennan's telegram arrived at the State Department, it received little attention, except for its exceptional length. It was discussed by James Forrestal, Secretary of the Navy, who had received the telegram text from the US Ambassador to Moscow, Harriman. Forrestal advocated a hardline policy toward the USSR; he immediately embraced the idea of containment and sent the text on his behalf to top officials, including the President. When Kennan returned to Washington, Forrestal gave him a job at the National Army College and the opportunity to interact with the government's top political-military experts.

---

[16] It may have contributed to the fact that before the 1944 election, Roosevelt had long hinted to Byrnes that he was willing to take him on as vice president.

[17] Kennan says in his memoirs that the telegram was in response to a question from the US Treasury Department as to why Moscow did not want to support the activities of the World Bank and the International Monetary Fund. A few years after Kennan's death, John Gaddis, in his book (Gaddis, John Lewis (2011). George F Kennan: An American Life), provides evidence that Kennan responded to the request by telegram in late January.

The First Brick

After Byrnes resigned, General George Marshall, who had recently turned 66 and already dreamed of ending his government career, was appointed US Secretary of State. For Marshall, whose entire life was linked to the army, foreign policy remained terra incognita to him. Yet, the general was an excellent organizer who knew his staff's strengths and recognized that one man does not win the battle alone.

After receiving notice that Britain was going to withdraw from Greece a month after his appointment, the newly appointed Secretary of State was not very surprised—for him, the collapse of the British Empire was inevitable, with obvious consequences; the only question was whether they could be controlled. Asking his deputy Dean Acheson the obvious questions for a general—how long could British troops hold their ground in Greece? By whom and how quickly could they be replaced? How much would it cost?—Marshall was told more time was needed to gather the answers. Fine, he said, and sent his deputy to look for answers he needed to prepare himself for the Moscow meeting of foreign ministers to be held next month.[18]

Whether it was a premonition of global upheaval, or the respect that Marshall enjoyed in military circles, or both factors, friction and rivalry between the State and War Departments evaporated. Within three days a draft directive proposing immediate financial and military aid to Greece and Turkey reached the President's desk. Truman liked the decision, but being an experienced politician, recognized that asking Congress at once to fund nations beyond the traditional orbit of US interests would likely fail. Two days later, he invited eight congressmen, four from each party, to the White House, and painted for them a picture of impending geopolitical collapse: once the Soviet Union had gained control of Greece, nothing would save Turkey from repeating its fate, after which one should expect the Kremlin to move into the Eastern Mediterranean and the Middle East, from where the roads to Africa and South Asia open up. Therefore, support for Greece and Turkey should not be perceived as aid to the British Empire but as a defense of US national interests. America was offered either to win by acting quickly and decisively or to accept defeat in advance. "*The developments in the Mediterranean are impressive and even startling*" declared the chairman of the Senate Foreign Relations Committee, Republican Arthur Vandenberg, who would play a decisive role in consolidating support for aid to the two countries and, a few months later, support for the Marshall Plan.

[18] Benn Steil. The Marshall Plan. At the Dawn of the Cold War. Simon & Schuster, 2018, p. 43.

New Deal

On March 12, 1947, President Truman delivered an address to Congress in support of Greece and Turkey,[19] which would go down in history as the "Truman Doctrine"—a declaration that the United States was ending isolationism and stood ready to use its resources, including military force, to defend its interests anywhere. "*I believe that it must be the policy of the United States to support free peoples who are resisting attempted subjugation by armed minorities or by outside pressures… If we falter in our leadership, we may endanger the world's peace—and we shall surely endanger the welfare of our own nation*."[20]

The second major shift in US policy was that financial assistance shifted from loans to grants. Although the President's speech was met with a standing ovation in Congress, passage of the legislation was by no means smooth. The choice of countries for aid was questionable: the Greek government was corrupt, and Turkey had been neutral for the entire war. Advocates of a soft line in relations with the USSR feared Moscow's retaliatory reaction. The followers of President Roosevelt demanded that the problem of Greece be brought to the newly created UN for discussion. And, most importantly, if we start giving out money irrevocably, where is the guarantee that tomorrow, China, where there is also a civil war, will not ask for it? Nevertheless, six weeks later, Congress passed the bill, and it became law a month afterward.

The Partition of Germany Is on the Horizon

A few days after the congressional vote, Secretary of State Marshall returned from Moscow, where a conference of foreign ministers had just concluded. During this meeting, Moscow and Washington's disagreement over Germany's future became so acute that no compromise was possible. The Potsdam agreements envisioned Germany as a single state. Its division into occupation zones was not meant to disrupt a unified economy: the Allies set up controls on key goods, distributing them country-wide at uniform prices, irrespective of

---

[19] It should be noted that Washington greatly overestimated Moscow's willingness to use force to change the situation in Greece—Stalin understood the strategic importance of that country. "*What do you think that Great Britain and the United States—the United States, the most powerful power in the world—would allow their transportation arteries in the Mediterranean Sea to be severed? Nonsense. We don't have a navy*," he told Yugoslavia's deputy prime minister, Edward Kardel, who had come to Moscow. (Milovan Djilas. Conversations with Stalin. Posev, Frankfurt, 1972, p. 172).

[20] National Archives. Truman Doctrine (1947). https://www.archives.gov/milestone-documents/truman-doctrine

where they were produced. However, if the US and Britain hoped to rebuild Europe, exports from their zones—undervalued for reparations—should have strengthened neighboring economies instead of being siphoned off as reparations agreed in Yalta as quickly as possible, and a significant part of the production of the enterprises located in these two zones was sent as reparations instead of being sent to consumers in other zones. In May 1946, the commander of the American zone of occupation, General Lucius Clay, prohibited further reparations shipments to the eastern zone and the associated dismantling of equipment.[21]

Building on previous Allies' decisions to preserve a unified Germany, the United States favored the rapid formation of a unified government that could take responsibility for addressing domestic problems. However, the idealistic scheme—a neutral Germany, equally influenced by the Allies, worked only on paper. The same fate befell Stalin and Churchill's attempt to divide postwar influence in other countries under the "percentages agreement." After Clay halted deliveries to the Soviet zone, Deputy Foreign Minister Maxim Litvinov said prophetically in an interview with American journalist Hottelet: "*Both sides (West and East) want to control Germany in its entirety … [this country] must obviously be divided into parts. There is no other solution in sight.*"[22]

At the same time, Great Britain proposed to the United States that their two zones be placed under joint control. The realization of this idea was expected to benefit both sides. The British occupation zone was the most developed. In contrast, the American zone had underdeveloped industries, and the unification should have created a more balanced situation and become a step toward a unified economic Germany, which was Washington's goal. On the other hand, Britain's dire financial situation made it ever harder to finance basic services in its German zone, and unification allowed this burden to be shifted to the US. This idea was transformed into the creation of Bizonia, formally established on January 1, 1947.

During the Moscow meeting, all participants reaffirmed the desire for a unified economic and decentralized political Germany, consistent with previous agreements. However, Stalin and Molotov, rebuking Washington for ruining this idea by creating Bizonia, made no concessions when it came to limiting reparation payments or forming a unified German government. After six weeks of fruitless negotiations, an exhausted Marshall returned to Washington convinced that Western Europe was on the verge of 'total

[21] By the Allies' agreement, if German factories could produce more of any product than was deemed necessary, some of the factories were to be dismantled.

[22] The Ambassador in the Soviet Union (Smith) to the Secretary of State. June 21, 1946. FRUS, 1946, Eastern Europe, The Soviet Union, vol. VI, doc 517.

collapse' and that the United States must act decisively—working with, or if need be against, the USSR. The next day, the Secretary of State gave a radio interview in which he said that Europe could no longer wait for a compromise between the two superpowers and that "*while the doctors confer, the patient may die.*"

We Need a Plan!

On the same day, Marshall invited Kennan to head the Political Planning Staff in the State Department, which was to determine the strategic direction of American policy. The basic ideas of the Long Telegram, which defined the goals of containment, had already been embraced by the American foreign policy establishment, and the first weeks of this group's work were devoted to developing the thesis contained at the very end of Kennan's telegram. "*We must formulate and put forward for other nations a much more positive and constructive picture of the sort of world we would like to see than we have put forward in the past. It is not enough to urge people to develop political processes similar to our own. Many foreign peoples, in Europe at least, are tired and frightened by experiences of the past and are less interested in abstract freedom than in security. They are seeking guidance rather than responsibilities. We should be better able than Russians to give them this. And unless we do, Russians certainly will.*"

On June 5, 1947, Marshall delivered a speech at Harvard announcing the beginning of the development of a major program for the economic recovery of Europe. Ten months later, on April 3, 1948, President Truman signed the Economic Recovery Act—America's most ambitious non-military foreign policy program, one that would shape postwar history. The Marshall Plan's main ideological rationale was to fight communist expansion, but its real aim was to restore Europe's economic prosperity rather than wage an ideological battle. "*There is no choice between being a communist on 1 500 calories a day and a believer in democracy on a thousand. It is my sincere belief that our proposed ration allowance in Germany will not only defeat our objectives in middle Europe but will pave the road to a Communist Germany,*"[23] wrote Lucius Clay.

[23] "Food Situation in US Zone. March 27, 1946. Personal for Echols and Petersen." The papers of General Lucius D Clay: Germany, 1945–1949 (ed Jean E Smith). 1974, vol. I, p. 184.

… Built on New Principles

While preparing and approving the bill in Congress, US officials and politicians needed to destroy several basic principles on which US foreign policy has been built virtually since the nation's founding.

First, America had abandoned its isolationism. The devastating war in Europe undermined the resilience of the economies of all European countries, which did not even have the strength to rebuild, let alone maintain order and stability in their colonial possessions. A return to a policy of detachment from European and Asian affairs, as had happened after World War I, was all too obvious in its consequences. Although American public opinion demanded turning its back on Europe, withdrawing its troops, and allowing European countries to solve their own problems, it was obvious to politicians that this would leave two possible future scenarios, and it was not clear which one was worse: either the Soviet Union would occupy all of Germany or Germany would repeat the history of the Weimar Republic.

Moreover, America must not only contribute money to the rebuilding of Europe but also design and implement the project. "*The United States must run this show*," wrote Clayton.[24]

Second, the Marshall Plan was not a set of plans to help individual countries but a plan to support the economy of Western Europe as a single economic system. One of the competitive advantages of the American economy was the size of the market, which contrasted strongly with the economic fragmentation of Europe. At the insistence of the United States, the plan was based on the ideas of a European economic federation, support for intra-European trade, and movement toward a customs union,[25] which was strongly opposed by Great Britain, which did not want to open the markets of its colonies to goods from other European countries. The Paris Conference was originally convened to develop the Marshall Plan, which was positioned as a European initiative. The US pushed Great Britain and France to act as its

[24] FRUS. 1947. Vol. III. Doc. 136.

[25] The first European customs union was the union of Belgium, the Netherlands, and Luxembourg, established as early as 1921. In October 1943, the emigration governments of the three countries, based in London, signed an agreement to regulate mutual payments post-war and strengthen economic relations between them. At the beginning of September 1944, they signed the Customs Convention, which came into force on January 1, 1948. From then on, trade between the three countries became duty-free, and a single, lowest external customs tariff in Western Europe was imposed on third countries. The Benelux example prompted US Undersecretary of State for Economic Affairs Clayton, who was the chief US negotiator and persuader at the Paris Conference and during the parallel negotiations on the creation of the GATT, to the idea of extending the customs union to all Western Europe. The GATT agreement was signed on October 30, 1947, and entered into force on January 1, 1948. The Soviet Union refused to participate in the IMF and the World Bank and did not join this organization.

initiators, clearly hinting that a single European request—if any—would receive the necessary financial support from Washington. At the same time, American representatives officially did not participate in the work of the conference, carefully observing "from behind the scenes" what was happening. In addition, Germany was not invited to participate in the conference.[26]

Sink or Swim

Left on their own, the European countries failed to agree on a common plan because their interests diverged too sharply. France, fearing the restoration of militaristic Germany and wishing to replace it as the continent's leading economy, demanded international control over the Ruhr and that as much of the coal and steel produced there as possible be sent to French factories.[27] This was opposed by the Benelux countries, for whom the recovery of the German economy opened the way to increased trade. Great Britain, by right of the victorious country, wanted to maximize the amount of American money received to maintain trade within the empire and keep the British pound zone stable.

Having received a "unified" request from the participants of the Paris Conference in mid-September 1947, American officials sighed: there could be no question of any unity there, and the total request for American aid was the result of arithmetic summation of the deficits of the balance of payments of the participating countries and amounted to ≈$29 billion—roughly one-and-a-half times what the program's architects deemed feasible. Most importantly, it was obvious that after four years, the economies of European countries would not become self-sufficient and would require the allocation of new funds.

As a result, the reworking of the European proposals was undertaken by American experts, who managed to get support from the conference participants for the ideas of economic federation and reduction of customs duties, promises to increase production of basic goods (coal, steel, electricity) and expanded use of available credit for economic recovery, reduction of requests

[26] The conference in Paris opened on July 12, 1947, and by this time, it was clear that the establishment of independent governing bodies in Germany was inevitable; their emergence was a matter of time. On May 23, German representatives were included in the Economic Council of Bizonia despite strong protests from France.

[27] As one of the behind-the-scenes compromises, the US agreed to slightly increase coal and steel shipments to France in exchange for France agreeing to annex its zone of occupation to Bizonia. The resulting Trizonia thus began its movement toward the emergence of West Germany. In addition, France agreed to include Germany in the perimeter of the Marshall Plan.

for housing construction, and agreement to consider any sensible amendments to the submitted applications.

Most importantly, the conference participants gave the green light to German involvement, although the report did not contain any clear formulations. While there was no doubt in anyone's mind that the German economy should be integrated into the European economy, no one understood how this could be done based on political realities: Germany remained under Allied occupation, and all questions about the country's future had to be resolved with the participation of the Soviet Union.

Third, in 1934, the United States passed the Johnson Debt Default Act, which prohibited the US government from lending to countries with outstanding debts to America and prohibited those countries from placing their debt instruments on the US market. The Law was a reaction to the fact that after the onset of the Great Depression, many countries that had received American loans during and after World War I found themselves unable to service them. The Law prohibited new US loans to such countries.[28] Obviously, after World War II's end, European countries' financial situation became even worse, and they needed a reprieve. As part of the Marshall Plan, the US removed the recipient countries of American aid from this law[29] and required the recipient countries to postpone making demands on Germany for repayment of accumulated debts.

Fourth, just as in the case of aid to Greece and Turkey, Marshall Plan funds were to be grants, not loans, at Kennan's insistence.

Fifth, it was a plan to rebuild all of Europe, including Eastern Europe and even the Soviet Union. Soviet Foreign Minister Vyacheslav Molotov participated in a meeting of foreign ministers with their French and British counterparts in June 1947, at which the decision to convene the Paris Conference was formalized. Stalin's initial position, which Molotov broadcasted, was cautiously positive: the participation of the USSR and the countries of Eastern Europe was possible if the sovereign rights of individual states were not infringed upon in the decision-making process. American experts feared Stalin's consent to participate in the Marshall Plan the most: by entering the Marshall Plan, the USSR could quite easily sabotage its implementation, as the experience of the Control Council for Germany showed.[30] And how relieved they were when, a few days later, Molotov received a telegram from Stalin ordering him not to support the American idea under any

[28] Johnson's Law continues to be in effect at present.

[29] A similar decision was made for Great Britain when the Lend–Lease program was approved in 1941.

[30] That was the recommendation by Novikov, the Soviet ambassador to the United States.

circumstances. A few weeks later, similar orders were received by the Kremlin-controlled governments of Eastern Europe.

The Plan Is Good, but It Needs Support

In addition to putting together a plan that was fiscally sound yet optimistic and persuading European countries to accept it,[31] the Truman White House had two more difficult tasks to accomplish: persuading Congress that, after the 1946 mid-term elections, had been controlled by Republicans who had begun by cutting the budget for fiscal years 1947 and 1948, and persuading American voters that support for European countries was consistent with the intergovernmental process.

Agree with Your Opponent

In the first task, the administration received invaluable help from Arthur Vandenberg, chairman of the Senate Foreign Relations Committee, who had become deeply immersed in foreign policy issues while working on the aid package for Turkey and Greece. He suggested that President Truman "step aside" after the bill was introduced, putting the entire initiative for further discussion in the hands of Congress. The proposal seemed more than risky, but Truman and Vandenberg's personal relationship and mutual trust ensured success.

Three congressional committees were set up to pick apart the administration's proposals, make officials explain every figure, and advocate the administration's plan. From August through November 1947, more than 200 congressmen traveled to European countries, and it was explained to them that they would travel without spouses, formal attire, or ceremonial dinners. The congressmen traveled through towns and villages, visited factories, and talked to officials and ordinary citizens. After their return, the opinion was firmly established in Congress that without American support, Europe would be devastated, and the Communists would come to power.

Of course, this did not mean that Congress would accommodate all the administration's requests. The US economy was going through a difficult transition at this time, as the war orders that had propelled it forward for

[31] One of the arguments that prompted European politicians to soften their positions was the US promise to provide for the basic needs of the participating countries until the Law was passed. The US fulfilled its promise: in December 1947, President Truman signed into Law a temporary aid bill worth about $600 million.

six years disappeared, and hundreds of thousands of returning soldiers turned into hundreds of thousands of laborers. The growth in demand outstripped the increase in supply—the industry needed time to readjust to peaceful ways—which fueled inflation. The interests of businesses and voters demanded adequate solutions from politicians, including cutting budget expenditures.

The Truman administration initially sought $16 billion for the Marshall Plan. Congress cut the budget request to $14.2 billion, trimmed authorized spending to $13.4 billion, and finally appropriated $12.5 billion.

Convince the Voter

The "advertising" campaign for American voters was no less creative. A month before Marshall's speech at Harvard, his deputy Dean Acheson gave a speech in the middle of a farmer's field in Mississippi and articulated why the average American should support aid to Europe—economic reconstruction of war-torn countries would expand the market for American goods. The wartime Secretary of War Henry Stimson published an article in Foreign Affairs.[32] Having won the war at great cost, America cannot afford to lose the peace.

> The immediate and pressing challenge to our belief in freedom and prosperity is in Western Europe. Here are people who have traditionally shared our faith in human dignity. These are the nations by whose citizens our land was settled and in whose tradition our civilization is rooted. They are threatened by Communism—but only because of the dark shadows cast by the hopelessness, hunger, and fear that have been the aftermath of the Nazi war. Communism or no Communism, menace or no menace, it is our simple duty as neighbors to take a generous part in helping these great peoples to help themselves.
>
> Americans can decide to stand apart from the reconstruction of Western Europe only if they wish to desert every principle by which they claim to live. And, as a policy decision, it would be the most tragic mistake in our history. We must take part in this work, take our full part, and be sure that we do enough.

After Stimson's article, numerous private initiatives emerged in America, including the Committee in Support of the Marshall Plan. Iowa farmers sent their delegation to Europe to "*find out exactly what food was needed, what it would cost to get it there, and how to make Great Britain solvent again so that she could trade with us.*"[33] A "friendship train" traveled across America to collect

---

[32] Henry L. Stimson. The Challenge to Americans. Foreign Affairs, October 1947.

[33] "European Aid Top Interest in Iowa; it is Put on a Par with Break in Grains—Rural Opinion is Strongest for ERP." The New York Times, February 16, 1948.

items and food for starving Europe. In February 1948, the American Society for the Prevention of Cruelty to Animals called for the implementation of the Marshall Plan "for the least of these" in Europe and announced a collection of animal feed and money to transport them to Europe.[34]

In July 1947, fewer than half of Americans had heard of Marshall's plan, and only 57% of that informed group supported it. This situation persisted until mid-fall, and it was not until November that public opinion shifted. But they were not unequivocal: although the proportion of Americans who had heard of the European support plan rose to 61% in November, the proportion who viewed it favorably fell to 47% (due to an increase in the proportion of those who could not make up their minds; the proportion who opposed it remained unchanged at 15–16%). By early March 1948, the proportion who knew of the Marshall Plan had risen to 79%, and those who supported it rose again to 57% (of those who knew). In November, already 82% of Americans were aware of European support, more than half were satisfied to varying degrees with the results, and two-thirds agreed with continued funding of the Marshall Plan in the next fiscal year.[35]

Rising from the Ashes of War

On March 13, 1948, the US Senate voted in favor of the Economic Cooperation Act by a vote of 69 to 17.[36] On April 2, the House approved the bill 318–75. President Truman signed it on 3 April, and by 20 April the first ships laden with food, fuel, chemicals, and machinery sailed from US ports to Europe. On April 3, President Truman signed the act into law, and on April 20, the first ships carrying food, fuel, chemicals, and industrial equipment headed from US ports to the shores of Europe.

The approval of the law and the beginning of the Marshall Plan's implementation, the inclusion of Germany in the list of aid recipients, and equal participation in the economic union under construction, in fact, meant the transformation of West Germany into a full-fledged member of economic Pax Americana. The only thing left was to fix the division of Germany into two

[34] "ASPCA Suggests ERP Project for Animals; Society Solicits Funds for Pets Abroad." The New York Times, February 18, 1948.

[35] The Gallup Poll: Public Opinion 1935–1971, vol. 1, pp. 661, 683, 715.

[36] An important factor that turned the position of many opponents of the law in Congress was the Communist coup in Czechoslovakia, organized with the support of the Kremlin in February 1948. Thus, former US President Herbert Hoover, who was the consolidator of the Republicans who resisted approval of the program of aid to Europe, demanded in January 1948 to reduce by one-third the expenditures for these purposes in the first year, declared in mid-March reduction of spending was out of the question.

states, for which Washington was already ready. There was no constructive cooperation with the Soviet Union on building a unified German state or on economic development; Moscow blocked any projects to solve the existing problems and was not shy about creating new ones.

The London Conference of Foreign Ministers of the four countries, held in November–December 1947, was the last attempt by the recent Allies to agree on a unified system of government for the whole of Germany. The US and British plan, which envisioned the gradual formation of a single government for all zones of occupation, as well as the establishment of a parliamentary council, met with fierce resistance from France, which demanded that the Saarland be handed over to it and that international control over the Ruhr be established. The Soviet delegation, headed by Molotov, refused to discuss any issues until guarantees were given that the full $10 billion in reparations would be received, mainly at the expense of the Western Zone.

The coup d'état in Czechoslovakia in February 1948 effectively ended any attempts at political dialog between Moscow and Washington. The London Conference of the six powers (the United States, Great Britain, France, and the Benelux countries), which began next day, initially convened as a consultative meeting, was immediately transformed into a substantive discussion on the establishment of a democratic and federal government on the territory of the American, British, and French zones of occupation. During the second phase of the conference, which lasted a month and a half and ended in early June, it was decided to establish the West German Parliamentary Council, which included delegates from the state parliaments. The task of this body was to draft the Basic Law of West Germany. In addition, in the middle of May, the London Conference decided on a monetary reform in the Western zones. On June 20, the Economic Council of Trizonia announced the introduction of a new monetary unit, the Deutsche Mark, on its territory.

The Parliamentary Council began its work on September 1, 1948, and adopted the Basic Law of West Germany on May 8, 1949. Two weeks later, on May 23, the official signing ceremony took place, and the Federal Republic of Germany was proclaimed.

On November 29, 1949, the Petersberg Agreement was signed, beginning West Germany's exit from the occupation regime. The FRG could apply to join the Council of Europe as an associate member. In exchange for the recognition of the Ruhr's international status, West Germany was allowed to send representatives to the International Authority for the Ruhr, and the Allies agreed to stop the dismantling of industrial facilities. The FRG was authorized to participate independently in international trade and to open consular offices in other countries.

It's Time to Finish

It was no secret that Stalin wanted to establish Soviet control over all of Germany,[37] but the natural obstacle to this was the American military presence. Of course, numerically the Soviet Army far outnumbered to the combined US-British forces, but knew the army's combat effectiveness still relied on Lend-Lease supplies, yet he was unwilling to start a war with his recent Allies without a clear pretext. In such a situation, the Kremlin's German policy was twofold: in its zone, the USSR acted unilaterally, while demanding that Allied policies in their own zones be coordinated with Moscow. The Kremlin was counting on the US to honor its Potsdam commitments and withdraw from Europe. Until then, Moscow's tactic was to maintain joint quasi-institutions but to take a hard line on substantive issues, leaving little room for compromise. This stance sowed uncertainty in the minds of US policymakers and military officers, who received conflicting signals from various Soviet interlocutors.

Harry Dexter White, Morgenthau's undersecretary of the US Treasury during the war, was the chief US negotiator at the Bretton Woods Conference in July 1944, when the postwar world financial system took shape under his guidance, including the creation of the IMF and the World Bank. White played an important role in developing the Morgenthau Plan and did his best to implement it in the first postwar months. At Bretton Woods, White refused any exceptions for the USSR; after his death, the FBI discovered that he had passed documents to Soviet intelligence.[38]

When Clay, a brilliant administrator and military governor of the American zone of Germany, who ensured the operation of the air bridge during the siege of Berlin in 1948/49, accused the State Department in 1946 of suffering from anti-Soviet complexes, Kennan told him the General had fallen under the charm of Marshal Zhukov. After the beginning of the Berlin blockade, Clay proposed breaking it with armored forces.

The President's widow, Eleanor Roosevelt, strongly influenced the Democratic Party leadership. After Marshall's speech at Harvard, she supported the Morgenthau Plan and advocated aid to European countries.

Haunted by the Red Army's wartime advance across Eastern Europe, Army Secretary Kenneth Royall argued that the United States should make

---

[37] In the summer of 1946, at a meeting with the leaders of Bulgaria and Yugoslavia, Stalin said, "*The whole of Germany should be ours, that is, Soviet, communist.*" (Milovan Djilas. Conversations with Stalin. Posev, Frankfurt. 1972, p. 144).

[38] FBI Memorandum identifying Harry Dexter White as agent Jurist. https://en.wikisource.org/wiki/FBI_Memorandum_identifying_Harry_Dexter_White_as_agent_Jurist

whatever concessions were necessary to avoid direct confrontation. After the siege of Berlin began, Royall stated that the US was not obligated and should relinquish control of the city to avoid a humanitarian catastrophe.

John Foster Dulles, then advisor to the Secretary of State, aligned himself with the French position and ardently backed the Soviet-backed proposal to place the Ruhr under international control, believing that this would avoid the militarization of Germany.

Although Winston Churchill delivered the famous Fulton speech in March 1946, in which he stated that the Iron Curtain had come into being, a year later, many **in** Washington still believed a negotiated settlement with Moscow was possible. The man who finally dispelled these hopes was George Marshall. In the first weeks after his appointment as Secretary of State, he recalled the successful experience of military cooperation with the Soviet Army in the last months of the war and believed it might be possible to reach agreement with Soviet leaders on a politically and economically united Germany. But, having spent five weeks in Moscow in April 1947, 43 rounds of four-power negotiating sessions, and despite his willingness to compromise, despite President Truman's instructions to take a hard line, he left Moscow with the realization that to achieve his goals of dominance in Europe, Stalin was ready to sacrifice the interests of Europe and its inhabitants and was not prepared to find solutions or to help anyone. Flying to Washington, Marshall spoke to members of the American delegation about the need to avert a looming disaster in Europe. The Secretary of State recalled a phrase from Kennan's Long Telegram—"*if the adversary [the Soviet Union] is strong enough and clearly shows a willingness to use his force, he seldom has to use force. If one chooses the right line of behavior in such situations, [Washington] will not need humiliating negotiations with the enemy,*" and the very next day invited the author of these lines to his office. A day later, the State Department began working on what became known as the Marshall Plan.

Birth of an Alliance

In December of the same year, 1947, Marshall returned from London, where another meeting of the four foreign ministers took place, with little positive progress. On the last evening, British Foreign Secretary Ernest Bevin invited the Secretary of State to his home for a private dinner and frank conversation. Bevin, after his morning conversation with French Minister Bidault, was in a depressed mood—the economy of Western Europe had not yet begun to recover, leading to growing leftist sentiment in France and Italy. It seemed that a little more, and the Communists would come to power in these countries, after which Moscow would control all Europe. The British minister had no concrete proposals; instead, he shared his thoughts. "*We must devise some Western democratic system comprising the Americans, ourselves, France, Italy, etc., and, of course, the Dominions. This would not be a formal alliance but an understanding backed by power, money, and resolute action. It would be a sort of spiritual federation of the West... The essential task was to create confidence in Western Europe that further communist inroads would be stopped ... the spiritual consolidation of Western civilization was possible... The form in which it should be done requires more study.*"

Marshall tempered the idea of a union—he focused on winning Congressional approval for the European recovery plan, a task growing harder by the day. "We *must distinguish between the material and spiritual aspects of this program... it was not necessarily to write everything down in detail. What was needed was a clear understanding*."[39] Marshall was ready to begin the discussion but without any commitment. With a presidential election approaching, and Republicans, inspired by their victory in the 1946 mid-term elections, were confident they could capture the White House as well.

The next morning, however, Marshall relayed the contents of the conversation to his staff, suggesting that they ponder the idea of a European political-military alliance with US material assistance. He understood the only way to contain Soviet expansion was for the United States and Western Europe to join forces. However, Marshall was not ready to voice concrete commitments on behalf of the US during the difficult discussions in Congress on the plan to restore Europe. Sometime later, he wrote a letter to Bevin suggesting that Western European countries first show what they were willing to do for themselves and each other, after which the United States would consider how it could help. As a model, the Secretary of State suggested looking at the recently signed and ratified by the Senate Rio de Janeiro Treaty, by which the countries of the Western Hemisphere formed a collective defense agreement under the UN Charter to respond individually and collectively to any armed aggression.

The idea of a collective defense agreement appealed to Bevin, who initiated negotiations with France and the Benelux countries. The coup d'état in Czechoslovakia spurred the negotiators, and on March 17, 1948, the Treaty of Brussels was signed, creating the Western Union (Western European Union since 1954). Whereas the Dunkirk Treaty between Britain and France, signed the year before, provided for mutual aid in the event of renewed German

---

[39] "British Memorandum of Conversation." London, December 22, 1947. FRUS, 1947, vol. II, doc 317, p. 818.

aggression, the new Treaty was a response to a new threat—a threat from the Soviet Union.

By this time, a coalition of hard-liners had formed in Washington toward the Soviet Union. Its leader was Secretary of Defense James Forrestal, who was sympathetic to Kennan's concept of containment, including its military dimension.[40] Although no pledges of support for the new alliance were forthcoming from the US, the militaries of the US, Canada, and Britain held secret talks in Washington to define the terms of a political-military alliance that could include Western Europe, the US, and Canada.[41] The resulting text was later used to draft the North Atlantic Treaty.

When US Deputy Secretary of State Robert Lovett decided to try out the idea of a new treaty on Senator Vandenberg, he received a resounding "*No!*" in response. However, it was a no with a positive connotation. The senator was seriously contemplating his presidential run as the Republican Party's nominee and was eager to seize the opportunity to score points ahead of a possible race. "*Why should all the credit go to Truman?... Why not get the Senate to ask the President to negotiate such an alliance? Wouldn't that give you a long way toward possible bipartisan Senate approval?*".

On April 28, 1948, Canadian Prime Minister Saint Laurent publicly announced the idea of a treaty. Speaking in the House of Commons, he proposed a system of collective mutual defense involving Canada, the United States, and the parties to the Brussels Treaty. On June 11, the US Senate passed the Vandenberg Resolution, which opened the door for the US to join peacetime collective security agreements outside the Western Hemisphere.

The Kremlin Has "Helped" Again

Ten days later, on June 20, the Allies announced the monetary reform[42] in Trizonia, after which the Soviet Union accused the West of intending to split Germany, refused to find a compromise on the issue, and declared a blockade of West Berlin. Initially, the pretext seemed justified: the Soviet officials feared economic and social chaos that could arise from the influx of withdrawn

[40] Ironically, Forrestal's main ideological opponent was Kennan, who believed that policymakers in Washington greatly overestimated Moscow's willingness to take risks and use force to achieve its goals in Europe. This would cause Kennan's desire for government work to cool, and he would soon resign.

[41] Moscow most likely knew not only about these negotiations but also about their progress—one of the members of the Cambridge Five, Donald Maclean, was working at the time as the first secretary of the British Embassy in Washington and had access to all diplomatic correspondence.

[42] Marshal Sokolovsky, commander of the Soviet military administration, received this information from his vis-a-vis late on the night of June 18.

Reichsmarks into the Soviet zone. However, this threat was very quickly removed—4 days after the introduction of the Deutsche Mark in Trizonia, the Soviet administration announced a monetary reform in the eastern zone of Germany. The blockade's purpose was to drive the Allies out of West Berlin.

Stalin was internally prepared for Germany's split—as early as February that year, at a meeting with Bulgarian Communists, he said: "*The West will make its own state out of West Germany, and we will make our own state out of East Germany!*"[43] But he wanted to hold the West responsible for it, and Moscow was voicing deliberately unacceptable demands not only to roll out monetary reform but also to abandon plans for a German government in Trizonia and to halt the work of the Parliamentary Council. At the very least, it would have been a good idea to take advantage of the situation and force the former allies out of Berlin.

The blockade of a city of nearly 2.5 million caught Washington completely off guard; the improvised "air bridge" was a desperate stopgap rather than a long-term strategy. An attempted relief train was halted by Soviet tanks, which blocked the tracks and forced it to return. Although almost half of the airplanes available to the army were allocated for goods transportation, it was impossible to provide the city with everything it needed until the end of the summer. The military clash in the city clearly made no sense—the Soviet army grouping in East Germany numbered 318,000 soldiers, almost 25 times the number of Allied troops. On September 13, President Truman held a meeting to discuss the possibility of using nuclear weapons in a military conflict that seemed almost inevitable. American Air Force Deputy Chief of Staff Loris Norstad flew to London to prepare bombers stationed there for possible atomic strikes.[44] Relief came unexpectedly: a new leader, General William Tunner, well versed in Taylor's theory of scientific management, arrived at the Headquarters of the Berlin air supply operation. After implementing little-publicized procedural changes based on his recommendations, the airlift's performance improved dramatically, and doubts about the ability to supply the city disappeared.

On July 6, the US, Canada, and Western Union member states began talks on issues related to the defense of the Atlantic region, including the possibility of a treaty.

By September 1948, the draft treaty was almost ready, and the conversation began about who should become parties to it. At France's insistence, Italy was

[43] Milovan Djilas. Conversations with Stalin. Posev, Frankfurt. 1972, p. 144.

[44] Daniel Harrington. Berlin on the Brink. The Blockade, the Airlift, and the Early Cold War. University Press of Kentucky, 2012.

invited. In case of mass troop movements across the Atlantic, intermediate airfields were essential, so Denmark (controlling Greenland) and Portugal (with the Azores) had to be invited. With Denmark under the American umbrella, Norway agreed to join, while Sweden chose to remain neutral. An attempt to involve Ireland, which occupied a strategic position in anti-submarine warfare, failed—replied that the country would join, but only if Washington could convince Britain to return the six northern counties.

On April 4, 1949, the North Atlantic Treaty was signed.

To Be or Not to Be?

The question of the possibility of Germany's participation in the emerging political alliance had no obvious answer. On the one hand, Great Britain believed that its accession to the new alliance was only a matter of time "when circumstances permitted."[45] On the other hand, France was categorically opposed to the restoration of Germany's military potential, did everything possible to weaken its economic potential, and demanded that the new alliance be created should provide for measures in case of new aggression by Germany.[46] However, the restoration of a powerful Germany was not an obvious goal in Washington either. On the one hand, "*the role of the German people in any European alliance will ultimately be of paramount importance*, but on the other, … *such an alliance offers the hope of restoring the balance of power in Europe without allowing Germany to become the dominant power again,*" wrote Kennan.[47]

As a result, a compromise was found. On the one hand, Germany and Austria were included in the security zone of the future North Atlantic Treaty, i.e., the participating countries were to come to their aid in case of external aggression. On the other hand, these countries, as well as Sweden and Spain, were defined as not "natural participants of the North Atlantic community,"[48]

[45] "The British Ambassador (Inverchapel) to the Secretary of State." Washington, January 13, 1948. FRUS, 1948, vol. III, doc 3.

[46] "The Secretary of State to the Embassy in France." Washington, February 27, 1948. FRUS, 1948, vol. III, doc 23.

[47] "Memorandum by the Director of the Policy Planning Staff (Kennan) to the Secretary of State." January 20, 1948. FRUS, 1948, vol. II, doc 719.

[48] "Memorandum of the Fourteenth Meeting of the Working Group Participating in the Washington Exploratory Talks on Security, September 7, 1948." FRUS, 1948, vol. III, doc 147.

and the question of their membership in the emerging alliance was left to the future.[49]

On the eve of the signing of the North Atlantic Treaty, Dean Acheson, who became Secretary of State after Marshall resigned, sent President Truman a memorandum outlining US policy toward Germany.[50] The first paragraph of this document contains the essential thesis—the US President was asked to frame his policy toward the German people in inseparable intertwining with his interests and policy toward the other nations of Europe. "*The ultimate goal of the United States in its policy toward the German people is that they, or as large a portion of them as practicable, be integrated into the new common structure of the free peoples of Europe, to share in due time in equal obligations, economic benefits, and security. We recognize that the form and pace of development of such a structure is predominantly a matter for the Europeans themselves and that the final effective integration of the German people into this structure will depend on mutual willingness and faith in the long-term economic benefits and greater security which will be assured to all through mutual participation in it.*"

The memorandum explicitly mentioned the danger that Germany's industrial capacity and rapid economic recovery could threaten neighboring countries and the United States. Moreover, Marshall Plan funds could be used to recreate a military threat not only from Germany, but it expressed confidence that "*the establishment of satisfactory military strength by such [Western European] countries, combined with their economic recovery and the restoration of a free part of Germany, would, in the opinion of the United States, greatly reduce the possibilities of aggression throughout Europe, including [aggression by] Germany.*"

Acheson concludes the memorandum by discussing the US's responsibility for maintaining security in Western Europe and stating that the US "*has assured that it will not withdraw its occupation troops without consultation with the major Western allies and until peace in Europe is assured.*"

The creation of NATO, which in the early years was not an organization, remained a multilateral treaty, providing American security guarantees to European countries against Soviet and German aggression and at first satisfied everyone. Moreover, including Germany in the perimeter of the North Atlantic alliance did not cause significant debates. However, this situation did not last long—less than 15 months after the signing of the North Atlantic Treaty, the Korean War began, which, for the West, was clear proof that the Soviet Union was ready to use military force to achieve its goals.

---

[49] "Memorandum by the Participants in the Washington Security Talks, July 6 to September 9, Submitted to Their Respective Governments for Study and Comment." FRUS, 1948, vol. III, doc 150.

[50] German Policy papers. Memorandum by the Secretary of State to the President. Washington, March 31, 1949. FRUS, 1949, vol. III, doc 56.

Both Hungry and Thirsty

Assessments made by the US military and intelligence services before the outbreak of the Korean War indicated that the Soviet Union had a significant superiority in the number of armed forces and armaments stationed in Europe and that in the event of an attack on West Germany, the United States and its allies would be unable to defend that country from occupation and, subsequently, would be unable to liberate it. A few days after the outbreak of war, on the one hand, Marshall stated to Dean Acheson that the military grouping of the North Atlantic Treaty Organization in Europe should be significantly strengthened with the mandatory involvement of Germany; on the other hand, with similar ideas to Truman, German Chancellor Konrad Adenauer appealed to Truman, and by the end of the summer, the US President accepted the inevitability of restoring Germany's military capabilities. Soon, the "Spofford Plan" was laid on the President's desk.[51] The proposal, approved by the President before long, was comprehensive and involved increasing US ground forces in Europe by creating four to six divisions German divisions, without creating a German Army and General Staff, increasing the number of British and French troops stationed in Europe, uniting the forces of all the members of the alliance under a single leadership and creating the position of Supreme Commander of NATO forces, creating a NATO headquarters structure, including a special group to coordinate the military production. "Spofford Plan" was submitted to the NATO session for discussion as a "single package," and its support from the US was conditioned on the Allies' agreement with all its points and demonstration that the commitments made were beginning to be fulfilled.

As could be expected, these proposals, or rather their part concerning the creation of German military units, caused categorical rejection from France. However, the adamant position of the United States and pressure from European countries forced French politicians to seek compromise ideas. At the end of October, the French Prime Minister Pleven proposed the creation of a single European army of 100,000 people under the leadership of a committee of defense ministers of European countries, accountable to the Parliamentary Assembly of the Council of Europe, and the Supreme Commander-in-Chief, with its command and staff structure. The army was to be composed of Allied and German military units, though the size of German units would be limited to a battalion while the Allies units should retain

[51] Charles Spofford was at this time the deputy US representative to the North Atlantic Council, the alliance's main political body.

normal regimental structure. For the duration of hostilities, the European army was to be placed under the command of the Supreme Commander of NATO forces.

The Pleven Plan was indeed a compromise, requiring concessions from all sides, but at the same time, meeting the basic demands of the key participants. The US received an increase in the military participation of European countries and, most importantly, the inclusion of Germany in forming a unified armed force. At the same time, the US had to put up with the fact that the army building structure proposed by France was not optimal and, at times, confusing.[52] France, agreeing with the appearance of German military units, sought a ban on creating a German army and received leading roles in the European military. Germany did not get NATO membership, which was the dream of Adenauer, who understood only the United States could guarantee his country's security, but agreeing to the French plan opened the way to the end of the occupation regime. Great Britain retained maximum independence: it was impossible to oppose the American idea of a unified command in NATO, but having supported the French proposals, London refrained from participating in a unified European army, remaining an independent military unit within NATO.

After a year and a half of negotiations, the Treaty establishing the European Defense Community (EDC) was signed in Paris on May 26, 1952. The same day, in Bonn, the US, Great Britain, and France had signed the Convention on the Relations of the Three Powers with the Federal Republic of Germany (the General Treaty or Bonn Convention), which provided for the end of the occupation regime and the transfer of all power on the territory of the Federal Republic of Germany to the German officials after the entry into force of the Treaty establishing the European Defence Force. However, three more years passed before this point, and things did not go as planned.

We Invented It, We Broke It

On August 30, 1954, the EDC Treaty was submitted for ratification to the French National Assembly and rejected by its deputies.[53] Two months later,

[52] Integrated Forces and European Army. Paper Prepared in the Department of State. [Washington,] January 26, 1951. FRUS, vol. III, Part 1, doc 415.

[53] This was facilitated to some extent by easing tensions in the world after Stalin's death and the end of the Korean War. A particular role was played by the fact that during the negotiations, the operational control of the European army was transferred to the Supreme Commander of NATO forces, which was perceived as an infringement of French interests. In addition, the stability of the Fourth Republic could not withstand the blows of different political forces.

the Bonn Convention was amended: the EDC Treaty was annulled, and Germany received an invitation to join NATO. For Germany, this invitation came at a cost—the country agreed to maintain the special status of the Saarland.[54] However, it soon turned out that this sacrifice was short-lived.[55] On May 5, 1955, the agreement on Germany's accession to NATO was ratified by all alliance members. Thus, the occupation of West Germany was completed, and the country became a member of the West's most important military and political alliance.

A Miracle or ...

The "German Economic Miracle" is a term often used to describe what happened in postwar Germany. The country, which in 1929 was about 15% behind France and a quarter behind Great Britain in terms of living standards, caught up with the former a decade later and, in another 15 years (by 1970), caught up with the latter.[56] In 1951, German exports rose 64% over the previous year; over the next four years, they rose another 77% having surpassed the prewar high (1929).[57]

The main result of US policy toward Germany after World War II—as a peaceful, democratic, prosperous country—can hardly be questioned by anyone. Germany became the economic engine of European integration and the largest donor to the integration of Eastern European countries after the fall of the Berlin Wall and the collapse of the Soviet bloc. One could probably stop

[54] After the end of the war, France demanded that the Saarland be handed over to it, to which Great Britain strongly objected. A compromise between the two countries was found in creating a special so-called European Statute: political sovereignty of the territory under international control and its participation in an economic, customs, and monetary union with France.

[55] The status had to be approved in a referendum at France's request. Paris was so confident of a positive outcome of the vote that it did not envisage the possibility of rejecting it. However, the inhabitants of Saarland voted against it, effectively obliging France to accept Saarland's accession to the Federal Republic. On January 1, 1957, Saar became a state within the Federal Republic of Germany after a transition period.

[56] I am wary of statistical comparisons from that time because, before World War II, countries embarked at different times on armament programs that had a marked impact on gross economic and industrial performance, their economies suffered differently during the war, and at the end of the war, countries received different amounts of US financial aid, and their currencies were not in equilibrium. These comparisons are based on estimates of GDP per capita from the Maddison Project of the University of Groningen. https://www.rug.nl/ggdc/historicaldevelopment/maddison/

[57] There is a widespread belief that the Korean War played an important role in the economic rise of Europe in the 1950s. However, statistics do not support this: while in Japan 80% of the increase in exports in 1948–1953 was accounted for by the countries that actively participated in the Korean War (USA, Great Britain, Korea), for Germany this figure amounted to 22%, more than half of the increase was accounted for by shipments to the countries of continental Europe. Statistical Office of the United Nations. International Trade Statistics. 1900–1960 (draft). May 1962. https://unstats.un.org/unsd/trade/imts/Historical%20data%201900-1960.pdf

there, especially since it would be wrong to attribute all economic achievements solely to the Marshall Plan and political outcomes to Germany's accession to NATO. If that were the case, today, France, Italy, or Great Britain would boast a more efficient and sustainable economy, and Turkey would be a more democratic and peace-loving country, which would make the actual partition of Cyprus impossible.

Undoubtedly, Germany's success can and should be attributed to the people who led the country in the postwar period. Despite sometimes very sharp disagreements, they were able to agree on the basic principles of building a new state and adhere to them for decades.

It is pointless to deny that the influence of the American military/occupation administration during the reconstruction of Germany was strong and, at times, decisive.[58] However, it is essential to note that this policy was flexible and responsive to the emerging situation. Naïve dreams that Germany's liberation from Nazism and movement toward democracy would inevitably lead to the invisible hand of the market providing economic prosperity collided rather quickly with the harsh reality of financial devastation, starvation, and impoverished populations. The hope that the Allies could agree on common principles of financial management and the process of building a unified German state was shattered by the mighty walls of Kremlin ideology; moreover, it soon became apparent that compromise among the Western Allies was becoming increasingly problematic, and the only solution that offered any hope of success was the unification of the three zones of occupation and the involvement of German representatives in economic decision-making long before the creation of West Germany. The belief that the German economy could withstand the payment of postwar reparations, which were substantially less than those imposed on Germany after World War I, and the dismantling of industrial equipment that Western experts would deem superfluous, collapsed a little more than a year after the end of the war when Lucius Clay banned reparations shipments of goods from the Western Zone in favor of the Soviet Union. But after that, it took another two and a half years to persuade the British government to refuse to dismantle German factory equipment.

One could attribute the Marshall Plan's success to the notion that "cash is king"—that unprecedented US aid alone drove Europe's recovery. If this were

[58] After 71% of the population of the state of Hesse voted in a referendum in 1946 for the inclusion in the state constitution of an article on the "socialization of industry," which provided for state participation in management and the inclusion of union representatives in the management of companies, Clay, head of the US military administration, decided to postpone the entry into force of this norm and repeated his refusal several times thereafter. John Gimbel. The American Occupation of Germany. Politics and the Military, 1945–1949. Stanford University Press, 1968, p. 117.

true, the European economies should have recovered much sooner—from mid-1945 until April 1948, when the Marshall Plan was authorized by law and began to be implemented, the US spent $15.4 billion in support of Western Europe,[59] the same amount that was eventually spent on the Marshall Plan over the next four years. For the money to become an engine for rebuilding the postwar economies, it was necessary first to understand and convince the European countries that their economies could not be rebuilt in isolation and that they had to be treated as a single system. And then to take another step—to incorporate the German economy into the economy of a united Europe.

As is often the case, even a good plan ceases to be realistic the moment it encounters reality, and new solutions are needed for its survival, which may require overturning previously established rules.

In the fall of 1949, it became apparent to Marshall Plan administrators that European economies lacked sufficient dollars to finance needed imports. Since the source of the dollars was no secret, the Economic Cooperation Administration (ECA) and the US Department of Commerce formed a joint group that prioritized expanding US imports from Europe to prewar levels: before the war, imports from European countries accounted for 2% of US GNP; after the war, they did not exceed half that level. The proposed measures included substantial reductions in import tariffs, easing customs procedures, and relaxation of "buy American" requirements established at the federal and lower levels. Already in six months, they began to give a noticeable return.[60]

In the postwar years, the Bretton Woods financial system, based on gold, the dollar, and the International Monetary Fund, was established worldwide. Trade settlements between countries were either in bilateral clearing arrangements or in US dollars. Despite massive aid, the recovery of European economies until the end of 1949 was not very fast, and one of the main obstacles was that trade flows between countries were objectively unbalanced: the matching of exports and imports was rare, and exports to the US, which was the source of dollars, were small (7% for Western Europe as a whole, 5% for France and Germany[61]). Again, it was necessary to be flexible and look for new solutions—in mid-December 1949, the US proposed[62] the idea for a

[59] Out of this amount, 44% were grants and the remaining were credits. William Adams Brown, Jr. and Redvers Opie. American Foreign Assistance. Washington DC, The Brookings Institution, 1953, p. 116.

[60] Ibidem, pp. 211–212.

[61] International Trade Statistics, 1900–1960. United Nations, 1962. https://unstats.un.org/unsd/trade/imts/Historical%20data%201900-1960.pdf

[62] Kurt F. Flexner. The Creation of the European Payments Union: An Example in International Compromise. Political Science Quarterly, vol. 72, No 2 (Jun 1957), pp. 241–260.

European Payments Union (a system of multilateral clearing, the operation of which is supported by US credit). By the middle of May 1950, it was possible to remove Great Britain's objections and work out all the terms of the EPU, which began to function on July 1.[63]

Overall, the success of the European reconstruction plan, of which the Marshall Plan was the core, was so evident that in May 1955, more than half of Americans (56%) thought it was a good idea to create a similar program for non-communist Asian countries.[64]

"Make a Friend Out of an Enemy"

It's All Hands-on Deck

At first glance, Japan's postwar fate should have been easier than Germany's. The countries' leaders participating in the anti-Hitler coalition scarcely discussed the issue at Yalta or Potsdam. Having lost the war, Japan avoided an unconditional surrender and retained a national government (though severely limited in autonomy). The country was not divided into zones of occupation. To maintain the regime of occupation of Japan, the Allied Joint Command was established, yet in practice virtually all authority rested with General Douglas MacArthur;[65] the Advisory Commission on the Far East, established in the fall of 1945, had very little power. In addition, the right to veto its

[63] Although the Treaty creating the ENP was only signed in mid-September, its potential benefits were so obvious that the participating countries agreed to put it into effect retroactively.

[64] The Gallup Poll: Public Opinion 1935–1971, vol. 2, p. 1330.

[65] During the Potsdam Conference, the Allies agreed on the transfer to the Soviet Union of South Sakhalin and the Kuril Islands and the secession of Korea as an independent state. After Japan capitulated, Stalin approached President Truman with a proposal to station Soviet troops on the northern island of Hokkaido, stating that a Soviet occupation zone should be established there, but it was rebuffed. The US thought all occupation forces should be subject to a single command. "*I must say that neither I nor my comrades expected such an answer from you*, "Stalin said with restraint. (John Emerson. The Japanese Thread. Holt, Rinehart, and Winston, New York, 1978, p. 281). But this refusal did not upset him much. As early as October 1945, Stalin told US Ambassador Averell Harriman in Moscow that it made no sense to send additional troops to Japan to facilitate MacArthur's work, and the following January, when Harriman was leaving Moscow to complete his mission, Stalin himself started talking about Japan and said: "*Things are going well in Japan because the United States and the Soviet Union have found common ground.*" (Averell Harriman and Elie Abel. The Special Envoy to Churchill and Stalin, 1941–1946. Random House, New York, 1975, p. 531). Apparently, Moscow was willing to accept Japan as part of the US sphere of influence in exchange for Washington's "calm attitude" to what was happening in Eastern Europe. In addition, China and its future appealed to the Soviet dictator (as did the Truman administration) much more, given the civil war that had begun between the Communists and Chiang Kai-shek's government.

decisions granted to the US, the USSR, Great Britain, and China excluded any conflicts with MacArthur's decisions.

President Truman's administration made no secret that the United States would be the only country to determine what would happen in Japan after the war. In late August 1945, MacArthur received a document entitled "Initial US Policy Toward Japan After Surrender,"[66] which defined the tasks of the occupation forces. The general, accustomed to the brevity and clarity of military commands, summarized the text of the five-page document in eight lines:[67]

> First, destroy military power. Punish war criminals. Build a structure of representative government. Modernize the constitution. Hold free elections. Give rights to women. Free political prisoners. Free the farmers. Create a free labor movement. Encourage a free economy. Abolish police pressure. Develop a free and responsible press. Liberalize education. Decentralize political power. Separate church and state.

In early November, Douglas MacArthur received Directive JCS1380/15, which granted him virtually unrestricted decision-making authority.[68] *"In addition to the usual powers of a military occupier of enemy territory, you have the right to take whatever steps you deem appropriate (and expedient) to implement the surrender and the provisions of the Potsdam Declaration… Your supreme authority as Supreme Commander of the Allied Powers in Japan will extend to all matters in the economic sphere… You will establish control over all Japanese foreign trade in goods and services."*

The general objective was well defined—"*to create conditions which will give the greatest possible assurance that Japan will no longer become a threat to world peace and security and will enable it eventually to become a responsible and peace-loving member of the family of nations.*" To this end, the occupation administration, militarily named "Headquarters," was to develop and implement comprehensive political, economic, and social reforms, including the drafting of a new constitution for the country, to define the principles and put into practice the purge of the state apparatus at all levels to remove officials and employees involved in war crimes or actively supporting the militarist regime,

[66] https://www.presidency.ucsb.edu/documents/statement-policy-approved-the-president-relating-post-war-japan

[67] Douglas MacArthur. Reminiscences. McGraw-Hill, 1964, pp. 282–283.

[68] "Basic Initial Post Surrender Directive to Supreme Commander for the Allied Powers for the Occupation and Control of Japan (JCS1380/15). Political Reorientation of Japan. September 1945 to September 1948. Report of Government Section. Supreme Commander for the Allied Powers. Washington DC, US Government Printing Office, 1949, vol. II, pp. 429–439.

to destroy the foundations of the economic system based on large financial and industrial groups (zaibatsu).

While quite detailed in some respects, the Directive gave wide latitude to its interpretation and left MacArthur free to act. It spoke of writing a new constitution or political cleansing without defining its basic terms and principles. While speaking of broad economic reforms, the Directive was silent on such trivial matters as the sustainability of the Japanese economy and its ability to provide the population with sufficient food and essential goods. "*This Directive does not purport to formulate a definitive long-term policy for the treatment of Japan in the postwar world, nor does it seek to prescribe in detail the measures you should take during your occupation of Japan to implement the surrender and the Potsdam Declaration. This policy and the appropriate measures for its implementation will be primarily determined by developing circumstances in Japan.*"

By granting MacArthur the broadest powers, the Directive effectively shielded him from accountability for the effectiveness of his decisions. "*You will assume no responsibility for the economic recovery of Japan or the strengthening of the Japanese economy... The Japanese authorities will have to make every effort to maximize the production of agricultural and fishery products, coal, charcoal, materials for home repair, clothing, and other necessities...*" Moreover, economic stability was declared to be a secondary objective of the policy of the occupation authorities. "*Serious inflation would significantly retard the achievement of the ultimate objectives of the occupation... However, the prevention or control of inflation cannot be a justification for restricting withdrawal, destruction, or reduction of production capacity in the course of reparation, restitution, demilitarization, or economic disarmament programs.*"

To implement large-scale plans for the transformation of Japan, up to 5000 people were employed at Headquarters at a time, not counting the numerous experts and consultants sent from Washington on their initiative or at MacArthur's request by various agencies. Formally, normative acts were prepared and issued by the Japanese government. Still, the principal guidelines of these documents, and often the specific wording of certain provisions, were drafted at the Headquarters, and no document could be issued without MacArthur's consent. Although one of the most important tasks of American policy was to democratize the political system, the separation of powers and the establishment of a government based on a parliamentary majority, as early as September 1945, an imperial decree was issued that allowed the government to prepare and issue decrees (imperial decrees until the new constitution came into force in 1947, later cabinet decrees) that defined the norms and rules traditionally established by law without the consent of parliament.

Having entered the West Point Military Academy at 18, Douglas MacArthur had spent nearly half a century in military service by the time he was appointed Supreme Allied Commander in Japan. The general was never a public politician and was not "his own man" in the bureaucratic corridors.[69] However, in late January 1946, meeting with the members of the Advisory Commission who had arrived in Tokyo, MacArthur proposed to begin preparing a peace treaty with Japan, surprisingly precisely defining the task of his mission in this country: "*The most proper way to ensure the development of a peaceful and democratic Japan is to make a friend out of an enemy.*"[70]

Decisive Measures

In the first months of the occupation, Headquarters' main efforts were directed at political reform—after years of military dominance, the public consciousness was militarized, as well as the nature of government institutions.[71] Meeting for the first time with Japan's newly appointed first postwar Prime Minister Kijuro Shidehara, MacArthur read aloud from a slip of paper the Japanese government's five top priorities, handing the piece of paper to his interlocutor. The list included granting women the right to vote, supporting the formation of trade unions and liberalizing strike practices, establishing a more liberal education, eliminating the intimidation system that relied on the secret police, and moving toward a broad distribution of income and ownership of the means of production in society.

It is believed that many Headquarters officials, sympathetic to Roosevelt's New Deal, sought to achieve in Japan what they had been unable to implement at home. This explained the speed of decision-making. Conversely, few understood Japanese culture or daily life, which helps explain some of the unexpected results once their decisions were put into practice.

[69] Douglas MacArthur had no doubt that he understood the problems he was dealing with better than anyone. From the beginning of his work as the head of the occupation administration in Japan, he was dismissive of people sitting in Washington. He often did not think informing them of his intentions and plans was necessary. At times, even President Truman was kept in the dark about what MacArthur intended to do.

[70] Richard Finn. Winners in Peace. University of California Press, 1992, p. 69.

[71] It is believed that even during the war years, anti-war politicians continued to exist in the Japanese government. These politicians had no discernible influence on decisions but were able to discuss plans for Japan's postwar transformation based on the hypothesis of its defeat. Richard Finn. Winners in Peace. University of California Press, 1992, pp. 39–40.

Hungry Bellies Have no Ears

In mid-December 1945, new electoral legislation was adopted: women were given the right to vote, the minimum voting age was lowered from 25 to 20, and the number of voters doubled. At the same time, the House of Representatives, elected in 1942, was dissolved, and elections were scheduled for April 1946. The result of the elections surprised many: the Liberal Party, whose leader Ichirō Hatoyama, according to the decision of the majority coalition, was to be appointed prime minister of the coalition government, received the maximum number of votes, but was caught in a political purge and imprisoned.

The second surprise was that the Japanese Communist Party, first legally established in the country in late 1945, whose leader Kyuichi Tokuda spent 18 years in prison, from which he was released only in October 1945 along with other political prisoners, was able to overcome the 3% threshold and enter the parliament, winning five seats.[72]

Simultaneously with the adoption of the election law, new labor legislation was introduced, largely copying the American Wagner Act of 1935, which created a system of collective bargaining, initiated the creation of national trade unions, and fixed the procedures for announcing strikes. At the same time, none of the initiators of the law paid attention to the fact that granting the right to strike to employees of state-owned companies jeopardized the stability of the most important industries—unlike in the US, in Japan railroads, electric power, and communications were owned by the state. A year after the law was passed, Japan had over 17,000 labor unions with over five million members.

The difficult economic situation of 1946–1947, with high inflation, shortages of essential goods, and huge unemployment, became a breeding ground for social protests. The strike movement gradually expanded, strengthening the political position of the left-wing parties.

---

[72] Unlike in West Germany, where the Communist Party was not authorized until 1968, the US did not oppose Communist activities in Japan, believing them to be rather nationalistic and not ready to "dance to the tune" of Moscow. In an interrogation at Headquarters a few days after his release from prison, Tokuda said: "*One of the aims of the Japanese Communist Party will be to convince the United States that we have no connection with Soviet Russia… Communism may not come to Japan for another hundred years… The Communists will fully support the policies of Britain and the United States.*" In the manifesto he prepared in connection with his liberation, Tokuda put forward ideas that differed in content from MacArthur's plans only in that he demanded the abolition of the institution of monarchy, naming the emperor as responsible for starting the war. John Emerson. The Japanese Thread. Holt, Rinehart, and Winston, New York, 1978, pp. 257–259.

Four years later, in January 1949, in the parliamentary elections, the Communists achieved an impressive success, winning nearly 10% of the vote and securing 48 seats. In October of the same year in China, the Communist Party finally won the civil war, and the People's Republic of China was established. In June 1950, the Korean War began. All this provoked an upsurge of anti-Communist sentiment, which was transformed into the Red Purge, during which tens of thousands of Communists and sympathizers were repressed and lost their jobs.

Land to the Peasants

Agrarian reform was not Headquarters' original intention, but the existing agricultural land use practices were deeply problematic. About 40% of the population of postwar Japan lived in villages and farmed, but they owned only half of the land available for cultivation. The other half belonged to landowners who leased it out at the standard rate of half the crop. The average size of a farm was 1 ha, and half of the farmers had no more than half a hectare at their disposal.

In December 1945, the Japanese government initiated agrarian reform, realizing the archaic nature of the existing system, but its proposals seemed insufficiently progressive to MacArthur—after a visit from Washington experts led by Wolf Ladejinsky, the General became an ardent supporter of transferring land to those who worked it. The development of an alternative law took considerable time and saw the light of day only in the fall of 1946. Landowners who leased land had to sell it to their tenants at low prices, receiving payment in government bonds and retaining only 1 ha of fertile land. The land transfer, land distribution among tenants, and the determination of the redemption price were left to local committees, most of which belonged to farmers and tenants. On the one hand, the reform was successful—the number of tenant farmers was reduced from 73% of the farming population to 30%, of which only 5.5% were tenants without own land. On the other hand, it was unfair to landowners, who discovered at the time of redemption of government bonds that their property had, in effect, been expropriated—they received the price of a block of cigarettes per hectare of land.[73] In addition, the reform was technically very complex and stretched over time—land

[73] Peter Frost. Debating the Allied Occupation of Japan. 2016. https://www.asianstudies.org/publications/eaa/archives/debating-the-allied-occupation-of-japan-part-two/

distribution did not end until late 1951—which disrupted sustainable agricultural linkages. Rice production in Japan exceeded prewar levels starting in 1955.[74]

Down with the Oligarchs!

The most important task of Headquarters concerning Japanese industry from 1945 to 1947 was the policy of forcing the unbundling of the powerful conglomerates, the zaibatsu. On the one hand, by the end of the war, the ten largest zaibatsu controlled the production of two-thirds of machinery and equipment, half of the output of extractive industries, and nearly 40% of the country's chemical production; they owned more than half of the banking and insurance business.[75] But on the other hand, they were all diversified; none of them was a monopolist in any industry. In addition, each conglomerate created its own "support group" of medium and small companies that received steady orders. From the point of view of American experts, all zaibatsu were active participants in the militarist machine, which could not be denied. However, Japanese experts clearly distinguished between the "old" zaibatsu, which emerged at the turn of the century and grew organically for decades, and the "new" zaibatsu, which grew during aggressive wars on government orders.

Raymond Kramer, head of the economic section of Headquarters, who had extensive experience in managing big business before the war, could get an adequate assessment of the state of Japanese industry during his short time there. In October 1945, he told President Truman's special envoy Edwin Locke that in 15 years, Japan would be one of the world's largest industrial exporters, competing with the United States and Great Britain.

Kramer was determined, and as early as October–November 1945, a plan to unbundle the four largest conglomerates was approved. The unbundling procedure was not simple. Companies within the zaibatsu were bound by intertwined ownership, management contracts, overlapping directors, and banking arrangements, and it was not quick. It might have proceeded at a faster pace, but Kramer's mission ended in December 1945, and MacArthur appointed his good friend, Artillery General William Marquart, whose knowledge of economics and business was minimal, to this position. Marquart looked arrogantly at Japanese industrialists and politicians who genuinely

[74] USDA. Agricultural Statistics. (Annual publications, 1945 to 1960).

[75] Richard Finn. Winners in Peace. University of California Press, 1992, p. 57.

wanted to build partnerships with America, mistaking their peculiar politeness for subservience. He saw the future of Japanese industry in the production of clothing and shoes, overlooking that during the war, the country had created modern companies with advanced technology in engineering, shipbuilding, chemical industry, optical products, and electrical appliances.

In November 1945, the Special Commission for the Liquidation of Holdings (SCLH)[76] was established to transfer the shares of 18 holding companies owned by the four zaibatsu in the first wave of unbundling and the shares of 326 of their subsidiaries. One year later, the number of holding companies whose shares were transferred to SCLH had increased to 83. Former stockholders were compensated with 20-year government bonds whose value had fallen 90% by the time they matured. The task of the SCLH was to organize the sale of the shares received. Still, it turned out that the savings in the Japanese economy before the war depreciated due to inflation, and no buyers were willing to pay an adequate price except… banks, including the banks that were part of the zaibatsu. The fact is that different groups of experts reformed the industrial and financial sectors, and those charged with reforming the financial sector saw their task as making the banks sustainable as quickly as possible without having to unbundle them.

As a result, of the 83 holding companies designated for liquidation, 16 were dissolved, 26 were dissolved and reorganized, 11 were reorganized, and no action was taken with respect to the remaining 30. Two hundred and fifty subsidiaries were declared independent. The separation of conglomerates had the effect of retarding economic activity. Typically, more than 60% of the shares of companies within holding companies were cross-owned by the holding companies, and banks used these holdings to assess the soundness of borrowers. Once the cross-shareholdings were eliminated and the "freed" shares were transferred to SCLH, the companies were left with only their productive assets and lost dividend flows, reducing their ability to attract bank loans.[77]

The Economy Is Not Reviving

During the occupation of Germany, the US self-financed the costs of providing for the military and civilian personnel stationed there and purchasing critical food and industrial supplies. Thus, the German economy was supported, albeit slightly, by the occupying authorities. The policy toward Japan

[76] Holding Companies Liquidation Commission (HCLC).

[77] The zaibatsu separation policy was greatly relaxed in mid-1948 after a visit by Kennan, who was highly critical of it, believing it weakened the country's economy.

was different—the defeated country had to fully fund the costs of the US military stay, and all costs associated with Headquarters operations. During the occupation, Japan spent $3.3 billion for those purposes while the US grants came to $2.2 billion.

Cut off from foreign trade, the Japanese economy did not receive the necessary imported raw materials, and the recovery process was extremely slow. Unemployment continued unabated, and shortages of goods led to prices soaring and a thriving black market. Social tensions were growing daily; a general strike of government employees, scheduled for February 1, 1947, could be stopped only by MacArthur's firm order, who threatened to use force. This was the end of political liberalization, and the most active unions and their leaders began to face pressure from the officials.

World War II's economic and geographical results were more severe for Japan than for Germany. Japan lost half of the territory it consisted of at the beginning of the twentieth century: Korea, Taiwan, South Sakhalin, and the Kuril Islands.[78] According to a population survey conducted in 1945, the country lost about 4% of its population, but half of this loss was offset by the repatriation of military and civilian personnel from outside Japan. The economy lost about a quarter of its tangible assets compared to the prewar period. Still, these losses were uneven: three-quarters of its military and civilian vessels, more than a third of its industrial equipment, a quarter of its industrial structures, and a fifth of its housing stock were lost; at the same time, the industrial and utility infrastructure: communications and water supply (15.9%), electricity and gas (10.8%), and rail and road transportation (9.9%) were destroyed to a lesser extent.

Headquarters' efforts in the economic sphere focused on structural reforms but did not improve matters in the least. It was the Japanese government's responsibility to solve existing problems, but it could not boast of success. The preoccupation with planning economic activity under conditions of limited resources was characteristic of all countries affected by the war—Japan was no exception. However, the inability to obtain key imports made these efforts pointless, and some of the steps taken by Headquarters only worsened the situation.

In the spring of 1947, the two largest trading companies, part of the Mitsui and Mitsubishi conglomerates, which had served much of the foreign trade before the war, underwent a split. None of the managers of the companies that were part of the trading holdings were allowed to buy more than 1% of

[78] Japan gained control of Korea in 1910, Taiwan in 1895, South Sakhalin in 1905, and the Kuril Islands in 1875.

the stock, and no company they newly created was allowed to hire more than 100 employees.[79] As a result, two large companies were replaced by 360 small companies,[80] none of which could attract bank loans in the amounts necessary to finance export and import operations. In addition, any foreign trade transaction had to be approved by Headquarters, and individual exchange rates were determined for each transaction, which added to the confusion of businessmen, who could not assess the profitability of a transaction until they received an opinion from Headquarters.

In 1948, exports from Japan were a little over a quarter of the prewar level (1934/36), and imports were as high as 70%,[81] but more than half of that was the US humanitarian aid.[82]

Familiar Consequences

In mid-1947, the Japanese government began implementing a "priority production" policy in key industries, which included steel, coal, electricity, chemical fertilizers, shipbuilding, maritime, and rail transport. Calculations showed that an increase in coal production led to a rise in steel production, which made it possible to mine more coal, produce more steel, and then begin to rebuild shipbuilding—Japanese fishermen needed ships to fish. The government could support the priority industries with a well-known set of tools: government orders, allocation of scarce resources, and budget subsidies for "price adjustment," the amount of which in the 1949 fiscal year increased 7.5 times compared to 1947[83] and exceeded a quarter of all budget expenditures.[84] Unsurprisingly, all subsidies were financed by the Bank of Japan's purchase of government bonds, i.e., by monetary expansion.

The results of this policy were contradictory. On the one hand, the production of basic goods began to increase; industrial production rose from 31% of the prewar level in January 1947 to 80% in April 1949. On the other hand, the negative effects soon became starkly evident. The growth of wages in basic

[79] Mitsui Trading House employed 7050 people before the split.

[80] Randall K. Morck and Masao Nakamura. A Frog in a Well Knows Nothing of the Ocean: A History of Corporate Ownership in Japan. In A History of Corporate Governance around the World: Family Business Groups to Professional Managers. NBER, 2005, p. 427.

[81] Warren Hunsberger. Japan. New Industrial Giant. American-Asian Educational Exchange, 1972, p. 74.

[82] Fiscal and Monetary Policies of Japan in Reconstruction and High-Growth—1945–1971. Office of Historical Studies, Institute of Fiscal and Monetary Policy, Ministry of Finance of Japan, April 2020, p. 7.

[83] Ibid., p. 7.

[84] Special Monthly Economic Report, Bank of Japan, Research Department, Tokyo, May 1949, p. 27.

industries without an increase in the production of consumer goods fueled inflation, which reached 300% a year.

A substantial share of the loan funds disappeared through graft and kickbacks, some of which even involved bribing Headquarters personnel. Large companies, which were not caught in the hammer of unbundling and were not among the priority industries, were paralyzed by uncertainty and waited for recommendations/instructions/decisions from American officials, being sure that they knew the secrets of economic recovery.

Shock Therapy

Unlike the Japanese experts who considered the policy of priority production a success and recommended that the government continue it, American economic experts took the opposite view. President Truman's economic views were very different from the ideas promoted by Franklin Roosevelt; Truman was critical of much of the New Deal, and his team included people with much more conservative views on economic policy. They saw that rising inflation was eating away at the achievements of which the government was proud and, most importantly, that the policies were not addressing the most pressing problem—the provision of basic goods.

Need a "Marshall Plan"?

In December 1947, General Draper, Deputy Secretary of War, who had previously been deputy head of the American occupation administration in Germany, flew to Japan. He readily saw many parallels between the two countries, and his recommendations were based on an analysis of the mistakes made in Germany. He sharply criticized the policy of destroying economic conglomerates and insisted that the dismantling of equipment be halted as reparations to Asian countries. He argued that preserving its industrial potential was necessary to rebuild the Japanese economy. Back in Washington, Draper initiated the development of a Marshall Plan–style program for Japan, which allocated $1.2 billion over four years to jump-start the economy. From the Truman team's point of view, the price was more than acceptable—by this time, the US was spending $400 million annually to support Japan, with little progress to show for it.

Following Draper, Kennan flew to Tokyo in February 1948. As head of Secretary of State Marshall's Political Planning Group, he was the highest-ranking State Department official to visit Japan after the end of the war. Kennan's recommendations dealt with politico-military issues and proved controversial. On the one hand, Kennan argued that the Japanese military machine was utterly destroyed and that Japan posed no threat to its neighbors and was incapable of offering any support to the United States if a military partnership agreement was signed. On the other hand, Kennan considered the policy recommendations of Headquarters too liberal and called for strengthening the role of the police, the beginning of the fight against leftist forces and, at the same time, considered it necessary to stop the prosecution of war criminals. On the economic side, Draper and Kennan had little disagreement, except that Kennan believed it was essential to reduce the presence of American soldiers and civilian specialists since their upkeep was the government's single largest expense.

Inflation Is the Main Enemy

In October 1948, President Truman signed Directive NSC 13/2,[85] which identified Japan's economic recovery as its highest priority. "*Economic recovery should be the primary objective of United States policy in Japan for the immediate period, second only to US security interests. It should be achieved through a combination of a US assistance program … and vigorous and concerted measures … to remove existing obstacles to the revival of Japanese foreign trade … We should make it clear to the Japanese government that the success of the recovery program will depend largely on … domestic austerity measures and rigorous control of inflationary trends, including efforts to achieve a balanced domestic budget as soon as possible.*"

By December, US agencies agreed on and presented to the Japanese government a "Nine-Point Stabilization Program" developed under Joseph Dodge's direction. The Detroit banker, who had been in charge of the procurement system for the US Army during the war and had become a key figure in planning and implementing monetary reform in postwar Germany, was very reluctant to take on the responsibilities assigned by the President—to propose a set of solutions that would stabilize the Japanese economy and ensure sustainable growth. Upon receiving Draper's offer to address Japan's problems, Dodge wrote to him, "*I see no quick or easy answers. They are non-existent,*" and he expressed doubt that MacArthur would accept the advice of an outsider,

[85] FRUS, 1948, vol. VI, doc 588.

much less a civilian.[86][87] Dodge believed that there was no mistake in economic policy that had not been made in Japan.

A hallmark of President Truman's personnel policy was that he often announced an appointment before meeting with the person in question, making rejection unlikely. This was the case with Joseph Dodge, who, on February 1, 1949, flew to Tokyo as a special representative of the President with the rank of minister (which put him equal footing with MacArthur[88]) to personally supervise the implementation of the stabilization program.

The "Dodge Line" stabilization plan called for eliminating the budget deficit and price subsidies, raising taxes, and introducing a unified yen exchange rate. Concurrently, a new tax system was introduced, designed by Professor Carl Shoup, which emphasized direct taxes (income and income tax).[89]

Out of the Frying Pan into the Fire

Joseph Dodge spent less than seven months in Japan, returning to Washington in late August with a sense of accomplishment. The chronic deficit budget turned into a surplus, which by the end of the fiscal amounted to 4.5% of GNP and was used entirely to pay off the debt to the Bank of Japan. Inflation, which had raged in the country since the mid-1930s,[90] was curbed within three months; moreover, prices for many goods began to fall: by June 1950, the country's composite price index had fallen by 17%. In one of his meetings with Dodge, Japanese Finance Minister Ikeda said that economic recovery had begun because he had been informed of it by the Tokyo police chief. To a surprised question—How could the police chief know this?—Ikeda said that police officers in the city began to record many pickpocketing incidents when

[86] Marie Thorsten & Yoneyuki Sugita (1999) Joseph Dodge and the geometry of power in US-Japan relations, Japanese Studies, vol. 19, No 3, pp. 297–314.

[87] It should be noted that, in this case, Dodge was wrong. According to Dodge's recollection, when he presented his recommendations to MacArthur, the General's face became increasingly cold and angry. At the end of the presentation of the stabilization plan, MacArthur was silent for a long time, looked out the window, then turned to Dodge, pointed his index finger at his chest, and said: *You're right—we will.* David Halberstam. The Reckoning. William Morrow and Company, Inc. New York, 1986, p. 127.

[88] "Japan in the US view second to Europe." The New York Times. February 11, 1949.

[89] The exchange rate of the Japanese yen, 360 yen to one dollar, remained unchanged until 1971 when the US refused to support the exchange of the dollar for gold. Based on Professor Shoup's recommendations, the tax system did not change until 1989.

[90] In April 1949, when the Dodge Plan began, consumer prices in Japan were 220 times the 1934–1936 level. Jerome Cohen, "Japan's Postwar Economy." Indiana University Press, 1958, p. 84.

the target of the thieves was money; "*until now, money has not made sense for stealing.*"[91]

Drawing on European experience, Dodge insisted that US aid be sold at market prices, using the new yen exchange rate, so that the government could generate "counterpart funds" and use them to finance its programs. In 1949, the Japanese budget received 129 billion yen in this way, half of which was used to pay off the debt to the Bank of Japan, thus reducing the amount of money in circulation. For 1949–1950, receipts to "counterpart accounts" amounted to 292 billion yen (over $800 million), almost 2% of GNP annually.[92]

At the same time, like any stabilization program, the Dodge Plan led to a serious recession: companies saw credit dry up and were forced to cut production and lay off workers. Japanese railroads laid off 100,000 workers; the Japan Postal Service and the Telephone and Telegraph Corporation released 30,000.[93] Those who failed to act risked bankruptcy. It was especially hard for those industries where the government continued to control prices, such as the automobile industry. As early as April 1949, the demand for trucks had already declined, and some dealers began to decline the vehicles assigned to them by the government. At the end of the summer, the government stopped controlling coal allocation and then released coal and steel prices, eliminating budget subsidies while retaining control over automobile prices. The car companies' financial problems were mounting. Japanese business ethics prevented executives from laying off workers. In late 1950, they could survive only after the Bank of Japan organized a consortium of banks to provide the necessary loans for a significant restructuring. To find the money to lend, the banks issued bonds, which the Bank of Japan bought, thus mitigating the effects of the ultra-tight fiscal stance.

In April 1950, Ikeda flew to the United States for talks with Dodge to get a relaxation of fiscal policy. The talks ended unsuccessfully for the minister; the Americans considered any easing of policy a mistake. Japan was facing the threat of a deep recession.

---

[91] David Halberstam. The Reckoning. William Morrow and Company, Inc. New York, 1986, p. 129.

[92] Fiscal and Monetary Policies of Japan in Reconstruction and High-Growth. Office of Historical Studies. Institute of Fiscal and Monetary Policy. Ministry of Finance of Japan. April 2020, p. 59.

[93] Uchino Tatsuro. Japan's Postwar Economy: An Insider's View of its History and Future. Kodansha International, Tokyo/New York, 1983, p. 52.

At a Crossroads

Five years after the end of the war, the Japanese economy was in a state of complete uncertainty. On the one hand, implementing the Dodge Plan led to the suppression of inflation and the normalization of the market economy after the abolition of massive budget subsidies and the system of government planning and resource allocation. On the other hand, the economy recovered very slowly: The country's GNP in 1949 was 15%, and exports were 45% below, prewar levels. The population lacked basic commodities; consumption of the population was 71% of prewar levels. Sugar consumption was four times lower than prewar levels, eggs and chicken nearly three times lower, and sake five times lower.[94]

Could the American aid plan developed by Draper help Japan? Perhaps. The $1.2 billion is about 10% of the aid received by European countries under the Marshall Plan, but in terms of GNP, the specific aid plan for Japan would have been one and a half times less. The strength of the Marshall Plan lay in restarting the mechanism of intra-European cooperation; Japan lacked this factor, and integration threads did not bind its economy. Imports from some countries and exports to others did not allow for synergies. If we consider the loss of Chinese market after the Communists came to power and the impending anti-colonial war in Indochina, it would be difficult to rely on the factor of external demand as an engine of Japan's economic growth in our hypothetical scenario.

Certainly, the Dodge Plan's well-intentioned goal of macroeconomic stabilization came at an unreasonably high price in terms of fiscal policy. A balanced budget and low public debt form the foundation of sustainable development, but maintaining a budget surplus of 3–5% of GNP annually to repay the debt to the Bank of Japan would have withdrawn national savings and thus reduced resources for investment.

Every Cloud Has a Silver Lining

Japan's recession may have been prolonged and would have taken many years to recover from, but an event radically changed the country's economic and political development trajectory. On June 25, 1950, the Korean War began between China-backed North Korea and Western-backed South Korea, which lasted three years.

---

[94] Ibid., p. 16–17.

MacArthur, in addition to his Japanese "portfolio," was appointed commander of the UN forces fighting on South Korea's side. Due to its geography, Japan was an ideal logistical hub: supplies of food, arms, and ammunition to South Korea flowed through Japan, reserves were gathered here to reinforce military units fighting on the Korean Peninsula, and wounded soldiers returned for treatment.

Soon enough, it became clear that the war would not be quick and easy; the need for the army began to increase, and the idea of using the idle capacity of Japanese industry was not long in coming. First, there was a demand for clothing, shoes, and dressing materials. Then, it became clear that the potential of arms and military equipment production accumulated by Japanese companies was not destroyed, and its quality did not lag European and American. Geographical proximity to the place of consumption and lower labor costs made placing military orders in Japan even more attractive.

Direct estimates of "special procurement" (as contracts for the belligerent army were called) show that between 1950 and 1953, the Japanese economy received an additional $1 billion in foreign demand annually, close to 5% of GNP. Including other expenditures by the UN forces, estimates of additional demand range from $2.6 to $3.4 billion per year, approaching 10% of GNP.[95] Although the level of development of Japanese industry was high enough to meet the growing needs of a belligerent army, new investment and technology were needed—foreign direct investment flowed into the country. In 1950, Japanese companies concluded 27 cooperation agreements, in 1951—101 agreements, in 1952—122 such agreements.[96] After the end of the war, Japan became one of the biggest beneficiaries of South Korea's reconstruction, which was financed at the expense of Western countries.

Not surprisingly, the threat of recession quickly faded; the Japanese economy grew at an annual rate of 11–15% during the Korean War, and industrial production grew even more strongly. The influx of foreign currency used to pay for war orders allowed for a rapid increase in imports to relieve bottlenecks in the production chain and supply the population with essential goods. The boom in demand for imports continued until 1957, by which time import volumes were more than triple their prewar level.

It would take Japan another decade before its economy would produce goods that would capture the world market—from 1965, Japanese exports steadily exceeded imports, and in 1968, the Japanese economy became the

---

[95] Ibid., p. 57.

[96] Richard Finn. Winners in Peace. University of California Press, 1992, p. 268.

world's second largest in terms of GDP. The share of engineering products in Japanese exports rose from 9.6% in 1938 to more than 25% in 1959. The share of Japanese goods in world trade in machinery products rose from less than 2% in 1953 to nearly 5% in 1960. Japanese goods made steady inroads into the US market: the US share of Japanese exports rose from 15% in 1938 to 26% in 1948–1958 and became nearly 30% after 1960.[97] The share of Japanese goods in US imports rose from 5.5% in 1950 to nearly 10% in 1960.[98]

In March 1973, after the outbreak of the first oil crisis, the finance ministers of the world's four leading economic powers—the US, Great Britain, France, and West Germany—gathered in Washington to discuss the emerging situation and agree on a joint policy. Very quickly, it became clear to the meeting 's participants that it was impossible to discuss the world economy without Japan, and the proposal of the US Treasury Secretary George Shultz to invite the Country of the Rising Sun was supported by all.[99] This was the origin of the "Five," which, after Italy (1975) and Canada (1976) were invited, became the "Seven."

What's This Japan Thing for?

A Springboard to Jump into the White House?

By the time World War II ended, American policymakers had no clear idea of what future relations with Japan would be like. The problems of Europe were closer and hotter, and energies were directed there. Japan was given "at MacArthur's mercy," who had specific views on this issue. The General believed that in 1948, he would have a good chance of being elected President of the United States—his victory in the Pacific had made him a national hero, and the declining popularity of the Democratic Party did not bode well for President Truman. Consequently, by the start of the campaign, he thought it was necessary to finish business in Japan and return home. Finishing business meant ending the occupation and signing a peace treaty. Thus, his initial prediction that the occupation would last two or three years seem understandable. A successful information campaign in the American media supported this. In June 1946, 60% of Americans believed MacArthur was doing a good

[97] Toshiaki Yoshihara, "Japan's trade with developing countries. A note based on foreign trade of Japan 1961." IDE-JETRO, The Developing Economies, Preliminary Issue, No 1 (August 1962), pp. 106–120.

[98] International Trade, 1960. GATT, Geneva, 1961, pp. 13, 57.

[99] George Shultz. Turmoil and Triumph: My Years as Secretary of State. Scribner's, 1993, p. 148.

job in Japan. In October 1947, more than half of those surveyed were confident that the next year would be better for Japan (29% gave an optimistic forecast for Great Britain, 31% for France, and 37% for Germany).[100]

Kennan shared the General's position on a short occupation, using a different argument: He believed that a rapid movement towards normalization of relations between the two countries would prevent the development of nationalistic and, consequently, militaristic sentiments in Japan.[101]

MacArthur's desire to conclude a peace treaty in a short period was shared by Japanese politicians but not shared in Washington. Soon after the signing of the surrender act, special study groups were set up in Tokyo to summarize the practice of concluding peace treaties, identify issues that could be included in them (reparations, territory, overseas assets), and begin to prepare a Japanese position. Memoranda prepared by the Japanese were sent to Washington, where no one paid serious attention to them. Although it was all fascinating, they heard there would be no peace treaty for a long time. When the time approached, the question of territory or reparations would be decided by the United States, not the Japanese.[102]

MacArthur's rapid failure in the 1948 presidential race[103] sharply reduced his desire to sign a peace treaty as soon as possible and ended the idea of a transition of power into the hands of a civilian administration, as had happened in Germany after the Basic Law and the proclamation of the FRG in May 1949. MacArthur decided to remain in Japan until the peace treaty was signed, retaining full authority.[104] The San Francisco Peace Treaty was signed on 8 September 1951, though McArthur was relieved of command by President Truman and left Japan on April 11, 1951. The reason for that was not Japan, but the Korean war—McArthur's public and unofficial statements contradicted administration's policy to avoid expanding of the war.

[100] The Gallup Poll. Public Opinion, 1935–1971, vol. 1, pp. 582, 677.

[101] The Association for Diplomatic Studies and Training Foreign Affairs Oral History Project. Ambassador Marshall Green. https://adst.org/OH%20TOCs/Green-Marshall.pdf

[102] The Association for Diplomatic Studies and Training Foreign Affairs Oral History Project. Richard B Finn. https://adst.org/OH%20TOCs/Finn,%20Richard%20B.toc.pdf

[103] MacArthur did not formally enter the race; to do so, he would have had to resign first. His supporters nominated him as a candidate in the Wisconsin primary election, which MacArthur resoundingly lost.

[104] The Association for Diplomatic Studies and Training Foreign Affairs Oral History Project. Richard B Finn. https://adst.org/OH%20TOCs/Finn,%20Richard%20B.toc.pdf

Controlling Japan Won't Help Anything

No one wanted to argue with the General, and no one in Washington was willing to deal with the problems of a distant country. Japan was not a significant figure on the geopolitical chessboard, and neither was the situation in Northeast Asia in general.[105] In February 1949, Secretary of the Army Kenneth Royall, during a visit to Japan, stated, "*I have my doubts about Japan's strategic importance. Her role must be seriously rethought. If, in the event of military conflict, the Soviet Union were to seize the industrial centers of Western Europe, control of Japan would not be very important. On the other hand, losing control of Japan would not change the balance of power in Europe. And in general, the US military is skeptical that the Communists are moving to take complete control of China—they have no idea of the magnitude of the problems they will face.*"[106]

Since no unified vision of future relations with Japan existed, each agency expressed its wishes for a peace treaty. Some demanded more reparations, disregarding the fact that much of it was going to China, where the Communists were approaching full control of the country; some insisted that America retain the right to keep military bases on Okinawa and the Ryukyu Islands; some argued heatedly with Great Britain, which feared the ultimate loss of prewar economic opportunities in Japan; some insisted that the signatories to the peace treaty must be the Soviet Union and China, but no one wanted to search for a compromise.

Alarm in Tokyo

Meanwhile, Japanese politicians, watching events in China and Korea, realized that a neutral Japan had no chance of survival and that the country needed protection from potential attacks. Shigeru Yoshida, who was at the helm of the government, understood that creating its armed forces, which had been discussed in Washington, was too dangerous for a country that had fought wars of aggression for a decade and a half. Consequently, he realized, the only way to ensure Japan's security was direct US support, which could be obtained in the only way possible—by concluding a peace treaty on terms Washington would formulate.

---

[105] *We had one staff member in our Office of Northeast Asian Affairs who dealt with Korea who knew very little about it.* The Association for Diplomatic Studies and Training Foreign Affairs Oral History Project. Ambassador Marshall Green. https://adst.org/OH%20TOCs/Green-Marshall.pdf

[106] "Japan in the US View Second to Europe." The New York Times. February 11, 1949.

In April 1950, Yoshida sent the finance minister to Washington, whose official mission was to negotiate with James Dodge on easing fiscal policy. Unexpectedly for an American banker, at one of the meetings, the minister said he had a message from the Prime Minister that should be passed on to the upper levels of government: Japan wanted "*an early conclusion of a peace treaty. Such a treaty may include a clause on the retention of American troops for security; if the American government hesitates to make such or other demands, the Japanese government says it will find a way to meet them.*"[107]

The Role of the Individual in History

Most likely, this statement would have disappeared in the bureaucratic archives (the same fate befell a similar appeal of the Japanese Foreign Minister Hitoshi Ashida, transmitted by him to Washington in September 1947[108]) if the right person—John Foster Dulles—had not appeared in the right place at the right time.

Dulles, a highly successful corporate lawyer, grandson of one US Secretary of State and nephew of another, who in 1919 had been a reparations expert on the US negotiating delegation after the Peace of Versailles, went to work in the administration of a Democratic President after his defeat in the Senate elections in the fall of 1949, as a Republican. In March 1950, he became an advisor to Secretary of State Acheson and was sent to prepare a peace treaty with Japan. "*You will never accomplish anything unless you pick a man you have confidence in, give him a task, and demand results. Look at the peace treaty with Japan—the Department has been discussing it for four years without results. Why don't you give someone one year to get it done, with the understanding that if he fails, he will fail? Give him a goal and enough authority to achieve it.*"[109]

By this time, Acheson had articulated his position: "*Western Europe and the United States could not simultaneously contain the Soviet Union and suppress Germany and Japan. Our best strategy was to make these former enemies willing and strong supporters of the free world structure.*"[110] But while basic decisions had already been made with respect to Germany, there was little energy, desire, or time to formulate a policy toward Japan, especially after Mao Zedong came to power in China. After some thought, Acheson came up with a proposal to

---

[107] Richard Finn. Winners in Peace. University of California Press, 1992, pp. 248–249.

[108] Goro Fujita. Reconsidering the Ashida Memorandum: the relations between the emergency stationing plan and police reform. *International Relations of the Asia-Pacific,* vol. 24, iss 2, May 2024, pp. 289–314.

[109] John Beal. John Foster Dulles, 1888–1959. Harper and Row, New York, 1959, p. 116.

[110] Dean Acheson. Present at Creation. Norton & Company, New York, 1969, p. 338.

appoint Dulles responsible for negotiations with Japan and received his consent.

Dulles had extensive experience in international negotiations, and he had good relations with both Republicans and Democrats—many saw him as the future Secretary of State regardless of the outcome of the 1952 presidential election—but no one knows whether his mission would have been successful if the Korean War had not broken out a month after he was authorized to negotiate. On the one hand, the war showed the miscalculations of Washington analysts, who were waiting for Soviet aggression in Europe and calmly looked at the establishment of the communist regime in China. After the outbreak of the war, they had to rapidly rethink the role and significance of Japan in the global confrontation. On the other hand, the war in Korea made representatives of various US agencies more treaty-capable, which allowed Dulles to discard the need to negotiate the text of the treaty not only with the Soviet Union but also with the Western allies.

The peace treaty with Japan was signed in September 1951 in San Francisco, 16 months after President Truman authorized John Foster Dulles. The peace treaty fixed Japan's postwar borders ended the occupation regime and opened the way for the country to join the United Nations. At the same time, the Security Treaty between the US and Japan was signed, which laid the foundation for a military-political alliance between the two countries. Under this treaty, Japan authorized the United States to maintain military bases on its territory after the end of the occupation and pledged not to grant other countries bases on its territory or rights related to military activities without the consent of the United States. The United States was authorized to use military forces stationed in Japan without prior consultation with the Japanese government. The treaty did not contain an obligation on the part of the United States to defend Japan in the event of an attack; this provision was introduced in the revision of the treaty and entered into force in 1960.

All Happy Families Are Happy in the Same Way…

The postwar trajectories of Germany and Japan are, at first glance, very different.

Germany was fragmented into zones of occupation, where it was difficult or impossible to agree on a standard policy or concerted action. Each victorious country had its own goals for which it was unwilling to make concessions. The division of Europe into spheres of influence gave Western politicians a sense of the inevitability of continued Soviet expansion, first ideological and then military and political. Perhaps if Stalin had been less straightforward and more cunning, he could have implemented his plan to preserve a united but weak and neutral country—remember the senseless blockade of Berlin or the categorical refusal to participate in the Marshall Plan at the very initial stage. Three years after the occupation's beginning, after the unification of the three western zones, the gradual transfer of power to German politicians and the replacement of the military occupation administration by civilian experts began. Although the formal signing of a peace treaty and its entry into force was still several years away, the de facto occupation of Germany ended in 1949 with the creation of the Federal Republic of Germany, and the launching of the Marshall Plan began the process of integrating the economies of Western Europe, where Germany was accepted as an equal. Washington's original plans called for a complete withdrawal of American troops from Germany, which made many politicians in Paris and London nervous, fearing a resurgence of German militarism. However, history itself solved the problem: the growing threat from the East and the adoption of the concept of deterrence, including the readiness for forceful confrontation, led to several hundred thousand American troops remaining in Germany until the end of the Cold War and, in addition to protecting against a potential Soviet invasion, guaranteeing the security of neighboring European countries against an even less potential new German aggression.

Japan, being formally occupied by the combined Allied forces, was under the complete control of the American administration, which, in the five years leading up to the Korean War, failed to achieve sustained economic growth and a standard of living above prewar levels. The decisive structural reforms accompanied significant adverse side effects that hampered achieving the goals. The failure to include Japan in the perimeter of strategic attention in Washington, on the one hand, and MacArthur's desire to retain full power in the occupied country, on the other, resulted in Japan's economic and political future being in a complete fog on the eve of the outbreak of the Korean War. One can only wonder what the future of this country would have been had Stalin not agreed to North Korea's request to launch a full-scale invasion of the South.

However, if we look at Germany and Japan in 1955, 10 years after the end of the war, by this time, both countries had become members of a political-military alliance led by the United States. The economies of both countries had begun a process of successful integration into the Western economic system that would place them among the world's leading nations in both size and technological development within a decade.

The Cold War was the flip side, or perhaps the engine, of the process of integrating Germany and Japan into the West's economic and political system. This confrontation would continue for almost half a century and end with the Soviet Union's defeat, after which the state vanished from the world map.

2

You're On Your Own

Perestroika Time

In the early 1980s, the Soviet economy had stalled: growth had flattened, plans went unfulfilled, and the technological gap with the West was widening. The Soviet leadership realized that the creaking economic system could no longer foster growth, so the leadership launched a large-scale economic experiment, which affected about 500 enterprises producing industrial equipment and about a thousand enterprises producing food and consumer goods.

Launched on 1 January 1984, the experiment aimed to spur managers and workers to raise productivity, conserve resources, and expand output. For this purpose, it was decided to end centralized wage-fund planning by the ministries and instead tie any wage-fund growth to the rise in net marketable output (analogous to value added). In addition, it was decided to abandon the distribution of enterprise profits by the ministry, which decided which part of the profits to send to the Union budget, which to keep at its disposal, how much money to allow the enterprise to use for bonuses to employees and how much to finance social facilities. Instead, enterprises received cost- and productivity targets, and any gains they achieved allowed them to retain a larger share of profits.

The experiment's results showed that economic incentives worked in the Soviet economy; however, their impact was limited because enterprises had no freedom to decide what to produce, who to buy from, and at what price. Historically, the experiment's key legacy was to prod the Soviet leadership into a deeper—and more urgent—debate on reforms. It became clear that cosmetic tweaks to the old system could not improve the economy's efficiency.

S. Aleksashenko, *Post-Cold War Russia and the Missed Opportunity for Global Stability*,
https://doi.org/10.1007/978-3-032-01380-4_2

In 1985, the 54-year-old Gorbachev became General Secretary of the Communist Party, the real leader of the Soviet state. By this time, he understood that the Soviet economy needed profound changes, but neither he nor his entourage had a plan or even a contoured idea of what form those changes should take. In a speech to the first Communist Party Central Committee Plenum after his election, Gorbachev proclaimed the acceleration course first floated within the Kremlin leadership in late 1982 under Yuri Andropov. He believed that economic growth could be initiated by shifting resources toward agriculture and food processing, thus easing consumer shortages, and toward machine-building to modernize industrial capacity.

The plan soon proved purely theoretical: shifting resources to machinery and agriculture produced no immediate rise in output of consumer goods. Yet, the shift still diverted scarce resources, primarily foreign currency, previously allocated to other industries. In contrast to a market system—where prices adjust to rebalance supply and demand—a planned economy could address imbalances only through bureaucratic fiat. After detecting growing imbalances and their causes, Gosplan and Gossnab had to make decisions to redistribute output for certain goods, coordinating them with changes in the matrix of mutual supplies between industrial ministries. In their turn, the industrial ministries had to change the planning assignments for subordinated enterprises and, when necessary, secure price adjustments from Goskomtsen.

Clearly, the apparatus could respond rapidly only to minor issues; anything bigger required re-writing hundreds of enterprise plans. Moreover, decisions on significant investments were prepared for years, considering the territorial distribution of production and the availability of infrastructure, energy, and labor resources; such decisions became the basis for 5-year plans, which fixed the direction and scale of structural shifts in the economy. It was impossible to decide on new construction outside the framework of the 5-year plan.

When the Soviet government opened an anti-alcohol campaign in May 1985, they failed to anticipate its macroeconomic fallout. The drastic reduction in the production of alcoholic beverages cost the Union budget about 10% of revenue in 1986–87—as expected—yet, more crucially, reduced household supplies by roughly 10%[1] with no offsetting increase in other goods, imports, or prices. The public adapted swiftly: demand for sugar—as well as alcohol-laden medical and cosmetic liquids used for moonshining—spiked nationwide. On the other hand, consumer market got out of balance all over the country.

[1] *Narodnoe hozyajstvo SSSR v 1990 g.* (National Economy of the USSR in 1990.) Moscow, Finansy i statistika, 1991.

The fall in world oil prices from $30–35/bbl in 1982–1985 to $15–17/bbl in 1986–1988 deprived the raw materials industries of resources to maintain production volumes, which was followed by a rapid decline in the production of basic commodities: from 1987 to 1990, oil production fell by 10%, coal production by 11%, steel production by 6%, mineral fertilizers by 14.5%, and timber by 13.7%.[2] Exports plunged: oil by 52%, coal by 15%, pig iron by 49%, timber by 34%, and fertilizers by 32%. The decline in export revenues entailed a fall in imports, further slowing down investment activity and leading to a rapid build-up of external debt.

The Chernobyl disaster dealt another blow, demanding massive human and material resources for containment. According to official data, in 1986–1987, 260,000 people took part in the liquidation of the accident's consequences; by 1990, that number had risen to 525,000. According to the Soviet Ministry of Finance in 1986–1990, the costs for the Chernobyl cleanup amounted to 12.6 billion rubles (in 1986 prices).[3]

Economic imbalances kept widening. On the one hand, the Soviet authorities realized that it was impossible to alleviate it without a serious revision of the price system. On the other, they feared taking such an unpopular step. In July 1987, the Communist Party Central Committee and the Council of Ministers of the USSR issued a joint resolution "On the main directions of restructuring the pricing system under the new economic mechanism," which was never implemented before the collapse of the Soviet Union.

Paradoxically, measures meant to grant enterprises more initiative only deepened the overall imbalance. In 1987, the Law on State Enterprise was adopted, which granted significant autonomy to 2000 of the 46,662 industrial enterprises, replacing rigid targets with broad control figures and state orders. Enterprises were given the right to enter the foreign market independently, to carry out joint activities with foreign partners, etc.

The gravest shock to the planned system came with the May 1988 Law "On Cooperation"[4] struck the hardest blow: although it legalized private enterprise, it quickly upended the carefully managed balance between the wage fund and consumer-goods supply once policed by Gosplan (Central Planning Agency), Goskomtrud (Labor and Wages Agency) and Goskomtsen

---

[2] Ibid.

[3] We have no certainty that this amount includes all costs associated with the elimination of the consequences of the accident. At the same time, to understand the scale of prices, let us point out that the annual expenditures of the Union budget on health care and physical culture in 1986–1988 amounted to 20 billion rubles.

[4] The first step in this direction was made in 1987 when the district committees of the Komsomol began to create Centers of Scientific and Technical Creativity of Youth, but the scale of their activities in the first year was not very large.

(Pricing Agency). Wage outlays ballooned past projections, while consumer-goods output lagged and imports shrank. Under conditions of centrally set prices, this led to a growing deficit in the consumer market and the accumulation of inflationary potential.

In 1989, the USSR staged its first semi-competitive elections to the Congress of People's Deputies, televised live and suddenly stripping away limits on criticism. The sad state of the economy was evident to everyone, and many of the deputies' complaints against the officials were aimed in this direction. From the beginning of the nineteenth century, an unspoken order was formed in Russia: if the government faced a problem, the solution was not obvious, and a special commission was immediately created in parallel with the existing structures. In its attempt to solve the essential issues of the Soviet economy, the Soviet leadership created a Government Commission for Economic Reform, intended to serve as the brains and engine of future change.

The Commission did not begin from a blank slate. At the beginning of 1988, the government set up a special working group to prepare a plan for economic reforms. It included the heads of key government agencies (Gosplan, Gossnab [Distribution and Supply agency], Goskomtrud, Goskomtsen, and the Ministry of Finance), who met for a few hours at first to discuss emerging ideas and problems or to report on the results of their work to Prime Minister Nikolai Ryzhkov. By late 1988 the group was working around the clock, sequestered for weeks—sometimes months—outside Moscow.[5]

However, despite all efforts, the government failed to create a reform plan to solve the key problems. The main reason was the unwillingness of the top political leadership to take the decisive step and move to free prices. Even the implementation of the price system reform approved in 1987 was blocked personally by Gorbachev, who feared unpredictable social consequences. In addition, the "bureaucratic lobby" and the industry ministries defended the state-controlled pricing system, which knew that most of them would have to disappear after the transition to free prices.

As conditions worsened, the Kremlin remained paralyzed over what course to take.

[5] From the beginning of 1989, I became involved in this group, where I got to know the leaders of the Soviet government and gained knowledge about how the Soviet economy functioned, what problems it faced, and how and why the country's top leaders accepted or rejected the proposed ideas.

Something's Going on There …

On January 10, 1990, Nigel Wicks, British Prime Minister Margaret Thatcher's G7 Sherpa, wrote her a note on the outcome of a meeting with his G7 colleagues, where preparations for the July 1990 G7 Summit in Houston, USA, had been discussed.[6] Unexpectedly, the topic of changes in the Soviet Union and the attitude of Western countries toward what was happening in that country became one of the top items on the agenda of the G7 leaders.

> Everyone agreed that East/West issues, in one guise or another, would dominate the Summit. There was unanimous agreement that the success of President Gorbachev was a top priority, though no-one thought that Summit participants could do much to help him with his internal reforms. Only the Japanese, with the comment that perestroika and glasnost had still to appear in the Soviet Union's Far Eastern policies (their northern islands), struck a jaundiced note. Burney (Canada) suggested that the Chairman of the Summit, Mr Bush, should brief President Gorbachev after the Summit on its results. The US's initial reaction did not seem to be enthusiastic, partly, I think, because of their wish to keep the Soviet Union some distance from Western international organisations until there is real evidence of a drastic reduction in the Soviet military threat.

It was only six months after the previous G7 meeting in Paris, whose agenda looked entirely predictable; the meeting resulted in Economic and Political Declarations that did not mention the Soviet Union. Events in China after the suppression of the Tiananmen Square protests generated much more serious interest and discussion. Transformation in the countries of Eastern Europe had already begun, but no one could predict at what speed it would continue and to what results it would lead. In this regard, the Declaration on East-West Relations[7] was restrained, its key point being a reminder that the East and the West are military adversaries.

We see signs of this same desire for greater freedom and democracy in the East… We hope that freedom will be broadened and democracy strengthened and that they will form the basis, after decades of military confrontation, ideological antagonism and mistrust, for increased dialogue and cooperation… We call upon the Soviet Government to translate its new policies and pronouncements into further concrete action at home and abroad. Military imbalances favoring the Soviet Union, both in Europe and in Asia, remain an

[6] MTF 213783. 1990 Summit. Nigel Wicks Minute to Prime Minister. January 10, 1990.

[7] G7 Declaration on East-West Relations. Paris, July 15, 1989. http://www.g7.utoronto.ca/summit/1989paris/east.html

objective threat to each of us. Our Governments must therefore continue to be vigilant and maintain the strength of our countries. For the foreseeable future, there is no alternative for each of us, within existing alliances, to maintaining a strategy of deterrence based upon an appropriate mix of adequate and effective nuclear and conventional forces.

Although it was too early to talk about the victory of democratic forces in the countries of Eastern Europe, the G7 singled out the "leaders," Poland and Hungary, promising them moral and economic support. Moreover, the Declaration made a direct appeal to the Paris Club of creditors to restructure Poland's foreign debt and to the IMF to conclude negotiations on a program of support for economic reforms in this country as soon as possible, although at that time there was no government in the country and no program of economic reforms.[8]

> We welcome the process of reform underway in Poland and Hungary. We recognize that the political changes taking place in these countries will be difficult to sustain without economic progress… Each of us is developing concrete initiatives designed to encourage economic reforms, to promote more competitive economies and to provide new opportunities for trade… Concerning concerted support for reform in Poland and Hungary, we call for a meeting with all interested countries which will take place in the next few weeks… We are in favor of an early conclusion of the negotiations between the IMF and Poland. The strengthened debt strategy is applicable to Poland, provided it meets the conditions. We are ready to support in the Paris Club the rescheduling of Polish debt expeditiously and in a flexible and forthcoming manner.

Unlike Poland, there was no place for the Soviet Union and its economic problems in the declarations at the end of the Paris Summit, Soviet leader Gorbachev[9] addressed a letter to the French President as the host of the meeting.[10] The letter was written in florid diplomatic language and did not describe

[8] In early June 1989, Poland held semi-free parliamentary elections in which the ruling party (PORP), thanks to the quota method, won the most significant number of seats in the lower house (173 out of 460) but failed to win a single mandate in direct elections to the Senate. During the Summit in Poland, negotiations continued the future of political and economic reforms, the fate of which was still uncertain. On August 19, President W Jaruzelski handed the mandate to form a government to Tadeusz Mazowiecki, elected to the Sejm from Solidarity, the country's main opposition force. On September 12, 1989, the Sejm approved the composition of the government, in which 11 out of 23 seats went to Solidarity representatives. This government became the government of reforms, which implemented an exemplary "shock therapy" program in early 1990.

[9] At that time, Gorbachev was General Secretary of the Communist Party and Chairman of the Supreme Soviet of the USSR (the country's parliament).

[10] Text of the Letter Sent by Mikhail Gorbachev to the President of France. July 15, 1989, Paris [Unofficial Translation} http://www.g7.utoronto.ca/summit/1989paris/letter_english.html

the changes taking place in the USSR or the problems of the Soviet economy. The Soviet President's address in the economic part could be interpreted as a proposal for a full-scale partnership, although the letter did not say what it might consist of.

> We observe with interest the efforts made by the seven most highly developed States of the Western world to enhance the coordination of macroeconomic policy. Thanks to this coordination, we consider it possible to make world economic processes more predictable. This is an important premise for guaranteeing international economic security.
>
> On the topic of economic security, we have in mind above all else the formation of bases for stable, de-ideologized, and mutually advantageous co-creation and for joint development.
>
> Like other countries, the Soviet Union seeks to complete the task of adapting its national economy to a new structure of the international division of labor which is developing. Our perestroika is inseparable from the policy that aims at full and complete participation in the world economy. That orientation, which is in keeping with current political thought, is equally determined by our direct economic interest. But it is clear the rest of the world can only gain from the opening up to the world economy of a market like that of the USSR. Of course, mutual advantage implies mutual responsibility and respect for the rights of all the participants in international economic relations.

In this regard, the G7 position toward the USSR, declared by the French President Mitterrand at the final press conference, gave no hint that East-West relations could radically change. The Soviet Union has a long way to go before attitudes toward it change.[11]

Question: *"Mr President, how do you see East-West relations, particularly with the Soviet Union, after the Summit?... What have the reactions of the Summit been to the letter sent by President Gorbachev?"*

The President: *"The Summit has not profoundly changed the nature of relations between the Soviet Union and the participants in the Summit. That wasn't the objective of the Summit... This letter does not call for a collective response. Our agenda was already extremely full, so there was therefore no response by the Summit of the Arch to Mr Gorbachev...*

As for the nature of the relations, it has not changed fundamentally... We hope that the attempt at democratization in the Soviet Union succeeds... But there are many aspects to the situation: economic, political, military and other serious

[11] Press Conference of François Mitterrand, President of France, on the Conclusion of the 15th Summit of Industrialized Countries. July 16, 1989, Paris [Unofficial Translation]. http://www.g7.utoronto.ca/summit/1989paris/press_english.html

advances must be made, especially in disarmament, before any general conclusions can be drawn."

Question: *"Does it seem conceivable to you that he might participate someday in a Summit such as the one that was just completed here at the Arch?"*

The President: *"The Soviet Union is a very large country which plays a considerable role in the world. It is one of the two greatest military powers on the planet, so its role is pre-eminent... The countries that gather in the bosom of the Summit of the Seven are countries whose basic definition is democracy, furnished with adequate institutions, with democratic institutions... The countries which are evolving toward democracy have not yet defined the rules for a democratic existence to the same degree that we have defined ours through institutions and practice—since it is not what is written, it is what is done. Whatever the remarkable interest on the plane of political ethics which I have in the evolution of the Soviet Union, we are not all at the same point; we are not."*

Trust but Verify

This position was hardly surprising. The last military conflict of the Cold War period was still in everyone's memory—five months before the G7 summit in Paris, in mid-February 1989, the Soviet Union withdrew its troops from Afghanistan, ending a 9-year occupation of the country. Democratic stirrings ignited by the first Congress of People's Deputies had only just begun and had yet to reshape the political structure. The Soviet Union continued to spend more than 10% of GDP on the military complex, and the signing of the Strategic Arms Reduction Treaty (Start I) with the United States was still more than two years away.

It is hardly surprising that the Sherpas and American politicians could not or would not believe that Gorbachev was in an agonizing search and was moving further and further away every day from the views with which he had come to power in 1985. Thus, at the time, Defense Secretary Cheney openly referred to Gorbachev as a "Marxist," based on a conversation with him in 1987.[12]

> I'd met Gorbachev [in 1987] when he came on a state visit during the Reagan years, We got into a debate with Gorbachev, this is still the heyday of the Gorbachev era on economic policy. We're asking him if there weren't lessons to be learned by the Russians from the Asian tigers, the Taiwans and Singapores and Koreas that had done so much to rejuvenate their economies and grow and take off. What we got back from him was absolute, utter, total, 100% Marxist

[12] Miller Center. George H.W. Bush Presidency. Dick Cheney Oral History.

BS. You know, it was, They're exploiters, they were being exploited, the masses were being exploited. I mean, the man didn't have a clue about what to do with his economy other than try to make Communism work.

Brent Scowcroft also made no secret of his distrust of Gorbachev's words and promises, believing that the Soviet leader was not changing the essence of a political system built on fear and repression. According to Scowcroft, Gorbachev wanted a warming of relations with the West so that the Soviet economy would be given time to restructure and, after some time, could provide a dramatic increase in the Soviet Union's military power.

By the time we came into office people as important as Maggie Thatcher and a number in the Reagan administration said, "The Cold War's over." I said, "The Cold War is not over. All of the elements of the Cold War are still in place. The only thing that's changed is the rhetoric… Europe was basking in the thought that here was a new man and that the Cold War was over, despite that fact that nothing fundamental had really happened, and that the end result—if my worst fears were realized—was that we would unilaterally dismantle the defenses of the Cold War all the time that Gorbachev was restructuring a creaking Soviet economy to become more efficient. And we'd wake up one morning with a rejuvenated Soviet Union and a West that was in shambles. I thought that was fundamentally what we had to guard against… Gorbachev never showed any interest in transforming the Soviet Union. He did do one thing. He did remove terror as the instrument that drove the Soviet Union…[13]

Skepticism of the Soviet leader, his statements and actions remained with the President's national security aide until Gorbachev's final days in the Kremlin, and undoubtedly this had a significant impact on Bush's position and influenced the decisions he made.

After the coup, … Gorbachev came back from the Crimea and defended the Communist Party… I don't think President Bush ever bought on completely to my theory, but he listened carefully, and I think it affected the way we operated early on.

It should not be forgotten that the East and the West at this time existed as separate economic systems. After the end of World War II and Stalin's rejection of Eastern Europe's participation in the Marshall Plan, the Soviet Union built an isolated economic system, Council for Mutual Economic Assistance

[13] Miller Center. George H.W. Bush Presidency. Brent Scowcroft Oral History Part I.

(CMEA), which was generally self-sufficient and did not need active trade ties with the West. The CMEA countries needed Western technology, resulting in occasional large industrial project purchases using imported equipment. Starting in the 1960s, the Soviet Union began to need grain imports, which became the subject of constant negotiations with Canada, and later with the United States. The "gas-pipe" deal was implemented, which provided for the delivery of gas from Western Siberia to Germany through a pipeline, for the construction of which large-diameter pipes were imported from Germany. In 1987, the Soviet Union's trade with socialist countries was almost three times as large as its trade with developed countries.[14]

Little wonder, then, that the Sherpas struggled to grasp Soviet dynamics, economic conditions, and looming problems. They frankly said that the G7 could not see how it could help Gorbachev, but at the same time, a set of strict conditions was beginning to form, without the fulfillment of which the USSR could not count on Western help.

Money? What Money?

On May 22, 1990, Nigel Wicks sent a note to the Prime Minister on the results of another preparatory meeting.[15] On the one hand, the Sherpas voiced the political task of supporting perestroika in the Soviet Union and finding ways of rapprochement with the USSR, but, on the other hand, no one proposed concrete steps to achieve this goal. Moreover, the US strongly rejected the USSR's membership in the IMF and the World Bank, with which no one argued.

> There was a recognition that the West should do all it could to support President Gorbachev; to keep perestroika on the rails; and to draw the Soviet Union into the international community so that Soviets do not believe themselves sidelined by the West. But no-one had practical initiatives to suggest other than limited technical assistance, etc., including closer links with the OECD. There was no dissent to strong US opposition to Soviet membership of the IMF/IBRD.

[14] *Narodnoe hozyajstvo SSSR v 1987 g.* (National Economy of the USSR in 1987 Moscow, Finance and Statistics, 1988. p. 602.)

[15] MTF 213784. Sherpa Meeting, Paris, May 19–20, 1990. Nigel Wicks Minute to Prime Minister. May 22, 1990.

On June 13, a memo from Margaret Thatcher's aide (Private Secretary), Charles Powell, first broached the subject of possible financial aid to the Soviet Union.[16]

> The Americans are likely to be very guarded about substantive assistance, though the Germans may possibly want the West to offer economic help to keep the Russians afloat until reunification is tied up.

On May 29, representatives of 40 countries signed an agreement to establish the European Bank for Reconstruction and Development (EBRD), which began its work a year later in April 1991. This organization was designed to facilitate investment in companies and banks in Eastern Europe to spread international business practices and technologies.

Although the Soviet Union co-founded the bank, the US vehemently opposed allowing Soviet banks and companies to receive its loans. On March 22, the US spoke at a hearing before the Senate Foreign Relations Committee. Under Secretary of the Treasury, David Mulford made this point bluntly.[17]

> The status of the USSR [in EBRD], remains an open issue. There is general agreement that eligibility to borrow should be conditioned on a continued commitment to political and economic reforms and creditworthiness criteria. Under our proposal, the EBRD Board of Directors would have the authority to restrict or cut off lending for backsliders. We continue to believe that Soviet borrowing from this bank should be limited for a period of time to the capital they contribute to the EBRD.

A month later, US Treasury Secretary Nicholas Brady, speaking before the Budget Committee of the US House of Representatives, declared that an agreement limiting the Soviet Union's options for the next three years had been reached, indicating that the US administration was confident that no significant changes in the Soviet system would occur during this time.[18]

> While the Soviet Union is eligible to be a borrowing member of the EBRD, its borrowing will be limited for a three-year period to the amount of their paid-in subscriptions to the Bank and will be confined to loans for the private sector or

[16] MTF 213785. Houston Summit. Charles Powell minute to Prime Minister. June 13, 1990.

[17] US DoT. vol. 296. Statement by the Honorable David C Mulford, Under Secretary of Treasury for International Affairs before the Senate Foreign Relations Committee, Subcommittee on International Economic Policy, Trade, Oceans and the Environment, March 22, 1990.

[18] US DoT. vol. 297. Statement by Brady before the Committee on Ways and Means, US House of Representatives, April 18, 1990.

> to help enterprises operating competitively and moving to a market orientation. Any expansion of Soviet borrowing after the three-year period will require agreement by members holding 85% of the voting power.

On June 18, Wicks briefed the Prime Minister on his conversation with Jacques Attali, ideologue and future President of the EBRD, who had expressed high anxiety about the situation in the Soviet Union. The memo stated that discussing Western aid to the Soviet Union was part of the Summit agenda and that Gorbachev would ask for money from the G7 members. Wicks meanwhile urged against extending loans, arguing they would merely finance consumer imports and solve nothing.[19]

> Attali, who has hitherto taken a sanguine view of the Soviet Union's and President Gorbachev's prospects, is now full of foreboding: the situation is our of control with division among leaders and advisors; … and there is a desperate shortage of cash. President Bush has already, I understand, told Summit leaders that he wants to discuss at the Summit aid for the USSR. The Soviets have already asked Chancellor Kohl for $15–20 billion over three years; the French banks were that day (last Friday) in Moscow, at the Soviet's invitation, discussing possible loans (and had been given a political hint from the French Government to do no more than listen and report). President Gorbachev had asked Mr Mulroney for grain credits during his recent Canadian visit and right at the end of his US visit he had mentioned assistance to President Bush. My German colleague believed that Chancellor Kohl would suggest positive support for the USSR, though he thought the US should take the lead. My US colleague responded that there were legal (Congressional) difficulties in the way of US lending. The Canadian Sherpa wondered whether loans might not be made available to the Soviet Union to help them buy Polish/Czech etc. goods. I said … that it was doubtful whether the Soviet Union was in a position to benefit from large chunks of credit; they would be dissipated on consumer goods and only debts would remain. There was a large measure of agreement for this view.

On June 22, Nigel Wicks spoke about the differences in the positions of the G7 members regarding financial assistance to the USSR. They emphatically reiterated his recommendation to refrain from participating in such a program.[20]

---

[19] MTF 213786. Houston Economic Summit. Nigel Wicks Minute to Prime Minister. June 18, 1990.
[20] MTF 213786. Houston Economic Summit. Nigel Wicks Minute to Prime Minister. June 22, 1990.

> Of the Summit participants, Kohl will be the most keen to offer support. He may be joined by Mitterrand. Bush has publicly warned against any "bold new initiative" at Houston. Kaifu will be very cautious, The Canadians face severe budgetary stringency, but will want to be part of any bandwagon. The Italian position is uncertain. Our own approach, for both Dublin and Houston is as follows. We want to encourage the reform process in the Soviet Union but to keep this separate from German unification. "Know-how" and technical assistance can be a catalyst of reform. But to offer large credits would be a serious mistake.

On June 27, the British Foreign Office received a telegram from the Japanese embassy informing them of Japan's negative stance toward supporting Soviet reforms.[21]

> Japan understands the FRG's wish to extend financial support for the Soviet Union, but they do not wish to join in any international arrangement, because of the Soviet occupation of the Northern Territories, the continued Soviet military threat in the Far East and the risk that such aid would simply go into a bottomless pit.

Just before the Summit began, the Sherpas noted that they had not implemented one of the first recommendations of Kennan's Long Telegram—"*to study it* [the Soviet Union] *with the same determination, impartiality, objectivity, and emotional literacy with which a physician studies a recalcitrant and unreasonable patient.*" They recorded that the situation in the Soviet economy was complex and unclear. They recommended that a joint analysis of the situation in the Soviet Union be undertaken by the international financial organizations, which would contain recommendations to the Soviet government on significant areas of reform that the G7 could support. No promises of financial assistance to the Soviet Union should be made until then.[22]

> The Summit could give a remit to these organizations [IMF, World Bank, OECD], and some others, to make a common analysis of the Soviet economy… As to what followed, there was no point in writing the Soviet Union a large cheque, for example to spend on consumer goods. But assistance in know-how and techniques of running a market economy could bring benefit.

---

[21] MTF 213823. Houston Economic Summit: Japanese Political and Economic Scene. UKE Tokyo Telegram to FCO. June 27, 1990.

[22] "Sherpa Discussion: USSR, Trade (Agriculture) and Environment." Nigel Wicks record of conversation. July 9, 1990. https://www.margaretthatcher.org/document/213789

The German Sherpa's attempt to convince his colleagues that the situation required greater speed of decision-making—he "*argued that perestroika needed support now. He was worried that calls for analysis were simply intended to gain time*"—found no support. In a private conversation, the American Sherpa admitted to Wicks that "*President [Bush] was taking a much tougher line the Soviets than either Secretary Baker or General Scowcroft.*"[23] No urgency was seen by Washington, and the recommendation to the heads of state was very specific, discouraging any discussion of financial aid to the USSR.

It may be possible for the heads to agree on the following:

- Agree on an analytical study of: the USSR's economy; the progress achieved in reforms to date; what still needs to be done; and the assistance, through the transfer of know-how, advice on techniques, etc., which could be provided in support of that reform effort;
- Stipulate that any assistance should be contingent not only on economic reform but also on improved international behavior, e.g., Cuba, the Kurile Islands and reduced expenditure on arms;
- Indicate that judgements on financial assistance should await the outcome of the study.

After the end of World War II, when preparing for decisions regarding Germany and Japan, Washington began by conducting a thorough analysis of the situation and devoting substantial human resources to this task. Now that it was obvious that the Soviet Union was entering a phase of serious transformation, US policymakers took the exact opposite position: the responsibility for analyzing the situation in the Soviet economy was shifted to organizations that had never dealt with the problem in their history and had no experience in dealing with planned economies. In short order, Washington took the more consequential step of refusing to discuss Russian reform plans and programs to support them, saying that the IMF and the World Bank should handle this.

We Need to Figure It Out

The G7 Summit in Houston was held from July 9 to 11, 1990,[24] and at the session devoted to the Soviet Union, there was an active discussion in which the positions of Germany, France, and Italy diverged from that of the United States.

[23] MTF 213788. Houston Economic Summit: Final Sherpa Meeting. Nigel Wicks Minute to Prime Minister. July 2, 1990.

[24] GB M&T. Memorandum of Conversation. First Main Plenary Session of the 16th Economic Summit of Industrialized Nations. July 10, 1990.

As host, Bush opened the discussion. He outlined the position agreed upon by the Sherpas and proposed three principles on which policy towards the Soviet Union could be based:

> The Soviet economy does indeed face serious challenges. We want Soviet political and economic reform efforts to succeed. It is in our interest to have a reformed, fully functioning and market-oriented Soviet economy integrated into the world economy.
>
> The three principles … are the following:
>
> 1. Any Western assistance, technical or financial, should be linked to an economic system and the USSR's integration into the world economy;
> 2. Soviet steps to reduce the proportion of their economic output devoted to the military will have an effect on our decision to provide assistance;
> 3. Equally, Soviet decisions to provide foreign aid to regimes that consistently act contrary to the objectives of the international community of states will also affect our willingness to offer assistance. The Soviets should make good faith efforts to build a cooperative and stable international environment.

As for Gorbachev's appeal for massive financial assistance,—"*At present, the Soviet leadership is looking for ways of supplementing the internal transformations with outside financial and economic support. These efforts are directed toward securing credit assistance, attraction of foreign capital, transfer of managerial experience, personnel training… Perhaps, it would be possible to talk about working out long-term agreements on large-scale credit and investment cooperation which in effect would be a serious factor of stabilization and a transition to the market economy in the USSR,*"[25]—Bush proposed simply ignoring the appeal—"*In response to Gorbachev's request in his July 4 letter, we could also pledge to consult with the Soviets on their reform program.*"

In doing so, he spelled out US conditions for the USSR: "*We remain concerned about Soviet aid to Cuba and continued high military spending in relation to GNP … Step up the pace of our negotiations with the Soviets on the Tsarist and Kerensky debts to the US Government. An agreement would overcome one of our legislative restrictions.*"[26] This stance was paired with only vague promises of US market access for Soviet companies.

---

[25] GBPL&M. Letter from Mikhail Gorbachev to George H.W. Bush, President of the United States of America. July 4, 1990 (back translation from English).

[26] This was the Johnson Act, which prohibited US loans to countries that were in arrears with their debts to the United States. The total debts of the Tsarist and Provisional Governments amounted to about $300 million, on which several billion dollars of interest had accrued since 1917.

> [Tsarist and Kerensky's debt settlement] would allow Soviets to gain access to our private financial markets for loans and to sell Soviet debt instruments in the US… Accelerate current negotiations on the Bilateral Investment and Tax Treaties. A successful conclusion to both would provide more favorable conditions for our firms and would encourage them to do more business in the USSR… Agree to a Soviet request to extend the repayment period for Lend-Lease claims totaling $674 million owed to the US upon successful conclusion of a trade agreement.

Bush ended with a harsh, unambiguous message: the Soviet Union should expect no immediate assistance.

> Movement towards considering lifting restrictions on our ability to provide government guarantees and direct credits will await further Soviet actions to liberalize their economy and to address the various political concerns we have… We need to give the Soviets an incentive to reform, to shift resources from the military. This approach would be in our mutual interests. It is impossible for the US to loan money to USSR at this time. I know, however, that others won't agree.

Mitterrand was the first to enter the discussion. He suggested softening the language of the statement prepared by the Sherpas and thinking about whether Soviet reforms could be realized without Western assistance.

> We are too timid in this text regarding aid to the USSR. We have a chicken or egg problem—whether to provide aid first or demand reform first. Which comes first? One could lead to the other. Much has been achieved in the USSR in past months… We need to prime the Soviet engine.
>
> In the third paragraph of the text, the concerns expressed are standard and straightforward. In our language, these represent harsh political conditions as a preliminary to extending aid… The US language is too brisk, too much like an ultimatum. The USSR is already unstable, and we are sending the wrong and too harsh—a message to the USSR, It is too patronizing in tone. We can't proceed like this. It would be pointless, irritating and patronizing to the USSR.

Kohl, who spoke after him, tried to walk between Scylla and Charybdis, avoiding a clash with Bush yet acknowledging Moscow's need for support.

> We have to speak so openly about controversial matters like this. I do not support the text either and request the Foreign Ministers to take it up and modify it.
>
> The Germans have provided support to the USSR, but, clearly, this is not a long-term way to do business. We need to coordinate our approach, if possible.

> I do not think that a decision can be taken today. We need to start the process of a study so that we can make decisions in December.
>
> What do we really want from the USSR? We all want Gorbachev to succeed. His successor is likely to be much worse.
>
> Gorbachev's letter represents a positive development. We should not treat it as we would a letter from the Congo. We cannot reply in a discouraging way to Gorbachev.
>
> We are mindful of America's Cuban problem. I support President Bush's point that our aid should not be mindlessly thrown at the USSR. It must be addressed at a concrete program of reform. Experts, specialists must be provided. We should make our response positive.

After two speeches in which his proposal to postpone aid to the Soviet Union was criticized, Bush lost patience and decided to dot the i's and cross the t's: "*The US would be prepared to stand alone if need be on the issue of aid to the USSR.*" Discussion continued, yet the tone softened.

Italian Prime Minister Giulio Andreotti avoided the fraught issue, hoping Finance Minister Carli would supply the right words. "*The Soviets ... need help and advice… We should help Gorbachev… We must take some risks in helping Gorbachev. It is necessary, as requested by Gorbachev, to have a close dialogue, a direct dialogue, not just through the international organizations. Maybe the IMF will not understand the full complexity of the USSR situation. We need a dialogue to help us think about what kind of aid would be needed and well used by the USSR. There is the risk of misuse, but we need to run it.*"

Canadian Prime Minister Mulroney backed the U.S. line, placing security first and insisting the West focus on helping Moscow craft a reform plan. "*Cuba is a problem. There are political and military problems for the US with the Cuban situation. It is a hostile regime being helped by Gorbachev which creates problems for President Bush…The question is whether to help now or study the question first… We need to help Gorbachev design an engine that will work with his economy… We should use the IMF in consultation with the EBRD to help him fix his economic design.*"

Japanese Premier Kaifu was blunt: without progress on the Northern Territories dispute, aid would remain off the table.

> We need to provide intellectual support for perestroika—training, advice, etc. We have sent two economic survey missions to the USSR. But large-scale credits to the USSR and long-term agreements on investment are something that I am doubtful about. I doubt that financial support will be effective in helping the USSR. The USSR is still a military superpower. Financial support will help them to maintain their military machine. And we still have our problem with

> the Northern Territories. It would not be appropriate to provide financial assistance to the USSR at this time.

Thatcher, the last speaker at this session, did not fully agree with the position of her Sherpa and admitted that the Soviet Union would need help, not only with loans under IMF programs but also with grant support. That was true; all this could happen only after the USSR formulated its reform plan and began to implement it.

> We helped Poland. We provided grants, not loans. But on larger aid, we insisted on an IMF program first. Aid to the USSR not accompanied by reform will accomplish nothing except to accumulate new debts. We need to recognize that our aid must be limited, and we need to target our aid skillfully: food processing, transportation system reform, accountancy arrangements, statistics.

"*We have a consensus*," Bush summarized the discussion. The G7 took note of Gorbachev's economic plan but found no arguments to seriously support it; only technical assistance was promised to the Soviet Union for the coming year. The leaders of the participating countries agreed that they lacked an understanding of how the Soviet economy was organized, what processes were going on in it, and what the transition to a market economy should look like. Four international organizations were tasked with finding answers to these questions, with a mission to be completed by December 1990. As preconditions for potential assistance, the G7 statement demanded that the Soviet Union reduce military expenditures, cease aid to countries involved in regional conflicts, and reach an agreement with Japan on the southern Kuril Islands.

"*While the Soviet Union is providing $5 billion of aid to Cuba, while their missiles are trained on our city, while 18% of their GNP is dedicated to defense, it would be very hard for the American people to understand a loan*," told US Treasury Secretary Nicholas Brady at a July 10, 1990, press conference.[27]

Indeed, in the mid-summer of 1990, Moscow still lacked a coherent economic or political reform plan, and the West had no desire to support slow changes whose logic was unclear, but which did not affect the central element of the planned economy, the system of state price controls. "*Production is not done by planners, but by price signals. The Soviets don't know how to respond to price signals or to organize an economy that is based on this principle,*" said the Italian finance minister Carli with whom it was hard to disagree.

---

[27] Press Briefing by Brady (Houston Economic Summit), July 10, 1990. https://fraser.stlouisfed.org/title/6111/item/587143?start_page=203

However, the United States and the Soviet Union had signed numerous arms limitation treaties. The danger of military conflict had been eliminated, still the Cold-War ghosts still haunted Houston: Washington refused to back Moscow's entry into the IMF or World Bank. There was no talk of a political alliance between the two superpowers.

Only 533 days remained before the Soviet Union collapsed.

Gorby's Looking Around

Poland

In early October 1989, a month after its formation, the Polish reform government publicly presented its plan, which was later called "shock therapy." Two months later, in early December, the Sejm approved the necessary laws to come into force on January 1, 1990. The reform plan was aimed at quickly quelling inflation, primarily by balancing the state budget, prohibiting the National Bank from lending to the government and setting a real positive interest rate on loans (above the inflation rate). On January 1, the liberalization of prices was completed[28] and a single exchange rate was established for the national currency, which was devalued by more than 30%.

Prices almost doubled in January–February 1990, but inflation then fell sharply; from March it stayed below 5% a month—clear evidence of reform success. The US actively supported Polish reforms: already on December 29, the Treasury announced a $200 million loan to Poland to offset the creation of a stabilization fund to support the exchange rate of the national currency;[29] the announcement of the creation of this one-billion-dollar fund was followed three days later. In addition, the US announced that within a year Poland would receive $600 million in grant aid under the SEED Act 1989 and that the Paris Club of creditors[30] had decided to write off $5 billion of

[28] Poland, under socialism, retained a substantial private sector that was powerful in agriculture. This did not allow the government to establish total control over prices, and, unlike in the Soviet Union, where inflation took a suppressed form (deficit), in Poland, price increases could only be partially restrained by freezing prices for the products of state enterprises. Thus, in the first seven months of 1989, open inflation in Poland exceeded 60%. On August 1, a month and a half before the emergence of the reform government, the liberalization of state prices began with the decision of the country's last communist government. In the last five months of 1989, retail prices rose almost fivefold. This played an important role in future popular support for the reforms—the political responsibility for the price hikes fell on the shoulders of the communists, not the reformers, as happened in Russia in 1992.

[29] US DoT. vol. 294. Treasury Statement on Bridge Loan to Poland, December 29, 1989.

[30] The Paris Club brings together creditor countries that provide official loans. The Paris Club accounted for three-quarters of Poland's foreign debt, which amounted to $44 billion (64% of GDP).

Poland's foreign debt by reducing the payments due in 1990–1991. In April 1994, the Paris Club agreed to write off half of Poland's debt, with the US waiving 70% of its claims.[31] In October 1994, the London Club of creditors united commercial banks and wrote off 49% of Polish debt.

On February 5, 1990, the IMF Board of Directors approved the Polish government's program and granted a loan of $700 million. This was followed by the World Bank's decision to grant Poland six loans totaling $1 billion during 1990. In 1991, the IMF provided Poland with an additional $1.6 billion loan,[32] and the World Bank agreed to six more loans totaling $1 billion.[33] The total amount of financial aid that Poland received in the first two years of its reforms from Western countries amounted to $11 billion or almost 16% of 1990 GDP.

Program, Program, and More Program

In early February 1990, at the request of the Council of Ministers of the USSR, a group of employees of the Commission for Economic Reform and academic experts traveled to Warsaw to observe Poland's early reforms and learn firsthand about the pitfalls of market transition. As a result of this visit, the USSR government received a detailed report, which concluded bluntly that transition to a market economy is impossible while state price controls remained. The Soviet leadership rejected this approach, and the report was archived. The Soviet government continued its painful search for language that would convince the political leadership and public opinion that there was another way to build a market economy that would avoid the shock of price liberalization.

In May 1990, after the first free and competitive elections held in the Russian Federation, Yeltsin became the leader of the Russian parliament. He immediately began a power struggle with the union center, specifically

[31] US General Accounting Office. POLAND. Economic Restructuring and Donor Assistance. Report to Congressional Committees. August 1995. GAO/NSIAD-05-150. https://www.gao.gov/assets/nsiad-95-150.pdf

[32] It should be noted that Poland did not fully utilize IMF loans: the country received 65% of the 1990 loan and 6.2% of the 1991 loan. Poland's transition to a single exchange rate, which had been sharply weakened before, led to a decrease in demand for imports and an increase in the attractiveness of exports. Combined with a reduced burden of servicing foreign debt, this normalized the balance of payments. Poland did not use the established Stabilization Fund, which played an important role in repaying devaluation expectations. Poland, Republic of: History of Lending Commitments as of September 30, 2017. International Monetary Fund. https://www.imf.org/external/np/fin/tad/extarr2.aspx?memberKey1=805&date1key=2017-09-30

[33] World Bank Group. Project List. Poland. https://projects.worldbank.org/en/projects-operations/projects-list?status_exact=Active^Closed&prodline_exact=GU^PE&countrycode_exact=PL&os=40

Gorbachev. Draft economic programs, covering the entire spectrum of opinion from conservative adherence to the planned system to anarcho-adventurous, were submitted to the deputies for discussion. In June, the Russian parliament almost unanimously adopts the Declaration of State Sovereignty, which proclaims the priority of the Russian Constitution and laws over those of the USSR. Two centers of power emerged in the USSR, neither could act independently, yet each could block the other's initiatives.

At the end of July, Gorbachev and Yeltsin, realizing that delaying the start of economic reforms would only worsen the situation, took a step toward each other and agreed to prepare a joint reform program. This work was entrusted to a group of experts, which the two politicians formed on a parity basis. Written by the end of August, the program was called "500 Days."

This program envisaged a comprehensive macroeconomic stabilization program based on the example of Poland, a set of steps for de-monopolization and competition development, social support measures, and some elements of structural reforms. Unlike the programs presented by the government, 500 Days contained a set of priority bills that would create the basis for reforms. In addition, 500 Days considered the changing political reality and proposed the conclusion of an Economic Union between the republics.

In early September, Gorbachev held two meetings in the Kremlin at which a detailed comparison was made between the program presented by the Ryzhkov government and 500 Days. In closing the discussion, Gorbachev said that he was choosing 500 Days as his program. Prime Minister Ryzhkov immediately announced that he would resign from office in such a case because he was not ready to implement a program with which he disagreed. Nevertheless, Gorbachev agreed to have a group of experts travel to Washington to present the reform program at the fall meeting of the IMF and World Bank. However, when the delegation was already on the flight, Gorbachev took a step back and declared that it was necessary to preserve the government, for which purpose he instructed to combine Ryzhkov's program and the 500 Days program. Combining the two programs, based on different principles, proved impossible. Moreover, Gorbachev destroyed the already tenuous alliance with Yeltsin with this decision.

The Soviet parliament approved the program's text that Gorbachev personally presented, but it could not help in solving any problems. Due to the rapid growth of nominal wages while production stagnated, the imbalance of the economy was growing daily. Falling revenues from exports forced imports to be cut, which deprived many enterprises of the possibility to continue normal operations. The alternative to reducing imports could be foreign loans, but the Soviet government's requests were so large and chaotic that very quickly, all available limits for increasing foreign debt were exhausted. There was no longer time to develop a proposal to change the entire structure of state prices; however, the power of the line ministries over enterprises was rapidly disappearing. On the one hand, electing directors of state-owned enterprises—permitted by law—brought opportunists and profiteers to the helm. On the other hand, Yeltsin's government began lured enterprises into "Russian jurisdiction" with promises of lower taxes and freedom from administrative oversight.

In December 1990, Prime Minister Ryzhkov was hospitalized with a heart attack and was unable to return to full-time work. In his place, Gorbachev appointed Finance Minister Valentin Pavlov, one of whose first decisions was to confiscate large-denomination banknotes. Economically, the move achieved little, but public distrust of the government soared to unprecedented heights.

Pavlov's government did not change its approach to the general logic of possible reforms. First, it was necessary to increase the volume of production and/or import of consumer goods, which would balance the economy, and only after that could it be possible to talk about price liberalization. Since there was no time, equipment, or free material resources to increase production, in April 1991, Pavlov's government offered Gorbachev, who had become President of the USSR, a way out by asking the Western countries for emergency financial aid. The Soviet leadership estimated the size of the desired aid package to be $100 billion.[34]

At the same time, Grigory Yavlinsky[35] obtained the Soviet President's agreement to develop, together with Harvard professor Graham Allison, a reform plan that could receive financial support from developed countries. The resulting document was not much different from the 500 Days program and did not help Gorbachev in his search for a painless transition to the market. Finding nothing better and realizing that before the G7 meeting in London, he needed to secure the support of the US President, Gorbachev decided to send two groups with two programs to Washington at once in late May: one headed by Vladimir Shcherbakov, First Deputy Prime Minister of the USSR, and the other headed by Yavlinsky. To ensure control and overall guidance, Gorbachev sent his trusted representative, Yevgeny Primakov, a member of the Security Council, to Washington.

This visit ended the idea of massive Western aid to the Soviet Union.

[34] "Gorbachev pleads for $100 billion in aid from the West." The New York Times, May 23, 1991.

[35] Grigory Yavlinsky was one of the leaders of Soviet reform-minded economists in 1989–1991, being initially in Yeltsin's team and moving toward Gorbachev afterwards. After Yeltsin had chosen Gaidar as his chief economist, Yavlinsky moved to political life and established his political party, Yabloko. He is the leader of this party until today.

Those Are Words We Can Applaud. But...

On January 20, 1989, George H.W. Bush took the oath of office and became the 41st President of the United States. He inherited from Ronald Reagan the positive dynamics of change in Soviet-American relations in terms of limiting the arms race and reducing the military threat. In such conditions it was natural to think about other aspects of relations with the Soviet Union, and on February 15, the US President signed a directive to conduct a full-scale review of relations with the USSR.[36] The purpose of the review was to understand the nature and possible consequences of changes in the Soviet Union, to assess Gorbachev's chances of success and the consequences of his failure, and, most importantly, to identify which pre-2000 scenario best served US interests—and whether Washington should help Gorbachev.

> Remarkable changes are taking place in the Soviet Union and in Soviet foreign policy. It is therefore necessary to undertake a comprehensive forward-looking review of the US-Soviet relationship, and clearly articulate our long-term objectives and strategy. What kind of relationship do we wish to see in the year 2000? We may be standing at the door of a new era in our relationship with the USSR, with potential for significantly reducing military forces and resolving longstanding international disputes… My own sense is that the Soviet challenge may be even greater than before because it is more varied…
>
> … What are the broad internal and external goals of Soviet leadership in the short term (3–5 years)? Do they have longer term (10 years) objectives? … What would constitute "success" for Gorbachev in both economic and political terms? [this document] should consider the possibility of the failure … [and] the impact on both domestic and foreign policy if Gorbachev to be removed from office…
>
> … What should be the long-range goals of US foreign and security policy toward the Soviet Union? Is it in the US interest to "help" the Soviet leadership in the attainment of some of its internal or external objectives? What are the potential dangers and benefits to US national security interests in a negative or affirmative response?

The presidential team was given the task of developing proposals for radical changes in relations with the strategic adversary, with only one month allotted—hardly a sign that the new administration intended a major shift toward the USSR.

[36] GBPL&M. National Security Review—3. Comprehensive Review of US-Soviet Relations.

The final document, NSD-23, "United States Relations with the Soviet Union," appeared in the traditional-style, seven months later, in September 1989. There was no room for positive scenarios; in fact, the document was a detailed explanation of the maxim favored by Ronald Reagan after the first disarmament talks with Gorbachev in November 1985: "Trust but verify." The document clearly stated that the reality of Soviet reforms could be discussed only when the Soviet leadership radically changed the course of its foreign policy, agreed to a unilateral reduction in military power, and undertook meaningful domestic reforms.

> We may be able to move beyond containment to a US policy that actively promotes the integration of the Soviet Union into the existing international system… But a new relationship with the international system cannot simply be declared by Moscow. Nor can it be granted by others…
>
> We will not react to reforms and changes in the Soviet Union that have not yet taken place… The foundation of that relationship will grow firmer if Soviet reforms lead to conditions that will support a new cooperative relationship between Moscow and the West. Those conditions include:
>
> - Deployment of a Soviet force posture that is smaller and much less threatening… Soviet Union has legitimate security interests but Soviet military power is far greater than that needed to defend those interests;
> - Renunciation of the principle that class conflict is a source of international tension and establishment of a record of conduct consistent with that pledge;
> - Adherence to the obligation that it undertook at the end of World War II to permit self-determination for the countries of East-Central Europe. Moscow must authoritatively renounce the "Brezhnev Doctrine";
> - Demilitarization of Soviet foreign policy in other regions of the world and serious participation in efforts to ameliorate conflict, including bringing pressure to bear on Soviet clients who do not recognize the legitimate security interests of their neighbors;
> - Participation in cooperative efforts to stop the proliferation of ballistic missile technology, as well as nuclear, chemical and biological weapons;
> - Institutionalization of democratic internal laws and human rights practices, political pluralism, and a more market-oriented economic structure.

There was no mention of any steps toward or assistance for the Soviet Union, except for a few phrases about the possibility of expanding economic ties and a brief directive to the Secretary of State to begin preparing public opinion for the repeal of Jackson-Vanik.[37]

[37] This law was passed in 1974 and prohibited the administration from granting most-favored-nation treatment in mutual trade, government loans, and loan guarantees to the Soviet Union and other socialist countries that restricted Jewish travel to Israel.

> The United States supports the expansion of mutually beneficial non-strategic trade on strictly commercial terms... In the short run, we are prepared to streamline, in conjunction with our allies, the COCOM list. In the longer run, as the Soviet Union meets appropriate political and economic criteria, the United States will remove or reduce the legislative, administrative and other obstacles to non-strategic trade and normal commercial and financial ties.
>
> The Secretary of State is directed to encourage public debate on Jackson-Vanik and consult closely with Congress and the relevant public groups. With the requisite support, we will consider a waiver of the Jackson-Vanik amendment if the Soviet Union codifies emigration laws that meet international standards and demonstrates its intent to implement them faithfully.

The Glass Will Always Be Half-Empty

Bush's ultra-cautious stance was based on the principle that "the glass is always half-empty." The steps that the Soviet leadership took in foreign policy were seen in Washington as forced or mistaken reactions made under pressure and lacking a clear plan.

Glasnost and freedom of speech had not yet curtailed the Communist Party's monopoly on power; Gorbachev remained the leader of the party. Although the Soviet Union had signed the Convention on the Prohibition of the Development, Production, and Stockpiling of Bacteriological and Toxin Weapons and Their Destruction, the Soviet biological weapons program was not curtailed; instead, the program accelerated. US intelligence agencies received documentary evidence of this in 1989 after the escape of Vladimir Pasechnik, who worked at the Biopreparat NGO, but despite repeated appeals to Soviet leaders, including Gorbachev himself[38] the work did not stop until the fall of 1992 when Yeltsin agreed to Russia's compliance with its international obligations under pressure from the US and Britain.[39]

"This was a typical case of the Soviets lying, cheating, stealing—call it what you will—and failing to honor a solemn agreement with the US to end the biological weapons program. The evidence was irrefutable. It wasn't just "maybe they're doing it," it was a clear violation,"[40] said Dick Cheney, and understandably, such conduct heightened distrust of Soviet leaders on other issues. *But this does not mean that nothing is happening inside the country's political leadership.*

---

[38] For example, GBPL&M. President's letter to Gorbachev on Soviet Biological Program. June 19, 1991.

[39] Milton Leitenberg and Raymond A. Zilinskas. "The Soviet Biological Weapons Program: A History." Harvard University Press, 2012.

[40] Miller Center. George H.W. Bush Presidency. Dick Cheney Oral History.

On November 3, 1988, at a Politburo meeting, Gorbachev unexpectedly asked, "Why do we need such a large army?… The military doctrine we have announced diverges from what we are doing in military construction. After all, if we publicize what the situation is: we spend 2.5 times more than the United States on the military, and no state in the world … spends more per capita than we do. If we make this public, all our new thinking and all our new foreign policy will go to hell…" Further down the line, Gorbachev talked about reducing the Soviet presence in Eastern Europe. "*If the situation in Hungary worsens. Then, it will not be us who will leave, but we will be asked to leave… I suggest that the Defense Council consider all this. And then we'll return to the Politburo.*" And at this moment, Prime Minister Ryzhkov's tense voice suddenly sounded: "*I must responsibly declare here: if we do not do this, we will not be able to make the XIII Five-Year Plan. Any rise in living standards is out of the question. Put any government, it will not solve this problem.*"[41]

Two years later, in May 1991, Gorbachev would say that the Soviet Union had stopped the growth of military spending, which amounted to 9% of GNP;[42] meanwhile, the CIA and other analysts claimed that the Soviet Union was spending a disproportionate share of its financial resources on the military (between 12% and 20% of the gross national product).

In May 1989, before his trip to the United States, Gorbachev gave an interview to the Washington Post and The New York Times, in which he explicitly stated that the Soviet Union would not interfere in other states and that there would be no repeat of the 1956 Hungarian or 1968 Czechoslovak interventions.[43] On October 25, 1989, Gennady Gerasimov, head of the Information Department of the Soviet Foreign Ministry, was asked on Good Morning America to comment on Shevardnadze's statement two days earlier about the Soviet Union's refusal to interfere in the affairs of other countries. In response to the Soviet Union's de facto rejection of the Brezhnev Doctrine, Gerasimov compared Gorbachev's foreign policy line to Frank Sinatra's cult hit song "My Way": "*From now on, the states of the Warsaw Pact Organization, like the American singer, are free to choose their own path of development.*"[44]

But none of this convinced Scowcroft and his colleagues, who had weathered the vicissitudes of the Cold War and were skeptical of what was happening. "*As we started out in Eastern Europe with our strategy toward Eastern Europe, Gorbachev also had his strategy toward Eastern Europe, which was to*

[41] A. Chernyaev. Sovmestnyj iskhod. (*Joint Exodus.*) Moscow, Rospan, 2008, pp. 770–771.

[42] "Soviet Military Budget: $128 Billion Bombshell." The New York Times, May 31, 1991.

[43] Truthout, May 23, 1989.

[44] Dmitry Okunev. *Zabyt' pro Brezhneva: kak SSSR prinyal «doktrinu Sinatry».* (Forgetting Brezhnev: How the USSR adopted the "Sinatra Doctrine.") https://www.gazeta.ru/science/2019/10/25_a_12776000.shtml?updated

create in the Bloc little Gorbachevs, little reforming Gorbachevs, totally misunderstanding the character of Communism in Eastern Europe. There was no halfway house between a Soviet system and a non-Soviet system the way he was seeking to do it in the Soviet Union. There maybe wasn't one there either. But there certainly was not any way to relax Soviet control over the satellites and have little Gorbachevs who would help him make his own reforms inside the Soviet Union.

So he looked benignly, or at least indifferently, to what we were doing, and to what was happening inside Eastern Europe until the Wall fell. Then he got scared. But up 'til then, he was very relaxed. In fact, he was helping us—helped us in Poland, helped us in East Germany."[45]

I Should Be the One Setting the Prices!

However, it was impossible to ignore the changes in the USSR. Michael Boskin, head of the President's Council of Economic Advisers (CEA), set up a special working group to analyze the situation in the Soviet Union, which met at least once a month. John Taylor, one of the most prominent American economists working at the intersection of theory and practice, began to deal with the problems of the Soviet economy.[46]

Dealing with Soviet ministries made a lasting impression on Boskin. He later described a meeting with Yuri Maslyukov, Chairman of the USSR State Planning Committee, in 1990:[47]

> We're talking and ... all of a sudden he says, "Who sets the prices in your economy?" So I go, well, for most goods and services, of which there are millions, it is the interaction of millions of consumers and thousands of producers, and for some it's dozens of producers, whatever. We have a small regulated sector where there are a very few number of firms, but primarily these are set by market forces and the interactions of suppliers and demanders.
>
> I went through Adam Smith's invisible hand of the market, that it is not to the beneficence of the baker but to his greed that we owe our bread and so on, and so forth. I've won a lot of teaching awards, but this guy had no idea what I was talking about. I was the economic advisor to the President of the United States, so I must be the guy who set the prices!
>
> So he takes out a 1960s-era computer output, from this old mainframe, these big wide sheets that you'd flip over with holes in the side. And it's the price list

[45] Miller Center. The George H.W. Bush Presidential Oral History. Brent Scowcroft, Part I.

[46] In 1992, John Taylor formulated the principle of monetary policy targeting, named after him as the "Taylor rule."

[47] Miller Center. George H.W. Bush Presidency. Michael Boskin Oral History.

from the Soviet Union. He's been told by Gorbachev that he's got to reform prices. I'm the President of the United States' economic advisor, so as we're sitting there, he wants to cross out the old prices and me to fill in the new prices.

After four international organizations presented their three-volume Study of the Soviet Economy in February 1991, one of the strongest Sovietologists, Ed Hewett, joined the National Security Council and became the "think tank" of policy toward the Soviet Union. In short, by May 1991, understanding of the situation in the USSR and the problems facing the Soviet system was adequate.

The Soviet delegation, which in addition to Primakov included First Deputy Prime Minister Shcherbakov, Chairman of the USSR State Bank Gerashchenko, and Yavlinsky, left Washington with a chaotic impression: each member offered a different version of the economic program, ignoring their contradictions. Yavlinsky's presentation was particularly discordant, though he claimed to speak for Gorbachev.

To remove all suspicions as to "Who's boss?" at a lunch with Bush,[48] Primakov repeatedly emphasized that he alone had the authority from Gorbachev and that Yavlinsky was not independent.

> Mikhail Gorbachev has named me as the coordinator of the assistance. Yavlinsky is able, but he wasn't involved at the beginning. He works for me. Don't overestimate him -- he is a bit immature. He works on instructions he got from Gorbachev…. We must get together, and not have competing plans. We will use the result of Yavlinsky's work in Boston as an "overlay" on our basic plan.

Primakov said his task was to secure Bush's approval of $100 billion in aid to the Soviet Union. "*What we need now is large-scale assistance. The issue is taking on strategic importance.*"

The President made no promises, aware that staff would analyze the talks and draft proposals before his departure for the London G7 summit. *"The Economic Summit is a more complicated issue. We have to work it out so that Gorbachev doesn't ask, then go away empty-handed,"* is how he set the task.

On June 3, 1991, Scowcroft met with key officials[49] and all of them strongly advised the President against promising aid to the Soviet Union.[50] The main

[48] GB M&T. Memorandum of Conversation. Luncheon Meeting Between the President and Yevgeniy Primakov, member of the USSR Security Council. May 31, 1991.

[49] GBPL&M. National Security Council. Memorandum for Files. Meeting on U.S.—Soviet Economic Relations, June 3, 1991.

[50] GBPL&M. Brent Scowcroft's Memorandum. "The US Economic Relationship with the Soviet Union," May 31, 1991, for the meeting on June 3, 1991.

argument was that the Soviet government was not ready to undertake meaningful reforms, and that the money would be spent without any effect.

John Taylor explicitly pointed out that there were irreconcilable differences between the programs of Yavlinsky and Primakov: "*Despite claims by Primakov to the contrary, there are substantial differences between Yavlinsky and the Primakov anti-crisis program. Most important Yavlinsky is against the continuation of administrative controls, while Primakov maintains that these are needed as part of the anti-crisis program.*"

Boskin did not hold back; he argued that the Soviet leadership was not ready for market reforms. "*I came back and wrote a report to the President and to the head of the CIA and the Federal Reserve, and the Secretary of the Treasury, etc. We went through the National Security Advisor and we had a meeting over this and I said that my view is it's going to be a decade or more before they can really start having a serious functioning market economy.*"[51]

The Scowcroft Memorandum clarified that the US disagreed with the logic of Gorbachev's program and could not support it.

> In economics we have always argued to the Soviets that we cannot provide significant assistance until they are committed to a market economy. When Gorbachev rejected the 500 Day plan, he also undermined any hope of significant international financial assistance tied directly to reforms… Soviet leaders hold strongly to the notion that administrative measures are the only way to stabilize the economy and get to markets.
>
> Prime Minister Pavlov's Anti-Crisis Program, which has been through many variants over the last few months, was in that vein. At this point we are, therefore, in the interesting position that Soviet leaders—particularly Gorbachev—espouse a full commitment to markets. The issue on which we and they disagree is how, and how quickly, to move to markets.

Discussing Gorbachev's request for financial aid, Taylor came to an unexpected conclusion: even Yavlinsky, who had made Western aid a key element of his program, could not explain for what purposes the Soviet government intended to spend the money received.[52]

---

[51] Miller Center. George H.W. Bush Presidency. Michael Boskin Oral History.

[52] Taylor was correct in his assessment. The Yavlinsky-Allison program did not provide quantitative assessments of the problems of the Soviet economy that would dovetail with Gorbachev's request. In addition, the program's text said that the Soviet Union needed grant aid in one place while it talked about providing loans in another. "Window of Opportunity. The Grand Bargain for Democracy in the Soviet Union," by Graham Allison and Grigory Yavlinsky. Pantheon Books, New York, 1991.

> Yavlinsky also discussed how his plan might be affected by support from the West. For example, he said "Depending on interaction with the West, the fleshing out of the general guidelines will be different, and the same goes for the timeline and sequencing." However, "parts of the reform program do not relate to financing from the West." He gave few details, stating "On the question of the impact of the Western support on the plan, this is something that has yet to be answered…
>
> … There are good arguments that general financial support from the Western governments will have a negative impact on the reform: it will help to preserve inefficient state enterprises and put off needed budget cuts.

Primakov's position prompted Boskin to burst into Homeric laughter, who thus recounted the conversation that had taken place:

> Primakov heading the delegation … wanted to open up his trench coat and show us the list of things he could sell us. Pay for this factory, pay for this dam, etc. This is what we really need you to do and we could sell you—It would be kind of like a university selling signs on buildings. Give us this money and we'll make good use of it and your name will be in lights blah, blah, blah.
>
> So I bored into it and asked him, "What did you do with the money that the Germans gave you to regarrison the Russian troops? We want to go inspect the housing. And you have all this gold, is it clean or dirty, do you really own it? How do we know that other Soviet republics aren't saying they own it?" He couldn't even answer. This went on for two days and I was supposed to go brief Bush and then we were going to have a meeting so he could hear from Primakov directly and then talk to Gorbachev, and I just told him that I thought we should be doing it if they would agree to decommission all of their nuclear weapons. Otherwise, the money would be wasted, stolen, misused.
>
> I think one of the best things we did was not throw that money away.

In the memorandum, Scowcroft was not so categorical and left it to the Soviet government to make a second attempt to explain why it needed Western financial assistance: *"They* [the Soviets] *said that if Yavlinsky was successful in negotiating a deal between the West and the USSR on a step-by-step process of reform with western assistance, that they would be willing to radically speed up the move to markets. They are going to a market economy in any event; but if we are forthcoming with aid, they will get there quicker… The Soviets offered very few details on the second point, what some call the "grand bargain," the details of which may be available late next week.*

… The "grand bargain" is a very long shot, since it is not at all clear that Soviet leaders understand and fully support the market rhetoric they now use."

In conclusion, Scowcroft implicitly pointed to the budgetary constraints that would later hinder US aid to post-Soviet Russia. The US economy was in recession at this point, and the budget deficit was growing rapidly: from $150 billion in the late 1980s to $270 billion in 1991 and $290 billion in 1992 (from 2.7% of GDP in 1989 to 4.5% of GDP in 1991–1992). In such a situation, he sees no possibility of helping the Soviet Union without reducing aid to Eastern Europe, which seems highly undesirable: "*The economic situation among Europe's new democracies is getting worse, as noncompetitive industries are feeling the full brunt of transformation; any shift of resources—or even apparent shift of attention—away from helping Central and Eastern Europe could have adverse economic, political, and even security consequences.*"

To ensure Bush did not arrive empty-handed in London, the Scowcroft memo proposed the usual mix of promises and grain credits.[53]

> We should also do what we can now to do the relatively easy things which will signal our willingness to be forthcoming with the Soviets. In this regard, Soviet passage of an emigration law and the results of the recent visit of our food distribution team, offer possibilities to make some moves on MFN, the Trade Agreement, and grain credits, subject to conditions that show the Soviets are ready to make some practical steps in the right direction.
>
> In the end we gave them some technical assistance and some CCC [Commodity Credit Corporation] wheat because they allegedly were having a bad agriculture year. Now there was some discussion that that might have actually hurt their agriculture more than it helped them, but our Secretary of Agriculture with a straight face declared them creditworthy. So we had an agricultural component, some technical assistance.

So, in early June 1991, it became clear in Washington that the Soviet Union could not count on financial support for economic reforms, as it was widely believed that the measures proposed by the Soviet government would not be able to ensure the transition to a market economy. To be more precise, the reform plan lacked one solution—the abandonment of state price controls, which Gorbachev could not bring himself to accept for the rest of his political life. Even on December 3, 1991, when Yeltsin's government announced that prices would be liberalized on January 1, Gorbachev was sure there was a way to avoid it: "*One must not think that the reform agenda was concluded with the liberalization of prices. Rather, one ought to stimulate production, satisfy farmers,*

[53] GBPL&M. Brent Scowcroft's Memorandum. The US Economic Relationship with the Soviet Union. May 31, 1991, for the Meeting on June 3, 1991.

provide incentives for the employees in the industrial sector, and stabilize the tax system to stabilize the entire economic balance."[54]

A Humiliating Summit

Gorbachev's visit to London for the G7 meeting in July 1991 was presented by Soviet propaganda as a symbol of recognition of the Soviet Union's new role in the world and a move toward its inclusion in the system of relations between developed countries. In fact, for the Soviet President, the visit was an outright humiliation: he was to hear from Western leaders—either directly or second-hand—extremely unfavorable assessments of his economic policy and the reform program that he had staunchly defended, yet none of his interlocutors believed it. He was denied a large aid package and other requests he had laid out during the negotiations. At the same time, the set of demands and conditions placed on the Soviet Union was expanding, Yeltsin increasingly overshadowed Gorbachev. No issue concerning the USSR could now be discussed without factoring in Yeltsin's stance. Proposals to aid the USSR or speed its integration remained slogans the participants never seriously considered. The idea that priority in supporting reforms should be given to Central and Eastern European countries was clearly voiced.

Opening of the London Economic Summit, July 15, 1991[55]

Mitterrand: "*I favor specific assistance for the USSR, but no guarantee… We need to consider our obligations to others.*"

Bush: "*His [Gorbachev's] plan is short on specifics and not clear as to the role of the Republics. Who do businessmen deal with?*

… We cannot write out checks or give money until the reforms that have been talked about are implemented… We need to encourage Gorbachev to go ahead with Baltic independence…".

Kohl: "*We need to provide the Soviets with the opportunity to change. I'm not sure what Yeltsin will do… It can't be in our interest for instability to exist in the USSR… We need to integrate it into the world economy… Our resources are limited…*".

---

[54] Wilson Center. The Chancellor's Telephone Conversation with President Mikhail Gorbachev, Tuesday, December 3, 1991.

[55] GB M&T. Memorandum of Conversation. Opening Session of The London Economic Summit. July 15, 1991.

Mulroney: *"We don't want to waste money. We want to help, and do so in an effective way. I'm not sure what the effective way is."*

Kaifu: *"On the USSR, we support their integration into the world economy. I hope to see concrete reform… there is a political context, as well as economic necessity: the Baltics, human rights, the union republics process, the global application of "new thinking" in foreign policy (Cuba, Afghanistan)… We will test the USSR's interest through the Northern Territories."*

Lubbers: *"We have responsibility to integrate the Soviet Union into Europe, not only politically, but in the world economic system. We shouldn't single out the USSR because the Central and Eastern Europe are also important. We might bring the USSR into the GATT, maybe also into the IMF."*

Major: *"The Soviet Union is still divorced from our system. He [Gorbachev]'s submitted his plan; we've had limited time to examine it, to see how it will be implemented. What does he mean by … price reform? … What will he do to help himself?"*

First Plenary Session, July 16, 1991[56]

Andriessen: "[Since G7 summit in Paris, July 1989] *the G24 and IFIs have allocated $40 billion in Central and Eastern European assistance. This comes to $9.4 billion from the Bretton Woods Institutions, and $30 billion from the others in the form of $20 billion in loans and $10 billion in grants… We need to be concerned about displacing Central and Eastern Europe as we consider support for the USSR."*

Second Plenary Session, July 16, 1991[57]

Lamont: (summing up the discussion between ministers of finance) *"The Soviet economy has weakened more quickly than the reform plan foresaw… We've all felt that reform plans lacked details and credibility. Under these circumstances, there could be no financial assistance… We had strong reservations on creating funds for stabilization and to supply goods. On restructuring debts, there are difficult problems. We lack information on assets… Debt rescheduling is undesirable.*

We see five criteria for reform: (1) achieving a balance between the Center and the Republics; (2) radical reform (no less than in Central and Eastern Europe); (3) tightened macroeconomic policy in the near future; (4) a commitment to drastic

[56] GB M&T. Memorandum of Conversation. First Plenary, London Economic Summit. July 16, 1991.

[57] GB M&T. Memorandum of Conversation. Second Plenary, London Economic Summit. July 16, 1991.

reductions of military expenditures; and (5) adequate conditions for foreign investment. These we've seen as the main tests of good Soviet intentions."

Hurd:[58] *"We agreed that our response to the Soviets should be forward leaning… Key points: 1) no cash, 2) Special Association [with the IMF and the World Bank]."*

Major: *"We're all agreed: there can be no bag of money; there should be IFI Special Association (though the question of whether this leads to membership remains open)."*

Kohl: *"A special relationship with the IMF and the World Bank must be well established. Let the future decide; I'm against saying membership is not possible."*

Andreotti: *"In 1947 our government was weak, the Communist threat was great, and we [Italy] got the [US] Ex-Im loan. We got the Communists out… There are times one needs to decide with political foresight. This doesn't mean writing a blank check."*

Delors: *"The EBRD was created for Eastern Europe. It has $10 billion in funds. This means only 180 million ECU for the USSR. Can we increase it since Eastern Europe has gotten $40 billion?… East Europeans are now paying market prices for Soviet goods. Soviet import from the region are down 40%. Could we require Soviet purchases from Central and Eastern Europe if we assist them?"*

Bush: *"We set up the EBRD last year to help Central and Eastern Europe. At the last minute, we decided to fit in the USSR. Now some of us are calling for bank loans to the USSR. Why should we raise the limits if the Bank hasn't made any loans to the USSR? … Why should the EBRD loan to the USSR when no one else is? If everyone wants to raise limits, then there should be a footnote that the US is against it."*

Baker:[59] *"The Soviets spend 25% of their GNP on defense.*[60] *It would be hard for President Bush to bring around the American people to helping the Soviets under such circumstances."*

Nakayama: *"Japan is against to changes in the EBRD cap."*

… Being Unheard

On July 17, the G7 met with Gorbachev for four hours.[61] While describing the reform plans, Gorbachev stumbled at important points, demonstrating that he had not yet decided what was right and how to do it.

[58] UK Foreign Secretary.

[59] US Secretary of State.

[60] The source of this estimate is unknown.

[61] GB M&T. Memorandum of Conversation. G7 Meeting with President Gorbachev. July 17, 1991.

> Step by step, we'll liberalize prices. We'll move from a situation in which "of our prices are unregulated to one in which 70% are unregulated... Regarding macroeconomic stabilization... We will go as far as socially acceptable. Neither of us would want to see the process become socially impossible... We will freeze deposits... Convertibility is under study... Paying debts—we will pay them...

The Soviet leader's attempt to emphasize the integration of the Soviet Union into international institutions and the world economy and to make some progress in lifting trade restrictions failed. The position of the G7 had already been agreed upon, and no one wanted to resume its discussion. Good improvisation is always well prepared. The G7 members were well prepared.

> I understand the real historical context and that this dictates what's possible. But it also dictates the need for a new level of trust.... Changing international institutions. The USSR wants to be part of the world economy. There are questions about how to organically incorporate it. We believe it is in our long-term interest to integrate ... This will help us ... to overcome our distorted economy; perhaps the most distorted economy in the world.

> We expect reciprocating steps from you. Like lifting legislative barriers; letting the USSR participate in international economic institutions; and a number of other steps. I have long lists on reciprocating. Let me be frank: Will you be well-wishers, onlookers, or active supporters? I'll answer your questions, but want you to answer mine.
>
> We've decided on irreversible moves. But it will be impossible to move on to radical reform outside the world market...
>
> We want to move into the international economic arena. If we're not admitted into the IMF, the World Bank, GATT and the EBRD, it won't work. We need them to provide oxygen to breathe. We're talking about mutuality. If I'm going too far, or am too optimistic, then let me know. I hope not.
>
> Some ask why isn't Gorbachev cutting military expenditures, when he will solve the question of links with Cuba and Afghanistan. I've tried to tell you about the real process of arms procurement. We've cut 29% since 1988. Procurement of APCs is down by a factor of four. I'll cut more...
>
> As for Cuba and Vietnam, our relations have changed radically. We've cut aid to Vietnam three-fold. Aid to Cuba has been halved...

None of the questions Gorbachev raised were answered. He was asked many minor questions, but the main wish of the G7 participants was that at the press conference that followed the meeting, Gorbachev would not express disappointment and resentment and would not criticize the position of the participants. As Canadian Prime Minister Mulroney recalled, this would be unlike Polish President Wałęsa, who, after one of the previous G7 meetings, criticized the decisions taken to cancel Polish debts, which journalists supported.

Gorbachev lacked the strength to argue, persuade, or fight. So, after hearing the closing words of the host of the meeting, British Prime Minister Major, "*What we'll say at our press conference … we need some message. It should be a positive one and will be historic…,*" the Soviet President uttered exhaustedly: "*I'll be positive.*"

Thirty-three days later, on the eve of the announced signing of the new Union Treaty, which was to create the basis for the continued existence of the Soviet Union, an attempted coup d'état would take place in Moscow. Gorbachev would be removed from power for three days, Yeltsin would become the leader of a public protest that would overturn the putschists, and the Soviet Union would effectively cease to exist. Before the legal disappearance of the USSR from the day of the putsch, another 128 days would pass, during which the world asked how life on one-sixth of the globe would now be organized.

Who's That?

In September 1989, Yeltsin visited the United States, which created a serious protocol problem for the American bureaucracy. Formally, Yeltsin was chairman of the Commission of the Council of Nationalities of the Supreme Soviet of the USSR, which could be considered a rough analog of a US Senate Committee. Moreover, thanks to this position, Yeltsin was a member of the Presidium of the Supreme Soviet of the USSR, which in the Soviet Union served as a legislative body between sessions of the Supreme Soviet, which were held twice a year and lasted two or three days. In principle, nothing prevented the President of the United States and the leaders of the houses of Congress to meeting the Moscow guest. However, it was no secret that Yeltsin had become an irreconcilable critic of Gorbachev and had been elected to the Supreme Soviet of the USSR against the latter's will through an unusual procedure.[62]

[62] When voting at the Congress of People's Deputies, Yeltsin did not get the necessary number of votes to be elected to the Supreme Soviet. When this was announced at the Congress session, unexpectedly, the deputy Alexei Kazannik, who had been elected to the Supreme Soviet, announced his refusal accept the mandate he had received. Since, according to the announced voting results, Yeltsin won the largest number of votes among the candidates who were not elected to the Supreme Soviet, the vacated mandate went to him. In October 1993, Yeltsin appointed Kazannik as the Prosecutor General of Russia, but he resigned four months later in a violent confrontation with Yeltsin. The Russian President demanded that the

With this in mind, they decided to stage a carefully orchestrated "chance" meeting: Yeltsin was invited to the White House to Scowcroft's office, where the organizers planned that Bush would "accidentally" drop by since the General's schedule included a meeting with Secretary of State Baker and eight high-ranking senators. To prevent journalists from learning about this meeting, Yeltsin was not told about the plan, and he was to enter the White House by going via an underground corridor from a neighboring building while all the members of the delegation accompanying him were to remain in the dark, waiting for the return of their leader in the guest room. Once in the underground, uncertain where—or why—he was being led, Yeltsin "rebelled" and sat down in a chair, saying he would not go anywhere until all delegation members joined him. For almost half an hour, the White House staff tried to persuade Yeltsin to go further; at some point, Scowcroft came down to him, but Yeltsin did not believe him immediately.

Bush "peeked" into Scowcroft's office, was "very surprised" to see the Moscow guest there, and chatted with him while standing for about 15 min. Coming outside after the meeting, Yeltsin upended the entire plan by immediately telling reporters that he had just met the President, where they discussed "ten important steps that should save perestroika." After that, it became impossible to hide what had happened; Bush spokeswoman Marlin Fitzwater and Secretary Baker confirmed the meeting, noting that the Russian politician's position was frank, direct, and at times provocative, but that Yeltsin's ideas lacked specificity. Baker was blunter, saying that when Yeltsin began asking for incentives for U.S. businessmen to invest in the Soviet economy, he responded, "*In order to make the Soviet Union an attractive place for Americans to invest, the Soviet Union needs to address price reform and the convertibility of the ruble.*"[63]

The episode left a lasting impression on Scowcroft; Yeltsin's "underground rebellion"[64] led him to doubt the Russian's seriousness as a statesman. Bush did not trust the latter after meeting Yeltsin and carefully analyzing his

Prosecutor General not implement the State Duma resolution on amnesty for participants in the putsch of August 1991 and the October 1993 armed conflict in Moscow, writing on the document, "Do not implement it and release no one from Lefortovo." Kazannik stated that he could not go against the law, released all those under investigation, and wrote a resignation letter. The Federation Council did not accept the Prosecutor General's resignation, but security guards at the Prosecutor General's Office building refused to let him enter his workplace. Two months later, Kazannik submitted a second resignation, which was accepted. "*Vas kak snimali?*" (How were you fired?) Kommersant, December 11, 2001. https://www.kommersant.ru/doc/301240

[63] "Yeltsin Asks Bush to Aid Soviet Reform Process." The Washington Post, September 13, 1989. The Washington Post, September 13, 1989.

[64] During this trip, Yeltsin did not seem to hide from the American officials accompanying him his craving for alcohol, and rumors about it spread actively in Washington.

statements and actions. He and his closest aides often expressed doubts about the political and human qualities of the Russian opposition politician and his political future. Scowcroft said many years later: "*I doubt Yeltsin was a democrat. I'm not sure. Not much of a convinced Communist; he was an opportunist and a populist. He saw, as his way to power, a finger on the pulse of what was popular. He split with Gorbachev in the Politburo in favor of more far-reaching reforms because he thought that was the popular thing to do.*"[65]

When Singaporean leader Lee Kuan Yew told Bush during their meeting, "*I doubt that Yeltsin could actually run the country.*" CIA Director Robert Gates, who was present, added, "*Everyone agrees that Yeltsin is a real opportunist without depth... He has accomplished very little since he became the President of Russia.*"[66,67]

In March 1991, in a meeting with Canadian Prime Minister Mulroney, Bush said, "*The thing about Yeltsin is that his values are good, but I don't know about him. I don't know how Yeltsin would deal with us... Yeltsin is not all bad, but we are not sure how to deal with him.*"[68]

In July, Baker, who was in Moscow on a visit, invited Yeltsin to a meeting at the American Embassy, which he declined without explanation.[69] This caused outright bewilderment and heightened doubts about the Russian politician's unpredictability, a fact that CIA Director Gates frankly expressed.

> What became apparent after Yeltsin was elected President of Russia was that he understood that communism was no longer an alternative for Russia. He was willing—he was really the first major leader in the Soviet Union to come around to the view that communism would no longer work and to say so... I don't think Yeltsin had a clue where he wanted to take Russia. One of the things that as an intelligence officer I spent a lot of time telling senior officials including Presidents, is that it is very hard for me to forecast to you the actions of a man who doesn't know himself yet what he is going to do.[70]

[65] Miller Center. George H.W. Bush Presidency. Brent Scowcroft. Oral History.

[66] GB M&T. Memorandum of Conversation. Meeting with Lee Kuan Yew, Senior Minister, Singapore. January 21, 1991.

[67] It is worth noting that, as often happened with American politicians, Gates made a factual mistake—Yeltsin became President of Russia six months later, in June 1991, while at that time he was chairman of the Supreme Soviet of Russia, a body with very narrow powers and opportunities.

[68] GB M&T. Memorandum of Conversation. Meeting with Brian Mulroney, Prime Minister of Canada. March 13, 1991.

[69] GB M&T. Memorandum of Conversation. President's meeting with President Ozal of Turkey. July 22, 1991.

[70] Miller Center. George H.W. Bush Presidency. Robert Gates Oral History. l

"Yeltsin is an excellent politician but he is also an ambitious opportunist of the first order and his credential as a democrat are suspect at best," Scowcroft wrote to Bush in an August 1990 memorandum analyzing the decentralization of the Soviet Union.[71]

Chained Together

The logic of the political struggle in the Soviet Union was *terra incognita* for analysts, and predictions centered on the potential ouster of Gorbachev by "hardline" supporters—figures in the KGB, the army, and Marxist ideologues in the Communist Party. "*Gorbachev could be gone tomorrow and a new guy come in and be exactly like the old crowd. I took it as a major responsibility for me as Sec Def to make sure we didn't lose what we had.*"[72] "*There is a strong chance that if Gorbachev were replaced, it would be by someone from the Right, not by Yeltsin.*"[73]

The scenario of Gorbachev losing against more reformist forces did not seem realistic. CIA analysts acknowledged that scenario but deemed it likely only toward the decade's end.[74] Although it was clear that Yeltsin was competing for power with Gorbachev, they were seen as allies in transforming the Soviet Union. Yeltsin, meeting with Western politicians, emphasized repeatedly that his differences with Gorbachev were merely tactical and that they shared the same strategic goal. "*Russia is firmly on Gorbachev's side. I cannot act without him.*"[75]

Even the attempted August 1991 coup, which all but shattered the USSR and stripped Gorbachev of leverage in preserving union, did not alter the stance Yeltsin presented to foreign interlocutors.

On September 5, 1991, Yeltsin told Kohl, "*Two weeks ago, nobody had been able to predict whether the President [Gorbachev] was really willing to continue democratic reforms. Meanwhile, today we may justifiably say that they collaborated well with each other. There was not a single question he did not discuss with Gorbachev. They found solutions together.*"[76]

---

[71] GBPL&M. Turmoil in the Soviet Union and US Policy. Memorandum for President. August 18, 1990.

[72] Miller Center. George H.W. Bush Presidency. Dick Cheney Oral History.

[73] GB M&T. Memorandum of Conversation. Meeting with Brian Mulroney, Prime Minister of Canada. March 13, 1991.

[74] GBPL&M. The Soviet Caldron. CIA. April 25, 1991.

[75] GB M&T. Memorandum of Conversation. Meeting with President of the Russian Republic Yeltsin of the USSR. June 20, 1991.

[76] Wilson Center. Memorandum. The Chancellor's Telephone Conversation with Russian President Yeltsin, Thursday, September 5, 1991.

On October 8, when asked directly by Bush in a telephone conversation about the fate of the Economic Union treaty, Yeltsin promised that he would meet with Gorbachev in three days to finalize all outstanding issues, after which "*Russia will sign the Treaty…to achieve the great political goal of preserving the Union… Even if eight, or nine, or ten republics sign [the Treaty]. The country as a single entity will be preserved … The Economic Union will become the basis for a formalized political* union."[77]

Yeltsin was trusted. "*We sense strong cooperation between Gorbachev and Yeltsin*," said Bush.[78]

On October 18, in Moscow, the leaders of the eight Soviet republics and Gorbachev, President of the USSR, signed the Treaty on the Economic Community, which provided a consensus method of forming common governing bodies and solving economic problems under common jurisdiction. A good treaty, by design, but there was no time left for its realization.

The situation in the Soviet Union was becoming increasingly chaotic: after a putsch led by the state's leaders and the government, the government was liquidated, and in its place, an ad hoc body emerged—the Committee for Operational Management of the Economy—which possessed no real powers. Union ministries lost their managerial authority—enterprises refused to execute any orders from Moscow; the Union budget did not receive taxes, loans from the USSR State Bank financed expenditures; the Russian government created an alternative center of monetary policy, declared the independence of the State Bank of Russia, appointed its chairman, who immediately began to execute decisions on lending to the republican budget.

Gorbachev had no opportunity to strengthen the negotiating positions, and each time, the seemingly final agreements began to be revised to weaken the Center further and strengthen the republics. It was impossible to miss. German Foreign Minister Genscher brought this to the Bush's attention: "*Gorbachev and Yeltsin agree that they must try to keep majority of republics together. But I'm afraid that their agreement might not go much beyond that.*"[79]

[77] GB M&T. Memorandum of Conversation. Telcon with Yeltsin, President of the Republic of Russia. October 8, 1991.

[78] GB M&T. Memorandum of Conversation. Expanded Meeting with Helmut Kohl, Chancellor of Germany. September 16, 1991.

[79] GB M&T. Memorandum of Conversation. Meeting with Foreign Minister Hans-Dietrich Genscher of Germany. October 3, 1991.

Everything Comes to an End

By the end of October, a group, committed to the maximum weakening of the Soviet Union, had formed around Yeltsin, and the Russian leader was making obvious steps in this direction. On October 28, Yeltsin addressed the Congress of People's Deputies of Russia and announced the formation of a new government that would implement radical economic reforms without consulting the other republics. Russia effectively terminated the Economic Community Treaty signed 10 days earlier: the remaining republics were given two weeks to reach an agreement with Russia on a common monetary policy. It was announced that Russia alone will liberalize prices, although the Treaty stipulated that the participating states "*shall pursue a coordinated policy of transition to free pricing,*" etc.[80]

This did not escape the White House's notice; the topic of increasing disintegration became the subject of discussion between Bush and Gorbachev when they meet in Madrid on October 29.

"*Yeltsin is under pressure by those who support a different concept. People who think Russia should shed other republics and go ahead alone. Yeltsin understands what that would mean… but he is easily swayed… he reaffirmed support for the Union, he retreated on some issues in the union treaty,*" Gorbachev said. "*Does Yeltsin's Russia want to take over the center?*"—Bush asked bluntly. "*That was happening when I returned from Crimea… That process was stopped…,*" Gorbachev replied, but immediately added that he did not understand the logic of Yeltsin's actions. "*His present situation is not entirely calculated.*"

Not surprisingly, Washington didn't know what to do—or whom to rely on. On the one hand, Gorbachev and the Center were weakening right before their eyes. However, Gorbachev ensured control over foreign policy, the army, and nuclear weapons. Soviet negotiators continued to discuss disarmament treaties and the settlement of the situation in Afghanistan; Gorbachev was under severe time pressure, facing the need to find solutions to many problems at once. His decisions appeared arbitrary and purposeless. America saw this clearly and capitalized on it. "*How did he want to get the reforms in? … What in fact he was doing was pulling apart the sinews that had kept the system together… We should squeeze every last agreement out of current leadership that*

[80] Speech by Russian President Yeltsin at the V Congress of People's Deputies of the RSFSR (October 28–November 2, 1991).

we can… Gorbachev made a lot of serious mistakes,[81] *and most of them were beneficial to us.*"[82]

We Just Let Things Happen

> The Soviet Union is indeed "disintegrating" [but] not so fast that the Gorbachev leadership is useless to us even as it becomes increasingly impotent at home. We will need to play a two-level game: a short-term policy that exploits diplomatic opportunities with the central government and a longer-term policy that begins to acquaint us with local leaders and the democratic opposition in support of decentralization. As hard as it is, we must resist the pressures that would force us to choose between the two.[83]

It is difficult to choose at all. Yeltsin, who is considered a democrat, has at times made strange statements that have made the White House wince. In late October, Vice President Rutskoi told an American diplomat, that Yeltsin's upcoming speech would assert Russia's duty to protect compatriots abroad and announce a decree abolishing the Soviet Foreign Ministry. An urgent meeting with the US ambassador persuaded Yeltsin to drop those passages.[84] "*What is in the US interests? Is it to keep the Soviet Union together? Break it up? What should our role be in the disintegration of the centrality?*" In Bush's entourage, two influential camps emerged, and both arguments were equally convincing or unconvincing.

> There was the debate about Gorbachev and Yeltsin themselves. The CIA was predominantly pro-Yeltsin, anti-Gorbachev when we had this debate. I thought they were wrong. Gorbachev and Yeltsin, as probably the two most influential in the system, were to me fairly clear-cut types. Gorbachev was an intellectual. He was not a democrat by any stretch of the imagination. He was not trying to transform the Soviet Union into a modern democracy. He moved more and more and more in that direction, but he was never right there. Even at the time when he came back from the Crimea and the attempted coup, he tried to defend the Communist Party… He had no rapport, no feel for the people. And he disliked Yeltsin, his protégée, who he thought had betrayed him.

---

[81] One such mistake with long-term consequences was that having obtained an agreement from the United States and Germany not to expand NATO eastward after German reunification, Gorbachev did not demand that this commitment be recorded in any way.

[82] Miller Center. George H.W. Bush Presidency. Brent Scowcroft Oral History, Part I.

[83] GBPL&M. Turmoil in the Soviet Union and US Policy. Memorandum for President. August 18, 1990.

[84] Wilson Center. Memorandum of Conversation. NATO Summit. November 7, 1991.

> … They're two very different kinds of people. We didn't have a real choice between them, although we were widely criticized for supporting Gorbachev. Gorbachev, after all, was the General Secretary and the President, but Gorbachev was also doing our work for us…
>
> We were split, badly split. Baker thought it was important that we try to keep the Soviet Union together—principally because of command and control over the nuclear forces. Cheney, at the other extreme, thought we ought to do everything we could to break up the Soviet Union. I thought that we were better off with a broken up Soviet Union, because it would fractionate the Soviet nuclear forces—and a large part of them, we could stop worrying about. But I disagreed with Cheney that we ought to actively pursue it, because if it didn't happen that way, we would engender great bitterness on the part of the Soviet Union. In the end, we took no position at all. We simply let things happen.[85]

One can hardly envy Bush in that situation. In October 1991, he hoped the two leaders could agree and act in concert. "*We don't know how everything will end up in the Soviet Union. Will there be a center, will there be independence or will there be a loose union*?"—he asked himself. And he could not understand how relations would develop in this strange alliance. "*I don't believe you can have Gorbachev and not Yeltsin… They need each other, although I think Gorbachev needs Yeltsin more.*"[86]

But a month later, when at a NATO summit, the German Chancellor bluntly asked: "*There is a rumor in Europe that the US is rethinking its policy toward the Soviet Union and that is has changed slightly. We have heard that you pin your hopes on the republics… Tell me, George, is the US position on the Soviet Union still the same*?"—The US President's confidence that the two bears can coexist in the same den was waning, which he was willing to admit. "*I support the Center, and I support Gorbachev even though I am criticizing the United States for doing so… Some people have said that this place is coming apart, but this is not my position… My answer to your question is yes. We support the Center or at least we support Gorbachev. Otherwise, we could have anarchy. I will give you the George Bush theory. Gorbachev and Yeltsin are not really getting along that well.*"[87]

---

[85] Miller Center. George H.W. Bush Presidency. Brent Scowcroft Oral History, Part I.

[86] GB M&T. Memorandum of Conversation. The President's Meeting with Secretary General of NATO Manfred Woerner. October 11, 1991.

[87] Wilson Center. Memorandum of Conversation. NATO Summit. November 7, 1991.

Unexpected Denouement

With just over a month to go before the collapse of the Soviet Union, Russia has a "reform government," and Parliament has given Yeltsin emergency powers to implement economic reforms. None of the republics had expressed a desire to be "in the same boat" with Russia, but Gorbachev and Yeltsin continue to send signals that they remain in agreement, that they communicate normally, and that they find solutions to existing problems.

On November 19, Gorbachev's closest aide, Alexander Yakovlev, arrived in Washington, where the President received him. Yakovlev told him that the situation was improving, that the last meeting of the State Council[88] was held in a constructive atmosphere, that the participants agreed that a unified foreign policy would be maintained, that unified control of nuclear weapons would be maintained, that Yeltsin had dropped his earlier demands for the creation of republican armies and agreed that representatives of all republics, including Russia, would work abroad as employees of Soviet embassies. At the same time, Yakovlev said, it came as a complete surprise to Gorbachev when the republics demanded the immediate closure of 70 Soviet ministries but strongly opposed the closure of the Ministry of Culture, which Yakovlev said should have been closed first.

In response to the President's question about what Yeltsin thinks and does, Yakovlev tried to combine moderate criticism and optimistic assessments. He criticized Yeltsin's decision to announce price liberalization well ahead of schedule, which unnerved the population. At the same time, Yakovlev said Yeltsin had become more aware of the situation and more adequate. [Gorbachev and Yeltsin] "*talk every day; seek each other's advice. They have frank conversations. (I see them). They will never be friends. But that's not necessary. They can have good business-like relations.*"[89]

Two days later, Yeltsin met with Kohl[90] and said that the Council of State was actively discussing a political union, that it was likely to be a confederation, and that he, as President of Russia, "*was in strong favor of a union and collaborating closely with Gorbachev.*" At his interlocutor's request, Yeltsin confirmed that the Union would retain a unified army and, among other things,

---

[88] The State Council was established in the USSR after the failure of the August putsch as a governing body for the coordinated resolution of domestic and foreign policy issues affecting the common interests of the republics. The members of this body were President Gorbachev and the leaders of the 12 Union republics.

[89] GB M&T. Memorandum of Conversation. Meeting with Alexander Yakovlev, Senior Advisor to President Gorbachev of USSR. November 19, 1991.

[90] Wilson Center. The Chancellor's [Helmut Kohl's] Meeting with Russian President Yeltsin on Thursday, November 21, 1991.

a unified energy system and a unified railroad system. Yeltsin said that the position of President of the Union, elected by universal suffrage, would remain, that the Supreme Soviet of the USSR would have to approve the law on elections, and that Gorbachev would retain the post until the elections.

Kohl summarized the conversation with satisfaction: "*The decisive thing for him was Yeltsin's support for a confederation. The major concern in the West was that the dissolution of the giant colossus of the Soviet Union would lead to explosive developments. Yeltsin says that Russia would stand up for the union.*"

Ten days later, on November 30, on the eve of the Ukrainian referendum, Yeltsin called Bush and told him that he had no doubt that the idea of independence would be supported in the referendum and that Russia would recognize Ukraine's independence. The Russian President was sure that, in this case, Ukraine would sign a political union, and "*That will dramatically change the balance in the Union between Slavic and Islamic republics. We can't have a situation where Russia and Belorussia have two votes as Slavic states against five for the Islamic nations… I cannot imagine a union without Ukraine.*"

Bush also had no doubts about the outcome of the Ukrainian referendum but believed that it would not prevent the Union from being preserved. "*We will be making a statement after the referendum that explains our approach. The statement will also note our desire to work closely with President Gorbachev. It would not be a recognition, but rather a statement about independence.*"[91]

On December 3, Bush called Ukrainian President Leonid Kravchuk, congratulated him on the results of the referendum, and informed him that US Assistant Secretary of State for European Affairs[92] Thomas Niles was coming to Kyiv to discuss US-Ukrainian relations and how Ukraine sees its relations with Russia regarding defense and foreign policy. Kravchuk responded that he would be happy to receive the envoy from Washington and informed him that he would meet with Yeltsin and Belarusian President Shushkevich in Minsk in three days. The three Presidents met on December 7–8 and decided to terminate the Treaty establishing the Soviet Union. Bush and Gorbachev learned of this almost simultaneously. Shushkevich spoke to the Soviet leader, while Yeltsin spoke to the US President.

Gorbachev still entertained illusions that the created Commonwealth of Independent States (CIS) would be a state in which he would find a place, but very quickly realized that the word "Independent" left no room for interpretation. On December 14, Gorbachev's aide Pavel Palazhchenko gave journalists

---

[91] GB M&T. Memorandum of Telephone Conversation. Telcon with President Yeltsin of the Republic of Russia. November 30, 1991.

[92] The Assistant Secretary of State for European Affairs is the fourth level of hierarchy in the State Department.

Beschloss and Talbott a confidential message for Bush and Secretary Baker that Gorbachev may resign soon.[93] On December 20, Gorbachev reported this as a fact in a telephone conversation with Kohl. On December 21, delegations from eleven republics signed an agreement in Alma-Ata on the dissolution of the Soviet Union. On December 25, Gorbachev announced his resignation. The Soviet Union ceased to exist.

Save Our Money

After the G7 summit in London, it became clear that the Soviet Union could not count on financial assistance from the West. After the August events, the Soviet leadership did not even attempt to conduct such negotiations. But this does not mean financial topics were pushed out of the political spotlight. On the contrary, both sides started talking about money at the slightest opportunity, but each had its own motives.

Unlike Poland, which requested and quickly received US support and the Paris Club's agreement to cancel half of its foreign debt, no creditor considered writing off the Soviet Union's debt. Moreover, after Gorbachev signed an agreement with Thatcher in 1986 to settle the debt of pre-revolutionary Russia,[94] the governments of other countries whose citizens and companies had lent to Russia before the October Revolution were no longer reluctant to receive similar compensation.[95]

The Debt Burden Was Growing Rapidly

Foreign debt was one of the most closely guarded topics, even for the top Soviet leadership. Even Gorbachev received such information based on a separate request; a document that came to the office of the head of state had to be returned to the Ministry of Finance after the President had familiarized himself with it.

Historically, the Soviet Union was very reticent to use foreign loans, but as the situation deteriorated, foreign loans proved to be the only way to keep the

[93] Michael R. Beschloss and Strobe Talbott. At the Highest Level. The inside Story of the End of the Cold War. Little, Brown and Company. 1994, p. 455.

[94] Great Britain undertook to compensate its citizens who held bonds of the Russian Empire with 5.5 tons of gold of the tsarist government stored in an English bank.

[95] And they achieved their goal. Russia signed agreements on the settlement of pre-revolutionary debts with the USA (1993), France (2000) and Belgium (2008).

economy in balance. By early 1980, the country's foreign debt had not exceeded $25 billion, but by 1985, it had risen to $40 billion. The fall in world oil prices in 1986 undermined the Soviet Union's balance of payments: in 1981–1984, the current account deficit averaged less than $1 billion, while in 1986–1990, it amounted to more than $16 billion a year. Lack of currency to purchase necessary equipment and production components, the anti-alcohol campaign that led to a drop in budget revenues, and the accident at the Chornobyl nuclear power plant posed new challenges for the Soviet government, and often foreign loans were the only way to cope with them: in 1989, foreign debt exceeded $57 billion, and by the end of the Soviet Union's existence it exceeded $70 billion.[96] More troubling, the Soviet government lost control of the debt-accumulation process.

Until the mid-1980s, Vnesheconombank was the only borrower on behalf of the USSR, while foreign countries acted as creditors of the Soviet Union. The reform of state-owned enterprises and liberalization of foreign trade led to the fact that state-owned foreign trade associations began to attract trade credits from foreign companies, which did not closely follow the events in the USSR and assumed that a mere change of letterhead by Soviet buyers would not jeopardize payment due. No authority in the USSR could track these loans, which totaled about $6 billion by the end of 1991.

Relations with CMEA member countries were even more strained. Trade between CMEA countries operated through bilateral clearing with settlements in the conventional currency unit, the transferable ruble; lists of mutually supplied goods, their volumes and prices were agreed upon within the framework of annual plans, and each country paid for exported goods and ensured payments for imports in its national currency according to its own rules. Until the end of 1988, this system functioned smoothly, and the USSR consistently acted as creditor to other countries. The destabilization of the Soviet economy in 1990/91 led to the destruction of this mechanism. On the one hand, Soviet exporters did not fulfill their obligations to supply goods to Central and Eastern European countries—some found more favorable consumers who were ready to pay in freely convertible currencies, and others could not produce their products due to the breakdown of economic ties. On the other hand, the importers, having obtained freedom of decision-making, began to place orders from CMEA countries without prior agreement on transaction volumes and prices. By the end of 1989, the USSR's debt to the

[96] "To V.V. Bogdanov, Assistant to the First Deputy Prime Minister of the Russian Federation.—Vnesheconombank. Materials on foreign debt as of January 1, 1992." Yegor Gaidar Archive. http://gaidar-arc.ru/databasedocuments/theme/details/3134

CMEA member states exceeded $6 billion; by the end of 1990, it had more than doubled, and by the time of the collapse of the USSR, it ballooned to $29 billion.[97] The Soviet government had no control over the build-up of this debt, and Western experts were unaware of its existence at the end of 1991. However, even later, the US administration did not recognize this debt[98] as part of Russia's foreign debt, although Russia had to repay it in full, except for $7 billion that Germany forgave.

Given that by the end of the Soviet Union's existence, it had accumulated overdue interest arrears of more than $5 billion and nearly $6 billion in clearing and barter accounts,[99] the total value of Soviet foreign debt at the time of its collapse exceeded $110 billion. Besides that, Vnesheconombank (VEB), where all enterprises and households were required to keep their foreign currency accounts and which made all foreign currency payments in the Soviet Union, used $24 billion of customer funds,[100] which were later structured as domestic dollar-denominated government debt.

... But No One Knew About It

Before his trip to London for the G7 meeting, Gorbachev received a memorandum from the Ministry of Finance on the size of the country's foreign debt, which, it said, was far from alarming: as of January 1, 1991, the USSR owed other countries $52 billion, the forecast for the end of 1991 was $64.3 billion.[101] During 1992, the Soviet Union was to pay just under $15 billion in debt repayment and service.[102]

---

[97] These data are contained in the document of the Balance of Payments Department of the Bank of Russia, which is [erroneously] attached to the letter of the USSR Ministry of Finance dated June 28, 1991, "To V I Boldin, Chief of Staff of the President of the USSR. Materials for the meeting of the USSR President in London." Yegor Gaidar Archive. http://gaidar-arc.ru/databasedocuments/theme/details/2506

[98] In 2001, CRS, in discussing the problem of Russia's negotiations with the Paris Club, consolidated information on the debts of the USSR and Russia from 1991 through 1998, where the debt to CMEA member countries was missing. (CRS Report to Congress. "Russia's Paris Club Debt and US Interests" Updated June 6, 2001. Order Code RL30617).

[99] "To V.V. Bogdanov, Assistant to the First Deputy Prime Minister of the Russian Federation.—Vnesheconombank. Materials on foreign debt as of January 1, 1992." Yegor Gaidar Archive. http://gaidar-arc.ru/databasedocuments/theme/details/3134

[100] Letter from the Deputy Chairman of the Central Bank of the RSFSR D. Tulin to the Chairman of the Special Commission of the Supreme Soviet of the RSFSR Ryabov N.T. December 1, 1992. https://gaidar-arc.ru/databasedocuments/theme/details/1624

[101] Materials for the meeting of the President of the USSR in London. Letter from the USSR Ministry of Finance to the Chief of Staff of the USSR President V.I. Boldin. June 28, 1991. Archive of Yegor Gaidar. http://gaidar-arc.ru/databasedocuments/theme/details/2506

[102] Later, when data on the USSR's debt (excluding debts to CMEA member countries) were consolidated, it turned out that the sum of payments for debt service and repayment in 1992 should have amounted to $25 billion.

The government reform programs of Ryzhkov and Pavlov did not mention the problem of foreign debt. The Yavlinsky-Allison program, although premised on Western financing, likewise ignored the question of restructuring the external debt. "A Study of the Soviet Economy," carried out by four international financial organizations, devotes a page and a half to the subject of debt without considering it essential. The figures the experts gave were not fundamentally different from those Gorbachev received before his trip to London. However, the text said that the size of the debt may be larger due to incomplete information and that by October 1990, the Soviet Union was in arrears on interest payments on debts of about $5 billion (almost 10% of the amount of debt at the beginning of 1991, which the experts used for their analysis). The problem of the Soviet Union's solvency was not even discussed. Everyone was sure that the USSR was a first-class borrower.[103]

Before the London summit, EU Commission representatives suggested that the restructuring of Soviet foreign debt be considered to[104] enable the Soviet Union to increase imports of goods from Eastern European countries facing sharp economic decline (very similar to Marshall Plan support for intra-European trade—was it not?). Although the US was not a major creditor of the Soviet Union, Bush, Baker, and Treasury Secretary Brady flatly refused to raise the issue at the G7.

Delors: *"I think a most helpful thing to do would be to restructure Soviet debt. If this is done, it would increase Soviet imports from eastern Europe and give them maneuvering room."*

The President: *"But to what end? What will they do with the maneuvering room? We need to have greater evidence that such restructuring would help promote significant economic reforms in the Soviet Union."*

Delors: *"Debt restructuring is the only measure that the G7 can take at the present time."*

---

[103] At a press conference on July 16, 1990, Gorbachev spoke of the advisability of *prolonging the repayment of Soviet debts on the most appropriate terms*. This statement caused panic in the Western media, which believed that the USSR intended to declare a moratorium on servicing its foreign debt and that the Bank of England had placed the USSR on a list of unsecured debtors. The Soviet government was bombarded with calls for explanations, and many foreign banks suspended operations with Soviet companies. On July 18, 1990, the Kremlin organized a special press conference on behalf of the Presidential Council, at which it was explained that it was not a question of a possible cessation of payments, but of improving the structure of the existing debt by attracting new long-term loans while restraining the overall size of the foreign debt. It was especially emphasized that all previously signed credit agreements will be observed without revision of their terms. "Regarding M S Gorbachev's statement concerning the necessity to prolong the repayment of our debts on new terms." Note by S A Sitaryan to N I Ryzhkov. July 31, 1990. Yegor Gaidar's archive. http://gaidar-arc.ru/databasedocuments/theme/details/2253

[104] GB M&T. Memorandum of Conversation. Meeting with Prime Minister Lubbers and EC President Delors. July 15, 1991.

The President: *"Do we have any assurance that the Soviet Union could repay even a restructured debt?"*

Baker: *"We cannot grant his request for a stabilization fund or debt restructuring. Nor do we like the idea of lifting the cap on EBRD lending."*

Andriessen: *"The collapse of Soviet trade with Eastern Europe is the Eastern European countries' greatest problem and one argument for restructuring Soviet debt."*

Brady: *"Any debt rescheduling for the Soviet Union is an admission of the Soviet Union's bankruptcy. Such a step could result in future credit being cut off to the Soviet Union…"*.

Baker: *"The US does not hold a lot of Soviet debt. The Paris Club seems to be the right forum to discuss the issue of Soviet debt rescheduling."*

Lacking adequate information, Gorbachev dismissed the country's solvency question at a London meeting in July 1991. "*Paying debts—we will pay them… We will earn currency to pay our debts. We accept the rules of the game…*" But four months later, in October 1991, meeting with Bush in Madrid, Gorbachev begged him to help with money—*"million in money is needed today … $2.5 billion is needed as a reserve in case of need and to deal with the dangers in this crisis situation,"* and asked him to press Saudi Arabia and South Korea, which had pledged one and two and a half billion dollars, respectively. But at the same time, the Soviet leader again assured his interlocutor that debt service was not a problem—"*$10–15 billion is not much for us and repayment is not a serious problem."*[105]

Yeltsin likewise showed little concern for the foreign-debt problem. In those moments when he discussed possible Western assistance, the foreign debt issue did not come up in conversation. However, as President of a republic within the USSR, he was aware of the limits of his authority in foreign policy. In June 1991, at a meeting with Bush, the Russian President's requests were limited to programs for processing and storing agricultural products, training of managers, conversion, and transport development without offering any parameters for these programs. To which Bush replied melancholy, *"We can help and we want to do… We can share our expertise—there are things we can do."*[106]

[105] GB M&T. Memorandum of Conversation. Meeting with President Gorbachev of the USSR. October 29, 1991.

[106] GB M&T. Memorandum of Conversation. Meeting with President of the Russian Republic Yeltsin of the USSR.

Gaidar's team remained optimistic, even though Russia would soon bear sole responsibility for servicing Soviet debt,[107] and it obvious that neither Gaidar himself nor any of his team had any idea of the gravity of the problem at the time. After delivering a speech in late October outlining his reform plans, Yeltsin wrote a letter to Bush: "*We re-affirm the international obligations of the Union and intend to ensure their fulfillment.*"[108] Even on November 29, when the scale of the economic disaster in the Soviet Union was clear to everyone, Yeltsin told Kohl: "*Russia was able to cope with its foreign debts and was even willing to shoulder the debts of two or three additional republics.*"[109]

This position of the Soviet and Russian leaders pleased the G-7—especially Chancellor Kohl, who repeatedly opposed any debt write-off, arguing that Berlin had already spent heavily to support transformation in Central and Eastern Europe, as well as financing the withdrawal of Soviet troops from Germany.[110]

Aware that the eventual division of powers was uncertain, the G-7 insisted the republics accept joint responsibility for Soviet debt—blackmailing, no loans would be forthcoming otherwise to either the Soviet Union or its republics. "*This is a rich country. It has energy exports. If they prefer to spend money on defense, that's their choice. They can pay their debts and they should,*" US Deputy Treasury Secretary David Mulford said stiffly.[111]

Negotiations between the republics[112] on this subject began in Moscow in the second half of September. In mid-October, the G7 finance ministers invited a Soviet delegation to their meeting in Bangkok to discuss the situation in the USSR economy. They unexpectedly heard that the problem of lack of foreign exchange resources and inability to service foreign debt was the most acute. Viktor Gerashchenko, chairman of the USSR State Bank, said the country's foreign currency reserves were nearly exhausted. Grigory Yavlinsky went even further and said that after November 10, the USSR would not be

---

[107] "Russia's foreign debt and currency policy." Note by G. Anulova (presumably to Y. Gaidar). October 23, 1991. Yegor Gaidar's archive. http://gaidar-arc.ru/databasedocuments/theme/details/2526

[108] GBPL&M. Letter to President Bush from Yeltsin. (unofficial translation by Russians). November 1991.

[109] Wilson Center. The Chancellor's [Helmut Kohl's] Meeting with Russian President Yeltsin on Thursday, November 21, 1991.

[110] "Kohl Urges Japan to Increase Help for Eastern Europe." The New York Times. May 6, 1992.

[111] James M. Goldgeiger and Michael McFaul. Power and Purpose: US Policy toward Russia after the Cold War. Washington, DC. Brookings Institution Press, 2003, p.69.

[112] Representatives of all 15 republics participated in these negotiations, although the Baltic states and Georgia took the position of observers.

able to pay its debts,[113] that by the end of the year, the arrears of payments would reach $5 billion, and that the country's foreign debt would have grown to $70 billion. But no decision was made. Speaking after the meeting, Brady said: "*In truth, what happened here was not a watershed; it's a way station.*" The US began to lean toward supporting debt relief, but the major creditors, Germany and France, were vehemently opposed.[114]

G7 was not sure that the republics would sign the Economic Union agreement and pressed hard to fix their obligations on the external debt of the USSR. In late October, the deputy finance ministers of the G7 countries came to Moscow to talk with representatives of the USSR and the republics. As a result of the negotiations, a "Memorandum of Understanding on the debt to foreign creditors of the USSR" was signed, which formulated the fundamental principle of payment of the external debt of the USSR by its successors—the principle of joint and several liability.[115] However, it was not possible to go further and agree on the mechanism of control and responsibility of the parties to the agreement. Negotiations continued: on December 4, 11 republics (except for the Baltic states and Uzbekistan) signed a treaty in which they confirmed their obligations and allocated the debt, the value of which had already approached $80 billion, and the costs of servicing it among themselves. The republics' commitments were enshrined in the agreement on the Dissolution of the Soviet Union, signed on December 21.

Why did the Russian reformers, aware that Russia would bear the brunt of the debt, still pressed for the "zero option"[116] yet failed to seek any debt relief remains a mystery. Perhaps creditors applied pressure, insisting that neither the USSR nor its republics would receive support unless they accepted full responsibility for all debts. It was risky and dangerous to resist such blackmail when everyone needed emergency external loans for the purchase of food and medicine, without which the situation could have turned into a humanitarian

[113] James M. Goldgeiger and Michael McFaul. Power and Purpose: US Policy toward Russia after the Cold War. Washington, DC. Brookings Institution Press, 2003, p. 69.

[114] "Brady Says Soviet Pact on Union Is the Key to Aid." The New York Times. October 15, 1991.

[115] This meant that the successor countries were jointly and severally liable for the whole debt, the entire amount, and any failure to service it would automatically result in the termination of credit for each and every individual successor state. If one of these states cannot pay its share of the debt, the other partners in the memorandum are to assume the obligation to repay that share.

[116] During negotiations on the fate of Soviet debt, the subject of Soviet assets abroad, which was also shrouded in secrecy, constantly came up. For some reason, the negotiators believed that the loans, which the USSR provided to its satellites largely through arms deliveries, and which exceeded the volume of the Soviet Union's debt, would be repaid. Russia offered its partners a "zero option," under which it would assume responsibility for the Soviet debt while at the same time becoming the owner of all Soviet assets abroad. Eventually, all post-Soviet countries agreed to this option, except for Ukraine, which signed a treaty with Russia but did not ratify it.

catastrophe.[117] And the creditors were deluding themselves and exaggerating the problem's severity.

On November 5, 1991, Bush met with his economic and foreign policy team on the problem of Soviet debt. The situation was catastrophic: Vnesheconombank was on the verge of bankruptcy. To avoid this, the Soviet Union needed an immediate loan of $1 billion, although even in this case, the amount of overdue debt payments by the end of the year would amount to $4 billion. The Treasury's memorandum offered an unusual assessment: the USSR faced not a balance-of-payments crisis but a liquidity crisis. The Soviet economy could service its foreign debt, but the state (if there was one) could not control currency flows within the country and could not take it away from state-owned companies.[118]

Perhaps, as is often heard, by agreeing to accept responsibility for Soviet debts in full, Yeltsin's team wished Russia to be seen as the USSR's legal successor—and thus, in effect, to secure the Soviet Union's permanent UN Security Council seat. However, no documents or evidence support this version. There is no trace of any discussion of the subject of a seat on the Security Council in the disclosed transcripts of the negotiations. This version does not correspond to the recollections at the time of the US and Soviet ambassadors to the UN, Robert Pickering[119] and Yuli Vorontsov.[120] However, the problem of transferring the seat in the Security Council to Russia became apparent only in December, after the Treaty "On the Termination of the Soviet Union" was signed, and two months before that, hardly anyone was ready to put this scenario into the basis of the debt agreements.

Perhaps in the second half of October, Yeltsin had very little time to devote to economic matters, and the negotiation of foreign debt was entrusted to officials whose qualifications did not match the scale of the problem and who, without guidance, could not imagine seeking partial cancellation of Soviet debt. Yeltsin formed a reform government on November 6, but by this point, Russia had accepted responsibility for the Soviet debt.

* * *

[117] This, in particular, was mentioned by Gaidar, who claimed that Mulford threatened to cut off grain supplies if only Russia dared to raise the issue of debt forgiveness. James M. Goldgeiger and Michael McFaul. Power and Purpose: US Policy toward Russia after the Cold War. Washington, DC. Brookings Institution Press, 2003, p. 71.

[118] GBPL&M. Meeting on Soviet Debt. Memorandum from Brent Scowcroft to the President with attachments. November 5, 1991.

[119] Thomas Reeve Pickering. Oral History, Interviewed by Charles Stuart Kennedy, Foreign Affairs Oral History Collection, Association for Diplomatic Studies and Training. April 18, 2003. https://adst.org/OH%20TOCs/Pickering-Thomas-Reeve.pdf

[120] From the archives of UN Radio: Ambassador Vorontsov on how Russia became a "successor of the USSR." https://news.un.org/ru/audio/2015/10/1030441

On December 13, Gorbachev called Bush; it was more monologue than dialogue. For half an hour, Gorbachev tried to convince himself that all was not yet lost, that there was still a chance to preserve the unified structure, but his words sounded doomed. It was especially hurtful to the Soviet President that on that day, Secretary Baker, speaking at Princeton University, said that "*The Soviet Union has ceased to exist.*"[121] Gorbachev believed that those or other words could have made a difference.

Baker's speech[122] outlined the goals of US policy toward the former Soviet Union. In the presence of Kennan, the author of containment theory, Baker spoke of the need for a global partnership to help turn a former enemy into a friend, and that failure or abandonment of such a partnership could have dire consequences for both sides. "*If during the Cold War we faced each other as two scorpions in a bottle, now the Western nations and the former Soviet republics stand as awkward climbers on a steep mountain. Held together by a common rope.*"

If Marshall's June 1947 speech was permeated with anxiety, Baker's speech radiated optimism and hope.

> We have the chance to anchor Russia, Ukraine, and other republics firmly in the Euro-Atlantic community and the democratic commonwealth of nations.
>
> … Together with the new Democrats in the former Soviet Union, we can help create pathways of hope so that the new Russian revolution can fulfill the promise of the next generation. We alone cannot determine whether these new Democrats will succeed. Their success, of course, lies in their hands and in the hard choices that they make. But history will count our efforts to success if we help the Democrats hold open opportunities to develop a better future.
>
> … What this means for America is that we face a simple choice. We can follow our fears and turn inward, ignoring the opportunities presented by the collapse of the Soviet Empire, or we can answer the summons of history, and we can lead toward a better future for all…
>
> We can prevail over political paralysis to forge a bipartisan consensus about what has to be done, and then united at home, we can join with our allies to form a new coalition, a coalition for a diplomacy of collective engagement, a coalition to create pathways of hope, a coalition to make of the end of the Cold War a beginning, a new beginning for all the nations of the world. Ladies and gentlemen, history and the American people expect no less of us…

However, surpassing his great predecessor in the level of optimism, James Baker was far less generous. In 1947, President Truman's administration was

[121] There were no such words in Baker's speech, but he uttered "former Soviet Union" several times.

[122] James Baker at Princeton before and after the Cold War. Reel Mudd Manuscript Library. https://blogs.princeton.edu/reelmudd/2011/03/james-baker-about-post-soviet-policy-1991/

prepared to spend $16 billion on the postwar reconstruction of Europe. In late 1991 prices, this amount was equivalent to about $100 billion.[123] The Secretary of State was prepared to spend no more than 1% of that amount on support for the post-Soviet countries: $400 million for a program to eliminate Soviet nuclear weapons, which was "*an investment in America's security,*" just under $300 million in humanitarian aid, and $100 million in technical assistance. James Baker emphasized: "*This money, of course, will not come from domestic spending, but from aid to other foreign countries.*"

The Secretary of State seemed to get ahead of himself and gave an important reason why Russia and the other republics could not expect to receive serious aid. According to the President's economic team, the US budget could not afford it. However, according to many observers, the President did not think helping a defeated enemy was a priority in his policy these days.

[123] US Federal Reserve inflation calculator. https://www.minneapolisfed.org/about-us/monetary-policy/inflation-calculator

3

Bad Year

If Russia could choose when to start its reforms, it would be hard to find a less favorable year than 1992 given the domestic situation in the United States. It was a presidential election year, which shifted the administration's focus to campaigning and sidelined many other matters. The original intent of Bush's campaign staff was to emphasize foreign policy successes (Gulf War, victory in the Cold War)—in March 1991, the President's approval rating stood at 90%. However, Cold-War euphoria led many voters to embrace the "end-of-history" narrative and drift toward isolationism. This shift was compounded by a deteriorating US economy: recession in late 1990 and early 1991 led to a rapid increase in the budget deficit. In January 1990, the deficit for the 1990/91 fiscal year was estimated by the White House at $65 billion; by the time the budget was approved in early October, it had risen to $170 billion and reached $221 billion by year's end. "*We had a terrible time with Treasury and OMB… The President was trying to reduce the deficit, and so … if you wanted to propose any new programs, you had to find the money from other programs to fund them.*"[1]

To support the budget, the White House, under pressure from Democrats in Congress, went for a tax increase, anathema to voters inclined toward Republicans, who have not forgotten that Bush had promised not to raise taxes during the previous election campaign. Unemployment crept up, peaking at 7.8% in June 1992—by then the economy had shed over 1.6 million jobs; 75% of voters on the eve of the election believed that the country's main problems lay in the economy.

[1] Miller Center. George H. W. Bush Presidency. Brent Scowcroft Oral History Part I.

S. Aleksashenko, *Post-Cold War Russia and the Missed Opportunity for Global Stability*,
https://doi.org/10.1007/978-3-032-01380-4_3

A powerful wake-up call came when then-Attorney General Richard Thornburgh, being the governor of Pennsylvania from 1979 to 1987, lost a special Senate election in this state in November 1991. Thornburgh ran on foreign policy successes and lost, which, according to Scowcroft, caused panic inside the campaign team. "*The campaign people simply panicked. From that time on, foreign policy was anathema. And the consequence was we moved right over onto the agenda of his opponent… I did tell him [President] I thought it was a mistake, for example, to stay away from foreign policy just because the polls showed the American people weren't interested in it.*"[2]

Compounding matters, Lee Atwater, Bush's 1988 campaign manager and head of the Republican National Committee, died in March 1991. His unexpected death eroded donor support and weakened a key campaign apparatus. In December 1991, the White House Chief of Staff John Sununu resigned because of a scandal involving the use of official vehicles, paralyzing the administration and leaving Bush without a dynamic advisor.

However, the incumbent's position is always an advantage in elections, and the strong Democratic candidates, Mario Cuomo, Bill Bradley, and Jesse Jackson, were so unlikely to win that they declined to enter the race, giving way to a little-known newcomer, Arkansas Governor Bill Clinton. Clinton's outsider status—he had yet to make enemies in Washington—worked to his advantage, and he was able to rally the party at a crucial stage of the campaign. In June 1992, before Clinton was officially nominated as the Democratic nominee, only 25% of voters supported him in polls. On the Election Day, Clinton, whose main slogan was "It's the economy stupid!", won 43% of votes, well ahead of Bush's 37.5%.

A major element of unpredictability in the election race was the participation of independent candidate Ross Perot, who in June was leading in the polls with 39% against 31% for the incumbent.[3] In July, Perot abruptly left the race, which sent his ratings plunging; he still captured nearly 19% of the vote, but failed to win any states and to receive a single electoral college vote. Polls showed Perot taking votes equally from Clinton and Bush, and it is believed that his participation in the election didn't favor Clinton.[4] Nevertheless, out that in 23 states, the number of votes cast for him was three

[2] Miller Center. George H. W. Bush Presidency. Brent Scowcroft Oral History Part II.

[3] "The 1992 Campaign: On the Trail; Poll Gives Perot a Clear Lead." The New York Times, June 11, 1992.

[4] E.g., "Examining Ross Perot's Impact on the 1992 Presidential Election Results" https://split-ticket.org/2023/04/01/examining-ross-perots-impact-on-the-1992-presidential-election/

or more times the difference between the two major candidates.[5] In eight states, this ratio exceeded ten times.

In short, budget funds were depleted, foreign policy had slipped to the sidelines, the campaign sagged, Bush appeared listless, his team failed to woo voters, and the resulting defeat left him a "lame duck," paralyzing the administration. In such a year, Russia started reforms.

Total Fog

The Belovezha Accords were signed on December 8, and Yeltsin informed Bush the same day. However, no one knew or could predict how and when the Soviet Union would disappear—the president of the country continued to sit in the Kremlin and hold the "red button" in his hands, the deputies of the Union Parliament elected from Russia and Belarus first announced their withdrawal from the assembly but soon returned.

On December 13, Yeltsin called Bush and, in effect, informed him that on December 21, representatives of the ten republics would meet in Alma-Ata and sign an agreement to dissolve the Soviet Union. But again, there was no clarity about what would happen next. Yeltsin said he talked to Gorbachev daily and that "*in late December or early January, the Commonwealth of Independent States will be formed, and the structures of the center will cease to exist.*"[6] Bush immediately called Gorbachev, who said that Yeltsin had *radically changed course* and that he did not fully understand the nature of what was happening. Gorbachev mumbled that the process must be constitutional and that he would abide by the decision of the republics. In the end, Gorbachev admitted that the process of the country's disappearance was continuing and that his fears were justified. "*I want the other republics to participate in the process; otherwise, it would be against the constitution. I want the concept of the commonwealth to acquire more meaning… If the commonwealth is an amorphous organization with no mechanism for foreign policy and defense and economic interaction, then I do not see any role for myself.*"[7]

One thing was clear: a few more days would pass, and the Soviet Union would disappear. It is no coincidence that the transcript of the telephone conversation lists Gorbachev's position as president of ***the former*** Soviet Union.

[5] Clinton won in 15 of these 23 states and Bush won in eight. 1992 Presidential General Election Data—National https://uselectionatlas.org/

[6] GB M&T. Telephone Conversation with President Yeltsin of Russia. December 13, 1991.

[7] GB M&T. Telephone Conversation with President Mikhail Gorbachev of the FSU. December 13, 1991.

Yes, the Soviet Union would disappear, but what would happen to economic reform? Who would take responsibility for its realization? On the one hand, formally, the Soviet Union continued to exist, although there was no one in any Soviet ministry with whom to discuss what would happen to the economy. On the other hand, Russia in early November declared that it was ready to do it alone, and on December 5, two key people in the reform government, Gennady Burbulis, the first deputy prime-minister and Yeltsin's strategy advisor, and Gaidar met with US Ambassador Strauss in Moscow and said that the next day Yeltsin would ask the G7 to give Russia directly (until then, the Soviet Union was the recipient of all foreign loans) "*a loan of several billion dollars to stabilize the economy during the reforms.*" The request astonished the ambassador; Gaidar's remark surprised him even more: the money was needed "*to pay three thousand dollars to each serviceman to buy time with the military to keep the reforms on track.*" The ambassador assumed that he was referring only to officers but given that there were one and a half million of them, "*this would amount to a staggering sum.*"[8]

The next day, Gaidar met with the G7 ambassadors and handed them a letter from Yeltsin requesting a loan. The letter outlined the Russian government's plans yet omitted the details the G7 sought. Gaidar promised to hand over more information and data, "*everything we have.*" Explaining the logic of the reforms and the need for a loan to create a stabilization fund, on the one hand, Yeltsin said in his letter that without it, the ruble would rapidly devalue after price liberalization and retail prices could rise 20-fold. On the other hand, Gaidar said in his speech that Russia "*does not expect to receive a loan in the next few days and that the loan request is political in nature.*"[9]

The IMF mission to Moscow in early December generally endorsed the core ideas of the announced reforms but drew attention to two essential points. First, no one could explain how inter-republic relations would be structured or how monetary policy would be managed. Second, the team of reformers was tiny and could not organize interaction with bureaucrats inherited from the Soviet system.[10]

On the one hand, the discussion of the Russian leader's request at an informal meeting at Boskin's office yielded a positive result: the $6 billion figure was deemed appropriate for the scale of the Russian economy and set as a reference point. On the other hand, the discussion only accentuated the

[8] GBPL&M. Cable from Ambassador Strauss for Secretary Baker. December 5, 1991.

[9] GBPL&M. Cable from Ambassador Strauss for Zoellick, Niles, McAllister, Treasury Secretary Baker and under Secretary Mulford, NSC for General Scowcroft and E Hewett. December 6, 1991.

[10] GBPL&M. IMF Views on the Russian Reform Program. (In Boskin Group Meeting on Soviet Economy. December 10, 1991).

questions raised earlier without finding answers and outlined the main risks that could be encountered in creating a stabilization fund. Lack of agreement between the republics on the monetary system, loose fiscal policy, lack of free foreign trade, and ruble non-convertibility could derail macroeconomic policy and squander the stabilization fund's resources.

On December 17, 11 days after receiving Yeltsin's formal appeal to the G7 for a stabilization loan, British Prime Minister John Major, the "host" of the last G7 meeting, wrote a letter to Bush. In the letter, the British Prime Minister suggested that the Russians would discuss and agree on an action plan with the IMF before discussing financial support for reforms. "*In many respects the Russian Republic's reform plans are impressive... On the other hand, there must be some doubts about the Government's ability to deliver everything that it proposes in these areas. I am also concerned that the monetary policy and some of the structural adjustment reforms which are being suggested look weak. What is urgently required now is for an IMF team to discuss immediately the nature and scope of what the Russians are proposing.*"[11]

Bush's reply letter began by agreeing with the Prime Minister's suggestion that he take his time responding, hoping to get more information about what was happening in the Soviet Union. "*I share your view on the need to provide an early response by next week.*" [Monday of next week would be December 23]. The President expressed his surprise that neither Yeltsin nor Gaidar had discussed the subject of financial aid with Baker, who was in Moscow. Moreover, in response to a direct question about the "*request for 4–5 billion ... Gaidar ... did not provide us with much useful information.*"

In such a case, the US President continued, the G7 position was straightforward. "*We do not believe the G7 can seriously consider assistance to support the reform plan until we first see a coherent plan on paper, and I would suggest that you make this clear to Yeltsin in your letter.*" Moreover, Bush clearly articulated his position for the future: any negotiations on aid could proceed only after the IMF approved the reform program and Russia became a full member of the IMF. "*Furthermore, the purposes of any stabilization fund need to be more clearly defined before the G7 would be in a position to consider a specific request for assistance... Early IMF membership for Russia would be particularly important in responding to Yeltsin's request... The IMF could play a critical role in clarifying these issues and in developing and implementing a comprehensive reform program.*"[12]

[11] GBPL&M. Message dated December 17, 1991, from the Prime Minister [Major] to the President.

[12] GBPL&M. Presidential Message to Prime Minister Major (Draft), attached to Brent Scowcroft's memorandum for the President (not dated, presumably December 18–19, 1991).

In short, the reform program did not deserve support, but there were no serious arguments to stop Yeltsin from implementing what he had planned. Let them begin, and let it be what it would be. "*The Russians did not take the advice either of our own technical experts or the IMF, or the World Bank. Therefore, we didn't think it was worthwhile. The non-Union program was pretty vague on the background for it. I know we didn't initiate it. We didn't oppose it.*"[13]

IMF Membership

Initially, the Soviet Union intended to join the IMF. In January 1944, the Soviet government sent a group of experts to Washington to discuss the draft articles of agreement for creating the Fund and the World Bank. The USSR wanted to make sure that the peculiarities of its economy, centralized planning, a non-market exchange rate, and state-controlled prices, would not be an obstacle to participation. The Soviet delegation participated in the discussion of the Bretton Woods agreements and supported the adoption of the conference's Final Act. The head of the Soviet delegation signed the documents, after which the USSR's membership of the IMF and the World Bank depended solely on whether Stalin signed them before the late-December 1945 ratification deadline. Stalin chose not to do so, apparently unwilling to disclose data on the state of the Soviet economy.

After that, the IMF question lay dormant until Gorbachev came to power. In the late 1980 s, the Soviet probed IMF membership, but Western governments quickly rebuffed them. However, Hungary was admitted as a member in 1981 and Poland in 1986. Before the G7 summit in Houston, Gorbachev wrote a letter to Bush saying that "*the USSR's contacts with the International Monetary Fund, the World Bank, and the Economic Cooperation Organization are expanding,*" but the Soviet leader did not dare to ask for IMF membership. However, the first step in this direction was taken: the IMF took the lead of a working group tasked with preparing a "Study of the Soviet Economy." A large group of IMF experts traveled to Moscow, got acquainted with Soviet officials, and gained access to information that no one in the West had ever seen before.

The Soviet government continued to raise this topic, and, unexpectedly, on December 12, 1990, after talks with Soviet Foreign Minister Eduard Shevardnadze, Bush announced: "*to promote fundamental economic reform I will propose that the World Bank and the IMF work out with the Soviet Union a*

---

[13] Miller Center. George H. W. Bush Presidency. Brent Scowcroft Oral History Part II.

special association to give the U.S.S.R."[14] It is unclear who initiated the idea; it came as a complete surprise to US allies and IMF management, and the Fund's charter did not provide for such an option. The governments of Great Britain and Germany reacted negatively to the proposal, so the initiative was shelved.

But membership of the IMF was not forgotten by Gorbachev, who on June 5, 1991, accepting the Nobel Peace Prize, spoke about the main directions of reform in the USSR, among which were noted: "*decisive steps to open the country to the world economy through convertibility of the ruble, recognition of civilized 'rules of the game' accepted in the world market, through joining the World Bank and the International Monetary Fund.*"[15]

Before the G7 summit in London, the participants agreed on a common position toward the Soviet Union: public encouragement of reform but only token financial aid and a "special association" label with the World Bank and IMF. The main argument in favor of the limited participation of the USSR in the IMF was that it would allow the G7 to obtain information on the state of the Soviet economy. The "carrot" for the Soviet Union was the promise of technical assistance from international organizations.[16]

With the details settled, all that remained was a meeting with Gorbachev and a formal announcement, but … three days before the start of the summit, Gorbachev sent a letter to each of the participants, where he again raised the issue of membership of the IMF. "*In the last few months there have taken place vigorous contacts related to the potential Soviet membership in the International Monetary Fund and the World Bank. We realize that membership in the two organizations, which play a key role in the world financial system, will require that we take some major steps.*"[17] And on July 15, the first day of the summit, Gorbachev sent an application to the IMF and the World Bank to join these organizations. For unknown reasons, the letters did not reach their addressees until a week later, and during the meeting with the leaders of the G7 member countries, Gorbachev kept silent about it.

When the Soviet leader's letter became known, it had an explosive effect. The first to react was the host of the summit, British Prime Minister John Major: *"Our position is … that we would favor associate membership status and*

---

[14] Presidential News Conference. December 12, 1990. https://www.c-span.org/video/?15333-1/presidential-news-conference

[15] Mikhail Gorbachev. Nobel Lecture. June 5, 1991. https://www.gorby.ru/userfiles/nobelevskaya_lekciya.pdf

[16] GBPL&M. M Boskin's Meeting with Deal, Hewett, Mulford, Zoellick, et al. [re: Soviet Union]. June 27, 1991.

[17] Personal Message from President Mikhail S Gorbachev to Heads of State or Government Attending the G7 Meeting in London. July 12, 1991. http://www.g7.utoronto.ca/summit/1991london/personal.html

that full membership is premature."[18] Four days later, on the eve of Bush and Gorbachev's meeting in Moscow, US Treasury Secretary Nicholas Brady made an even tougher statement, calling the Soviet Union's bid "counterproductive." *We were completely surprised by their move*," he says, adding: "*there will* be *no Soviet membership."*[19] Brady dramatically reverses his position two months later when he meets with IMF chief Michel Camdessus in Moscow: "*I'm a little disappointed in the bureaucratic inertia … it's the most important event in the last 100 years and … we still haven't got started.* He shouted and demanded that the Foundation *invade the place … with staff and advice and not worry about the details or the eventual outcome."*[20]

But that would be two months later, and in the meantime, on the same day, July 28, Senator Connie Mack introduced an amendment to the 1992 foreign aid bill that directed the US Representative to vote against granting the Soviet Union membership of the Fund and Bank until "*the President first certified to Congress that the Soviet Union was instituting certain free-market economic policies, adopting democratic political structures and shrinking military and other Government spending."*[21]

At a meeting in the Kremlin, Gorbachev hesitated to bring the issue of IMF membership up for serious discussion and only brought it up when the Presidents were talking to each other.[22]

Gorbachev: *"Could we avoid that long [pre-membership] time period in the IMF? We would like to benefit from it, and a long waiting period will hold us back."*

Bush: *"Associate status was not to put the Soviet Union down."*

Gorbachev: *"I understand. This is not prestige but pragmatics. But within this status could we get something more concrete and practical than advice?"*

Bush: *"Lots of things can be done. But before big loans can be made, there are certain preconditions. Not US rules, but IMF."*

Gorbachev: *"Maybe we can make association more alive than dead?"*

Bush: *"That we can do."*

The full or associate membership in the IMF was a matter of substance. The IMF and the World Bank can only lend to their members, and associate

---

[18] "Soviets, in Surprise, Apply for Full World Bank Status." The New York Times. July 24, 1991.

[19] "Toward the Summit; Soviet Bid to Join IMF Still a Puzzle." The New York Times. July 29, 1991.

[20] Memorandum from Massimo Russo to the Managing Director, "USSR-Back-to-Office Report" and attachments. September 24, 1991. IMF archives, OMD files, "Russia 1991- (1) Country Files," Box 21980, Accession 1995-0180-0007.

[21] "Toward the Summit; Soviet Bid to Join IMF Still a Puzzle." The New York Times. July 29, 1991.

[22] GBPL&M. Memorandum of Conversation. President Bush with Mikhail Gorbachev. July 30, 1991. (ne-on-one). (10.30 am–12.30 pm; there were another two meetings that day).

membership status, since it was explicitly designed for the USSR, did not imply the possibility of loans. At this time, the IMF was short of lending resources after providing its support to the reforms started in Central and Eastern Europe. The only option for a loan to the USSR was to tap a special IMF–US credit line.[23] To do this, the administration had to get congressional approval, which it wanted to avoid at all costs. Everyone realized it would be impossible to persuade lawmakers to extend loans to the Soviet Union at US expense.

Potential congressional resistance and reluctance to expend negotiating resources to assist the Soviet Union were the real reasons for the White House's opposition to Soviet participation in the IMF and World Bank. Contrary to such claims, IMF membership did not actually require a fully market economy or a convertible currency. The IMF charter says that any country that agrees to comply with the IMF's requirements, which are the same for all, can become a member of the organization. In addition, by joining the IMF, a country agrees to pursue policies consistent with the IMF's objectives (maintaining the stability of the world financial system and international settlement system, developing international trade, etc.) and to move toward convertibility of its national currency. Nothing in the Fund's charter prevented the Soviet Union from joining the organization. The US, with its blocking vote on charter or capital changes, could veto Soviet membership because approval required prior quota-redistribution agreement among members.

Only after the failure of the August putsch did Bush and Prime Minister Major, under pressure from Germany, France, and Italy, which had supported Gorbachev's application for Soviet membership in the IMF, agree to fast-track on the Soviet associate membership. On October 5, the relevant agreement was signed. The IMF opened its representative office in Moscow and began more systematic work.

The Soviet Union never became a full member of the IMF, but all 15 countries that emerged from its ruins could soon go that route. Russia, having submitted its application on January 7, 1992, would be able to announce it on June 1.

Russia's non-membership at the start of its reforms proved a handicap. The G7 required Russia to coordinate its program with the Fund, but the IMF staff did not understand well what was required of them. The fact was that traditionally when the IMF discussed a program with a country, it would be

[23] The provision of this credit line, General Arrangements to Borrow (GAB), totaling SDR 17 billion (just over $22 billion) was agreed upon by 11 countries in 1990. The US accounted for 25% of the total, but Congress did not ratify the agreement until 1993.

linked to the loan the government would receive from the Fund. When the Fund was created, the main purpose of its loans was to maintain stable exchange rates on which the international financial system was based. Currency instability resulted from balance-of-payments disequilibrium, which could be systemic or temporary. Consequently, in designing the program, the Fund's staff focused on eliminating disequilibria that could be quantified.

Working with Russia in early 1992 did not include any loan, so it was impossible to assess the adequacy or inadequacy of the measures taken by the Russian government, or to assess their effectiveness in the traditional way for the IMF: the Fund could not give a loan to a non-member country, and the G7 from time to time started discussing the possibility of a stabilization loan to Russia, but made no decision. This disrupted the work of IMF staff, who struggled to draft program conditions without any guaranteed support from the Fund or the G7. Jeffrey Sachs, working with Gaidar's team in Moscow, informed Ed Hewett of this in his January 21 letter. "*The Western policy presence (read: IMF) is far too small and cautious, while the IMF feels that it can't guarantee a package of G7 financial support even after the right economic policies are in place. The IMF says nothing (I mean nothing) about a string of bad policy calls in the past two weeks by the Russian bureaucracy, feeling that it can't interject itself too vigorously. As Odling-Smee said to me, he feels the IMF can't push, because it has so little indeed to offer in the way of real support.*"[24]

Informed of this letter from Deputy Secretary of State Robert Zoellick, Hewett points to the main obstacle, the position of the Ministry of Finance. "*My impression is that so far the IMF is not seriously engaged … [because] … they feel they can't say a lot because they have no money behind their statements; anything you can think of to light a fire under the IMF or Treasury would be great.*"[25]

To change the "cool" position of the Treasury, which was manifested not only in relation to the Soviet Union, probably could only be down to Bush himself, but, for various reasons, he did not do it until the end of his presidency. "*The federal budget is a marvelous instrument… But it takes a cooperative approach. We got no cooperation either from OMB or from Treasury. They were fundamentally against what we were trying to do… We never did really resolve that issue.*"[26]

[24] GBPL&M. Jeffrey Sachs' Message to Ed Hewett. January 21, 1992.

[25] GBPL&M. Ed Hewett Message to Bob Zoellick. January 22, 1992.

[26] Miller Center. George H. W. Bush Presidency. Brent Scowcroft Oral History Part I.

Debts Must Be Paid

If the US Treasury Department was unwilling to lend to Russia, and in that case the IMF was unsure how to respond to Russia's reforms, the approach to Soviet debts was precisely the opposite. The G7 position had been formulated at the Houston meeting, and no one wanted to weaken it: all Soviet debts should be recognized and repaid in full, no matter who did it. This made the IMF's work easier because its cooperation with the Paris Club had been refined over the previous decade.

The G7 and IMF obviously did not have adequate information about the situation with the external debt of the Soviet Union by the end of 1991. In all discussions, only the volume of interstate debts (from \$60 to \$70 billion) was mentioned,[27] while overdue interest, commercial bank claims, and debts to CMEA partners—which would have doubled the total—went uncounted. In addition, Western experts had a poor grasp of the Soviet Union's external assets, which were carefully concealed by the Soviet officials. For example, experts placed gold reserves at 2500–3000, and when Yavlinsky reported in September 1991 that they were only 240 tons, few believed him. The G7 finance ministers' meeting in Bangkok and the alarming news brought by the guests from Moscow forced more serious attention to the debt problem—US Treasury Secretary Brady noted that the Soviet Union might need Western help to solve the problem of debt payments at the end of the year.[28] It was not until January 1992 that an IMF mission learned that the Soviet Union's foreign exchange reserves, totaling \$14.5 billion at the beginning of 1991, had virtually disappeared by the end of the year, leaving only \$16 million.[29]

The joint-liability agreement pleased every party except Russia: the creditors were assured repayment, while the other republics—lacking stable export—saw little risk in refusing to service the debts themselves. Further negotiations on the debt were taken over by the Paris Club, which on December 19 established a Committee of Creditors, including representatives of 17 states. After four rounds of negotiations on January 4 in Paris, an agreement postponed all arrears and 1992 maturities until year-end. The

[27] US DoT. vol 314. On February 5, 1992, US Deputy Treasury Secretary David Mulford, speaking before the House Committee on Banking and Finance, stated that the Soviet debt was \$65 billion. Statement by Mulford before the House Subcommittee on International Development, Finance, Trade, and Monetary Policy (Events in the Former Soviet Union and the US Response), February 5, 1992.

[28] Much of the Soviet Gold is Sold, Economist Says. The Washington Post. September 28, 1991.

[29] These data are contained in the Balance of Payments Department of the Bank of Russia document, which was [erroneously] attached to the letter of the USSR Ministry of Finance dated June 28, 1991 "To V I Boldin, Chief of Staff of the President of the USSR. Materials for the meeting of the USSR President in London." Yegor Gaidar Archive. http://gaidar-arc.ru/databasedocuments/theme/details/2506

document said that the deferment did not cover loans granted after January 1, 1991, which was the main goal of the US delegation. The fact is that all loans granted by the US to the Soviet Union were short-term, 1-year loans—issued to finance grain purchases—and, if paid within 12 months, they were prolonged for another year. Thus, the heirs of the USSR had to repay the US loans in full during 1992, as Deputy Treasury Secretary David Mulford proudly declared.[30]

In addition to obtaining the consent of the heirs of the USSR to repay grain loans, the US Treasury had two other smaller tasks: it had to confirm the agreement signed with the Soviet Union on the repayment of lend-lease debts and pre-revolutionary debts. The situation was not very complicated. In 1972, the USSR and the USA signed an agreement to fix the total amount of the Soviet Union's obligations, $722 million, and a 30-year installment plan to pay this sum. However, the following year, relations between the countries deteriorated, and the Soviet Union stopped servicing this debt. In 1990, Presidents Bush and Gorbachev signed a new agreement to repay the remaining $674 million by 2030.

The story of the pre-revolutionary debts was longer. In 1938, despite the Bolsheviks' refusal to pay the pre-revolutionary debts, Stalin proposed to the American ambassador in Moscow, Davis, that the debts be recognized and repaid. The parties discussed a debt of between $100 and $150 million during the discussion, but Stalin imposed two conditions. First, he wanted to repay the debt with a new US loan twice the amount of the debt; second, he wanted the US government itself to settle relations with the holders of these debts in the US, i.e. that all claims against the Soviet Union be dropped. The US categorically refused to discuss the second of these conditions, and discussion of the subject ceased.

The USSR returned to it in the late 1980s, when there was a desire to normalize economic relations with the US and gain access to the US financial market. The initial positions of the parties differed tenfold: the Soviet Union was ready to pay $100 million, and the US insisted on it paying $1 billion. In the end, the recognized debt amounted to $192.6 million. The sum was modest, and long instalments kept the servicing burden light, and Russian negotiators did not object to including this debt in the total body of the debt.

[30] US DoT. vol 314. Statement by Mulford before the House Subcommittee on International Development, Finance, Trade, and Monetary Policy (Events in the Former Soviet Union and he US Response), February 5, 1992.

Overall, the IMF estimates that the Paris Agreement gave the USSR's heirs a $3.2 billion respite[31]—clearly insufficient to materially improve the economic situation in Russia and other countries that agreed to assume Soviet debts.

On February 6, members of the IMF Board of Directors received a balance-of-payments forecast for the former Soviet Union (twelve republics), which stated that if $7.2 billion in external debt payments were deferred, the balance-of-payments deficit in 1992 would range between $14 billion and $18 billion.[32] At the beginning of the year, the IMF estimated total Soviet debt payments for 1992 at $14.6 billion, of which $5.6 billion was interest. However, like the US Treasury Department, the IMF assumed a substantially lower debt ($71-$75 billion) than was owed. By the end of the year's first half, overdue debt service payments totaled about $11 billion, of which $4.9 billion was overdue interest.[33]

In 1992, Russia paid $5 billion in interest and repayment of foreign debts inherited from the Soviet Union and received a single $1 billion IMF loan; the World Bank, having decided in July 1992 to lend Russia $600 million, did not disburse the funds until early the following year.

Very quickly, it became clear that none of the post-Soviet countries (except Russia) intended to fulfil their obligations to service Soviet debts. The special account in Vnesheconombank received two small payments from the other republics that had signed the December 4 Treaty in early 1992, after which there were no more payments. The unsettled debt posed a serious problem for Russia, which was trying to mend relations with the outside world. In the summer of 1992, Russia offered creditors, and other post-Soviet countries a "zero option"—under which Russia would assume all obligations for the USSR's debts, and the other countries would renounce their claims on the Soviet Union's external assets. Gradually, one by one, the CIS countries (except Ukraine[34]) signed corresponding agreements with Russia, and on April 2, 1993, the Paris Club gave its consent to the "zero option."

---

[31] Report on the Agreement on the Deferral of the Debt of the USSR and its Successors to Foreign Official Creditors. Document of the International Monetary Fund. SM/92/5. January 9, 1992. IMF Archive.

[32] Recent Economic Developments and Policies in Former USSR Republics. Republics. Document for Members of the IMF Executive Board. February 6, 1992. IMF Archive.

[33] Russian Federation—Review of Development Under the Stand-By Arrangement. Document for Members of the IMF Executive Board. December 1, 1992. IMF Archive.

[34] Ukraine agreed to the "zero option" only at the end of 1994, when it signed an agreement with Russia on December 9. However, the agreement was not submitted for ratification to the Verkhovna Rada, Ukraine's parliament, and thus did not enter into force.

Ready to Go!

Having defeated Gorbachev in a scramble for power, Yeltsin took up the cause with determination. First and foremost, he wanted to demonstrate his willingness and ability to address the accumulated problems in Soviet–US relations, which US politicians had long used to derail Soviet initiatives aimed at developing ties. The list of such issues was long, and the problems themselves varied in nature: from the Soviet Union's unwillingness to eliminate its biological weapons program to clarifying the fate of US military personnel missing during World War II, the Korean War, and the Vietnam War, from the transfer of documents related to the destruction of passenger flight KAL007 in the Far East by the Soviet military to the fate of Swedish diplomat Raoul Wallenberg. Some of these problems were easy for Yeltsin to solve. For example, to hand over information about the American military missing during the wars[35] or the "black box" from Korean Boeing flight KAL007[36] he only had to pound his fist and demand that these documents be put on the table. But what to do with the demands for immediate correction of the situation with the unregulated protection of intellectual property in Russia?[37] How can one explain to American politicians that Russia inherited virtually no legislative framework from the Soviet Union, even on the most critical issues for the life of the country? The Soviet Union lacked a basic document for economic relations, the Civil Code, which no one could prepare in two or three months. How can one explain that members of the Russian parliament were elected in another country and other political realities, that they were elected as members of the parliament of a republic within the USSR and suddenly became members of the federal parliament? In short, there were a lot of problems; you didn't know where to start…

Yeltsin began with the primary issue—the military confrontation between the two powers. Gorbachev's dialogues with Ronald Reagan and then with Bush seriously thawed the Cold War. The signed treaties created a good foundation for further reducing the threat of global military conflict, and the Russian President decided to propose to the United States a shift from confrontation to partnership. This was his "pet project" before he met with Bush on February 1, 1992.

[35] GBPL&M. President Yeltsin's Letter to the US Senator. Fax Dated June 12, 1992. Working Papers for June Summit 1992.

[36] GB M&T. Telcon with President Yeltsin of Russia. September 10, 1992.

[37] GBPL&M. Transmittal to the Congress of the U.S.-Soviet Trade Agreement. Memorandum for Brent Scowcroft from Ambassador Clara Hills, the US Trade Representative. June 13, 1991.

He's Some Kind of...

In Washington, Yeltsin had been viewed warily from the moment he became one of the leading Soviet politicians. Gradually, they grew accustomed to him, and his impulsiveness and decisiveness sometimes looked good against Gorbachev, who often couldn't make up his mind to do what needed to be done yesterday. But still, he was somewhat unusual...

Discussions of Yeltsin's personality and character were not uncommon during meetings between US politicians and foreign partners, and one can only guess what was discussed at internal White House meetings, the contents of which remain classified.

"Yeltsin may be a true demagogue. It's very easy to attack the system, which is what he does. It's not clear what he would actually create. Yeltsin does not appear to be a constructive force," Scowcroft told Canadian Prime Minister Mulroney in March 1991. As this conversation continued, Bush admitted that he did not understand how to communicate with Yeltsin and where developing ties with him might lead. *"I guess Yeltsin is not all bad, but we are not sure how to deal with him. If we overplay our relationship with him, we could play into the hands of the worst elements within the Soviet Union."*[38]

The cautious attitude towards Yeltsin persisted until August 1991, after which it changed radically. In those days, the Russian leader demonstrated his commitment to democratic values and openly opposed the attempted coup d'état in the Soviet Union. It became obvious to everyone that Yeltsin was emerging as the principal driver of change in the Soviet space, and the direction of that change appeared clear. Baker, writing to Bush about his meetings in Moscow in September 1991, praised Yeltsin's contribution to reaching an agreement on Afghanistan and claimed that it was Yeltsin who convinced Gorbachev to withdraw Soviet troops from Cuba before the end of 1991.[39] From late September to early October, Bush gradually switched to using his first name when addressing the Russian leader, an essential sign in political dialog.

Confidence in Yeltsin grew in the fall of 1991 as he demonstrated his willingness to constructively discuss the future of the Soviet Union with Gorbachev and to reach an agreement with him on issues that were important to the United States: nuclear arms control, a unified army, and a unified foreign policy. It was increasingly clear that Gorbachev-Yeltsin was a successful

[38] GB M&T. Memorandum of Conversation. Meeting with Brian Mulroney, Prime Minister of Canada. March 13, 1991.

[39] GBPL&M. Memorandum for the President from James Baker III. September 11, 1991.

tandem that would allow for reforms and preserve the structure of a unified state.

However, the sudden and chaotic collapse of the USSR revived doubts about whether Yeltsin was capable of being a politician leading a country with enormous nuclear capabilities, the collapse of which could lead to destructive processes throughout the former Soviet Union. During a visit to Tokyo, Bush, in a conversation with Japanese Prime Minister Kiichi Miyazawa, said, "*Although Yeltsin may have good intension, there are doubts as to whether he is mature enough to resolve this matter, and he is also inexperienced…* Miyazawa replied, *I also think that Yeltsin is not a stable leader.*"[40]

But everyone soon became convinced that Yeltsin was not only able to take power but also hold it, make difficult decisions, and withstand serious pressure in the first weeks of reform. Bush said this to Austrian Chancellor Franz Vranitzky on January 31, 1992, before meeting Yeltsin in Washington. "*There was a time when we doubted whether he was real and whether he could stand the test. Now, I must admit … he did it and did not waver. My respect for him is much higher … he will not be a toy in someone else's hands.*"[41]

Are We Allies? No, of Course, Not

Don't Let Me Starve to Death

The end of 1991 was challenging for the inhabitants of the Soviet Union. No one wanted to live in the old way, and no one knew how to live in a new way. Obligations given by one republic to another, one region to another, and one enterprise to another lost validity almost as soon as they were signed. The previously unified monetary system split into parts, each of them continuing to use the Soviet ruble as a currency unit. The office of the Soviet Gosbank in each republic turned into an independent central bank when financing its own budget. The regional branches of state banks became independent commercial banks. Still, since there was no system of prudential supervision in the Soviet Union, the banks' autonomy in decision-making was neither restricted nor controlled by anyone. The archaic system of settlements between regional branches of the Gosbank failed to curb the volume of settlement loans.

[40] The Visit of the US President George H. W. Bush and First Lady Mrs. Bush to Japan. Bush and First Lady Mrs. Bush to Japan. Japan-US Summit Meeting (Working Lunch). January 8, 1992. Japan Foreign Ministry Archive. https://www.mofa.go.jp/mofaj/annai/honsho/shiryo/shozo/pdfs/2023/gaiyo.pdf

[41] GB M&T. Memorandum of Conversation. Meeting with Franz Vranitzki of Austria. January 31, 1991.

Enterprises producing scarce consumer goods were best positioned, allowing them to barter exchange with suppliers of components. If the goods produced were not in great demand among the population, they could be used for settlements with employees, who had to find buyers on their own. Regional officials, fearing social unrest, erected customs barriers on the borders of the regions, prohibiting the export of the scarcest goods.

The households' and corporate nominal incomes rose even as the economy contracted. If there had been free prices in the Soviet economy, this situation would have resulted in high inflation, but prices were fixed, and shortages replaced inflation. Store shelves were empty, and any goods that appeared were snapped up within minutes. In all regions, local officials tried to introduce a rationing system by distributing coupons, but no one guaranteed that you could buy the goods you needed with a coupon. With the beginning of a new month, the coupons left over from the previous month lost their power. The main task of Soviet citizens was to "use it before."

Foreign visitors found the scene horrifying. The stores were empty, and the population's survival was a mystery. The first wish of Western politicians who received reports from diplomats and businessmen returning from the Soviet Union was to prevent starvation deaths. So, the bulk of the aid the Soviet Union received in the last months and weeks was humanitarian—food for people and livestock, and medicine. However, the aid was not altruistic; it consisted chiefly of loans, with grants below 10% in 1990–1991.[42]

When James Baker gave a speech at Princeton, he did not know how long the Soviet Union's agony would last, whether any central government would remain in the Soviet space, or what its functions would be. A sense of catastrophe hung in the air, with nightmarish television images of Soviet stores forcing politicians to react. During his speech, Baker, on behalf of Bush, announced a coordinating conference in Washington "*to discuss how best to meet ongoing humanitarian needs over the course of the next year… This conference should work toward helping the Soviet peoples help themselves to get through the winter and to ensure that together we take the right steps this winter, spring, and summer. To ensure a better situation next winter, our work should focus on critical short term needs, food, medicine, fuel, shelter.*"[43]

No delegation could ignore such a call—or arrive unprepared. The British government prepared meticulously: a 12-page memorandum awaited Prime Minister Major, who could not but be pleased with three main conclusions.

[42] Food Assistance to the Former Soviet Union. Memorandum to S. Wall from L. P. Neville-Jones. The UK National Archives, PREM 19/3562.

[43] James Baker at Princeton before and after the Cold War. Reel Mudd Manuscript Library. https://blogs.princeton.edu/reelmudd/2011/03/james-baker-about-post-soviet-policy-1991/

First, the food situation in the USSR was challenging but not critical; there was no threat of mass starvation. "*Food shortages in the (former) Soviet Union are severe but not critical … there is no immediate danger of widespread starvation or malnutrition.*" Second, no additional resources were needed to help the Soviet Union; the main difficulties were logistical and related to the breakdown of the Soviet trade system. "*The volume of aid committed … is substantial. The problem is not the financial commitment but the implementation of decisions already taken.* Third, *there is a good story to tell publicly.*"[44]

The note highlighted the unresolved distribution of humanitarian food aid. On the one hand, there were obvious groups of people with the most significant difficulties. Still, Western governments had no means of identifying and accessing them, and non-governmental organizations in the Soviet Union were weak and helpless. On the other hand, the most appropriate solution would have been to sell the food received in regular stores, but the broken systems of centralized distribution of goods did not allow this. As a result, some of the food was given to the regions, and Western governments created special structures to distribute the other part, the costs of which were counted as "technical assistance."

Curiously, neither American nor European officials recalled that under the Marshall Plan most aid arrived as commodities, not cash. European countries received the most needed goods to restore normal economic activity. The goods received from America were sold at market prices, and the funds received were deposited into special government accounts ("counterpart funds") and could be used to pay off debts (as Britain did), to invest in critical sectors (as Germany and France did, investing in energy and rebuilding transportation infrastructure), or to support macroeconomic stability (as Italy did).

No comparable mechanism existed in Russia. In June 1992, after Russia became a member of the IMF, this problem surfaced as the Board of Directors prepared to discuss the first loan to which Russia was applying. A note by A Premchand, Deputy Director of the IMF's Fiscal Department, stated that all intergovernmental aid was a grant in favor of the government, not the population. The government should ensure that the food it received was sold at market prices and that the money received was collected in the budget. The Russian government sent the received goods to the regions, where the local officials handed them over to the stores for sale, and vanished before reaching the federal budget.[45]

---

[44] Food Assistance to the Former Soviet Union. Memorandum to S. Wall from L. P. Neville-Jones. The UK National Archives, PREM 19/3562.

[45] A. Premchand. Russia: Budgetary Treatment of Food Aid. June 24, 1992. IMF Archive.

In a letter to Ed Hewett, Jeffrey Sack emphasized the issue, making an emotional addition: "*On the food aid, for heaven's sake, just auction the damn stuff… The revenues from the sales of the food can be earmarked to social spending, to give the humanitarian angle to it. The key point, though, is to get more food to the market. Sales (even to the "mafia") is infinitely better than dealing with the state bureaucracy and with the German security forces! If the food is sold, we further the market reforms; if it is distributed by the Western aid agencies, we invite a continued run of stories of corruption, misappropriation, etc. From a macro as well as distributional point of view, please push the State Department towards market remedies!*"[46]

Unfortunately, neither Jeffrey Sachs nor Ed Hewett could recall the details of the Marshall Plan. Neither did the State Department recall them.

Although London quickly judged existing aid sufficient—Major's memo listed about £600 million, over 80% of Britain's share in the EC support—such parsimony could hardly satisfy Bush's team. Given that the note on John Major's desk singled out Britain's "leading role as chair of the G7" as a particular merit, the White House needed to present something impressive to public opinion.

On January 17, 1992, five days before the Donors' Conference, Deputy Secretary of State Lawrence Eagleburger, appointed coordinator of all US aid to the former Soviet republics, informed James Baker[47] that something impressive was being worked out, and there were some details. The US was expected to announce at the conference that the total aid package for 1992–1993 would be $1.4 billion, while counting $3.75 billion in grain loans as aid, it ballooned to $5.2 billion. Was that not impressive? Especially if you forgot that the grain loans were due in one year and were guaranteed to be repaid as they were not subject to deferment and/or restructuring under the Paris Club. But… here was where the details came in.

Only $735 million of the $1.4 billion did not require congressional approval. Therefore, "*we need to be very careful in discussing publicly the $705 million*[48] *that … [is] a pending request of Congress and in no way a deal. If Congress senses the latter, we will be in a big trouble.*" Even within the $735 million, there were details, "*Even if we avoid this trap we can expect some problems in moving forward* "and not all of it could be used without consulting Congress and the Treasury Department. Reallocating spending between areas without

[46] GBPL&M. Jeffrey Sachs' Message to Ed Hewett. January 21, 1992.

[47] GBPL&M. Memorandum for the Secretary. Soviet Assistance. From Lawrence Eagleburger. January 17, 1992.

[48] Opening the conference, President Bush announced that he had submitted a request to Congress for a small amount ($645 million) for humanitarian and technical assistance to the countries of the FSU.

changing the total amount would have to be negotiated with them, but each had its priorities.

The outlook for spending in 1993 was even more dubious. "*The proposed funding for 1993 will be caught in a lengthy appropriations process. Given the election year politics and the need to finish the FY 1992 cycle, we can expect FY 1993 action to drag out.*"

The conference, which took place on January 22–23, was attended by foreign ministers from 47 countries and representatives of seven international organizations. Baker demonstrated the highest level of diplomatic skill. First, he declared something similar: "*There is no money, but you hang in there!*" Realizing that White House requests for money to help the (even former) Soviet Union would not be popular in an election year, the Secretary of State stipulated that the conference participants would forgo talk of new aid. Instead, they would focus on coordinating distribution of assistance already pledged to the CIS states.[49]

The paradigm shift defused the indignation of the European delegates who had come to Washington. In the institutional jockeying, the meeting organizers forgot to mention Europe as a co-organizer. In their view, America had talked too much about helping the Soviet Union and done too little. They recalled that the United States had not merely "coordinated" the Marshall Plan to rebuild Europe in 1947, financing it from the budget. "*France regrets that the United States, which provided only 20% of emergency food aid, is responsible for coordination,*" French Foreign Minister Roland Dumas said.[50]

As a result, the Secretary of State proposed the creation of five working groups to coordinate assistance in five areas (medical, food, energy, housing, and technical assistance). These groups, led by different countries, "*should prepare work plans—documents that the co-chairs of the working groups and other participants can use as a guide for action.*"[51]

Summarizing the results of the conference, Ed Hewett wrote to Scowcroft[52] "*Baker et al, did a first-rate job* "of pleasing the Germans, who spent the most on aid to the USSR, and the French by not demonstrating US claims to leadership. In addition, the Secretary of State managed the process "*without ruf-*

[49] The US GAO estimates that between 1990 and 1992, various countries promised the Soviet Union 91 billion in aid, of which 79% was in loans. And only ≈ 44% of that amount was spent. "Former Soviet Union. Assistance by the United States and Other Donors." US GAO Report for Congressional Committees. December 30, 1992.

[50] "US is Criticized on Aid to Russia." The New York Times. January 22, 1992.

[51] "Bush to Press Congress to Approve $645 Million for Ex-Soviet Lands." The New York Times. January 23, 1992.

[52] GBPL&M. Memorandum for Brent Scowcroft and Jonathan Howe. Results of coordinating conference. January 24, 1992.

fling the easily-ruffled feathers of *Europeans and Japanese*." The State Department leadership was "*almost ecstatic over results.*"

There was a small snag: it was necessary to explain to Yeltsin that the conference results were precisely what he needed.

Preparation: Yeltsin

The collapse of the Soviet Union and the Yeltsin's assumption of full power presented him with a daunting task: what to tackle? Should he prioritize economic reform—already launched on 2 January—work with the Supreme Soviet to develop priority legislation, or define new federal relations? Gradually, it became clear that despite radical change, life went on and even acute problems could be deferred. The need to communicate with the outside world came to the fore: everyone wanted to understand what a state claiming succession to the Soviet Union would look like. On the one hand, if Russia were a complete analogue of the USSR, why would it be necessary to break it up? On the other hand, what would it look like if Russia were to change as radically in its relations with the outside world as it was changing inside?

The special meeting of the UN Security Council was chosen as the platform for outlining the new state's foreign policy course, and Yeltsin's speech was agreed upon on January 31. On the way to New York, a stopover in London was planned. After the UN speech, the Russian President requested a meeting with Bush.

Foreign policy remained peripheral to Yeltsin's attention until early 1992; the Soviet republics had no authority in this sphere, international visits were rare and served mainly as courtesy introductions, with little substantive negotiation. After the August putsch, the Russian President's role in the life of the Soviet Union increased dramatically. Communication with him became an obligatory part of any visit to Moscow. Still, until the end of November, the whole world lived with the understanding that, in one form or another, the Union of the Republics would continue. Foreign policy would be given to the central government, however weak it might be. Much of Yeltsin's international effort focused on requests for financial or humanitarian aid. At the same time, he promised that the resources received would be used equally by all republics.

Apparently, Yeltsin considered this scenario the most likely until the end of November. At least, this was his opinion in his conversations with Bush and Kohl. In their turn, Western politicians in the fall of 1991 viewed Yeltsin leading a renewed Union as a real possibility[53] and drew him into discussions of international issues. Bush raised these topics particularly often; he was understandably interested in the Russian leader's views on the most important issue for America—limiting military capabilities.

On 27 September, President Bush sought Yeltsin's view of his proposals on nuclear weapons, which had previously been sent to Gorbachev. The Russian President was unprepared for such a discussion: "*I understand this proposal covers a broader range of issues. I would not go into detail now, but I appreciate this proposal very highly,* and did not hesitate to say outright that he did not envision dealing with the issue. *I believe the USSR will proceed along these lines. Your initiative is just a beautiful concept.*"[54]

Ten days later, President Bush phoned Yeltsin, who said he was finishing treatment and would soon return to Moscow. Bush's chief concern was the likelihood of a Union Treaty and Russia's stance toward it. Unexpectedly, Yeltsin raised the topic of arms control and declared that Russia was ready to play an independent role while inside the Soviet Union. "*We had a long, detailed conversation [with Gorbachev] on arms control, and on the role of Russia and what we could do. You see, Russia could … take even more radical cuts in the context if the Soviet cuts… Also Russia could provide an additional measure of verification. Let me assure you, the work is going on, and we are working with Gorbachev.*" Yeltsin argued that taking the lead would build "*more confidence in us, and confidence vis-a-vis Russia and the Union's intentions.*"[55]

However, until early December, the Soviet leader remained the United States' leading partner in discussing international issues and bilateral relations.

After becoming the head of an independent country and overdue but largely spontaneous and unplanned domestic reforms, Yeltsin turned to international affairs with the same determination. Yeltsin embraced the concept of "democratic solidarity," the notion that democracies share interests and will act together in foreign affairs.

Yeltsin began to drag skeletons out of the Kremlin's closet that had long plagued Soviet-American relations for years to demonstrate a break with the past. On January 20, Yeltsin told Secretary Baker that the Soviet Union had broken its pledge to terminate its biological weapons program.[56] On January

[53] *Does Yeltsin's Russia want to take the place of the Center?*— Bush bluntly asked Gorbachev when they met in late October in Madrid. GB M&T. Memorandum of Conversation. Meeting with President Gorbachev of the USSR. October 29, 1991.

[54] GB M&T. Telcon with Yeltsin, President of the Republic of Russia. September 27, 1991.

[55] GB M&T. Telcon with Yeltsin, President of the Republic of Russia. October 8, 1991.

[56] GBPL&M. Cable from the UK Ambassador in Moscow Braithwaite to the Foreign Office. January 20, 1992.

28, Russian Foreign Minister Andrei Kozyrev handed Secretary Baker documents relating to US military personnel held in the Soviet Union, North Korea, and Vietnam.[57]

Between 25 and 28 January, Yeltsin gave an interview to ABC News, in which he aired an unfinished proposal about the possibility of Russia refusing to target American cities with its nuclear missiles. The proposal did not appear in Yeltsin's briefing notes, and in a 29 January meeting he could not explain how it might be carried out.[58] On the same day, James Baker met with CIS Defense Minister Marshal Shaposhnikov, who had control over the "red button" at that time. For Shaposhnikov, Yeltsin's idea was also unexpected, and he could not explain how it could be implemented. Moreover, he denied Yeltsin's statement that nuclear missiles could be redirected in two hours.[59]

In the run-up to the Washington summit, Bush and Yeltsin unveiled competing disarmament initiatives in public speeches. The American President's proposals were deliberately modest.[60] *"After completing 20 planes for which we have begun procurement, we will shut down further production of the B-2 bomber. We will cancel the small ICBM [intercontinental ballistic missile] program. We will cease production of new warheads for our sea-based ballistic missiles. We will stop all new production of the Peacekeeper missile. And we will not purchase any more advanced cruise missiles."*[61]

Yeltsin, by contrast, was far bolder. He made a statement on Russian television, "On Russia's policy of arms limitation and reduction,"[62] in which he reaffirmed that Russia would fulfill all commitments made by the Soviet Union and voiced decisions made and new ideas. Russia promised to:

---

[57] NSA. Cable from USDEL Secretary in Russia. Subject: Secretary's Meeting with Foreign Minister Kozyrev, January 28, 1992. Department of State, National Security Archive FOIA.

[58] NSA. Cable from Secretary of State to US Embassy Moscow. Subject: Secretary Baker's Meeting with Russian President Yeltsin, January 29, 1992.

[59] NSA. Cable from Secretary of State to US Embassy Moscow. Subject: Secretary Baker's Meeting with Defense Minister Shaposhnikov; Ministry of Defense, January 29, 1992.

[60] The essence of the mutual proposals was not a secret: On January 17, Russian Ambassador to the UN Yuri Vorontsov asked American vis-a-vis Robert Pickering to ask the White House to share with the Kremlin the content of the American initiatives so that "*they would not take President Yeltsin by surprise.*" NSA. Cable from Ambassador Pickering to Secretary of State and NSC/Scowcroft. Subject: Message for the President from Yeltsin. January 17, 1992. On January 27, the Russian President sent a letter to Bush outlining his initiatives to be announced the day after the US president's address to Congress. NSA. Cable from the US Embassy in Moscow. Letter from Yeltsin to Bush. (Unofficial Embassy Translation). January 27, 1992.

[61] NSA. President Bush's Address on the State of the Union. January 28, 1992.

[62] Text of the statement of the President of the Russian Federation B N Yeltsin January 29, 1992. https://yeltsin.ru/archive/paperwork/11342/

- Unilaterally de-alert about 600 strategic ballistic missiles with about 1250 nuclear weapons before the START treaty enters into force;
- Eliminate 130 silo launchers for ballistic missiles;
- Dismantle missile launchers on six nuclear submarines;
- Cease production of the Tu-95 and Tu-160 strategic bombers;
- Cease production of long-range air- and sea-based cruise missiles;
- Reduce tactical nuclear weapons stockpiles by 35–50%, including the complete elimination of stockpiles of nuclear artillery shells and mines.

Russia generally intended to fulfill its obligations under the START treaty in three years instead of the seven years fixed in the document.

In addition to unilateral decisions, Yeltsin voiced radical new disarmament initiatives directed at the United States. He proposed to:

- Continue negotiations on START reductions to reduce the number of warheads to 2000–2500 for each side (against 6000 under the START treaty);
- Agree to eliminate existing anti-satellite systems and establish a joint global system of defense against attack from space to replace SDI;
- Completely ban nuclear weapons testing;
- Negotiate and sign a global Chemical Weapons Convention.

Addressing a special UN Security Council session in New York, Yeltsin argued "*the new political situation in the world makes it possible not only to put forward original ideas, but to make even the boldest of them feasible,*" briefly recounted the content of his disarmament initiatives and formulated the central thesis with which he was going to meet with Bush: "*Russia sees in the United States of America and the West, in the countries of the East, not just partners, but allies.*"[63]

Preparation: Bush

Whereas Yeltsin saw the visit as a watershed that would rewrite the rules, the Bush administration viewed the summit as important yet largely symbolic. Back in early January, when the prospect of such a meeting loomed, the administration discussed two possible scenarios: either full-scale talks on a wide range of issues or a short meeting that could launch "*new relationship … without having a full scale «summit» right after the President's State of the Union*

[63] Speech by the President of the Russian Federation, B N Yeltsin, at the UN Security Council meeting. January 31, 1992. https://yeltsin.ru/archive/audio/8987

Message." In the end, the second option was chosen because it allowed achievement of the main thing—"*to show we are taking him very seriously*."[64]

Unlike Yeltsin, who refined proposals up to his departure, Bush's preparations were completed well in advance. A few days before the arrival of the Russian President, Scowcroft signed a document that fixed the main goals of the meeting from the White House's point of view.[65] While Yeltsin wanted to discuss global problems, Bush was asked to "come down to earth": to demonstrate support for Russian reforms, show interest in strengthening economic relations between the two countries, support disarmament initiatives in principle, and give them to the military for discussion.

Three points were recorded in the description of the Russian President's political behavior: first, his personal courage and determination, his willingness to make unpopular decisions; second, his idealism in his views on world politics (he thought that "*Russia would join the community of advanced nations as a democratic state, whose security is based on cooperation rather than confrontation*); third, his weak personnel policy, in which *Yeltsin puts up with unbelievable levels of infighting and intrigue within his government, which … make it very difficult for the US and other countries to deal with Russia on small or big issues*."

The most challenging part of formulating Bush's position before the meeting was balancing his enthusiastic support for Russian economic reforms with his frank unwillingness to commit any meaningful resources to them.

On the one hand, the actions of the Russian reformers were decisive to the point of adventurousness: with minimal preparation—Gaidar and his associates entered the Russian government on November 6—almost complete liberalization was carried out and most state-owned enterprises[66] were given full economic freedom. On the other hand, US experts were quite justified in saying that the reforms were not comprehensive.[67] Russia did not move to a unified ruble exchange rate, a significant part of revenues from commodity exports was redistributed by the government outside the budget and according

[64] GBPL&M. Possible Washington Meeting with Yeltsin after the likely UNSC Meeting on January 30. January 6, 1992.

[65] GBPL&M. Memorandum "Meeting with president of the Russian Federation Yeltsin. February 1, 1992" by Brent Scowcroft.

[66] There was no state ownership as such in the Soviet Union; the Soviet constitution enshrined "nationwide property." The power of the line ministries rested on their right to remove and appoint managers of enterprises, to decide on the distribution of their profits, and on their ability to guarantee that enterprises received the necessary materials and components. The liquidation of the line ministries at the end of 1991 led to the directors of the enterprises becoming their beneficiaries without being responsible to the state. Mass privatization of large enterprises began in the fall of 1992.

[67] GBPL&M. Economic Reform in the Former Soviet Union. January 24, 1992.

to unclear rules, and, most importantly, the government had no working contact with the Central Bank, which was pursuing a soft budget policy at a time when the government was pursuing a policy of hard budget consolidation.[68]

The White House was very skeptical about the work of the IMF and the World Bank in Russia, pointing out that these organizations did not send "heavyweights" to Moscow. Especially odd was the criticism of the IMF for focusing "*solely on macro microeconomic and structural stabilization, and ignoring changes needed to foster competition, entrepreneurship and markets.*" On the one hand, these areas were the purview of the World Bank, and on the other hand, it was not clear how specific proposals in these areas could be formulated, let alone implemented.

A separate rebuke to the Russian government was that it did not involve international organizations in "economic policy planning." In this connection, the White House asked the Kremlin to include Gaidar in the Russian delegation so that he could meet in Washington with American Treasury Department officials and answer their questions about the logic and progress of reforms. As a "home run" in the President's folder was a piece of paper written, "*I have asked Congress for $645 million for technical assistance and further humanitarian aid for the next two years… This brings to $5 billion the level of our assistance to the states of the former Soviet Union since January 1991…*[69] *I understand that you want and need longer-term financial support for your courageous reforms… Frankly, before the G7 can consider assistance, we will need to have a much better understanding of your plans…*".[70]

Today, the US and Russia Are Ushering in a New Era in Their Relationship

Differences in expectations of the meeting came to the surface before it began. First, Bush, addressing Congress, declared "*communism died this year… By the*

[68] In addition, unfounded claims were made against the Russian reformers. For example, they were blamed for the high monopolization of the economy, the lack of a plan to privatize large enterprises, and the absence of a plan to dissolve collective farms. Of course, these problems were present, and their solution was important from the point of view of the reform strategy. Still, none of them could be solved quickly, especially since Yeltsin's government had gained real power in the country only a month before.

[69] According to US GAO, in 1991–1992, the US approved appropriations for noncredit assistance to the USSR/CIS in the amount of $787 million; actual programs implementation was $501 million. The amount of grain loans and insurance program financing provided during this time was $4.73 billion. "Former Soviet Union: information on US bilateral program funding: report to Congressional committees." US GAO. December 15, 1995.

[70] Memorandum "Meeting with President of the Russian Federation Yeltsin. February 1, 1992" by Brent Scowcroft. GBPL.

grace of God, America won the Cold War… Now we can look homeward even more and move to set right what needs to be set right."[71] The next day, while in London, the Russian President said he was not satisfied with this interpretation of history. "*It was not the United States, but we all won the Cold War. However, one cannot fail to see that equal partnership will be difficult if one side considers itself the winner and the other the* defeated."[72]

The White House plan worked perfectly. The choice of Camp David, the American President's country residence, and sweaters instead of jackets and ties initially gave the meeting an informal character that did not imply serious negotiations. Two hours were allotted for the meeting, with the Russian leader using the first 45 min, when, at Yeltsin's request, the President spoke one-on-one to unburden himself. "*I wanted to see you alone Mr President, in the hope that by being completely candid and open with you and by unloading several extremely sensitive questions that I have been carrying around with me, I might be able to begin this new era between us and between our two countries without any of this "baggage" that is on my heart.*"[73]

Yeltsin told Bush in great detail how Gorbachev had deceived him. First, it was about the Soviet biological weapons program, which Gorbachev thought was closed but never bothered to check. Yeltsin promised that all employees involved in this program would be transferred to different cities in the country, the heads of the program would be fired, and the program itself would be completely shut down in two and a half months.[74]

After thanking the Russian President for his candor, Bush decided it was safe to proceed with his advisors' agenda. Still, just in case, he asked, "*Do you have anything else you want to talk about?*" It turned out he did.

The second topic was tactical nuclear weapons. The Russian President said Gorbachev did not have full information on this issue. In his talks with Bush, he mentioned 30,000 charges. After a trip to the Black Sea Fleet just before leaving Moscow, he found the total number of such charges was 35,000.

Bush again decided it was safe to move on to the planned agenda, but, just in case, asked again: "*Do you have anything else you want to talk about?*" It turned out he did.

---

[71] Address before a Joint Session of the Congress on the State of the Union. January 28, 1992.

[72] Dmitry Okunev. *30 let nazad El'cin i Bush zakonchili kholodnuyu vojnu. Pochemu nastoyashchij mir ne nastal?* (30 years ago, Yeltsin and Bush ended the Cold War. Why hasn't real peace come?) https://lenta.ru/articles/2022/02/01/deklaracija/

[73] GBPL&M. Memorandum of Conversation. One-on-One Meeting with Yeltsin, President of Russia. February 1, 1992. (Approximately 10.30 am).

[74] Yeltsin's promise proved to be unrealistic. It took him almost three months before the Decree banning offensive biological weapons was signed (April 27, 1992), while next two years Russian representative acknowledged that work was continuing.

Finally, Yeltsin explained how the Soviet military fooled Gorbachev when he decided to reduce the size of the Armed Forces by 700,000 men. In their calculations, the military showed the Soviet President an underestimated army strength (three million versus 3.5 million actual troops), which made the reduction less meaningful. Yeltsin promised that his reduction would be more serious, after which the army would be reduced to 2.5 million men.

Without giving Bush a chance to respond, Yeltsin turned to domestic problems and thanked his interlocutor for financial assistance during the reform period. The US President thought he was about to be deluged with requests for a large aid package and began to pre-emptively justify refusing: "*You know it is difficult for me to do all of this in view of the economic conditions that our citizens are experiencing currently.*" The Russian President noted sullenly that[75] he disliked the word "*help*" and preferred to hear "*support*," "*cooperation*," and similar words.

As was often the case, the entire delegation meeting was less substantive, and American politicians immediately steered it onto familiar ground. This time the "conductor" was Secretary of Defense Dick Cheney, who immediately offered Yeltsin a tempting opening, which he eagerly accepted. "*We at Pentagon are very interested in President's Yeltsin strategic and conventional initiatives. We look forward to the opportunity to discuss strategic reductions.*"

The Russian President was happy to discuss his strategic arms reduction proposals, noting that "*our initiatives close to each other.*" He then moved on to the idea of building a global space-based defense using Soviet/Russian developments, with the possibility of involving in such a project 2000 Russian nuclear scientists "*who are looking for work today.*" And lastly, he raised another proposal—a project to convert Russian weapons-grade Russian weapons-grade uranium into fuel for nuclear power plants (later realized and called HEU-LEU).

The latter idea seemed attractive to Bush, and virtually all the remaining time was spent discussing how such a project might be structured, how much it might cost, and who might be involved. "*I suggest we have lunch,*" said the host of the meeting. Then a pivotal moment occurred. Yeltsin realized that meaningful dialogue was ending, and his vision for a new US–Russian relationship remained unspoken. "*Are we still adversaries?*" he asked. "*No, we are not,*" Bush replied firmly, looking at the text of the prepared Declaration. "*I promise I will emphasize that at the press conference.* ".

---

[75] GBPL&M. Memorandum of Conversation. Meeting with Yeltsin, President of Russia. February 1, 1992 (11.15 am–12.35 pm).

"You have nothing here which says that we are no longer adversaries and are moving to be allies," Yeltsin grudgingly muttered. *"It says friendship,"* Baker rushed to the President's aid. *"No, no. We should say that we are moving from a stage of adversaries to allies. This gives a new quality," the* Russian President insisted. *"We are using this transitional language because we don't want to act like all our problems are solved,"* Bush concluded the discussion coldly and stiffly.

The sizable list of unresolved issues occupied negotiators for years afterward. However, the word "allies" was never heard again in conversations between Yeltsin and American Presidents. Stung by the "cold shower," Yeltsin refused to revisit the matter, and Presidents Bush and Clinton saw little reason to revive it.

Legacy of the Past

Political Barriers

For almost half a century, the ideological confrontation between the two systems has not escalated into direct clashes between the two military superpowers. Still, it has led to many points of tension along the line of contact between spheres of influence. The Bush administration expected that the Soviet collapse would lead Russia to discard the entire Soviet legacy, yet Moscow was not always willing to comply.

These problems were relatively easy to solve when Soviet support had been mostly political and carried little economic weight—in these cases, deescalation began in the late 1980s, and Yeltsin only had to clean up the "last crumbs."

In January 1989, Soviet troops were withdrawn from Afghanistan, but the Soviet Union continued to supply arms, ammunition, and fuel for the needs of the Afghan army. It was not until September 1991 that the USSR and the US agreed that Soviet aid would cease as of January 1, 1992, but this was not a political settlement agreement. The US did not commit to ending support for the Mujaheddin. On June 6, 1989, in a meeting with Pakistani Prime Minister Benazir Bhutto, Bush stated, "*We intended to work with Pakistan to continue our support to the Mujahiddin... We were not softening our position on Najibullah—he must go.*"[76]

[76] GB M&T. Memorandum of Conversation. Plenary Meeting with Prime Minister Bhutto of Pakistan. June 6, 1989.

On November 15, Soviet Foreign Minister Pankin signed a decision to cut off supplies to Afghanistan, which began to be implemented after the collapse of the Soviet Union.[77] A small group of Soviet/Russian military advisors remained in Afghanistan until March 1992 and left the country a week before the fall of Najibullah's regime.

In the summer of 1991, the Lisbon Peace Accords on Angola were signed, and opposition military fighters transformed into political parties. When they rejected the 1992 election results and the civil war dragged on for another decade, Russia nevertheless ended the Soviet-era arms support for the dos Santos government.

In the fall of 1991, negotiations between Gorbachev, Yeltsin, and Baker resulted in an agreement on completely withdrawing Soviet troops from Cuba. In the summer of the same year, the Soviet President announced that the Soviet Union had ended its economic support for the Castro regime and that the USSR was receiving more from Cuba than it was giving it.

It was much more challenging to find a solution in situations where the Soviet Union, and later Russia, had an economic interest, mainly related to the export of arms and nuclear technology. The main points of tension were India and Iran.

Tensions between India and neighboring Pakistan have existed since their independence. By the time of the collapse of the Soviet Union, Pakistan had invaded India three times, forcing the country to think seriously about its security. In the 1980s, the US made a clear choice in favor of Pakistan, which was largely due to the Soviet intervention in Afghanistan. Pakistan, because of its geographical location, was the best place to set up camps and training bases for the Mujaheddin who had fought the Soviet Army, and it was also home to three million Afghans who had fled the Karmal/Najibullah regime. In response, Pakistan has become a key US partner in South Asia. "*Our policy will continue to give priority to relations with Pakistan… [which] is vital for the achievements of US objectives in Afghani*stan," was recorded by Bush shortly after entering the Oval Office of the White House.[78]

Acting in line with its key regional ally, the United States tried to curb Soviet-Indian military cooperation and related economic links. *"Major US objective [in South Asia] include … reducing the influence of the Soviet Union in the region."*

Pakistan received large amounts of military and financial aid from the US, which caused tension and apprehension in New Delhi. To avoid spoiling

[77] Pierre Allan, Dieter Klei. Afganskiy kapkan. Pravda o sovetskom vtorzhenii. (*The Afghan Trap. The Truth about the Soviet Invasion.*) Moscow, Mezdunarodnye otnosheniya,1999, p. 322.

[78] GBPL&M. National Security Directive 20. August 29, 1989.

relations with Pakistan, the US had to refuse to supply advanced weapons and dual-use goods to India. "*The United States will follow a selective policy of providing military equipment for projects and mission areas in which we have agreed to cooperate. More sophisticated technology that would significantly enhance Indian military power projection, fuel regional arms races, or otherwise have a destabilizing effect on the region should be denied.*"

India's attempts to access arms purchases from other NATO countries were unsuccessful, and the Soviet Union remained the only alternative source of arms supplies. For the Soviet Union (later Russia) MiG fighters' contracts with India were among the few that generated hard-currency payments; most other Soviet arms clients could not pay. Washington's response was obvious—"*The United States should continue to reduce India's economic and technological dependence on the USSR through expanded economic and trade relations with India.*"

In 1980, the United States imposed sanctions against Iran, and German companies stopped participating in the construction of the Bushehr nuclear power plant. By this time, construction of the first unit was 85% complete and the second 50%. Iran's wish to finish the plant was understandable, and once again the only available partner was the Soviet Union. Negotiations on the entry of Soviet companies into the project were held for several years. Still, only in August 1992 did Russia and Iran sign a contract to complete the NPP construction, which began to be implemented in 1995. In 2010, the building was completed, and a year later, Bushehr NPP was connected to the national energy system of Iran.

Just as in the case of arms supplies to India, the Iranian contract was critical for the Russian nuclear industry to maintain minimal sustainability and prevent the loss of key personnel. The G7 recognized the potential brain drain from the Soviet/Russian nuclear industry and constantly surfaced when discussing issues related to potential assistance to the Soviet Union/Russia. However, the problem was never raised, and the only realized project in this area was the HEU-LEU agreement.

The UN did not support the sanctions against Iran, so they did not restrict Russia from cooperating with Iran on NPP construction. Moreover, Moscow, like Washington, was anxious about Iran's potential penetration into the Muslim post-Soviet countries of Central Asia, and Tehran's memory of the Soviet Union's intense support for Iraq in the Iran–Iraq war hindered the development of military ties. In this regard, for Washington, the threat of Saddam Hussein's regime building nuclear weapons seemed more real than in Iran. Yet a nuclear-power plant in Iran bolstered the economy, lessened dependence on oil exports, and allowed energy-intensive projects to proceed.

Washington knew this list of "claims" well; every item was raised with Gorbachev and later Yeltsin, and on each the United States adopted an all-or-nothing stance. Either Russia completely stops cooperation with India and Iran, or there will be no serious economic support for Russia at the expense of the American budget. Given that outright US grants were tiny next to the value of Iranian and Indian contracts, Russian officials opted for pragmatism: better a bird in hand than two in the bush—and US aid was a shadow of the bird in the bush.

Economic Barriers

As tensions in political relations between the USSR and the United States decreased, economic relations increasingly became the subject of internal discussions and bilateral negotiations. At the same time, the Soviet Union, due to the planned nature of its economy, mainly proposed individual projects focused on specific problems or narrow sectors. America, in turn, was more interested in traditional trade liberalization and freedom of access for American capital to attractive sectors of the Soviet economy.

Although economic contacts between the two countries were minimal after the end of World War II, by the time the Cold War ended, they were beset by a wide range of restrictions and barriers. In late November 1989, Mike Boskin, head of Bush's Council of Economic Advisers, received a memo outlining this list.

GATT/WTO

In the first place, it was a matter of principle—the Soviet Union was not a member of the General Agreement on Tariffs and Trade (GATT), which allowed all member countries of this organization to apply various restrictive measures to Soviet goods. The main obstacle to the USSR joining the GATT is opposition from the United States; the non-market price system existing in the USSR is incompatible with the market rules of the GATT. This US position certainly had its logic, but how could one explain that three CMEA member countries had been admitted to the GATT many years earlier: Poland in 1967, Romania in 1981, and Hungary in 1983?

In 1986, the USSR applied to join the GATT as an observer, but it was rejected. In mid-1988, Soviet representatives held informal consultations with the United States on this issue and again received a categorical rejection. It was not until May 1990 that the Soviet Union was granted this status. In 1993, Russia applied to join the GATT.[79] Two years later, negotiations began, which ended in December 2011.[80] The last country with which Russia was able to reach an agreement[81] was the United States.[82] On July 30, 2012, the lower house of the Russian parliament ratified the Protocol on Russia's accession to the WTO. Thirty days later, Russia became a full member of this organization, 18 years after the application.[83]

In very general terms, WTO accession facilitates the access of goods produced in the acceding country to the markets of other WTO member countries. On the other hand, accession to the WTO is accompanied by a reduction in import duties, which increases the competitiveness of goods produced in different countries and enhances competition in the national market.

The US was never an important trading partner for the USSR or Russia. In the late 1980s, the US share of Soviet exports was less than 0.5%, and the US share of Soviet imports was about 1.5% (mostly grain imports). As the Russian economy transformed, mutual trade grew, but even in 2021, the US share of Russian foreign trade was 3.5% (exports) and 5.8% (imports). Russia's share in US exports of goods in 2021 was about 1%, and in US imports, it was 0.6%. Given that Russian exports are chiefly commodities, a trade that is not regulated by WTO rules. In that case, it becomes clear that the gain from any concessions by Russia was extremely insignificant from the point of view of the US economy. According to the testimonies of Russian negotiators, US negotiators were extremely intransigent and haggled over Russia's slightest disagreement. Such bargaining is normal; in the absence of a prior political deal, each side seeks the best economic terms for itself. However, in this case, there

[79] On January 1, 1995, GATT transformed into the World Trade Organization (WTO).

[80] Again, Russia's accession to the WTO was not the best timing: The application was submitted at the moment of GATT transformation, which stopped all bureaucratic processes. Later, Russia's accession to the WTO was overlaid by a long process of ratifying the Kyoto Protocol to combat global warming, signed in 1997. Russia's unwillingness to ratify it by November 2004 blocked its entry into force and caused the suspension of negotiations on Russia's accession to the WTO with the European Union.

[81] When a new country joins the WTO, each organization member can propose its desires/requirements to soften the candidate country's terms of trade. After that, the candidate country's negotiation goal is to limit itself to minimal concessions. After Russia's application, some 60 countries indicated their desire to negotiate with the new candidate.

[82] Not counting Georgia, whose claims were related to the consequences of the 2008 Russian–Georgian war.

[83] Of course, Russia also bears its share of responsibility for such lengthy negotiations. The structure of its foreign trade is such that no sectors in the Russian economy would gain or lose much from WTO accession. Experts estimated the balance to be within 1% of foreign trade, with the sign of the balance varying depending on the order of the assessment. As often happens in such situations, the supporters of WTO accession did not lobby much for this process. On the one hand, the gains are small; on the other hand, loud accusations by opponents of damaging the economy could always provoke an unpredictable reaction from Vladimir Putin.

was no gain for the United States: the volume of mutual trade after Russia's accession to the WTO remained virtually unchanged.

Jackson-Vanik

The Jackson-Vanik Amendment, which was passed in 1974, was in honorable second place in the memo on Bush's counselor's desk. It prohibited the administration from granting most-favored-nation trade, government loans, and loan guarantees to the Soviet Union and other socialist countries that restricted Jewish travel to Israel.

This measure failed to achieve its goal. Significant emigration of Jews from the USSR began in 1971. In 1970, only 1000 people were able to leave the USSR on Israeli visas,[84] the following year, about 13,000 people had such an opportunity, and in 1973—over 34,000 people. After a "quiet" period, 1974–1977, when between 13,000 and 21,000 people left each year, the Soviet government eased restrictions in the late 1970s, and 1979 marked the peak of Jewish emigration in the 1970s: more than 51,000 left. After the Korean Boeing was shot down in 1983, severe restrictions were again placed on emigration: fewer than 7000 Jews left the USSR between 1983 and 1986.[85]

With the arrival of Gorbachev in the Kremlin, the acuteness of the problem was fading quickly, and the United States became the main destination for emigrants from the USSR. While in 1986, 787 people left the Soviet Union for permanent residence in the United States, in 1988 the figure topped 20,000. NSC forecasts projected 90,000 departures in 1989 and 150,000 in 1990.[86]

With the goal met, NSC estimated 360,000 emigrants in 1990, so the amendment could be repealed. By the end of 1989, experts in Bush's administration knew the repeal was symbolically important yet unlikely to boost Soviet exports to America because Soviet goods would not be able to compete in the market.

Moreover, the amendment started hindering US grain sales to Russia—the law barred guarantees for countries that were denied most-favored-nation

[84] The Soviet government imposed restrictions on the number of departures—until the entry into force of the USSR Law "On Entry and Exit," a Soviet citizen, regardless of the purpose and duration of the trip, had to obtain an exit visa. A visa was applied for at the Israeli embassy only when the exit permit had already been received.

[85] Tolts. The Post-Soviet Jewish Population in Russia and the World // Jews in Russia and Eastern Europe. 2004. No 1 (52).

[86] GBPL&M. US Policy on Soviet Emigration. PCC Paper for Deputies Committee Meeting on Soviet Emigration. August 24, 1989.

treatment in trade with the United States. To lift such a restriction, the President had to submit to Congress a justification, which was limited to one year. As a result, the President was caught between hammer and: on the one hand, he was under pressure from agricultural lobbyists who did not want to lose an attractive buyer who could contract huge amounts of grain at once; on the other hand, as soon as the President sent his letter to Congress, he was criticized by human rights activists in the Soviet Union.[87]

The anvil won: after discussion, it was decided that while the Soviet Union had decisively liberalized exit from the country de facto, it had not done so de jure. The Soviet government made departure decisions non-transparently and were not regulated by law. At the G7 meeting in Houston, Gorbachev was asked to regulate this issue legally. The law granting Soviet citizens the right to leave the country without hindrance passed in May 1991, but the law was not to take effect until January 1, 1993. By that time, a year had passed since the Soviet Union's collapse, and Russian citizens gained the legal right to travel abroad.

In this situation, Bush decided not to try to repeal Jackson-Vanik, which could have been very costly when the law was debated in Congress in an election year. Since the Soviet law was already in effect after the election, it was considered improper to draw attention to it when Bush decided to avoid foreign policy issues during the election race. The amendment text stated that the President could introduce legislation to repeal it after the restrictions on free emigration had been lifted. Therefore, no formal claims could be made against the President.

The Jackson-Vanik Amendment was repealed only in 2012. After joining the WTO, Russia, citing the effect of this law, which did not comply with the norms of the organization, could not fulfill its obligations to the United States and, moreover, impose discriminatory import tariffs on American goods. The threat of losing the Russian market, where US goods faced competition from manufacturers from other countries (primarily civilian airplanes), led Congress to support the bill.

Since the early 1990s, the amendment no longer trade—each year any President sent Congress a 1-year waiver, and Congress never objected. For Moscow the issue soon became one of principle: the law's conditions were met, yet waivers could vanish at any moment. Repeal stayed on every negotiating agenda, resurfacing again and again, yet Russia still fell short.

---

[87] GBPL&M. Memorandum to the President [from Clayton Yeutter, Secretary of Agriculture]. Soviet Export Credit Guarantees. October 22, 1990.

Stuff

Besides the two big hurdles, several other US laws impeded economic ties and absorbed scarce political capital to overturn.

In 1974, Congress passed Senator Stevenson's amendment to the Eximbank Act, which limited the amount of government loans or guarantees to support US exports to the Soviet Union to $300 million. In addition, a separate limitation ($40 million) was placed on support for exports of goods intended for the extraction of energy resources in the Soviet Union. These restrictions were lifted on September 30, 1994.

In 1974, Congress passed Senator Byrd's amendment to the Trade Act, which established that no government entity (other than the CCC—Credit Commodity Corporation) could provide more than $300 million in loans, guarantees, or export insurance to the Soviet Union. This restriction was lifted on October 22, 2005.

In 1978, Congress passed Senator John Chafee's amendment to the Eximbank Act, which prohibited financial support to the Soviet Union and other countries classified as "Marxist-Leninist" unless the President declared that providing such support was in the national interest of the United States. A similar ban was imposed on the Soviet Union in 1972 and applied to loans of $50 million or more. These restrictions were lifted on September 30, 1994.

Got the Package, no Money

The meeting at Camp David was over, and the Presidents returned to matters of primary importance. Both had their hands full.

Yeltsin in Moscow continued building the new state and transforming the economy: the first month of reforms brought no obvious successes and, most sadly, no glimmer of light at the end of the tunnel.

Bush plunged into a campaign fought on three fronts. First, although the recession had ended, macroeconomic data failed to convince voters: unemployment had only begun to decline in the mid-summer of 1992, personal income had not begun to rise, leaving budget revenues meager.[88] The deficit kept rising, leaving no funds for new programs in the 1992 or 1993 drafts. Second, the Clinton's campaign, who was gaining popularity in the Democratic

[88] The share of income-dependent taxes (income tax and social security contribution) in the United States exceeds 80%. If we add excise taxes, which depend on the expenditures of the population, the figure exceeds 85%. The White House. OMB. Historical Tables. Table 2.3. Receipts by Source as Percentages of GDP: 1934-2029. https://www.whitehouse.gov/wp-content/uploads/2024/03/hist02z3_fy2025.xlsx

primaries, was based on the thesis "It's the economy, stupid!" and criticism of the incumbent's economic policies. Third, an alternative candidate, Pat Buchanan emerged in the primaries, centering his campaign on the slogan "Putting and Keeping America First." His campaign began with the words, "*Phase Out Foreign Aid… Charity begins at home.*" In short, the President had no time for Russia and needed to turn his attention to domestic affairs.

Shock Without Stabilization

The transition from prices set by the state to market prices, from the administrative binding of enterprises to each other to freedom of economic ties, is the most important and necessary condition for transitioning from a planned economy to a market economy. In Russia, such a transition took place on January 2, 1992.

The starting package of reforms included not only price liberalization and freedom of economic relations but also a few other important components (liberalization of foreign trade, transition to limited convertibility of the ruble, launch of a comprehensive tax system, transition to a two-tier banking system), without which the new economic system could not exist. Some solutions were formalized in legislation but could not be implemented because of a lack of time or because these ideas could not withstand the collision with reality. Some solutions were ready at the level of ideas but were not formalized and approved in the form of normative documents, which appeared later. Some solutions were half-hearted, which slowed down or sometimes blocked the expected effect. But one way or another, the reform envisioned a comprehensive restructuring of the entire economy and all the rules of the game began.

The transition to free prices on January 2, 1992, was a real shock for the entire Russian population, including the country's political leadership. Although government forecasts in Nov–Dec 1991 anticipated an initial price jump of roughly 2.5–3 times, early-January reports from around the country were shocking: meat and butter prices had risen 5- to 20-fold, stark proof of how unbalanced the economy was.

But if the price hike became visible to the entire population almost instantly, the filling of counters was much slower—new economic chains were established slowly, trade enterprises lacked working capital, and mutual trust with wholesalers or manufacturers had not yet emerged, regional barriers preventing the movement of goods in the country could not be removed. Basic foodstuffs were not available in stores in most cities throughout January. Up to the end of 1992, the volume of sales in the retail trade was declining, reflecting the declining living standards of the population.

Even worse, the Russian government failed to repeat the Polish scenario. The budget deficit in the first quarter amounted to 10% of GDP, which was certainly better than the 30% deficit at the end of the previous year, but far short of the IMF's requirement to limit the deficit to 1% of GDP.[89] Given the fact that the budget did not include domestic debt servicing, the situation was even worse. When Gaidar accepted Yeltsin's offer to join the government, he overestimated Bank of Russia Chairman Grigory Matyukhin's willingness to cooperate. He had been actively involved in destroying the unity of the Soviet monetary system, as this made him the main man to implement monetary policy in the Soviet space, but when it came to transforming the economy, it turned out that he had unorthodox views on what should be done and how it should be done, which contradicted the ideology of the reforms. Arguably the reformers' greatest misstep was failing to adopt a market exchange rate for the ruble; the government kept in its hands significant portion of commodities exports selling the foreign-currency at subsidized rate according to its own priorities. As a result, the economy lacked an important anchor, the free exchange rate.

The lack of obvious successes led to the fact that anti-government slogans were becoming increasingly popular in the Russian parliament, and the chairman of the Supreme Soviet, Ruslan Khasbulatov, began to think about the possibility of pushing Yeltsin aside and taking power into his own hands. It cannot be said that these thoughts had no basis. The position of President was introduced into the Russian constitution in April 1991, and the first elections were held on June 12. At that time, Russia was part of the USSR, and the republican government had very little power, of which the President was given his share. However, the main power was the Congress of People's Deputies and the Supreme Soviet. In the fall of 1991, at the time of the formation of the government of reforms, the Congress of People's Deputies adopted a special decision on granting the President extended powers for the period of reforms,[90] which were to expire on December 1, 1992.

High inflation in January–February led to a significantly deteriorating budget situation. Tax revenues were paid based on previous months' results and had time to depreciate before reaching the treasury. On the other hand, inflation devalued public sector salaries and pensions; budget funds were

[89] This target was incorporated into the Memorandum on Economic Policy discussed between Russia and the IMF in March 1992. "Russian Federation: Back-to-Office-Report" (from I. Coelho to Ter-Minassian), March 23, 1992. IMF Archive, Fiscal Affairs Department Records, ref. #71807.

[90] The President could head the government and issue decrees with a legal force equal to the law.

insufficient to purchase necessary materials for schools and hospitals and to buy food for the army. State enterprises were losing working capital and could not get bank loans, as banks could not assess how sustainable they were in the new conditions. Enterprise directors, having been refused by the Ministry of Finance, went to the Supreme Soviet, where they found support from their former colleagues. The pressure on the government to soften its policy was growing daily, and by the end of March, it was clear that one question—will it or won't it happen?—had been replaced by another—when will it happen?

It Was all Nixon's Idea

In addition to all the problems Bush had, there was another that one could not dismiss or pretend did not exist. It was Richard Nixon.

After his scandalous exit from the White House in 1974, he was out of the spotlight and had to make Herculean efforts simply to be remembered. It should be remembered, Nixon, who entered the House of Representatives in 1946, experienced the entire Cold War, seeing it up close. As Vice President under Dwight Eisenhower, he was present at the end of the Korean War and was an important negotiator with the Soviet Union during the Khrushchev thaw. After becoming President, he inherited the Vietnam War, and after unsuccessful attempts to achieve victory, he negotiated an end to the war and withdrew US troops from Vietnam. In February 1972, he made a sensational visit to China, which initiated the normalization of relations between the two countries and later became the basis for the "Chinese miracle." His signature is on the first serious strategic arms limitation treaty with the Soviet Union, which he signed in May 1972 in the Kremlin.

With this kind of baggage of foreign policy successes, Nixon could not help but feel that the collapse of the Soviet Union could become a major point in world history. In addition, the disgraced President wanted to rehabilitate himself and use the situation to change his legacy in the eyes of historians.

Up until August 1991, Nixon, though praising Gorbachev, remained a skeptic. In June of that year, he criticized the "grand bargain" proposed by Yavlinsky and Allison, saying that the Soviet Union could only transform itself under pressure; conservatives would use any Western help to modernize and preserve the old system. The President's views changed after the putsch's failure when he fundamentally changed his attitude toward Yeltsin, who had become the protagonist of Russia's transformation.

In early 1992, Nixon saw golden opportunity to showcase America's new global role—beginning at home. The euphoria of winning the war with Iraq was fading, and Nixon didn't understand why the Bush team was adamantly refusing to use his foreign policy successes in the campaign. He decided that power is seized, not bestowed. At the beginning of January, Nixon began an active public campaign to explain the historical significance of what was happening in the Soviet Union. He argued forcefully for substantial aid to Russia. Nixon gave TV interviews and published op-eds defending the need for budgetary expenditures to help the former enemy.

On 11–12 March Nixon convened a Washington conference, "America's Role in the Developing World," aiming to press the case for major aid to Russia and to draw Bush into the debate. The week before, about 60 leading politicians and journalists received a confidential Nixon memorandum defending his position. "*We are rich enough to do everything important … we must be willing to bear our share of the burden… If Yeltsin is replaced by a new aggressive Russian nationalist, we may kiss the peace dividend good-bye… President Bush is uniquely qualified to meet this challenge.*" The Nixon memorandum became a major talking point in Washington.[91]

The bait was taken, yet Bush hesitated to bite. At a March 10 press conference, when asked directly whether the President had seen the document and whether he considered it a criticism of his policy, he delivered a cautious yet firm reply: "*There are certain fiscal financial constraints on what we can do, but we have a huge stake in the success of democracy in Russia… So there's a lot of taxpayer money going in this already… I didn't take it as personally critical.*"[92]

Nixon's speech the next day (he spoke at lunch) was met with a standing ovation, though it was neither energetic nor beautiful. But the room was filled with his supporters and admirers, members of his administration, selected journalists, and foreign policy experts for whom living Nixon seemed a political relic—in short, it was strange to expect anything different. The speech's novelty lay in Nixon spelling out, for the first time, possible aid parameters for Russia. As an experienced politician, he did not make his estimates to avoid getting into trouble when asked how he got them. Nixon cited estimates from the Financial Times and the New York Times—$20 billion a year for 3–5 years—and added that as late as 1990, the West was spending 20 times that amount on programs for military confrontation with the Soviet Union. It was not a bad security investment and was much cheaper.

At the same time, Eagleburger—aid coordinator for the post-Soviet states—told a House subcommittee that "*the US does not have unlimited resources.*"

---

[91] Marvin Kalb. The Nixon Memo. University of Chicago Press, Chicago, 1994, p. 74.

[92] GBPL&M. Remarks at a Meeting with Republican Congressional Leaders and an Exchange with Reporters. March 10, 1992.

Although Russia faces unprecedented challenges, "... *Simply throwing money ... will not solve these problems ... We must remain prudent.*"[93] The administration was ready to increase spending on aid to post-Soviet countries by $620 million in 1992–1993 only.

On that day, Bush was in a good mood: the day before, on Super Tuesday, he had won an overwhelming victory in the primary elections in all 15 states, and the question of competition in the Republican Party had been removed. Journalists cared less about the primaries than about Bush's response to Nixon's challenge—but they heard nothing new: "one *area where we might have difference ... we are living in a time of constraint. There isn't a lot of money around ... I don't have a blank check for all of that.*"

The President's evening speech at a conference organized by Nixon disappointed many of those in attendance. Yet after prepared lines—"We invested so much to win the Cold War. We must invest what is necessary to win the peace... leadership will cost money"—his conclusion fell short of expectations. "*We invested so much to win the cold war. We must invest what is necessary to win the peace. If we fail, we will create new and profound problems for our security and that of Europe and Asia. If we succeed, we strengthen democracy, we build new market economies, and in the process we create huge new markets for America ... carrying out a leadership role in determining the course of the emerging world is going to cost money...* "sounded quite different from what many expected. "*Many in Congress today ... are calling for a peace dividend. They would have us slash defense spending far below the reduced levels that we have calculated would be prudent. This must be resisted.*" The new "Marshall Plan" melted into thin air before it could materialize.

Competition Is a Great Force

Suddenly, Richard Nixon had new allies. On the one hand, there was Baker. He did not like Nixon and did not believe him. Still, as the man in charge of foreign policy in the administration, he did not understand why it was necessary to throw away the achievements of recent years and why they were not used in the election campaign. However, they could highlight the strengths of the President. At that time, the Secretary of State was thinking about his presidential ambitions in the next cycle, the situation was not in his favor, and he had no choice but to push the President to change his campaign strategy.

[93] State Department Budget Proposal. March 11, 1992. https://www.c-span.org/video/?24913-1/state-department-budget-proposal

On the other hand, there was Clinton, who, by the second half of March, had practically guaranteed himself victory in the Democratic primaries and could start thinking about the November elections. Realizing that the candidate could not ignore foreign policy, and that Russia was certainly the dominant theme, he decided to give a big speech in New York on April 1 about America's role in supporting Russia's transformation. Usually, the candidates' headquarters keep the main thesis of the speeches of their wards secret until the last moment, but this time, something went wrong—word that Clinton planned to borrow Nixon's main themes quickly reached Republican ears.

Bush was cornered; with little time to react, the White House announced he would deliver a major statement on Russia on 1 April. Half an hour before Clinton's speech,[94] Bush announced that the G7 had agreed on a $24 billion package to support Russia, which would consist of IMF and World Bank loans, bilateral loans and humanitarian aid programs of the G7 members, a stabilization fund to support the ruble, and a deferral of foreign debt service. The President announced he had submitted the Freedom Support Act to Congress and that securing its swift passage was a top priority.

I have always been puzzled by proposals for a stabilization fund. This idea was borrowed from Poland, which proved very effective. However, the proponents of using this instrument in Russia failed to consider the fundamental differences in implementing reforms between the two countries.

Firstly, the stabilization fund in Poland was created when the zloty exchange rate was devalued by 35% and then fixing the rate, providing an "anchor" for inflationary expectations: the prices of imported goods did not change during the inflation suppression phase, as the exchange rate was kept unchanged for more than a year. Secondly, by this time, Poland had already been living with free prices for many months, which allowed the normalization of the relative price structure. Thirdly, the Polish government did not redistribute export earnings or support "important imports," i.e. it did not influence the supply-demand balance on the foreign exchange market.

[94] Although Clinton spoke later and could not give specific figures, his speech had an offensive tone. He accused Bush of removing himself from the world's most important problem. *The President has left America on the sidelines of the democratic revolutions that toppled the Soviet empire and are changing the face of world politics….. Time and again, this administration has sided with stability over democratic change.* Journalists commenting on the unscheduled debate noted that the incumbent defended and justified himself, looking less convincing than his rival.

Initially, the size of the Russia package made a tremendous impression on the audience, who remembered well what the President had said a few days earlier. But very quickly, the thought began to creep in that the President had presented a "raw product" that had been hastily and incompletely prepared. "*It's not a tremendous amount of money*," the President responded to a reporter's question about whether it would be too much. And a few minutes later he said the opposite: "*Our commitment* [to help Russia] *is very, very substantial,*" after hearing a question about whether it would be enough.[95]

Even worse was that neither the President himself, Baker, nor Treasury Secretary Brady, standing by, could answer questions about what the US contribution would be and whether that meant that budget spending would be increased. Rather, it looked like they were trying to reassure everyone that "*taxpayers would not have to spend more money to finance the aid for the Russians in this election year.*" Subsequent comments from the Treasury Department made it clear: "*United States would contribute $4.35 billion, all of it from "existing," "previously authorized" or "already committed" funds.*"[96] Secretary Baker, declaring that there was "*no higher priority*" than this bill, said, "*I'm ready to go up there tomorrow and start fighting for this legislation.*"[97]

On the same day in Bonn, Kohl, the leader of the country that held the G7 presidency this year, made the announcement of the aid package for Russia. Of course, there was and could be no fundamental disagreement in the two speeches, but the comments made in Bonn only strengthened suspicions that the decision had been hastily prepared.[98] Crucially, Horst Köhler noted that Russia must first agree on an IMF reform program and begin implementation before aid could flow. He reminded that Russia was not yet a member of the IMF and could receive this status at the end of April, which made it impossible to receive the money before June. All details of the aid package, he said, would have to be agreed upon at the July G7 summit in Munich,[99] although Bush had designated the end of April as the time to finalize all the details.

This was the end of the unanimity of the G7 leaders and the start of disagreements and confusion. First, John Major, the British Prime Minister, whose presidency of the G7 ended on December 31, unexpectedly claimed

[95] GBPL&M. The President's News Conference on Aid to the States of the Former Soviet Union. April 1, 1992.

[96] "Aid to Russia; Bush and Kohl Unveil Plan for 7 Nations to Contribute $24 billion in Aid for Russia." The New York Times. April 2, 1992.

[97] Ibid.

[98] On March 21–23, 1992, Kohl was in Washington and had hours-long talks with Bush. The published records of these talks do not mention aid to Russia. On March 29, Bush congratulated Major on his birthday; no word about Russia was said in the conversation.

[99] "West Commits $24 Billion to Bolster Russian Economy." The New York Times. April 2, 1992.

that his country had led the process of negotiating the aid package.[100] Japan then stated that no agreement had been reached with it, including the deferral of debt service, and that the decision was "*inappropriate* and *premature*."[101] France then reported that "*It's all a bit mysterious… There are still discussions going on on the details*."[102] A few more days later, a spokesman for the British Treasury politely contradicted the Prime Minister's position: "*If you take a snapshot, at the moment we are in midair, about three-quarters through our double spin*."[103] Yet this, it turned out, was only the beginning…

The real complications befell the IMF and the World Bank.

On April 6, five days after Bush announced Russia bailout package, the IMF Board of Directors held a meeting at which participants bombarded IMF's Managing Director Camdessus with questions. His responses made clear that the package had not been cleared with the Fund and revealed three major obstacles. First, the post-Soviet countries were not yet members of the Fund, and the IMF could not grant them any loans. In addition to bureaucratic delays in admitting new members, there was one significant obstacle: each member's quota (which determines the amount of Fund's credits available) would have to be recalculated; the republics' combined share—around 5%— required reallocating other members' quotas, and talks had not even begun. Second, the IMF lacked available resources to lend to new members, and the main donor of the Fund was the United States, which blocked this process. The resistance stemmed largely from big US banks eager to lend to developing governments at market rates. With low credit ratings these countries paid high market rates, whereas cheaper IMF loans let them bypass commercial borrowing. Third, the Fund lacked reliable estimates of the republics' needs. This was yet to be calculated.[104]

A week later, World Bank Director Lewis Preston said that his organization could provide $1.5 billion to Russia that year and estimated the post-Soviet states would need $4.5–5 billion annually during the following three years.[105] However, he stressed that it would be possible to discuss all this more specifically only after the procedure for admitting new countries' membership in the Fund and the Bank was completed and the reform program was agreed upon with the IMF.

[100] "Specific Pledges for Money are Absent in Russia Plan." The New York Times. April 3, 1992.

[101] "Tokyo Calls Announcement of Aid to Russia 'Premature'." The New York Times. April 4, 1992.

[102] "What Japan Knew of Plan on Aid to Russia is Debated." The New York Times. April 5, 1992.

[103] "Aid for Yeltsin and Russians: A Package with Loose Ends." The New York Times. April 9, 1992.

[104] IMF. Minutes of Executive Board Meeting 92/44. April 3, 1992. IMF Archive.

[105] "Ex-Soviets to Get a $12 Billion Loan." The New York Times. April 12, 1992.

On 19 April, Camdessus estimated that beyond the $24 billion for Russia, the other 14 republics would need $20 billion immediately and $100 billion over the next four years.[106]

No one was prepared for this. The US remained silent. The UK, France, and Italy hinted that the issue should be considered by the European institutions first. Kohl said that his country had already spent $47 billion in various forms to support the Soviet Union and post-Soviet countries and another $65 billion to help Eastern Europe and had "*reached the limit of our capacity.*" Therefore, further assistance should be provided by someone else. "*Now especially it is time for Japan, an exporting nation, to assume a larger share of the West's common responsibility and, in keeping with her economic strength, to help insure the success of the reforms in Central, Eastern and Southeast Europe and in the Commonwealth of Independent States.*"[107] again said it had no objection in principle but insisted the Northern Territories dispute be resolved first. In short, the G7 could not agree on who should support Russia and the other post-Soviet states—or on when and how without a face-to-face meeting of its leaders. And since such a meeting was to take place in early July in Munich, so the matter was deferred until that summit.

IMF? Good to Go!

By the end of April, negotiations were completed between IMF and World Bank participants on the size of quotas for CIS countries, their distribution among newcomers, and which of the existing members should agree to a reduction in their shares. On April 27, Russia and 11 other countries (three Baltic countries were completing the accession process at the time) received an official invitation from the Fund and the Bank to become members of these organizations. Another month was needed for bureaucratic procedures, and on June 1, Russia became a full member of the IMF. The path to IMF lending was now open.

More precisely, it was only nearly open. To begin with, the organization's new members had to pay their capital subscriptions, and although the principal amount had to be paid in local currency, Russia had to find more than $1.5 billion to pay for its share. Most importantly, Russia had to agree with the Fund on the content of its reforms and the parameters of its monetary and budgetary policies.

[106] "Discord is Said to Stall Plan to Raise IMF Loan Aid to Ex-Soviets." The New York Times. April 20, 1992.

[107] "Kohl Urges Japan to Increase Help for Eastern Europe. "The New York Times. May 6, 1992.

By this time, the Fund began to see Russia not merely as a technical-assistance recipient but as a borrower and therefore applied its standard toolkit. Historically, since its inception, the IMF has lent to member countries for balance-of-payments purposes. The logic of such programs was straightforward. To restore equilibrium, a country had to tighten monetary and fiscal policy and, in most cases, devalue its currency. These steps allowed for the reduction of domestic demand and demand for imports and made exports more attractive, eventually achieving the goal. Implementing such programs took months to approve, with economic results appearing only after 2–3 years. After 4–5 years, the country could start repaying the IMF loan.

Because the Fund waived rules only for the poorest countries, Russia was held to the same standards. This proved the IMF's greatest misjudgment in designing assistance for Russia.

Russia Is (Not) a Special Case

Undoubtedly, Russia (as well as other post-Soviet countries) faced a balance-of-payments imbalance, and the burden of servicing foreign debt was one of the most important factors determining the scale of disequilibrium. The first assessment of the balance of payments for 12 countries, presented by the Fund's experts in early February 1992 (at that time it was not possible to separate the data by republics), determined a balance-of-payments deficit between $14 billion and $18 billion, with scheduled external debt payments of $14 billion.[108] By June, the estimate of the balance-of-payments deficit for Russia had increased to $24 billion (quite probably, so that there would be no disagreement with the size of the aid package). In any case, Russia's currency shortfall had to be addressed—in situations when a country cannot cope with the burden of payments on foreign debts, the Fund normally offers no loans; instead, it advises to negotiate cost-free deferrals or restructurings with creditors. It would be aid, yet very limited. Evidently, Russia was unable to pay, thus creditors had no choice but to defer their claims.

The Russian budget, however, was the principal case in need of support. Since the Soviet economy, together with the economies of other socialist countries, existed in an isolated economic system, it was impossible to assess the quality and competitiveness of manufactured goods. Liberalization of prices and foreign trade showed that there was no demand for many goods even within the country: production costs often exceeded the price consumers

[108] IMF. Memorandum To Members of the Executive Board. Recent Economic Developments and Policies in Former USSR Republics. Republics. IMF Archive.

were willing to pay and attempts by directors to solve the problem of unprofitability by raising prices further reduced demand.

Technological chains in the Soviet economy were built without backup for many products—often, only one company in the country could produce certain goods. As a result, if one of them stopped, its suppliers lacked demand, and consumers of supply were short of supply. The same thing happened if some enterprise's directors found a favorable export contract—the whole production chain stopped.

In the second half of the 1980s, the Soviet economy faced a shortage of foreign currency, which led to a reduction in imports of goods. Without these, many enterprises could not operate at full capacity or at all. In 1992, when the Russian government transferred the function of distributing foreign currency from Gosplan and Gossnab (they were liquidated) to the Ministry of Foreign Economic Relations, whose staff had never been involved, failures to obtain imported goods to support production became dramatically more frequent.[109]

Do not miss, the companies were now located in different countries with different foreign trade regimes and different and reform tempos. All that made CIS production links even harder to sustain.

The Soviet economy was overloaded with military orders, and the enterprises that produced military products could not make anything else. An attempt to convert them under administrative coercion in the late 1980s did not yield noticeable results: highly specialized enterprises could not produce anything new with the existing equipment. The sharp reduction in arms purchases in 1992 led to the complete shutdown of dozens of enterprises.

Economists would call this a supply contraction, which eroded budget revenues. Two-thirds of all revenues came from the corporate profit tax and the value-added tax introduced in early 1992. The fall in production, which was much greater than the government and IMF experts had predicted, inevitably led to a fall in budget revenues. At the same time, all Soviet budget obligations remained, and, except for investment and military expenditures, they could not be reduced.

Consequently, Russia required fiscal support more urgently than balance-of-payments aid. However, IMF rules did not provide for loans to governments—the balance of payments is the responsibility of central banks—so the recipient of most loans in Russia was the Central Bank, not the government, and this did not alleviate the budget crisis. Attempts of Russian negotiators to

[109] The market rate of the dollar in Russia at that time was 120–160 rubles per dollar, and when receiving currency from the government, the price of a dollar was 20 rubles. One can only guess the ministry officials' temptations when making their decisions.

explain the needs of the economy were not successful; their arguments were not heard at the initial stage of reforms—the IMF started to depart from its strict principles, agreeing to use part of the loans provided to Russia for budgetary purposes later, starting from the end of 1994.[110]

There's a First Loan!

The Russian officials believed Bush's statement about the aid package reflected the decision made by the G7 and that all that remained was to formalize all the necessary documents. On April 28, Gaidar, during his meeting with the US President, did not say a word about the package or ask his interlocutor for anything related to it. This did not go unnoticed—the administration's activity in discussing the Freedom Support Act in Congress decreased, and the recently ambitious goal of passing the law by the time Yeltsin came to the United States disappeared from the discussion.

The main topic in all discussions and debates was the content of Russian reforms and the prospects of reaching an agreement with the IMF, where there was no good news.

At the beginning of April, the first political crisis occurred in Russia. The Congress of People's Deputies, in which the share of industrial and agrarian leaders was much larger than in the Supreme Soviet, met in Moscow.[111] They did not hide their dissatisfaction with economic policy. Under their pressure, the government agreed to loosen monetary policy significantly. The Bank of Russia loaned the government money to finance additional expenditures and generously lent it to state enterprises.

IMF experts found it increasingly difficult to assemble a set of measures that would allow the Russian economy to rebalance on paper. By the Fund's standards, this required a serious tightening of fiscal policy, but the Russian authorities were going in the opposite direction—spending and the budget deficit continued to grow, followed by rising inflation and a falling ruble. Before Yeltsin's visit to Washington in mid-June, the disagreements spilled over into the public arena. Pyotr Aven, the head of the Russian negotiators, accused the IMF of nagging on trivialities and postponing the decision to grant the loan. IMF chief Camdessus responded by stiffly stating that the

[110] Even in August 1998, when the epicenter of the Russian financial crisis was in the budget, the IMF agreed to lend exclusively to the Central Bank. Only after the strongest pressure from the Russian government was an addendum to the Board of Directors' decision adopted, allowing 20% of the funds received from the Fund to be directed to the accounts of the Ministry of Finance.

[111] Congress meetings were held twice a year and lasted several days. The law did not require deputies to give up their work.

Fund would not start lending to Russia until it was convinced that the program it had put together would be strong enough to help reform.[112] "*If we gave the Russians the funds under the terms they want, the money would disappear into a black hole in two days*," an IMF executive said.

It took the intervention of US Treasury Secretary Brady, who found a formula for compromise: "*IMF should not delay a pact because of "the crossing of each and every 't' and the dotting of each and every 'i'.*"[113] After a public statement by the White House that the administration "*very much wants an agreement to happen by July 6* [the first day of the G7 meeting in Munich], *not having one would not be fatal*,"[114] a compromise was put on paper: the IMF agreed to soften its demands on the Russian program and provide a loan, which opened the way for the rest of the bailout package, but the size of the loan was reduced to $1 billion. To receive the rest of the loan, Russia needed to strengthen its program and demonstrate its ability to implement it.

In closing the discussion by proposing to the Board an unusual design for the Fund—supporting a weakened program with a small loan—the IMF chief bluntly stated that the Russian program did not fully meet the Fund's requirements. "*It was clear that the Fund was, inevitably, operating in the domain of second- or third-best solution.*" It became clear that Russia had been given a reprieve to prepare for negotiations on a stronger program. "*The program could only be considered a damage control operation, and much more would have to be done to get to the stage at which the Board could consider a full-fledged stand-by arrangement.*"[115] On July 8, at the G7 meeting in Munich, Gaidar spoke of his intention to conclude negotiations on a full-fledged program, which the IMF could support with a $3 billion loan, by October 1.[116]

On August 3, the IMF Board of Directors supported Russia's reform program and approved the loan, conditioning its disbursement on Russia's

---

[112] Not all the IMF's demands were reasonable. For example, the Fund agreed with the position of the Bank of Russia on the desirability of maintaining the ruble zone with other CIS countries, insisting on reaching an agreement on the principles of a common monetary policy. The argument in defense of this position was understandable: it allowed for preserving the established cooperative ties between enterprises located in different countries. However, on the one hand, the breakdown of relations between enterprises continued, although the ruble zone was preserved, and, on the other hand, Ukraine blocked any negotiations on this topic without giving up the use of the post-Soviet ruble. Most reformers who worked in the government favored separating the monetary systems as soon as possible. Still, they could not convince Yeltsin of the correctness of this step.

[113] "Summit in Washington; Russians Say IMF Demands May Nullify Benefits of Loans." The New York Times. June 16, 1992.

[114] "Russia and IMF Fail at an Accord. The New York Times." June 20, 1992.

[115] IMF. Russian Federation—Report by the Managing Director. IMF Archive. EMB/92/85—8 July, 92.

[116] Russia cannot develop such a program in 1993 or 1994. It will appear in the spring of 1995.

fulfillment of several promises. The IMF money arrived in Russia in mid-November[117] and was deposited in the accounts of the Central Bank, which did nothing to alleviate the Gaidar government's budgetary problems.

In early December 1992, the Congress of People's Deputies refused to approve Gaidar as prime minister, insisting that Yeltsin present alternative candidates. In the rating vote, Gaidar came in third place, and, according to the rules, the president could appoint him as prime minister. But he did not, giving preference to Viktor Chernomyrdin. Yeltsin hoped his decision would be recognized as a compromise and would allow him to prevent political escalation.

Still Indecisive

Bush, after declaring he wanted Congress to pass the Russian reform bill before the Russian President arrived, surprised lawmakers by failing to act. With the White House silent—and with an election under way amid a frail economy—almost no one in Congress was willing to champion foreign-aid legislation.

On April 9, Secretary Baker came to defend the bill before the Senate Foreign Relations Committee. Yet, he never answered the central question—why the administration had reversed course so abruptly. Only two weeks earlier the White House had offered convincing explanations that US support should be minimal and that the Russians should do the bulk of the work themselves.

In addition, the package's cost breakdown baffled members. It included grants, loans, guarantees, previously budgeted funds, new funds, plus items that did or did not need extra appropriations, making it hard for congressmen to understand what it would cost the American budget to support Russia.

The President held several meetings with lawmakers to discuss the bill but refused to discuss it during the campaign. On June 4, the President held a nationally televised press conference and did not mention the bill introduced in Congress. Senator Joe Biden called attention to this, saying that failure to support Russian reforms could lead to the defeat of democracy in Russia. "*Right now, the aid package for the former Soviet Union is stalled, because there is little momentum in the Senate, outright opposition in the House and a tepid*

[117] Russian Federation: Transactions with the Fund, Disbursements and Repayments. Detail from January 01, 1992, to December 31, 1992. https://www.imf.org/external/np/fin/tad/extrans2.aspx?memberKey1=819&valueDate=1992&yearType=C&acctType1=GRASDA&extrans_flag=Y

effort by the President ... Without a bipartisan bill we will make it harder to secure democracy in Russia."[118]

By the time the Russian President arrived, the bill had not been brought to either chamber for debate, and its prospects were bleak:[119] money was tight, Election Day was near, and lawmakers with competing agendas found compromise ever harder.

During his visit, Bush discussed the bill several times in meetings Yeltsin, but after the Russian guest left, he again took a vow of silence on the subject.

Nevertheless, the situation had shifted by mid-July. On the one hand, the clear and emotional appeal Yeltsin made in support of the aid package in his speech to a joint session of Congress made a strong impression. Yeltsin was in good form, and his speech impressed with its sincerity. But perhaps more important was the fact that the White House agreed to an "ultimatum" issued by the speakers of both houses, who said that the Russian aid bill would not come up for a vote until the administration supported a "program of national renewal." That program included providing aid to victims of the Chicago flooding and Los Angeles riots, offering summer jobs in both cities, extending unemployment insurance, and creating 50 enterprise zones to spur urban redevelopment and employment. In early July, the White House supported the passage of related legislation, paving the way for the passage of the Freedom Support Act.

The President signed the law on October 24, 1992. Ten days remained until Election Day.

Second Summit

On March 3, Bush announced the dates for the Russian President's state visit to the United States, June 16–17. This gave both sides enough time to decide how to shape their relationship, which issues would be primary and which would be secondary, and what outcomes they hoped to achieve.

[118] "Bill to Aid Former Soviet Lands is Stuck in Capitol Hill Quagmire." The New York Times. June 5, 1992.

[119] In early June, the White House discussed the possibility of not continuing the student exchange program between Russia and the United States, agreed upon during a meeting in Malta, because the $500,000 needed to pay for the flight of Russian students is not in the budget. GB M&T. New Exchange/Internship Initiative. Letter To Ed Hewett from Larry Napper. June 5, 1992.

Domestic Calculations: Yeltsin

The problems worrying Yeltsin—and what he hoped to gain—were spelled out in a telegram from the US Ambassador to Moscow Robert Strauss,[120] which he sent to Washington a week before Yeltsin's arrival.[121]

According to the ambassador, Yeltsin's main purpose in visiting would be to be perceived as "*an established friend and ally*" and to create a basis for "*a special bilateral relationship with the United States to secure its continued place at the big table.*"

Russia stood at a historic crossroads. "*One is Russia's westernized future of effective, legitimate, democratic institutions and a market economy, with close political and economic alignment with Western Europe and the United States. The other is Russia's dismal economic and political present which is complicated by legacies from the past: the distended militarized economy and society which evolved under Stalin, the economic impact of the loss of Eastern Europe, and the wrenching process of territorial—but not yet psychological—separation from the non-Russian republics.*" Even in Yeltsin's inner circle, Strauss wrote, there are those for whom the collapse of the Soviet Union meant a dramatic weakening of the country and a growing threat to its security. Even stronger resistance to Yeltsin's rapprochement with the West came from parliament, where his foreign policy had been harshly criticized. Voting in the UN Security Council to impose sanctions on Libya and Serbia was perceived as "selling out the national interests." In this situation, "*Yeltsin is going to bring the practical results of US–Russian relationship home to the Russian people.*"

Yeltsin openly declared that Russia should join the Euro-Atlantic community. At a meeting with NATO Secretary General Wörner, Yeltsin drew North America, Europe, and Russia together through pan-European security structures. In his cable, Ambassador quoted Kozyrev: "*We must join the club of states which are developing most dynamically, in order to occupy among them the worthy place preordained for us by history and geography.*"

And here came the main question that Strauss believed the West needed to answer as soon as possible. "*How much demilitarization, democratization, defense conversion, and evolution to a market economy must Russia undertake*

[120] GBPL&M. Yeltsin's World. Cable to Hill, Howe, Scowcroft, et al. From Ambassador Strauss.

[121] Robert Strauss was not a career diplomat and did not speak Russian, which was perceived by many as a serious problem. Bush chose him because of several factors. First, they had a very good personal relationship, and Bush had complete confidence in Strauss. Second, Strauss was an experienced negotiator, which was important given the large negotiating agenda with the Soviet Union. Third, Strauss supported the Democratic Party and had been Jimmy Carter's in his victorious 1976 campaign. This ensured that the ambassador's confirmation in the Senate was trouble-free.

before it is welcome as a full partner in Western councils? ... the longer process of Russia's rejoining the European world it abandoned in November 1917 will further complicate the current Atlantic institutional crisis."

The ambassador had no illusions; the Russians "*have the potential to be very difficult partners*"; and future dealings might resemble Washington's prickly ties with France. For Yeltsin, France's special status within NATO was a possible scenario for building future relations. The ambassador quoted the Russian President responding to a question about his attitude toward NATO: "*I believe that we need to go first of all for a political alliance as France did. Russia was with Europe from time immemorial and we need to integrate ourselves into European institutions—the Council of Europe, the EC and we need to enter into political and economic alliances.*"

According to Strauss, the outcome of the upcoming summit would be strategically important in determining the nature of international relations in the coming years. "*Whether Russia is in or out of various institutions, its size and its exigent concepts of co-equal treatment will generate different types of stresses.*"

The telegram ended with a sober assessment of the situation: Yeltsin was not ideal,[122] but it was impossible to find a "better" leader in Russia. The Russian President was no longer an idealist; he felt the West was not ready to perceive Russia as an equal partner. "*Yeltsin, a former backwoods politician, doubts his ability to be accepted as an equal. We should accept him on the sober calculation that Yeltsin is as good a Russian leader as we can get.*"

"Russia and America are becoming friends," Yeltsin declared as he stepped down the ramp at Andrews Air Force Base on June 16, 1992.

Homebrewing: Bush

Bush was unwilling to recast relations with Russia. With the presidential campaign looming, domestic issues dominated his thinking. The election campaign was not going well: the President seemed low on energy and decisiveness, and the absence of an experienced campaign manager left the operation unfocused. Samuel Skinner, who came to this post in December, enjoyed the full confidence of the President, but he lacked experience and competence in his

[122] A day earlier, Ambassador Strauss sent another telegram to Washington, where he analyzed the key figures in the Russian President's entourage, their views, aspirations, and mutual relations. He said that Yeltsin is consciously creating tension between different groups, and gradually the balance of power is shifting toward "Soviet apparatchiks" with "socialist" views, naively believing that their bureaucratic experience can be of benefit. GBPL&M. Power and Palace Politics in Renewed. Cable to Hill, Howe, Scowcroft, et al. From Ambassador Strauss. June 8, 1992.

new position.[123] However, he largely shaped the campaign's message, which left little room for foreign policy. The economy was coming out of recession, but the budget's capacity to finance new spending remained constrained; the budget deficit continued to grow.

To make a radical turn in foreign policy in such a situation and announcing that a recent military adversary had suddenly become a friend and ally seemed politically untenable. On the other hand, it was also impossible to alienate Russia and its President, who claimed to be a follower of democratic values. Besides, everyone remembered that four months earlier Yeltsin had proposed a radical reduction in offensive arms, which promised a "peace dividend," a reduction in military spending, and relief from budgetary strains.

Baker tried to solve the puzzle by briefing the President on his concept for the summit.[124] The main thesis was simple: unconditional support for strategic arms reductions, a show of support for the Russian President, and a strengthened personal relationship with him. At the same time, it carefully showed that there are unresolved issues between the countries and that Russia still has a lot of work to do to earn the status of a democratic country.

Russian democracy, according to Baker, was fragile and unsustainable. The gains made are limited. The conservatives in Yeltsin's entourage were hampering the process of internal transformation, and their consolidation because of the compromise reached at the Congress of People's Deputies in April raised doubts about Russia's commitment to democratic values. This should have confirmed the President's conviction that such a country could not claim a place "at the big table" and could not claim the status of a friend and ally. Moreover, the memorandum explicitly proposed to enshrine the position that any American assistance to Russia would be contingent on progress in building democracy.

The toughest task for the President would be crafting a response to Yeltsin's plea for financial aid. The White House believed the Kremlin misunderstood the $24 billion package, assuming the $18 billion earmarked for balance-of-payments support could be spent at its own discretion.[125] The position offered to the President was very clear: the fate of the aid package was in the hands of the IMF. The aid package would begin to materialize as soon as Russia could

[123] In August, the President will nominate James Baker to replace him as chief of staff.

[124] GBPL&M. Your Meetings with Yeltsin. Memorandum For the President, from James Baker. June 11, 1992.

[125] This view was so ingrained in the minds of Russian politicians, including Yeltsin, that Ambassador Strauss was required to meet with the Russian President and explain the contents of the aid package to him. GBPL&M. G7 Financial Assistance—Clarifying Its Nature and Conditions with the Russian Government. Cable to Embassy in Moscow from R. Zoellick. May 20, 1992.

agree with the Fund on a program that it would support with its loan. "*We must walk a careful line between assuring Yeltsin of our support, while underscoring the critical need to work with the IMF.*"

Since the summit schedule provided plenty of time for negotiations, including face-to-face talks, the Secretary of State compiled a comprehensive list of grievances to present to the Russian President:

- Support the US position on the participation of NATO forces in the OSCE peacekeeping mission in Yugoslavia;
- Finalize negotiations with Ukraine on the status of Crimea and the Black Sea Fleet;
- Explain that Russia should publicly and openly declare its respect for its neighbors' territorial integrity and sovereignty. Change its position on Abkhazia, whose support reduces Georgian President Shevardnadze's ability to mitigate the situation;
- Clarify the Russian position on the conflict in Nagorno-Karabakh and joining efforts with the OSCE to find a solution;
- Withdrawal of Russian troops from the territory of the Baltic States as quickly as possible. "*Russia is concerned, with some very good reason, about discrimination against ethnic Russians in the Baltics... We need to impress upon Yeltsin the necessity of concluding negotiations with the Balts ... while assuring Yeltsin that we will urge them to ensure equal rights for ethnic Russians";*
- Get out of the standoff with Japan over the "Northern Territories," which is the biggest obstacle to economic aid from Japan;
- Provide relatives of those who died on board KAL007 with all documents regarding the incident;
- Lubavitch Library.[126]

[126] The Lubavitch Library (Chabad Library) is a Jewish study center in Brooklyn, New York. The library is named after the village of Lubavitch, located in the Smolensk region. Since the eighteenth century, the Rebbes who lived there began collecting books, and by the outbreak of World War I, the library had become one of the largest collections of Jewish religious books and manuscripts. With the outbreak of the war, Rebbe Schneerson (the alternative name of the collection, the Schneerson Library, is associated with his name) moved the collection to Moscow, where it was nationalized in November 1918. Shneerson's heirs, who left for Europe, continued to collect the library, which was taken to Germany during World War II, and at the end of the war part of it was captured by the Soviet army as a trophy. In early 1990, Schneerson's heir initiated legal action in the Soviet Union, demanding the return of personal property. However, the Russian Supreme Arbitration Court made a compromise in November 1991 to transfer the collection to the specially created Jewish National Library, but the management of the Lenin Library, where the collection was kept, refused to comply.

There were a lot of problems, and until we resolve them all. In short, this visit was not meant to be historic. In James Baker's opinion *"this visit will be important in the run-up to the Munich Economic Summit, July 6–8."*

In his recommendations to the President, Scowcroft was more pragmatic.[127] He agreed with Ambassador Strauss's position on the goals that the Russian President would pursue during his visit: to bring evidence to Russia that cooperation with America was yielding tangible benefits for Russia, with an emphasis on gaining access to the promised $24 billion. He also offered his own version of the answer to the question, "*What can we offer at the Summit?*"

Scowcroft's top priority was to accord Yeltsin the fullest honors and respect. According to many NSC officials, Yeltsin was bound to compare the way he was received with the way Gorbachev had been received. "*The symbolism of a state visit is of great importance to Yeltsin because it conveys the respect he craves.*" In that regard, the trip to Annapolis and a boat ride put on the visit's schedule, which only the most important guests were honored with, would have to make the right impression on the Russian guest. In addition, at the end of the visit, the "Washington Charter" would be signed, drawing an analogy with the "Atlantic Charter" signed by Roosevelt and Churchill in August 1941, laying down eight principles for the postwar world order.

In addition, recent White House decisions that had removed some barriers to high-tech cooperation would need to be remembered.[128]

But regarding financial aid, Scowcroft wrote, "*we would have to be tough,*" and recalled the President's June 9 meeting with Baker and Brady, at which it had been decided not to interfere in the negotiations between Russia and the IMF.

All Honors Were Paid

The summit brought no surprises. The agreement on radical strategic nuclear arms reductions announced by the Presidents shortly after the Russian President's arrival unsurprisingly took center stage: Russia and the United States agreed to reduce the total number of warheads by a factor of three, from 22500 to 3000–3500 for each side (the future START-2 treaty). Russia finally

[127] GBPL&M. Overview for your Upcoming Meetings with Yeltsin, June 16–17. Memorandum for President, from Brent Scowcroft. June 13, 1992.

[128] On March 27, the United States announced decisions aimed at creating opportunities for technological cooperation between the two countries. In particular, the Department of Defense received permission to purchase Russian rocket engines, permission was granted to purchase uranium-238 from Russia, the requirement for licenses for private Russian companies to purchase civilian products was eliminated, and two-thirds of the COCOM restrictions were lifted.

agreed to a sharp reduction in its land-based missiles, which the US negotiators insisted on, expecting that this would speed up the receipt of the promised financial aid. Yeltsin called the agreement tangible evidence of "partnership and friendship" between the two countries and added, "*We know one thing. We will not go to war with each other.*"

The second highlight was the Russian President's speech to a joint session of Congress. The Russian President's emotional and sincere speech—interrupted by applause 13 times—changed the attitude of many members of Congress toward Russia and Bush's Russia aid bill. Before arriving in Washington, Yeltsin sent a letter to Congress detailing the results of a study of Soviet archives on American military personnel imprisoned in Soviet prisons during World War II, the Korean War, and the Vietnam War. The Russian President frankly said that it had not yet been possible to determine the fate of all POWs but promised to see it through. "*There will be no more lies. Never*!"[129]

But Yeltsin could not secure the main objective—recognition of the new status of Russian–American relations and the promised financial assistance. The "Charter of US–Russian Partnership and Friendship" signed by the Presidents stated at the outset the fundamental differences between the countries—"*The United States of America fully supports the Russian Federation's efforts to build a democratic state and society founded on the rule of law and respect for fundamental human rights.*" The words "partnership" and "friendship" in the title were not reflected in the body of the document, which was limited to the intention to expand contacts, consultations, and regular meetings between the two countries' leaders.

Every time Yeltsin asked about the promised billions, he was curtly told, "Take it up with the IMF." In turn, the IMF management, with whom Gaidar was negotiating at the time, sent optimistic signals that an agreement was about to be reached, but soon after the departure of the Russian delegation, the messages from the Fund shifted—the information received about the state of the Russian budget forced a rethink of the situation.

However, Bush and his team had another motive to minimize the discussion of financial aid to Russia: by this time, it was well understood that Yeltsin would receive no billions from the United States. "*The US contribution [to the $24 billion package] in cash is substantial but not all that substantial; it's in*

[129] However, he added later at a press conference that even the President of a country cannot always know the truth, as in the case of the Korean Boeing. The KGB archives are well buried, and the work to find the documents continues.

hundreds of millions, not in billions, Bush said frankly."[130] Reducing political-military tensions with an ideological adversary had allowed America to reap a $50 billion "peace dividend" in 1992 by cutting military spending. However, the country had domestic problems that also required money to solve. *"Our Government is operating at an enormous, enormous deficit. And therefore, those who say take the money … and spend it on some Federal project have to understand that the American people want to get something done about this deficit and want to get something done so that we can get this economy growing."*[131]

Everything went according to plan: Yeltsin received maximum ceremony, but Russia's status remained unchanged; any partnership—or alliance—would have to await Moscow's transition to a stable democracy with a functioning market economy. Mistrust of Russia, accumulated over the years of the Cold War, was difficult to dispel in a few months. The new country was perceived as a defeated enemy that needed time to recover.

Shortly before Yeltsin's arrival in Washington, Russia supported the imposition of sanctions on Yugoslavia in the UN Security Council. During the negotiations, sought the Russian President's agreement to NATO troop participation in the OSCE peacekeeping mission, while Yeltsin suggested looking for "softer" options to influence the Milosevic regime since the introduction of NATO troops into Serbia would definitely cause a surge of anti-American sentiment among the Russian military and nationalist politicians. No agreement was reached, with the US President saying he did not need Russia's help and saw no place for it in resolving the conflict. "*I do not believe the Soviets have any special role anymore… I think the role for them is in the United Nations… I don't see them having a special assignment, although in fairness, he [Yeltsin] did say that they would like to be helpful. But I don't think their history gives them … the special leverage that we might think just looking back a year or two.*"[132]

The Pentagon did not abandon previously planned exercises that played out military operations against a Soviet Union that no longer existed, but which kept the Russian military on edge and Russian politicians puzzled.

---

[130] Remarks and a Question-and-Answer Session with Industrial League of Orange County in Irvine, California. June 19, 1992. Public Papers of the Presidents of the United States. George Bush, 1992–1993, Book 1.

[131] The President's News Conference with President Yeltsin of Russia. June 17, 1992. Public Papers of the Presidents of the United States. George Bush, 1992–1993, Book 1.

[132] Remarks and a Question-and-Answer Session with Industrial League of Orange County in Irvine, California. June 19, 1992. Public Papers of the Presidents of the United States. George Bush, 1992–1993, Book 1.

> In January of this [1992] year, a Japanese-American command and staff exercise of ground forces "Yamasakura-21" was held on the island of Hokkaido ... organization of joint combat operations on the island of Hokkaido and the adjacent Kuril Islands ... actions to blockade the bases of Russian Pacific Fleet ships, search and destroy our submarines and surface ships deployed at sea, actions to blockade the strait zones to prevent deployment from the Pacific Fleet bases, landing actions to seize the islands. Special attention in all exercises is paid to the search and destruction of our strategic submarines... 4–5 American anti-submarine submarines are constantly stationed in the vicinity of our nuclear submarine bases in Kamchatka and Primorye, as well as in their patrol areas, and anti-submarine ships and aircraft of the US and Japanese navies are systematically searching for our boats.[133]

Intelligence-sharing faltered when the CIA gained the information it wanted yet failed to deliver its promised returns to the Russian side. "*I was under a lot of pressure from State, Baker and company, to build a more constructive relationship with the KGB or the SVRR (Foreign Intelligence Service of the Russian Federation)... I said, Alright, we would cooperate on proliferation of weapons of mass destruction and the Russians will make the first presentation and I want it to be on North Korean weapons of mass destruction. The Russians came back and said, No, you start, and we'll talk about Pakistan. And our guys said, Let's go ahead and do that. I said, Bullshit, we're going to talk about North Korea. And we went back and forth for probably four months and our guys kept wanting me to give in, and I wouldn't. Because I thought it was a matter of principle. I mean, we'd run the whole SALT negotiations on US intelligence data because we wouldn't force the Soviets to spring their own data, so I was determined. And, as it turned out, they made a presentation on North Korea... It was not very good on nuclear and I was persuaded they didn't know much about the nuclear, but we got a fair amount of information from them on North Korean chemical and biological programs, and then we didn't brief on Pakistan.*"[134]

Trade Is Better than Aid

In his talks with Soviet and Russian leaders, Bush constantly spoke of promoting economic ties between the two countries and eagerly discussed various

[133] Wilson Center. Conclusion of the Chief Staff of the Navy on Russian-Japanese relations and the problem of territorial separation between Russia and Japan. July 21, 1992.

[134] Miller Center. George H. W. Bush Presidency. Robert Gates Oral History.

investment ideas that his interlocutors proposed.[135] However, the President realized that he could agree on one or two major projects but could not consider dozens or hundreds. For US capital to flow to another country, the President had to establish a basic foundation of bilateral treaties to fix the "rules of the game." This work began during the Soviet era but progress was uneven.

The basic trade agreement between the USSR and the US was signed in June 1990, but Gorbachev was hesitant to submit it for ratification because the US did not commit itself to repealing the Jackson-Vanik amendment, promising to extend the most-favored-nation treatment for the Soviet Union every year, which was perceived as a diplomatic defeat. In America, both before and after the signing of the agreement, there was a powerful lobby against granting trade preferences to the Soviet Union under the pretext of restrictions on emigration, occupation of the Baltic States, human rights violations, etc. As a result, the Senate ratified it only in early December 1991, when the Soviet Union ceased to exist. After the collapse of the USSR, the US offered all post-Soviet republics the freedom to leave the document in force with minimal technical changes, which pleased the Russian parliament, which ratified it. On June 17, during Yeltsin's stay in the United States, Bush signed a 1-year Jackson-Vanik waiver giving Russia, de facto, a most-favored-nation status in bilateral trade.

An agreement on avoidance of double taxation was also prepared and signed with the Soviet Union, but it required more substantial revision, as the tax system in Russia had undergone significant changes. This document was also prepared and signed during the visit.

The hasty preparation of the Agreement on Mutual Protection of Investments did not provoke opposition in Russia, although the Soviet Union had no such experience. The fact that without the inflow of foreign direct investment, the Russian economy had no chance to modernize and become sustainable was realized by everyone; it was a dream that possessed the Russian President as well. "*Those will be direct investments from private companies … and that will be a matter of hundreds of billions of dollars. And that will be very important aid… It will support our private sector, which is what we want.*"[136]

---

[135] On July 30, 1991, Bush passionately discussed the Chevron project in Kazakhstan with Gorbachev and Nursultan Nazarbayev and, separately, in conversation with the Soviet President, discussed the Trans-Siberian fiber-optic cable project. GB M&T. Memorandum of Conversation. Luncheon with President Mikhail Gorbachev of the USSR. July 30, 1991; Memorandum of Conversation. Expanded Bilateral Meeting with Mikhail Gorbachev of the USSR. July 30, 1991.

[136] The President's News Conference with President Yeltsin of Russia. June 17, 1992. Public Papers of the Presidents of the United States. George Bush, 1992–1993, Book 1.

The agreements did not immediately affect Russia but were necessary "work for the future." However, Bush did not promise to repeal Jackson-Vanik, citing the difficult situation in Congress before the elections, and Yeltsin did not insist on it, not wanting to put his guest in an uncomfortable position. The symbols of the Cold War remained in place.

Munich

To Be or Not to Be?

Should we invite or not invite the Russian President to the next G7 meeting in Munich? If invited, then in what capacity, as a full participant or distinguished guest? This question had weighed on Kohl's mind since the start of the year; Germany was the presiding country, and he was to announce and explain to Yeltsin the decision that was to be made.

The Chancellor understood Bush would have the deciding vote in this case, but the American President was the first to raise the subject during the March 21 meeting when it came to the G7 meeting. "*Yeltsin asked me to discuss this with you. Can we do something like we did with Gorbachev*?" Helmut Kohl said he had no clear position, citing uncertainty about the future of the CIS as the main obstacle. What to do if the CIS falls apart? Invite Yeltsin and not invite Kravchuk and Nazarbayev? And in what format should he be invited?

By this time, Bush had no doubts that Yeltsin should be invited to Munich; the agreement on the format of his participation remained. In any case, the Russian President's status at the "big table" should not be lower than that of Gorbachev at the previous meeting. "*Yeltsin is very sensitive to comparisons to Gorbachev. I'm not arguing this one way or another. We may want to have him come afterwards as Gorbachev did. He may want to be there for the whole time.* "The Chancellor did not like the second option, suggesting that, in this case, the meeting would turn into an endless request for money for Russia.

"But George, he is going to ask you for money... He already has... But at Munich his request will be much more dramatic." Such a picture of the future did not appeal to Bush either, who said wistfully: "*I'm not sure what we will do if he comes with a huge demand.*"[137] Realizing that journalists would torment them at the end of the talks with questions about Yeltsin's arrival or non-arrival in Munich, the President and the Chancellor agreed on an evasive

[137] GB M&T. Memorandum of Conversation. Telcon with Helmut Kohl, Chancellor of Germany. March 21, 1992.

form—the Russian President would come to Munich in any case, but in preparation for the summit, the G7 participants would consult with the other CIS members.

The idea of inviting Russia as a full participant in the G7 did not arouse enthusiasm. Baker, who participated in the talks, suggested putting Russia "on the spot": "*It's important to begin to develop criteria as a host between Russia and everyone else. Maybe you could say that as Russia joins the IMF, the size of its economy is the basis for their inclusion?*" Bush suggested: "*Perhaps that would make it possible to turn the G7 into the G8 of major economies?*" The Chancellor wasn't sure about this approach: "*We don't even know what's left of their economy.*" Scowcroft supported him, "*That might include the Chinese.*" The US President kept looking for a formula: "*Maybe then it should be the eight largest democracies.*" But who would dare to call today's Russia a fully democratic country? The discussion stopped there.

A few days before the Munich meeting, Bush announced that the G7 was ready to discuss becoming a G8, with Russia being the obvious eighth candidate: "*Their size gives them a unique standing.*" And suddenly, unexpectedly, when asked directly if the President supported the idea of Russia becoming a permanent member of the G7, Bush replied, "*That's right.*"[138][139]

The discussion of Russia's status continued during the G7 meetings, but there was little disagreement by then. Russia was not a market economy and "*still has a long way to go,*" Bush said. A middle class of owners must be created, private ownership of land must be introduced, monopolies must be broken up, and the ruble must be turned into a hard currency—this was the brief set of preconditions he outlined. Kohl was even more categorical, the question of Russia's participation in the club should not be discussed. "*I wouldn't discuss a G8 or G7+1… You can't do that with an economy that's not a market economy.*" British Prime Minister John Major supported his partners: … "*What's really been done? There has been no real privatization. Laws and decrees are not carried out.*"[140]

French President Mitterrand frankly expressed his position to the US President during their meeting on the eve of the Munich summit and decided to abstain this time. In his opinion, the essence of Russia as a state had not

---

[138] The President's News Conference with Foreign Journalists. July 2, 1992. https://www.presidency.ucsb.edu/documents/the-presidents-news-conference-with-foreign-journalists

[139] In a press conference after the summit, Bush said that he was taken too literally to mean that the issue has a valid point, drawing a line between Russia and members of the "big club." "*We have big differences in the world economies. And perhaps the conclusion will be drawn that seven plus one is the answer; after all, that makes eight.*"

[140] GB M&T. Memorandum of Conversation. Private Plenary Session. 1992 Munich Economic Summit. July 7, 1992.

changed, and the threat level from its side had decreased. Still, there was no reason to believe that there had been radical political changes in Europe and that it was time to reconsider the role of NATO, turning the organization into a political one. "*Since the collapse of the Soviet Union, I haven't understood the reasons why you're trying to give NATO a new content. At the time that the threat of war is receding, it seems you want NATO's mission to expand ...Do you want a political role?...Look at the heads in the former Soviet Union, they are all apparatchiks. They save their skin by becoming super nationalists. They're not the ones to give us lessons on loyalty to the alliance... Russia has been rolled back from its achievements over three centuries.*"[141]

"*He is not a full-fledged participant... We could give him standing without putting him in the middle of the rest of our work. We could make him welcome, but not as a full member,*" was Bush's formula that satisfied everyone.

There's Still no Money

The participants in the Munich meeting were in a difficult position. On the one hand, everyone understood that Russia needed support, and such support had been promised. On the other hand, no one had spare funds, so every government tried to pass the costs to its partners.

"*What are your expectations from Russia's participation in the Munich meeting? What does it want?*"—asked the head of the Kohl's Chancellery. Eagleburger replied—"*Money!* "He quickly added, "*It is time to clarify that our aid has limits. First, we can't take money away from Central and Eastern Europe, which have a better chance of success. Second, the administration will have enormous difficulties in dealing with Congress if it tries to ask for foreign aid money. The administration,*" Eagleburger added, "*will never say this publicly,*" but he wants his partners to understand it clearly.[142]

In a meeting with Italian Prime Minister Amato, Kohl said he was against inviting Russia as a full participant in the summit and that all aid to Russia should be based on the principle of "help for self-help. "The Chancellor then turned to the topic of the potential threat from nuclear power plants built in the Soviet Union and talked about the need for a special fund to modernize them, adding, "*In terms of the German contribution, I have to say that I have reached the financial limit to our capacity of assistance.*" When Amato reminded

---

[141] GB M&T. Memorandum of Conversation. Meeting between POTUS and President Mitterrand. July 5, 1992.

[142] Wilson Center. Meeting between ChefBK Bohl and US Deputy Secretary of State Lawrence Eagleburger on June 2, 1992.

him that all aid programs to Russia are short-term loans aimed at overcoming temporary difficulties, Kohl said that Russia could do it independently. He even claimed that pipeline losses ran as high as 40% and fixing them alone would fund Russia's needs.[143] Where the Chancellor got this figure from remains a mystery.

The G7 leaders met in Munich and reaffirmed their positions around a common table. Bush embellished his policy by declaring, "*We've [the US] pledged over $7 billion in aid to the FSU.*"[144] Italian PM Amato, remembering that Germany was not ready to give money, decided that Italy shouldn't do it either and said that $1 billion from the IMF and a 2- or 5-year deferral of foreign debt service would suffice. Japanese Prime Minister Miyazawa noted Japan had already pledged $2.6 billion, plus $20 million for nuclear-science centers and $25 million for atomic-site security. Miyazawa told all partners before the Munich meeting that his country would not give Russia any other money until a solution to the "Northern Territories" problem satisfactory to Japan was found, and he would repeat the warning. Jacques Delors, President of the Commission of the European Community, supported the need to restructure the foreign debt and complained that the approved $2 billion technical-assistance programs could not be absorbed by the Commission because there was no unified structure in Russia to help. Prime Minister Major limited himself to a set of recommendations to the Russian government, briefly restating IMF requirements for fiscal and monetary policy. Canadian Prime Minister Mulroney said that his country had already spent $2.5 billion and urged his colleagues to follow Canada's example: "*Yeltsin could get $60 billion if everyone did the same per capita as we,*" adding, however, that Germany had spent more.

The panelists agreed. Yeltsin had almost no chance of making headway.

During the discussion, Canadian Prime Minister Mulroney tried to explain to his interlocutors that the Marshall Plan was a much larger aid program—"*We think we're doing a lot, but just compare.*" His appeal, however, inspired no one. Only Kohl concluded his talk by sharing his memories of postwar Germany, saying that the Marshall Plan had stopped the impoverishment of Europe, calling for it to be remembered with gratitude and dreamily saying—"*This is also a model for us now.*"

---

[143] Wilson Center. The Chancellor's Meeting with Italian Prime Minister Amato at the Four Seasons Hotel in Munich, July 5, 1992.

[144] On the morning of this day, US Deputy Secretary of State Robert Zoellick announced an even more significant sum, $7.5 billion, during Bush's meeting with European Commission President Delors. In all previous official statements, the US aid package to Russia was estimated at $4.35 billion.

Surprisingly, in none of the discussions about aid to Russia did the leaders of the leading countries try to recall what the Marshall Plan was and how it was implemented, much less that postwar European aid had been given as outright grants.

To Signal Optimism

The meeting of the leaders of the G7 member states with the Russian President[145] began with speeches by Kohl, Mulroney, and Major, who summarized the results of preliminary discussions, made their assessments, asked their questions, and made their demands to Russia.

As the host, the German Chancellor said that all those gathered were following the situation in Russia and wanted to support the reform process. "*Our idea is a comprehensive partnership,*" Kohl said, outlining ten topics to be discussed. None of these topics came up again during the discussion.

After saying that everyone wished Yeltsin success, the Canadian Prime Minister explained that the seven countries around the table were united by the freedom and democracy that Russia had yet to build. However, he continued, everyone was concerned about Russia's relations with its neighbors: ambiguity in relations with Ukraine over Crimea, the continued presence of Russian troops in the three Baltic states, the problem of "Northern Territories" in relations with Japan, the situation in Moldova, and Russia's position on Yugoslavia.

Prime Minister Major, while paying tribute to the efforts of the Russian government and recognizing the enormity of the challenges they face, listed a set of reforms that were to be implemented, said that cooperation with the IMF was essential, and the forthcoming $1 billion loan was only a first step. "*We have an interest in your success. We want work as partners.*"

Yeltsin, at the "big table" for the first time, sounded unexpectedly timid and unfocused. He went from summarizing the Cold War to the unsettled relationship with Japan, from a strategic view of the logic of reform to minor details, from foreign debt to nuclear security issues. It was hard to discern his main themes—or what he hoped to gain from the meeting.

After the correct thesis—"*The Cold War has ended. We're in transition towards partnership… We need radically new approaches in our relations*"—he offered no follow-up to explain his vision for relations with the West.

[145] GBPL&M. Memorandum of Conversation. Heads of Delegations Meeting with President Yeltsin at the 1992 Munich Economic Summit. July 8, 1992.

"We have about $70.7 billion in external debt. Frankly, we can't pay … We won't follow Bolsheviks of 1917 and renounce our debt. We will pay … I look to you for your support a realistic rescheduling time frame,"—but neither the Russian President himself nor Gaidar, sitting next to him, outlined the terms they sought for debt restructuring.

"You're closed to us [for export from Russia]. This costs us more than the assistance we get… Barriers exist. We need more export possibilities,"—but exactly what the barriers were and what Russian goods cannot reach European and American markets remained unknown.

Gaidar promised to negotiate a full-scale loan with the IMF by the end of September, which looked more than optimistic, given that a program based on which the IMF might provide a $1 billion interim loan had yet to be agreed upon. Yeltsin unexpectedly proposed to convert foreign debt into property, but what this might look like and why Russian assets should interest state leaders remained a mystery.

As the chaotic session wound down, host Helmut Kohl struggled to craft a communiqué for the press, "*Hard work has been done here … Your success will be our success … The most important thing is to signal optimism, confidence, and hope.*"

History Will Not Praise the United States

Russia Must Be Remembered

Upon returning home from Munich, Bush and his administration were bombarded with alarming news: Ross Perot's withdrawal from the presidential campaign (which turned out to be temporary) resulted in a sharp rise in Clinton's approval rating. The Arkansas governor's lead in mid-July exceeded 20 percentage points, casting doubt on the incumbent's ability to stay on for a second term. Although indicators showed the economy had exited recession, voters felt no such improvement. Inflation and the budget deficit were falling faster than mortgage rates. Unemployment (which is a lagging indicator) peaked in mid-summer 1992. It was difficult for the Bush team to counter criticism from a rival—no one believed in promises of a "bright future."

Foreign policy faded from view: post-Cold-War euphoria rekindled isolationist sentiment in the United States. It was extremely hard to persuade struggling voters that sending taxpayers' money abroad was necessary. Especially since this state, Russia, could not boast of much success in its reforms, and the power struggle between the President and the parliament that had begun forced serious consideration of scenarios for changing Yeltsin's political course.

With the campaign absorbing him, the President could not be pushed to tackle Russia's problems or unlock stalled aid. To keep the Russia file from disappearing, the White House convened a working group of senior officials from State, Defense, the Joint Chiefs, and the intelligence community, which was to determine the conceptual directions of policy toward the post-Soviet countries. For the first meeting of this group, held on September 15, Ed Hewett prepared a document whose title alone revealed the confusion and uncertainty inside the administration—"A Strategy for US–Russia Relations in the Coming Months."[146]

Indeed, the memorandum did not speak of any strategy, the horizon of proposals did not go beyond the end of the current year, and the main factor of uncertainty was the next Congress of People's Deputies, which, despite Yeltsin's objections, was to meet in Moscow in early December. The pressure from political opponents on the Russian President was increasing, which was in no small part due to the lack of obvious reform successes for the population. The memorandum said the crisis in the Russian economy was a consequence of accumulated problems and indecision in initiating reforms, but it was impossible to "sell this to the electorate." "*Economic crisis seems to many to be a western import, reflecting IMF-imposed austerity which government has apparently been forced to accept in order to attract Western assistance. Moreover, that assistance still seems more of a promise than a reality.*"

As usual, three scenarios for Russia's political course were put forward for consideration: Yeltsin would show intransigence and continue reforms, Yeltsin would make compromises, and the speed of reforms would slow down considerably, Yeltsin (in one way or another) would be removed from power—of which the second one was considered the most probable.[147] On that basis, a set of proposals for the administration was built, which were rather symbolic in nature and did not require Bush's involvement.

[146] GBPL&M. Memorandum for Policy Group. A Strategy for US-Russia Relations in the Coming Months. (From Ed Hewett). September 1, 1992.

[147] The idea of Yeltsin's unstable political position had been discussed at the expert level since Russia's emergence as an independent state. The unusual way in which power was seized because of the collapse of the state raised questions about how powerful and monolithic the coalition of forces on was which Yeltsin relied. The almost immediate contradictions between yesterday's allies only increased suspicions. See, for example, "Russia Over the Next Four Years: The Prospects for Democratization and Marketization," NIE 11/1-92; "Russia's Relations with the West: Will Cooperation Continue?" NIE 11/1-9/92.

Although Western aid to Russia was modest, the US could not increase it. The only hope was Japan, but this would have required "pushing Russia–Japan rapprochement." One could try to ask the IMF to be less stringent, but this should not compromise the Fund and its policies. It was necessary to use the available opportunities to expand technical and humanitarian assistance, including pressure on the European Community.

Although the memorandum said there was a good chance that the first scenario would be realized, no proposals could provide the Russian government with additional arguments in the dialog with its opponents. Instead, it was suggested that "lines of communication with conservative forces" be established to convey two ideas. First, the US supported and would continue to support reforms, believing they were heading in the right direction. Second, any attempt to restore "order" by increasing centralized control "would inevitably worsen relations with the United States."

In short, this was no moment to urge the President to step up support for Russia. Of course, the most important thing was to keep a close eye on what was happening and not miss a possible change.

The Law Passed, but ...

On October 24, Bush signed the "Freedom Support Act," which had been approved by both houses of Congress three weeks earlier.

Recall that this bill was introduced to the Senate in early April and was presented as a key element of large-scale US assistance to post-Soviet states. Nevertheless, because a lack of sponsors and weak administration support stalled the legislative process until two weeks before Yeltsin's visit to Washington. De facto, most of the programs included in the bill did not require congressional approval.[148] Many technical-assistance projects were already under way under existing authority in the 1961 Foreign Assistance Act. Many Cold War-era statutory restrictions could not be rescinded by presidential action.

[148] The largest expenditure item in the Act was the agreement to participate in the IMF's capital increase, which was decided by the Fund's shareholders in 1990. To fulfill this decision, the United States was required to allocate 12 billion, which became one of the law's most controversial aspects. These resources were not intended to support Russia but to allow the Fund to overcome a shortage of funds to implement support programs worldwide. However, the administration failed to explain this clearly to congressmen and public opinion. Similarly, they failed to explain that participation in the IMF capital does not increase the budget deficit but is, in fact, a line of credit that the Fund can use periodically. It was the difficulty in explaining the mechanism that caused the increase in IMF participation in the IMF capital to be included in the bill on support for Russia—the administration understood the passage of a separate law would be extremely problematic.

The White House intended the Act to be a tool for rallying Congress and public opinion behind a foreign policy program requiring higher foreign-aid outlays—an idea many voters opposed in a time of economic hardship. Aware of the administration's goals, members of Congress made it clear that support for the legislation would come only if the President personally lobbied for it. However, in the months after the bill was introduced, Bush was reluctant to make the issue a significant element of his campaign. Only in mid-June, on the eve of Yeltsin's visit to Washington, when the legislation was in danger of being derailed, did the President say he would do "*whatever it takes*" to persuade Congress to make a "*tough decision*" on the issue. But even after that, and after the Russian President's emotional speech to Congress, which managed to convince many that supporting Russia was the right thing to do, there was no progress on the legislation. The President remained on the sidelines. Only after Baker became the bill's chief lobbyist did the bill begin moving toward passage, but along the way, it was criticized, tweaked, and amended in ways that did not affect the scope of Russia's assistance but complicated the mechanisms for its implementation.

As a result, when the law approved by Congress reached the President's desk in early October, it turned out that there were numerous objections from White House lawyers who argued that certain provisions of the law violated the American Constitution. For three long weeks, the White House debated this issue. On the one hand, the lawyers' claims were valid. On the other, a presidential veto would undermine the administration's efforts, damage Bush's international image, and cast doubt on the law's fate.

In the end, a compromise decision was made: to sign the law and issue interpretive reservations. Speaking at the signing of the law, Bush stated that some provisions of the law would be interpreted as advisory, and some would be discussed within the administration as to whether they were consistent with established practices and/or limited the President's oversight authority, and presidential decisions would revise some provisions of the law.[149]

The White House's position met no resistance—the US political elite were preparing for a new president, and, as they say, a new broom sweeps in a new way.

The Bush administration and experts' fears about the confusing and bureaucratic difficulties of implementing the law were later fully justified. Non-credit aid programs for the former USSR used barely two-thirds of their

[149] Statement on Signing the FREEDOM Support Act. October 24, 1992. https://www.presidency.ucsb.edu/documents/statement-signing-the-freedom-support-act

$486 million allocation, while credit-and-insurance subsidies reached only $228 million.[150]

What Can We Do?

On November 3, 1992, Bush lost the election, and his administration began the transition. Traditionally, no major decisions are made during a transition unless there are exceptional circumstances. For Bush, such an exception was the completion of negotiations with Yeltsin on a radical reduction of strategic offensive arms. The goal was achieved, and the START II treaty was signed on January 3. However, for all its importance in international politics, it did not alter the nature of US–Russian relations. Instead, the treaty was the end of a long process, the initial impetus for which was given by the meeting between Gorbachev and Reagan in Reykjavik in October 1986. Many American politicians continued to view Russia as a potential adversary and tried to maximize asymmetrical concessions from Russia. Often, the Russian leadership agreed to such steps in the expectation that this would expedite the receipt of the desired financial assistance.

However, it was impossible to set Russia "aside" completely—the Congress of People's Deputies was approaching, from which experts expected serious changes in Russian policy. Even before the election, Jonathan Howe, deputy assistant to the President for national security, set a date for a large meeting[151] devoted to the situation in Russia.

The assessment of the situation was bleak. "*Yeltsin's critics have been quick to note that major pieces of G7 support promised at the Munich Summit have not materialized: not a rescheduling of Russia's debt, not an IMF standby program, and not a stabilization fund for the ruble. The impression of flagging Western interest in Russian reform has been reinforced by EC reluctance to give CJS states any significant access to its markets…*

Yeltsin has himself expressed impatience with lack of sufficient western assistance … he reportedly wryly remarked during a recent speech to the MFA "Long futile talks are taking place here with endless delays in making decisions of extreme importance to Russia."

… The political crisis in Moscow represents a clear challenge to the viability of the current approach to reform and to the tenure of Prime Minister Gaidar and other key members of the reform team… Yeltsin has publicly reiterated his support

---

[150] GAO. Former Soviet Union. Information on US Bilateral Program Funding. Report to Congressional Committees. December 1995. GAO/NSIAD-96-37.

[151] GBPL&M. Deputies Committee Meeting. November 6, 1992.

for Gaidar and Kozyrev and … at the same time, he … has privately acknowledged that he may, in the end, have to sacrifice Gaidar and Kozyrev in order to maintain control of the political process. We, therefore, focus on short-term steps to bolster the current reform program."

What can we do?—the meeting participants asked themselves and admitted that there was very little. For example, in a telephone conversation with Bush on October 29, Yeltsin asked the leaders of Western countries and heads of international financial organizations to support Gaidar and his reforms. Of course, Russia's reforms were fundamentally in the right direction, and Russia's trajectory was in the interests of the United States. In such a situation, not responding to the Russian President's request would have shaken his confidence in the reformers and raised doubts about whether American support for Russian reforms was consistent. On the other hand, who could say that Yeltsin's position in Russia was stable and that he would not be ousted tomorrow? "*Taking a certain distance from the unfolding political drama might make it easier to work with a successor government.*"

Yes, economic reforms were inconsistent and had failed to deliver the desired results. IMF requirements were unmet, and an extensive program could not be agreed upon, which blocked access to the announced $24-billion bailout package and a long-term agreement on external debt. It was clear that, at best, the program would not be available until next spring, and there was little opportunity to speed up the negotiation process. Of course, it was possible to persuade Bush to speak in favor of reforms or to send a delegation of Sherpas from the G7 countries or even IMF chief Camdessus to Moscow to meet with the Russian leadership and publicly support reforms. However, it was not certain that this would convince Russian society that the West was ready to help Russia by deeds, not words. The IMF could be "pressured" to lower the bar of demands, but by doing so, it could undermine the Fund's credibility in other countries. In short, "*The primary responsibility for moving forward with the IMF rests on the shoulders of the Russian leadership.*"

Yes, Russia was under pressure from a huge foreign debt that it could not service and, therefore, needed a long-term solution to this problem. In principle, the US government could have pressed its partners to make progress in negotiations before the opening of the Congress of People's Deputies. However, this was strongly opposed by the State Department, which demanded a neutral position and no interference in the endless fights between Russia and Ukraine on legal issues—who and how should be responsible for Soviet debts. The agreement signed in the fall of 1991 on joint and several liabilities for the Soviet debt was not being implemented by any of the states declaring themselves heirs of the USSR. Russia, as the only (limited) solvent debtor, had to service 100% of the debt, but it had no right to dispose of all Soviet assets (in particular, access to several bank accounts was blocked, and debtors of the Soviet Union refused to service their debts). Yeltsin declared Russia's readiness for the "zero option" (accepting all responsibility for Soviet debts and all rights concerning Soviet foreign assets), but this was opposed by "*most of the G7 and the Paris Club, including Germany, France, Japan, and Italy*. Besides "*Ukraine has not articulated a clear position, but has not found proposed Russian solutions [to settle relations between the countries regarding Soviet debts and assets] to be acceptable*." In short, there could be no talk of any long-term debt restructuring. The maximum that could be hoped for was to persuade the G7 partners to demand less in 1993 and to persuade Russia to agree to pay more.

It was hard to describe any of the above as genuine support for Russia, and no one disputed the point. But it was urgent to find at least something "*because the political deal-making that could determine the position of Congress has already begun… Our leverage in this situation is extremely limited, however. The US government has few additional resources to make immediately available.*"

The memo asked whether "*our willingness to begin a serious dialogue with the Russians about conventional weapons sales, in furtherance of the Camp David language and along the lines of discussions we have with major allies, could be a visible sign of bread-and-butter support?*" Or could we have supported Yeltsin in his concern about restrictions on the rights of Russian-speaking populations in the Baltic states and sent a non-public message to the governments of those countries, emphasizing, however, that the US considered this problem not a human rights issue but a problem of inter-community relations. Of course, it was hard to call this support for reform, but perhaps it would have helped calm down the nationalist forces in Russia a bit. Also, $275 million in "grain-loan" funds became available only after 1 January; maybe we could urge the Ministry of Agriculture to release these resources earlier? Also, Eximbank was stuck in negotiations on a $2-billion loan for exporting oil and gas production equipment to Russia. Eximbank's rigid demand was that the oil companies' export proceeds be deposited into offshore escrow accounts to guarantee repayment of the loan. However, Russia's export earnings had fallen dramatically, so we could we have found arguments to convince Eximbank to be more flexible.

What Will Be Our Legacy?

The meeting participants understood they would have to leave office in a few weeks, and that few perceived them as people with whom to negotiate anything seriously. *"The Russians, as well as our Allies, are likely to be skeptical of the Bush Administration's capacity to act in its remaining time in office. While Yeltsin has said he would welcome visible US support, our ability to help will depend importantly on whether we can generate broader Western initiatives. The difficulties of asserting US leadership with our Allies during a Presidential transition are substantial."*

The last thing they had to discuss was what they could pass on as a legacy to the new administration. *"The West cannot afford to turn its back on Russian leaders, such as Yeltsin and Gaidar, who represent Russia's best hope of becoming a responsible member of the international political and economic community."* However, it quickly became clear that the Bush Administration had failed to develop any strategy for Russia's integration; no serious processes were launched, and there was no vision of what those processes might be. The final set turned out to be more than modest.

Continued technical assistance at the micro level—assistance in privatization, the development of tax, antimonopoly, and civil legislation, and the establishment of the banking system. Assistance in the conversion of the defense industry. Normalization of trade relations, including abolishing the Jackson-Vanik amendment, and extending the trade preferences already granted to Eastern European countries to Russia. This set of recommendations was on the desk of outgoing Secretary of State Lawrence Eagleburger as he wrote the traditional memorandum to his successor.[152]

Eagleburger identified *"The gradual incorporation of a reforming Russia and Eastern Europe into a stable European system"* as one of the possible foreign policy achievements of the incoming administration, although he pointed out that the risk of a reversal of Russia's reforms and a return to authoritarianism remained high. *"If reform succeeds in Russia, it may not assure the success of reform in other states of the FSU; but if reform fails in Russia, it most assuredly will mean the failure of reform throughout the former Soviet empire,"* he wrote, responding to criticism, including from Henry Kissinger, that the Bush administration was paying too much attention to Russia to the detriment of other post-Soviet countries.

[152] GBPL&M. Parting Thoughts; US Foreign Policy in the Years Ahead. Memorandum for Secretary of State-Designate Warren Christopher from Lawrence Eagleburger. January 5, 1993.

Eagleburger was not convinced that Russia had broken with its Soviet past. This was reflected in the first recommendation: "*To hedge against future uncertainties, we want to fix the reduction of nuclear weapons and their elimination in Russia as soon as possible.*" Russia was still seen as a potential adversary rather than a potential partner.

The second recommendation was to continue to support reforms *together with other donors* and to open markets for Russian goods. There was also a call for increased mutual exchanges between the two countries, a dream that by 1996, the end of Clinton's first term, the number of Russian students in the United States and the number of Americans working in Russia under technical-assistance programs would be measured in the thousands.

The third recommendation called for close cooperation with Russia to end armed conflicts on the periphery of Soviet space.

"While the Russians themselves must ultimately make the hard choices, history will not judge the United States kindly if we fail to offer generous assistance," Lawrence Eagleburger wrote, leaving his memorandum to speculate on why the Bush administration could not (or would not) do so.

4

A Year Full of Uncertainties

Hopes that Yeltsin's concessions and the formation of the Chernomyrdin government would calm the political storm were quickly dashed. For all the conventional analogies, 1993 echoed the turmoil of two years earlier: an acute political confrontation, which eventually led to an armed rebellion and its suppression by army units, absorbed the energies of both sides, and economic policy, as is often the case in such situations, became an instrument of this struggle.

The Power Struggle Continues

The Soviet Union collapsed, but Russia remained governed by the 1978 Soviet-era Constitution, and even with many amendments it failed to reflect profound societal changes. Most importantly, the Constitutional Commission could not agree on the distribution of powers between the President and the parliament, which turned substantive debate into a contest for personal power among political actors. The inability or unwillingness of Yeltsin and Ruslan Khasbulatov, the speaker of the parliament, to reach a sustainable agreement became a frequent trigger of the political crisis, which culminated in the armed mutiny in Moscow in October 1993.

At the VII Congress of People's Deputies of Russia held in December 1992, the position of Yeltsin and the government was unenviable: the term of emergency powers of the President was over, the country had undergone a shock yet remained unstable, the economy continued to contract, and store shelves were still empty. It was extremely difficult for the government to hold on in

S. Aleksashenko, *Post-Cold War Russia and the Missed Opportunity for Global Stability*,
https://doi.org/10.1007/978-3-032-01380-4_4

such a situation: there was no serious discussion about what needed to be done and why the painful decisions made at the beginning of the year did not lead to the desired result. The delegates of the Congress were overwhelmed with emotions, and the government's proposals to tighten their belts a little more and be patient inflamed them further.

Two weeks before the Congress, the Supreme Soviet passed a law on government that gave parliament the right to appoint the prime minister and members of the government. Yeltsin vetoed this law, noting that it contradicted the Constitution, but it was clear that this was only the beginning of the crisis. The President stood at a crossroads: on the one hand, the destructive position of the majority of deputies made Yeltsin's team want to liquidate the Congress as a body of power; on the other hand, only the Congress could adopt a new Constitution or, at least, amendments to it, which would define the principles of parliamentary structure and the organization of elections. Whatever the case, a compromise had to be found, which frustrated Yeltsin, leaving him unsure how to proceed without forfeiting the initiative. The President's entourage could not offer him a clear line of action. Consequently, decisions were made impulsively, without serious consideration; verbal compromises were never codified, leaving opponents ample room to reinterpret—or ignore—them.

The President's speech to the deputies was unsuccessful: Yeltsin abandoned a rigid declaration of his position and preferred to discuss possible compromises, a move perceived as weakness. The pressure in the hall grew and led to the Congress' adoption of amendments to the Constitution, which effectively stripped the President of significant powers, redistributing power in favor of the Supreme Soviet. This galvanized Yeltsin, and he rushed into action, once again taking the podium. The President accused his opponents "*of slowing down economic reforms and constitutional restructuring of the country,*" of wanting to organize "a *creeping coup,*" and, stating that "*it has become impossible to work with such a Congress,*" proposed holding a referendum with the question: "Who do you entrust to lead the country out of the economic and political crisis, to revive the Russian Federation: the current composition of the Congress and the Supreme Soviet or the President of Russia?" Yeltsin had the speech broadcast live without warning, curbing deputies' desire to oppose him publicly. The President's public support remained extremely high. However, embarrassment followed: the President asked his supporters to leave the session hall, which could have deprived the Congress of a quorum. The move caught allies off guard—Yeltsin's staff had neglected to alert supportive deputies—and only a small number of Congress participants followed Yeltsin.

In the end, the parties to the conflict reached a compromise: the MPs rescinded the amendments to the Constitution. At the same time, the

President agreed to submit the main provisions of the new Constitution to a referendum. In addition, the President proposed five prime ministerial candidates to the deputies for a ranking vote, promising to choose one of the top three for approval.[1] Yeltsin was confident that Gaidar's candidacy would win more than half of the deputies' votes, but this was not to be: the leader of economic reforms suffered a resounding defeat with only 400 votes, behind Yuri Skokov and Viktor Chernomyrdin (637 and 621 votes, respectively). Although Yeltsin had a longer and closer relationship with Skokov,[2] his candidacy was strongly opposed by Gaidar, whose opinion was important to the Russian President then. By choosing Viktor Chernomyrdin, as time would show, Yeltsin did not make a mistake, gaining a reliable partner for the next five years.[3]

After the change of prime minister, only one minister from Gaidar's team, Pyotr Aven, resigned, while the others remained in their positions, which prevented any sudden shifts in economic policy.[4] The appointment of Boris Fedorov as deputy prime minister and finance minister demonstrated Yeltsin's desire not to deviate from the chosen course. The President was able to focus on foreign policy by shifting economic authority to the prime minister. The timing was more than opportune—a newly elected President, Bill Clinton, was coming to power in Washington.

Where to Start?

It's the Economy ...

Clinton felt a sense of gratitude and respect for Yeltsin in September 1992, when, during his visit to Washington, the Russian President fulfilled his promise and met with the Governor of Arkansas despite the fact that the

[1] Gaidar said that at an earlier stage of the negotiations, Yeltsin's opponents had proposed another compromise formula: approval of Gaidar's candidacy for prime minister in exchange for the President's agreement to appoint the heads of the power ministries with the consent of the Supreme Soviet—which Yeltsin liked. However, this was later abandoned. (Y Gaidar. Days of Defeats and Victories. Moscow, Vagrius. 1996. pp. 229)

[2] Skokov was a member of the Moscow Communist Party City Committee when Yeltsin was the leader of the Moscow Communists; from 1990, he worked in Yeltsin's inner circle, first as deputy prime minister of the Russian government, then as presidential advisor and secretary of the Security Council.

[3] Skokov and Yeltsin soon parted ways. In March 1993, Skokov refused to authorize Yeltsin's decree dissolving the Supreme Soviet, claiming it was unconstitutional. The decree was not issued, Skokov resigned, and he never returned to the highest levels of Russian power.

[4] The new Prime Minister's first action was the decision to freeze prices. However, it met such strong resistance in the government that the decree, which had been prepared and signed, was withdrawn and never saw the light of day.

White House administration was doing everything possible to disrupt the meeting.[5] Yeltsin was the first foreign leader to meet with a candidate opposing an incumbent president. At the same time, Russia and its problems, as well as foreign policy issues in general, were not the center of attention of the presidential campaign—Bush's authority in this area was so high that it was impossible to compete with him. The campaign's narratives concentrated on the economy and living standards, which was more understandable to voters.

A month after his election victory, Clinton held a major economic conference in Little Rock, where the main discussions revolved around economic growth, the budget deficit, the health care system, and investment. When the discussion turned to international economic issues, its focus shifted towards familiar issues such as international trade agreements (GATT and NAFTA) and the situation in Latin America. Larry Summers—then the World Bank's chief economist—was tasked to address Russia and Eastern Europe and tried to convey the scale of the task by comparing the situation to the end of World War II.

> The Cold War is the third war to end this century… Will the sad situation of World War I be repeated, or will a happier period await us, as it did after World War II? This question will have to be answered in the next 40 years. The answer will depend largely on the success of literally the most significant economic recovery effort in world history—the reform of the former communist economies of Eastern Europe and the Soviet Union.

However, after describing the potential of the Soviet economy, mentioning the natural resources and high level of education, and emphasizing that reforms must come quickly and consistently, Summers proposed no concrete remedies, merely hinting that the former socialist states needed outside support. "*Those who fight for the values we hold dear, democracy, markets, and capitalism, have promised Western support and expect that promise to be fulfilled.*"[6]

Not surprisingly, the discussion went no farther.

The new administration's main economic problem was the budget deficit, around which the entire campaign was built. However, Clinton and his team did not offer anything concrete during the election race, limiting themselves to ambiguous phrases. Attempts to translate slogans into hard numbers showed that "*the numbers did not fit very well.*"

[5] Miller Center. Bill Clinton Presidency. Anthony Lake Oral History (2002).

[6] Clinton Economic Conference. December 14, 1992. https://www.c-span.org/video/?36074-1/clinton-economic-conference

After the Little Rock conference, a group led by Robert Rubin, who would become head of the established National Economic Council, was directly tasked by Clinton to formulate specific proposals. Projections showed that no matter how the economy grew, the deficit was expected to rise from $290 billion in 1992 to $300–400 billion over the next few years. *"Everybody felt that this could not be allowed to happen. We had to reverse it. So there were various proposals for a target. In the end, the one that won out was that we cut the deficit in half in four years. So half of 290 is 145… when the package was put together, the politicians realized that it meant no money for all the things we had promised to do. They were very upset."*[7]

In short, there is no money, but you hold on … Reducing the budget deficit was prioritized; large-scale financial aid to Russia was out of the question after that.

People Make All the Difference

Hardly any of the governors of American states were well versed in foreign policy and ready to discuss seriously the global interests of the United States in the world, much less the problems of individual countries. In this respect, Clinton was no exception. When, 10 days after his election victory, the CIA began providing him and future Vice President Al Gore with Presidential Daily Briefings (PDBs), on the first day, representatives of the office were dumbfounded by "how *our two new clients immediately read every word of that day's PDB, obviously intrigued by what it contained.*"[8]

Russia was undoubtedly one of the most important topics of the PDB, but the format of this document presupposes a narrative of current events, leaving no room for backstory. To draw the future President's attention to the most important topics, CIA analysts began preparing appendices and background analytical materials on the most important topics that did not require immediate reading. "*The first of the Supplements included articles on reforms in Russia … Such materials were provided to the Governor for several days, but it was clear that, although he was interested in principle, he simply did not have time to read the materials … When it became clear that the Supplement was not being read, and we had to put it off from day to day, we experimented with a much-abbreviated version in which we provided one page of material on only one or two major issues. These also proved to be of little use.*"

[7] Miller Center. Bill Clinton Presidency. Alice Rivlin Oral History.

[8] John L. Helgerson. CIA Briefings of Presidential Candidates. May 22, 1996. https://nsarchive2.gwu.edu/NSAEBB/NSAEBB116/cia/CIA%20Briefings%20of%20Presidential%20Candidates.htm

No single person could master all the issues the President faced, and it would be wrong to accuse Clinton of not having enough time to read all the materials that came across his desk. A leader's strength rests on the strength of his team, whose job is to present options and analyze their consequences. Unfortunately, the composition of President Clinton's "Russian team" proved stellar but unbalanced, which may have been one of the reasons why it failed to demonstrate any special achievements.

Nicholas Burns, Jim Collins, John Byerly, and US Ambassador to Moscow Thomas Pickering, who worked in the White House, were truly "stars" of American diplomacy, whose experience and qualifications are beyond question. However, if you look closely, they all were excellent political analysts, which greatly distorted the Clinton administration's vision of Russia's problems. The set of strong political analysts led to a kind of competition between them: at every turn of Russian political life, they drew scenarios of radical changes, which were reduced to the weakening of the position or the fall of Yeltsin and the subsequent return of Russia to the authoritarian Soviet regime. This was roughly how Deputy NSA Sandy Berger viewed Russia at the time: "*One of the items on our agenda was to stabilize Russian democracy. Don't forget, Yeltsin was faltering … because he was being pushed around by … Zyuganov and the Communists … on the left. The nationalist Zhirinovsky was coming at him from the right, and the question of whether Russian democracy would survive was very much in doubt in 1992 and '93, '94 and '95…*"[9]

No expert on the Russian economy advised the President, even though Russia's economic problems were central. But, almost always, when it came to Russia, the President was accompanied by his Oxford friend, Strobe Talbott. Talbott was an excellent journalist who had worked for many years in the Soviet Union and spoke Russian well, but he had never worked a day in government before joining the Clinton administration, had no bureaucratic experience, and, as it soon became clear, was unable to build a strong "pro-Russian" partnership with his counterparts in other government agencies. The problem was compounded because Talbott had no slot in State's hierarchy, so a bespoke post was created for him—Ambassador-at-Large and Special Advisor to the Secretary of State for Newly Independent States. Although the friendly relationship between the President and Talbott was no secret to anyone, it did not help overcome bureaucratic barriers within the State Department and in relations with other structures. Besides, being a good journalist, Talbott could describe any situation in accessible language, but he

[9] Miller Center. Bill Clinton Presidency. Samuel R. Berger Oral History.

was not a foreign policy architect like Kennan, for example. Talbott told Clinton about the problems but did not propose original constructive steps, agreeing with the President's decision, which was formed under the influence of other advisors.

In addition, Talbott understood the problems of the Russian economy even less than his colleagues in the White House, which was evident to those around him, but few dared tell the President about it. One such "daredevil" was former President Richard Nixon, who in March 1994 wrote a personal letter to Clinton in which he bluntly said that Talbott was incapable of handling the administration's problems in dealing with Russia. "*I have respect and sympathy for Strobe Talbott. He is an outstanding political figure. However, his strong suit is not economics. What we need now is a new program, similar to what we had during the Marshall Plan, when aid is run by a top-notch businessman reporting directly to the President. Strobe should be big enough to embrace the idea and not insist that everything go through him and his staff.*"[10]

However, Talbott was happy to "outsource" economic issues related to Russia to the International Monetary Fund, which was to be overseen by Deputy Treasury Secretary Summers. Although Summers had joined the administration as Vice President and chief economist of the World Bank, he had the same career disadvantage as Talbott: he had never worked a day in the bureaucracy of the US government. Summers was the youngest economics professor in Harvard's history and often quickly overwhelmed his counterparts in other government departments with his intellect, but just as frequently, his theoretical constructs failed to translate into bureaucratic solutions, remaining little more than pretty phrases.

In addition, Summers was an excellent expert in macroeconomic issues and had never been involved in business. This led to the fact that specific single business ideas proposed by the Russian government aimed at promoting economic cooperation between the countries did not receive his support and, consequently, the support of the President or his administration. Summers enjoyed the President's confidence, and his position was crucial in setting the agenda for the Clinton-Yeltsin negotiations.

For example, before the G7 meeting in July 1993, where the two Presidents were to meet, Commerce Secretary Ron Brown, outlining his proposals, prioritized the urgent need for Russia to ratify the Mutual Investment Protection Treaty. The treaty was signed in June 1992 during Yeltsin's visit to Washington and ratified by the Senate. Such treaties protect the interests of medium-sized

[10] CDL #118841. Letter to William J Clinton from Richard Nixon. March 21, 1994.

businesses that cannot rely on direct support from their government. They are part of the standard set of bilateral agreements between countries that want to have a broader economic relationship with each other than trade, along with double taxation treaties.[11] Without Summers' support, the issue remained on the periphery of Clinton's attention, who mentioned it in passing and, without waiting for Yeltsin's reaction, moved on to the next topic. The Investment Protection Treaty between Russia and the United States has not been ratified to date.

In the first half of the 1980s, the Soviet Union was one of the world's largest civilian aircrafts' producers; however, by the time the new generation of airplanes appeared, the Soviet industry could not design and produce an engine with the necessary characteristics. When the Soviet economy began to open, the idea of putting American Pratt & Whitney engines on Soviet Il-96 airplanes was born. Design work on the idea began in mid-1980s, and in 1993 a prototype of such an aircraft was shown at the Paris Air Show. A year later, Russia's largest airline, Aeroflot, signed an agreement to supply ten Il-96Ts with PW-2337 engines and Rockwell Collins avionics. This became possible after active lobbying of the project by Yeltsin, who, starting from the meeting in Vancouver, constantly reminded Clinton about it, and, finally, Eximbank agreed to finance the engine supply to Russia.

As soon as this intention became known, the project faced active opposition from Boeing, which saw a potential competitor. At that time, Boeing was producing over hundred B-747/B-767/B-777 aircraft annually, and ten airplanes produced in Russia within 3–4 years were clearly no match.

P&W recently applied to Eximbank for $1 billion in financing for 20 engine/avionics packages [for IL-96 Project]. Boeing and McDonnell Douglas are deeply concerned about Ilyushin as a potential competitor and draw an analogy with the creation of Airbus. They want Eximbank to apply the same standard it has applied since 1972 to financing engines and parts for Airbus airframes, that is, refusing to provide financing or guarantees.

The US Trade and Development Agency (TDA) has funded a study which concludes: 1) the primary market for these aircraft would be Russia and other NIS states; 2) development of the IL-96 poses no threat to Boeing because the product is not competitive in western markets; and 3) potential sales would be limited to NIS customers who could not afford western aircraft. FAA certification, which Ilyushin is seeking, could in the long term alter this conclusion. Ilyushin benefited from past Soviet subsidization, but its current plant and equipment are antiquated, and the Russian government is in no position to subsidize it...

[11] The US has signed such agreements with 46 countries; Russia has 80 agreements, of which the State Duma has ratified 68.

Eximbank has asked other US government agencies for guidance on the wider political/economic aspects regarding Pratt's application and the NEC is leading this effort. There are sharp interagency divisions on this issue and sensitive domestic political considerations.[12]

Though in April 1994 Eximbank's board issued its preliminary commitment, it was suspended in 1996. Russia and the US entered protracted negotiations, following which Aeroflot pledged to lease ten B-767 s, which were no longer in demand on the global market, and the Russian government exempted the imported aircraft from import duties. Aeroflot and the Russian government fulfilled their obligations, while Eximbank ... was still refusing to provide the promised loan. Only after another round of negotiations in late 1997 did the bank sign an agreement to provide a loan for engines for only three (!) airplanes in March 1998. But in August 1998, there was a financial crisis in Russia, then a political crisis, and within 18 months three prime ministers changed, and finally, a new Russian President came. The new President, Vladimir Putin, felt that building a Russian airplane with American engines was deemed contrary to national security interest. In late 2001, he ordered to halt the project.

They Met and Became Friends

Preparing for a First Date

As a politician of a younger generation, Clinton did not cling to the shards of the Cold War and did not consider disarmament issues the only priority in relations with Russia. They were certainly important and necessary, but by the end of 1992, Bush and Yeltsin had "squeezed through" the negotiations and signed START II. It was a bold full stop set by the outgoing President, after which it was difficult for the new team to offer anything more in the same direction. Clinton decided to focus on other areas, such as ensuring that Russia never again became a source of irritation for the United States. Already in his first telephone conversation with Yeltsin after his inauguration, Clinton said that he was open to working together to "*build the closest possible partnership*" with Russia, assured that his government was "*ready to get off to a fast start,*" and offered to prepare a face-to-face meeting.[13] However, the topics proposed by the American President for discussion were limited to foreign policy "points of tension": Ukraine's movement toward a non-nuclear state,

[12] CDL #101272. IL-96 (Background material).

[13] CDL #101331. Telcon with President Yeltsin of Russia on January 23, 1993.

Bosnia, and Iraq… The problems of Russian reforms and potential American support for them were not included in this list, except for a favorable attitude toward the Paris Club's granting of a deferral of foreign debt payments. The Russian President, who had extensive experience communicating with American politicians, understood the importance of personal contact and proposed meeting as soon as possible, as early as the last week of February. Still, Clinton was not ready for such speed. On February 10, Yeltsin reminded him of his readiness for a face-to-face meeting and proposed a new date, around March 10, but again, this proposal went unanswered. On February 22, Christopher and Kozyrev, meeting in Geneva, announced that the Presidents would meet in Vancouver on April 4.

One reason was his team's inability to offer a meaningful set of steps that could support Russia's transformation. The scale of what was happening was already clear, the complexity of Russia's reforms was beyond doubt, the amount of financial assistance that could help was far beyond America's capacity, and the G7 allies, apart from Germany, were not as generous as one would like.[14] Moreover, any proposals for aid programs for Russia were met with resistance from those charged with implementing the budget deficit reduction policy that had been adopted as a priority. At one of his meetings with his "Russian team," after hearing one of his aides call, "*No new money! No new laws!*," Clinton couldn't stand it and said he was taking it upon himself to solve the problems with Congress.[15]

Bush had a $24 billion aid package announced, but it was obvious to everyone that even formally it was only half-fulfilled. In a meeting with Helmut Kohl, Yeltsin complained that the financial support promised to Russia had not arrived, that the G7 countries were not fulfilling their obligations, that the Paris and London Clubs of creditors were unwilling to grant Russia a reprieve on debt payments. "*Helmut, I'm sorry, but I'm getting the impression that someone is interested in seeing Russia collapse*," he said.[16]

---

[14] In turn, European countries froze in anticipation of the new administration formulating its policy toward Russia. "*We need to see clearly what the Americans want and what they will do … I am ready to do everything possible to support Russia and Yeltsin. A policy of 'sit and wait' is not the right policy … it is very important for us to know Clinton's goals,*" Chancellor Kohl told French President Francois Mitterrand. Memorandum. Wilson Center. The Chancellor's telephone Conversation with French President Mitterrand on Thursday, March 18, 1993.

[15] Strobe Talbott. The Russia Hand. Random House/New York, 2002, p. 54.

[16] Wilson Center. Memorandum. The Chancellor's Meeting with Russian President Yeltsin on Wednesday, March 3, 1993.

According to IMF estimates, G7 financial aid to Russia in 1992 amounted to $16.8 billion, with 94% of this aid being so-called "tied loans," which were issued for imports from creditor countries, including US "grain loans." Russia received only $1 billion in "live" money (IMF loan). The IMF estimates that in 1992, Russia paid $1.8 billion as interest on its foreign debt.[17] The Bank of Russia estimates this amount at $5 billion.[18]

Clinton set out to surpass his predecessor. The package to be announced in Vancouver should be "*something new … high impact, with an ambitious follow-through,*" to be locked in at the G7 meeting in Tokyo.

Surprisingly, the only person who could be called an expert on the Russian economy did not participate in these meetings—Summers' views and proposals were presented by Talbott. Summers' diagnosis was quite accurate: one of Russia's main problems would be the need to maintain social infrastructure and create a system of social support for the population at a time when privatization and structural adjustment of the economy would reduce the state's capacity and increase the number of unemployed. But since Summers was not present at the meeting to explain to the President that it concerned substantial financial support for the budget, Clinton decided that the meeting should be about creating "*a huge public works project … They [Russia and its economy] are in a state of depression, and Yeltsin should become their Roosevelt.*"[19] This project would soon morph into the idea of a Privatization Support Fund, which would become one of the biggest failures of the Russian aid program.

The original intent, as outlined by Summers, was to provide enterprises with financial support after privatization. In the Soviet economy, large enterprises maintained social and communal infrastructure in the surrounding neighborhoods, where housing for employees was usually built. After privatization, enterprises needed funds for investment and to offset infrastructure costs. The initial amount of such a fund, which the G7 countries agreed to create, was set at $2 billion, with the US willing to contribute $500 million. Soon, the Fund's capitalization was declared to reach $4 billion.[20] However, the G7 failed to agree on who should receive the money, for what purposes, or on what terms it should be disbursed. Any mentioning of the Privatization Support Fund disappeared after the G7 leaders met in Tokyo.

[17] B. V. Christensen. The Russian Federation in Transition. External Developments. IMF Occasional Paper, #111. February 1994.

[18] Annual Report of the Bank of Russia for 1993. Moscow, 1994.

[19] Strobe Talbott. The Russia Hand. Random House/New York, 2002, pp. 51–52.

[20] CDL # 101270. The Tokyo Economic Summit. Memorandum For the President from Anthony Lake, Robert E. Rubin. Russia. Special Privatization and Restructuring Program (SPRP), April 6–10, 1993.

Of the $440 million allocated in the budget for this purpose, a quarter was given to USAID [United States Agency for International Development] for the creation of two investment funds, FLER [Large Enterprise Fund in Russia] and RAEF [Russian American Enterprise Fund]. Nevertheless, the funds operated under stringent conditions. They were direct investment funds that had to earn adequate profits in competition with similar funds created by private businesses. It was well understood that the funds, whose working conditions were determined by the state, and which must report on the use of budgetary funds according to all bureaucratic rules, stood little chance of competing with private funds. In two years, these funds were able to invest only a quarter of the funds received, with annual management costs approaching 5%, which triggered a change in concept: the funds were merged into the US-Russia Investment Fund (TUSRIF), the management of which was transferred to a private company. TUSRIF operated quite successfully in Russia until 2008, with total investments exceeding $300 million, but it did not significantly assist Russian reforms.

The President's meetings continued, but no significant progress was evident. Clinton already knew Russia's problems by heart and was ready to discuss them in detail. But every time he heard various proposals from his aides the President was aware that the proposed solutions fell far short of the problems' magnitude. "*Go back [to your workplaces] and think bigger!,*" he urged.

Two weeks before the Vancouver meeting, the draft aid package still fell short of what the President wanted: though $1 billion was more than the $400 million already budgeted by the previous administration, and everything that could be found and reallocated from the approved budget had been included, but the President demanded that they keep trying.

On March 23, Kozyrev met with Christopher and talked about what Russia wanted to see come out of the Vancouver meeting. "*The time had passed for general expressions of support… It was very difficult to make progress when the West essentially said "tell us what you're up to and we'll see what we can do to help"… Russia had in mind a medium-term program of cooperation with the G7 over 5–7 years. There needed to be firm targets for financial and technical assistance, and investment. Russia wanted to see an early G7 meeting, preferably at summit level, not to take the place of the Tokyo summit, but to coordinate work on an immediate package of support for Russia.*"[21]

But this was a lone voice. The G7 leaders had already approved the mid-April meeting in Tokyo of finance ministers tasked with negotiating an aid package for Russia, and they had no desire to disrupt the approved schedules.

---

[21] CDL #118876. Secretary Christopher's Bilateral with Russian Foreign Minister Kozyrev: Lunch, March 23. Department of State's Cable to NSC, April 1, 1993.

A telegram from the State Department outlining Russia's position was issued a week later, on April 1, when all discussions on the aid package were completed. However, lag by drafters and coordinators was not solely to blame: ambitious programs were not considered during the discussions inside the White House. Even when Clinton echoed Summers' plea for major aid, his words floated unanswered. "*We're a big, rich country with deep pockets. We need big, bold ideas. We're not worth shit if we can't put together a bigger package than the one we've been talking about. We've got to remember that we really do have a dog in this fight.*"[22]

The President's team earnestly searched for unconventional funding sources to finance aid to Russia without changing the approved budget parameters. On the President's desk were some exotic proposals, such as using NATO's infrastructure fund or the funds intended for oil purchases for the strategic reserve to pay for Russian oil in advance, giving Russian companies the necessary funds to invest and increase oil production. However, they all had to be approved by Congress and would have increased the budget deficit or cut spending in other areas. No one in the administration was prepared to recommend that the President go down this path.[23]

Clinton tried to discuss the possibility of allocating additional funds to support Russia with Democratic leaders in Congress but, meeting stiff opposition, decided to stand down. In the end, the President accepted that there was no money and agreed to make a move that satisfied everyone: to reallocate to Russia the unused limit of $700 million in "grain" credits and announce a $1.6 billion package consisting of spending for 1993 and 1994 that had already been passed and approved by Congress, which included programs for all CIS countries, not just Russia. The sum was impressive—four times what the Bush administration had used for the 1993 aid program. Later, additional decisions could be made based on the discussion at the G7 ministerial meeting in Tokyo.

Meanwhile, urgent news arrived from Moscow: a new round of political conflict was brewing, fraught with serious upheaval. In mid-March, the Supreme Soviet refused to honor the agreements reached three months earlier and enacted "frozen" articles of the Constitution that fully transferred control of executive power from the President to parliament, simultaneously canceling a referendum on a new constitution scheduled for late April.

---

[22] Strobe Talbott. The Russia Hand. Random House/New York, 2002, p. 57.

[23] WCPL&M. US Economic Assistance to Russia. Memorandum from A Lake to POTUS. March 1993.

On March 20, Yeltsin made an address in which he declared that "*the possibilities of finding agreement with the conservative majority of the Congress of People's Deputies have been completely exhausted … I am forced to assume responsibility for the fate of the country… Any decisions of parliamentarians directed against the President and the government will not be valid.*" At the same time, Yeltsin announced that on April 25 he would hold a nationwide vote of confidence in the President and Vice President of Russia. In response, the Supreme Soviet decided to convene an extraordinary Congress of People's Deputies to consider the impeachment of the President.

A clear majority of deputies, 617 out of 1033, voted in favor of Yeltsin's resignation, but the law required a qualified majority for the decision. To remove the threat of a presidential popular vote, deputies called an official referendum, the wording of each of the four questions posing a danger to the President. The acute phase was past, yet the threat of renewed escalation lingered. "*If … in the first chapter … there is a gun hanging on the wall, in the second or third chapter it must surely go off,*" wrote Anton Chekhov. The shot from the Russian political gun would be fired in the fall. So far, Washington believed, Yeltsin had emerged victorious from the battle, but confidence in the stability of Russia's course toward democracy had once again been shaken.

On March 31, four days before the first meeting between Yeltsin and Clinton, Clinton's national security advisor Anthony Lake and Talbott conducted an off-the-record briefing at the White House, seeking to square that circle.[24] On the one hand, it was necessary to confirm that "*partnership has replaced competition,*" to prove that regarding support for Russia, "*the President's first law has been we must be able to do what we say we will and to deliver on what we promise,* and that in Vancouver, Clinton *will be presenting a very serious economic package.*" On the other hand, beautiful words had to be found to hide the fact that there would be no new money for Russia, and that the entire aid package "*will not be an exercise in repackaging existing efforts and calling it 'new,' but projects are either completely new or are expanded and reshaped versions of current programs.*"

Experienced White House press pool journalists were not taken in by the spin. They quickly realized the real situation, gauged the size of the "package," and began to grill the President's aides with questions, and that's all? So, what is the difference between the new and old administrations you criticized for insufficient assistance to Russia? As a result of persistent "grilling," the journalists grasped that there was not enough money, that the previous

[24] CDL #48595. Background briefing by senior administration officials. March 31, 1993. The White House. Office of the Press Secretary.

administration was unable to fulfill its promises and provide even the aid it had promised, and that the new administration would be different in that it would fulfill its promises.[25] Decentralization became a key feature of the package: "*Three quarters of these programs will be directed to the non-state sector;*[26] *and three quarters will be directed to regions outside Moscow.*"

The journalists did not receive any clarification as to how the aid program would be administered or whether a single steering committee would be set up to ensure that the decisions made would be implemented. "*That's a big concern for us as it is for Yeltsin, and we are discussing mechanisms to make sure that this time we get it right,*" was the response.

> Non-credit aid lacked central oversight; between 1990 and 1994 funds passed through 23 separate agencies, each left to devise its own procedures. Grant support for Russia in those years totaled $5.37 billion, of which only 65% was used. More than half of the programs were funded via the Defense Department and USAID, yet they coordinated only a quarter of those funds with other aid operators. The most effective operator of Russia's humanitarian food aid programs was the Department of Agriculture, which disbursed over 96% of its allotment.[27]

Future programs were left vague: their scale would be set only after Yeltsin outlined Russia's requests at the presidential summit and G7 finance ministers met in Tokyo to gauge what they—and the IFIs—could provide.

All Seemed in Order

The 3–4 April Vancouver summit mattered to both leaders.

Yeltsin did not give up hope that Russia and America could become partners. The Russian President recognized that Russia's integration into the global economy and global political institutions could not take place without the active position of the United States. In addition, Moscow understood the US Treasury Department had enormous influence on the position of the G7

[25] "*Don't say "hop" before you jump,*" says a Russian proverb. The aid programs approved by Congress and included in the budget for Russia were funded at 64.5% in 1992, 63.4% in 1993, and 57.6% in 1994. Former Soviet Union. Information on Bilateral Programs. United States General Accounting Office. Report to Congressional Committees. December 15, 1995. GAO/NSIAD-96-37.

[26] Given that of the total $1.6 billion, almost half were "grain" loans, and $215 million was for nuclear disarmament financing programs, it is challenging to figure out how administration officials could have arrived at 75%.

[27] Former Soviet Union. Information on Bilateral Programs. United States General Accounting Office. Report to Congressional Committees. December 15, 1995. GAO/NSIAD-96-37.

countries, the IMF and the World Bank, which could provide Russia with financial support. Confidence in large-scale US aid was steadily fading, yet the hope that the new President's words on the eve of the meeting—"*The opportunity that lies before our Nation today is to answer the courageous call of Russian reform, as an expression of our own values, as an investment in our own security and prosperity, as a demonstration of our purpose in a new world*"[28]—could be transformed into deeds remained.

For Clinton, Russia's transformation was becoming "*the toughest and most important foreign policy problem of … Presidency,* in which he was to demonstrate *personal commitment to a broad and sustained American commitment to the support of democracy and market economic reform in Russia, despite the budgetary stringencies that we confront.*"[29] The meeting with the Russian President was the first international meeting for Clinton outside the United States, at which the administration intended to demonstrate that "*Despite the problems Russia faces, its need for Western assistance … this is very much a meeting of equals.*"[30]

It was clear to the aides of the American President that all the discussions in Vancouver could be divided into two parts. On the one hand, the Russian President would emphasize economic problems. "*Yeltsin will wonder how your thinking has evolved on aid to Russia, what you intend to propose to Congress, and whether or not you can bring the G7 along for a realistic multi billion-dollar multilateral financial assistance package.*" On the other hand, US interests demanded a serious discussion of international issues. "*Russian cooperation is essential to all our efforts at the UN on Yugoslavia, Iraq, North Korea or Somalia. The opportunities for peace in the Middle East, for isolating Gaddafi or Saddam Hussein, for building a broader European security community, are significantly reduced if Russia turns away from us. Russia can no longer threaten us militarily as it once did, but we cannot curb the spread of nuclear technologies or advanced weaponry if Russia decides it is in its national interest to sell rather than to scrap its enormous stockpile of weapons.*"

The asymmetry of expectations was obvious; moreover, when preparing the agenda, Yeltsin's aides hinted that there might be "surprises"—for example, a

[28] Remarks to the American Society of Newspaper Editors in Annapolis. April 1, 1993. PPP 1993, book 1, p. 379.

[29] CDL #101269. Meeting with President Yeltsin of the Russian Federation. Memorandum to the President from Warren Christopher. March 31, 1993.

[30] CDL #101269. Meeting with President Yeltsin. NSC Scope Paper. Anthony Lake to President William J Clinton. April 1, 1993.

multibillion-dollar request for support for the social security system or for a conversion program. At the same time, "*He not only may want more, but he may want it sooner and without the conditionality which we have always attached.*" The worst-case scenario for the Clinton team was for the negotiations to degenerate into endless explanations to the Russian guest of why his requests were impossible: there was no money in the budget, the reform program was not being implemented, Congress was wary after the recent political escalation, etc.

Accordingly, aides proposed an "echeloned-defense" strategy:

- US assistance will be two-phased; the first phase will be immediately after the Vancouver meeting, when "you put a credible and innovative program on the table immediately… You will be able to focus the meeting on what we can deliver now and what we hope to deliver in the next few months, alone and in concert with our allies and friends. Yeltsin is likely to appreciate the fact that everything offered in the core package is for real—no smoke and mirrors and no empty promises. In this case at least, less is more. Your package will directly help the daily lives of the Russian people."
- The second phase will come after the G7 finance ministers meet in mid-April when Russia could receive "more substantial support, on both the bilateral and multilateral (G7) tracks over the next few months." As part of the agreement to be presented at the G7 meeting in Tokyo, America would develop a new package, and "you will be able to say that you have energized the G7 nations to take a more comprehensive, fast-track approach to assistance. You clearly are in this for the long haul and are committed to asking the Congress for additional funds."
- "*Any additional large-scale requests you can discuss it in general terms with Yeltsin without making any firm commitments.*" However, it should be emphasized that the scale of aid and its effectiveness would depend on how consistent and successful the economic reforms in Russia were, first, in terms of suppressing inflation.

The Vancouver talks proved both intense and successful. The two leaders quickly developed a warm personal relationship, which allowed them to soften the edges when discussing issues where the parties had opposing positions. The two Presidents agreed to create a Gore-Chernomyrdin Commission, which would be tasked with negotiating all the problems of a technological and/or commercial nature, thus freeing up the Presidents' time to discuss political issues. After that, Yeltzin handed over an extensive list of Cold-War-era US statutes that still constrained trade between the two countries. Clinton promised that these laws would be repealed, although he made a separate reservation about the Jackson-Vanik amendment,[31] and added that the US would support Russia's application to join GATT and include Russia in the international organization that would replace CoCom. Although it was not possible to agree on all the details in Vancouver, it became clear that a deal for Russia to sell $9 billion in weapons-grade highly enriched uranium to the US would be concluded, making it one of the two most successful US assistance programs to Russia.[32] The US had agreed in principle to Russia's entry into the international space launch market, although Clinton conditioned it on reaching an agreement with European countries.[33]

The day after the summit, the Paris Club announced Russia had received a deferral of $15.4 billion in foreign debt payments, which included overdue payments for 1992 and upcoming payments for 1993. Although the move cleared the way for new loans (in particular, US "grain" loans), Russia still faced a heavy debt burden that year and had to negotiate with the London Club of creditors and, according to IMF estimates, find about $11 billion in grants and intergovernmental loans to bring the balance of payments into balance.[34] In addition, the creditors reserved the right to withdraw from the agreement reached if Russia did not reach an agreement with the IMF by the fall.

A serious misstep on the Russian side was the absence of Defense Minister Pavel Grachev in Vancouver. At that time, the US military took the most pro-Russian positions and "opened the door" for close military-to-military contacts. Thus, US Secretary of Defense Les Aspin wrote in his memorandum to the President: "*We seek to build on the military-to-military contacts of recent*

[31] Moscow's requests to repeal the law were constant. However, *no one in Congress wanted to expend the energy or take the political risk of rescinding this anachronism, nor did anyone in the administration want to see Clinton waste his political capital on third-rate, mostly symbolic issues.* (Talbott S. The Russia Hand. Random House/New York, 2002, p. 63).

[32] Of course, another such program was US humanitarian food aid from 1992–1993, which amounted to about $2.5 billion for all post-Soviet countries.

[33] Two days before the Presidents met, James Currie, the European Commission's deputy representative in Washington DC and French Ambassador Jacques Andreani visited the State Department and protested the White House's decision to allow Russia into the space launch market. Talbott's deputy, Richard Kauzlarich, explained that it was a package deal in which Russia would forgo supplying missile technology to India, which had greatly troubled the US. CDL #118876. Commercial Space Launches: Demarches from EC Commission and French on Russian Entry into Market. Department of State's Cable. April 9, 1993.

[34] Russian Federation—Staff Report for 1993 Article IV Consultation. Report to Members of the IMF Executive Board, SM/93/96, Supplement 1. April 16, 1993. IMF Archive.

years towards a real partnership between our two defense establishments at all levels. We want to win their hearts, minds, and guts. Central truths we want them to feel in their bones: (1) the US recognizes and respects Russia as a great nation and great power (we are anti-Communist but pro-Russian); (2) we do not regard them as our enemy and don't want them to think of us as an enemy; (3) we genuinely want them to succeed and are eager to cooperate with them to that end; and (4) cooperation with the US offers their best/only hope for reconstruction of a Russia of which they can be proud patriots... We are pressing ahead with attempts to arrange joint peacekeeping exercises, search and rescue exercises, visits here by senior Russian generals, joint staff talks, staff talks between the respective services, and a variety of officer exchanges, including young cadets from the service academies."[35]

There was no fundamental change in relations between the countries. The Presidents communicated easily and joked a lot; the words "friends" and "partners" sounded sincere during the negotiations and in communication with journalists, but this was not reflected in the content. Yeltsin's bid to project a "business-like" style meant many of his proposals received only cursory discussion—he considered words "*we understand the problem*" and "*we are ready to discuss it*" as an agreement in principle, and the Russian President jumped the gun. Attempts by Deputy Prime Minister Boris Fedorov to start talking about larger-scale projects (a multi-year aid program, creation of a mechanism for insurance against political risks) were not supported by the Russian President, who wanted to "play first fiddle" all the time. On the other hand, the Clinton aides' "pet project"—a housing program for demobilized Russian officers departing the Baltic states—was perceived by Yeltsin as real support from a friend who understands your problems.

> Aides to the US President planned a housing program for 2000 families that was to be completed in 12–16 months. Yeltsin persuaded Clinton to scale up the program to 5,000 families, raising the cost to $160 million.

[35] Thickening our Defense Relationship with the Russian Armed Forces. Memorandum for the President from the Secretary of Defense. March 31, 1993. https://nsarchive.gwu.edu/sites/default/files/documents/rvqh5a-bhrmo/Doc-5-1993-03-31-Defense-relationship-with-Russians.pdf

By the end of 1993, it became clear that construction was going much more slowly and costing much more than planned (Helmut Kohl warned Clinton about this in late March 1993). It turned out that many finishing materials could not be bought in Russia; they had to be imported. The contracts with the Russian government stated that local officials would provide free land plots and finance the construction of public infrastructure, but the Russian government did not enter into any agreements with local authorities. In addition, the initial cost of single-family housing, which the builders were supposed to meet, was so low that in most Russian cities, the money could only buy a one-room apartment. The most optimistic estimates of the project's completion were pushed back by an additional one and a half to two years. To speed up the progress of the project and to keep within the budget spending limit, it was decided to build 4000 houses and issue 1000 vouchers that could be used to buy housing.[36] Demobilized officers could then buy more expensive housing using personal savings or financial assistance from regional governments. In June 1994, when the US pressed Russia hard to complete its withdrawal from the Baltics by the end of the summer, the number of vouchers increased to 1500, which helped alleviate the discontent of officers who were threatened with moving to nowhere.[37]

The final version of the program increased the number of vouchers to 2500. In 1995, Congress cut funding for the program by $15 million, which reduced the number of officers who received housing to 4498.[38]

Yeltsin badly needed to return to Moscow "with money" to reduce the heat of criticism from his political opponents who reproached him for capitulating to the West and ill-conceived reforms. But all he heard from his interlocutor was "old wine in new bottles." During Finance Minister Bentsen's speech, the Russian President couldn't stand it and handed him a note saying, "*It would be good if we could receive $500 million before April 25*" [a referendum was scheduled for that day in Russia].[39] Clinton, to whom the note was shown and translated, remained silent—he could not promise any money before the decision of Congress. The maximum that he could give Yeltsin was a set of promises: which programs of the "old" package would be implemented and

[36] WCPL&M. Russian Officer Housing Initiative: It's Time to Make Program Decisions. December 8, 1993.

[37] WCPL&M. Russian Officer Housing Initiative: Concerns over a Cost Overrun and Other Problems. Memorandum from Ambassador Tomas W Simons to Deputy Secretary. June 10, 1994.

[38] Audit of Russian Officer Resettlement Program under USAID Project 110–0008. USAID. Memorandum of the Regional Inspector General for Audit, Frankfurt. December 4, 1995. https://pdf.usaid.gov/pdf_docs/PDABM346.pdf

[39] Strobe Talbott. The Russia Hand. Random House/New York, 2002, p.68.

when, and that the "new" package, which would certainly be larger, would be formed based on the requests of "Boris's friend" in the coming days. And, most importantly, he would have to wait two weeks when the finance ministers would announce something big. "*We want a different kind of multilateral agreement to come out of Tokyo. That is, last year when the figure $24 billion was floated all across the United States and the world and Russia, a lot of it was contingent on all kinds of things which never happened and could not reasonably have been expected to happen. We are going to try to make sure that anything we say will be done, in fact, will be done. And that will be a big difference.*"[40]

When it came to allowing Russia to enter the market for technological goods (nuclear and space technology), the opposition from members of the US delegation, who argued that this would lead to a loss of control over atomic nonproliferation, support for terrorism, or upset the regional balance of power became so powerful and coordinated that the Russian delegation realized that the best solution was to pause. There was no attempt to talk about a political alliance, and the format in which Yeltsin would participate in at the next G7 meeting in Tokyo in July was not even clear.

Another Package

Yeltsin returned to Moscow in a mixed mood. On the one hand, the US President talked to him as an equal without trying to demonstrate superiority, listened attentively, though at times condescendingly, to his requests, and never immediately rejected anything. Disagreements on foreign policy issues were significant, but none of these problems were global in nature and did not threaten to destroy the potential partnership. On the other hand, it was becoming increasingly clear that the United States was unlikely to provide direct financial support; at best "friend Bill" could exert pressure on other G7 members and the IMF. The Fund not only could give money but was a key participant in the negotiations on foreign debt—without even an advisory vote, the Fund, by agreeing on a program, implicitly guaranteed creditors that the debtor's economic policy was going in the right direction.

While Summers confidently stated that the $1.6 billion provided by the US would be sufficient for the G7 to build a large-scale international aid package, the position of Washington's partners was more hesitant.

[40] The President's News Conference with President Yeltsin of Russia in Vancouver April 4, 1993. Public Papers of the Presidents of the United States. 1993, book 1.

A week before the meeting of the two Presidents in Vancouver, German Chancellor Helmut Kohl, with whom Clinton spoke extensively about Russia, went to Washington.[41] In addition to personal respect for his German counterpart, the US President realized that he had a unique experience with the Soviet Union and Russia, a deep understanding of Yeltsin's problems, and, most importantly, practical experience in solving similar problems gained after the reunification of Germany.

Helmut Kohl frankly admitted "*The package agreed at Munich was not bad, but it was never implemented.*" At the same time, he revealed the open secret that the US position determined the G7 position. "*It is very important that the [US] President take the leadership on Russia… I want to ask a very primitive question: do Americans care about us? Or only about their own budget problems, health reform, etc.? Aid to Russia may not be popular but it is important to make it popular.*" Unless the US changed its approach and allocated additional budget funds to support Russia, Germany should not be expected to be the main donor as before. "*[We need] to harmonize our assistance to Russia, and divide up the work that needs to be done. But Germany has reached the maximum of what it can do. 53% of the assistance to Russia so far come from Germany.*"

"*The US has not done enough and should do more… though no one alone can do what Germany already has done,*" Clinton responded, and the German Chancellor decided to turn the conversation in a different direction. "*The G7 meeting last year in Munich was a disappointment, because some countries did not do a lot.*" Apart from the US and Germany, Japan was the only country that could commit meaningful resources to support Russia, which took a tough stance—no aid to Russia until the "Northern Territories" issue was resolved. During a recent visit to Tokyo, Kohl said that he discussed the issue with Japanese Prime Minister Miyazawa and hinted that Japan "*should be more flexible on the Northern Territories issue if it wants to be a great power.*" Clinton agreed with this position, saying, "*Russia cannot give the islands back today,*" and promised to put a little pressure on the Japanese Prime Minister in the coming days.[42]

The formation of the multilateral aid package was very difficult. The Clinton administration did not find support for its initiatives in the public

[41] CDL #57651. Meeting with German Chancellor Helmut Kohl. March 26, 1993, and Luncheon. Meeting with German Chancellor Helmut Kohl. March 26, 1993.

[42] Clinton made good on his promise; before the finance ministers met in Tokyo, the Japanese Prime Minister announced that his country would provide $1.8 billion in aid to Russia, of which, however, more than 80% were tied to loans, i.e. loans to import Japanese goods.

and Congress, which had difficulty digesting the White House's tough stance on deficit reduction and tax increases. The instructions to the US delegation were unambiguous: "*We need to be careful about the size and use of new money. We may not want to go into much detail with other G7 members until we have complete Congressional consultations.*"[43] Counting on G7 partners to offer more than tied loans was unrealistic. One could only hope for the IMF and the World Bank. But first, the Russian government could not achieve even minimal success in suppressing inflation. To lend against future successes, the IMF had to develop and approve new types of loans. Secondly, the size of loans from international organizations was strictly regulated, and the desired amount was obtained only by applying various surcharges and hypotheses that Russia could receive two or three IMF loans within one year.

Yet no one dwelt on such "trifles" anymore and after the ministers' of finance meeting in Tokyo in mid-April, they announced that the G7 had created a bailout package that exceeded what was promised a year ago in Munich—$28 billion. And if you added to that the $15 billion deferral of foreign debt payments, you got $43 billion. Nobody mentioned that 90% of the sum consisted of loans Russia would have to repay,[44] especially since, in 10 days, a referendum would be held in Russia, the results and consequences of which no one could predict. And, incidentally, it seemed that Yeltsin's power was so fragile that he and his generals did not control the entire arsenal of nuclear weapons—the de facto leader of Chechnya, General Dudayev, had contacted the White House and invited American inspectors to visit the republic to examine the nuclear weapons at his disposal.[45]

... The Last One

Three months between the two Presidents' meeting in Vancouver and the G7 meeting in Tokyo, to which Yeltsin was invited, were not easy for Clinton. Although for a year and a half, the American economy had been growing steadily, unemployment refused to fall thereby stifling budget-revenue

[43] WCPL&M. Briefing on G7 Joint Ministerial Meeting. April 6, 1993.

[44] Russian Deputy Prime Minister Alexander Shokhin said at a meeting with representatives of countries that had expressed their willingness to help Russia that if the Russian government agreed to use all the loans in the aid package, the annual amount of interest payments would be equal to the amount of debt payments to the Paris and London Club members that had been agreed upon during the negotiations. Meeting of the Consultative Group for Russia (Paris, June 8–9, 1993). IMF Office Memorandum from Donal Donovan to the Managing Director. June 16, 1993. IMF Archive.

[45] CDL #57568. Telcon with President Yeltsin of Russia. May 10, 1993.

growth.[46] The deficit far outpaced projections, leaving no room for new spending initiatives. In February, the President introduced a bill in Congress intended to stimulate the economy. During the debate, congressmen cut the President's request by 20%, and in a Senate vote, the bill fell short after five Democrats voted against it.

Meanwhile the President's international agenda expanded by the day. Difficult negotiations with the European Community on transforming GATT into WTO (the so-called Uruguay Round) continued. Bush had signed the North American Free Trade Area (NAFTA) agreement on December 17, 1992, but a significant number of Democratic congressmen had demanded that it be expanded to include labor and environmental protection, which forced the new administration to begin additional negotiations with Mexico and Canada. Because of decisions of the previous administration, the US intervened in conflicts in Somalia, where the overthrow of the Barre dictatorship saw the central government disappear and the country descend into chaos, and in Haiti, where a military coup overthrew the legally elected President Aristide. In addition, the ethnic conflict in Bosnia was escalating by the day. As a foreign policy novice, Clinton decided that resolving these conflicts was his task. Consequently, much of his time and his administration became distracted by what Talbott would a year and a half later call "Godforsaken places."[47]

At the meeting of finance ministers in Tokyo, the US announced that its contribution to the program of assistance to Russia under bilateral agreements would be $2.5 billion,[48] but it was already clear that the budget could not accommodate such a sum. Officials resorted to accounting maneuvers, counting the Nunn-Lugar program ($400 million) in this amount and include $300 million intended for other post-Soviet countries. But in addition to the size of the aid package itself, it was necessary to find sources of funding, and the Pentagon came to the "rescue," agreeing to cut military spending by almost $1 billion with a redistribution of funds in favor of Russia.[49] The bill passed

[46] About 85% of America's federal revenue comes from taxes related to personal income (income taxes and social security contributions).

[47] US DoS. Case F-2017-13,804. Doc No C06835924. Strobe to Chris. August 21, 1994.

[48] During the negotiations, the US insisted that its contribution would be a quarter of the total bilateral aid, bringing it to $10 billion.

[49] US Assistance to the Former Soviet Union 1991–2001: A History of Administration and Congressional Action. CRS Report RL30148. January 15, 2002.

Congress with great difficulty on the last day of the fiscal year, September 30. If it had not happened, the $1.6 billion funding limit would have been lost.[50]

By May the IMF board had approved a new loan instrument, tailored as far as possible to Russia's circumstances, and the Russian government had concluded negotiations with the Fund, accepting all program conditions. But economic volatility in Russia was so evident that Fund management postponed the board vote, which was eventually held only after public criticism from the US Treasury Secretary. Russia received $1.5 billion, which was supposed to "open the door" for the entire aid package, but the likelihood that this would happen was becoming less and less likely with each passing day.

The Russian economy kept sinking—after contracting 19% in 1992, GDP slid a further 5% in the first half of 1993. Defense-oriented companies were shutting down because the government was cutting military spending. Civilian manufacturers closed as Eastern European suppliers pivoted to Western markets, abandoning Russian buyers. Cooperative ties with companies from Central Asian unraveled amid rising nationalism and the exodus of Russian-speaking workers, who had formed the backbone of large enterprises' production teams. The Russian economy was heavily dependent on import, starting from food, drugs and medical equipment to machine tools and industrial components required for the unfinished investment projects. Confronted with this, the government abandoned market forces and rejected a unified floating exchange rate. Exporters had to surrender a large share of earnings to the state at an undervalued rate.

Exporters had to surrender a large share of earnings to the state at an undervalued rate, while the government sold hard currency at even more subsidized exchange rate to importers of what the government considered necessary. On the one hand, it was a hidden tax on export; on the other, commodity exporters could not import the necessary components and equipment for their investment and current operations (e.g., oil producers lacked drilling equipment). On paper, tax receipts looked high as a share of GDP, but in real terms kept shrinking due to falling GDP and because of high inflation.[51] IMF loans are traditionally designed to support the balance of payments, and the Russian government needed money for the budget. The Fund relaxed its wording,

[50] Another factor contributing to the passage of the law was the sharp deterioration of the political situation in Russia in September, which increased pressure from Yeltsin's supporters in Congress. However, in the Senate vote, the law was substantially amended: $300 million was allotted to Ukraine and another $300 million from the grant portion was redirected to increase Eximbank's loans.

[51] In Russia, enterprises calculated taxes based on the results of the previous period (month or quarter); the accrued taxes went to the budget by the end of the next period, but at an inflation rate of 15% month they lost more than 20% of their real value by that time.

letting the proceeds reach the Finance Ministry, which immediately sold them to the Bank of Russia. This, in turn, breached the monetary targets agreed with the Fund.

In early June, it became clear Clinton's cherished Privatization Support Fund met heavy resistance from partner countries. The toughest of all was Japanese Prime Minister Miyazawa, who said that his country was ready to participate in such a fund, but only if it was not a social support program. They would not be ready to give money to lazy workers.[52] At a meeting of donor countries in Paris, it became clear that would-be donors could not settle fundamentals—size, eligible spending, social scope, quotas, governance, and so on.[53]

Ten days before the summit in Tokyo, presidential aides informed Clinton that the idea of creating the Fund was close to failure, that the G7 partners were extremely reluctant to make their pledges to participate in the project, and suggested that the President, who had "strongly associated himself with this initiative," make calls to the leaders of the G7 countries and persuade them to make minimum contributions that would allow the creation of the Fund in the amount of at least $500 million.[54] The American President's calls and requests could not be ignored by his partners, who pledged the necessary resources.[55] However, no progress was made in institutionalizing the Fund and clearly defining its goals and objectives.

However, by that time the G7 Sherpas had found an elegant solution that allowed them to hide from public attention the fact that the total amount of the G7's aggregate pledges were only one-quarter of the sum previously announced—the failed Fund was replaced by the "Special Privatization and Restructuring Program (SPRP)," the size of which would amount to $3 billion.[56] The fact that loans from the World Bank and the EBRD would be this program's primary source of funds was not mentioned; however, no one remembered the program itself in the future.

[52] Wilson Center. Record of Japan-United States Summit meeting. April 16, 1993.

[53] Meeting of the Consultative Group for Russia (Paris, June 8–9, 1993). IMF Office Memorandum from Donal Donovan to the Managing Director. June 16, 1993. IMF Archive.

[54] WCPL&M. Calls to G7 Leaders on Tokyo Summit. Memorandum for the President from Anthony Lake and Robert Rubin. July 1993.

[55] "Memorandum of Telephone Conversation—Chancellor Helmut Kohl of Germany," *Clinton Digital Library*, accessed March 3, 2024. https://clinton.presidentiallibraries.us/items/show/101324

[56] Summers briefed Treasury Secretary Bentsen on this idea on June 27, adding that after that "*We can declare victory on the Russia part of the summit* and that *it would be a big mistake for the President to get into a fight for any additional resources for this purpose.*" CDL #99884. Report from Tokyo on Summit Meeting and Quadrilateral Trade Minister's Meeting. Memorandum for Secretary from Lawrence Summers. June 27, 1993.

While briefing Clinton for Tokyo, aides had to concede that the vaunted $43 billion package sketched by finance chiefs weeks earlier was largely illusory. The results achieved by the end of June looked dismal: a deferral of foreign debt repayments, an IMF loan, and three small World Bank loans totaled $18 billion, and the next 2–3 months did not promise to bring significant changes.[57] If the G7 leaders had "allowed" Yeltsin to concentrate on the topic of financial aid during the meeting, they would have had to blush profusely. But the Russian President spared them that by deciding to chase two birds with one stone.

Yeltsin was eager to demonstrate the return of great power status as soon as possible, and he insisted that Russia sign the summit's Political Declaration, which would automatically turn the G7 into the G8.[58] However, none of the G7 was prepared to accommodate him, especially since it was impossible to predict how Russia's political situation would develop. If the "Russian bear" were seated in the "Big Club," how could he later be removed if "friend Boris" was replaced by one of his opponents, who were radically opposed to democratic and market reforms and Russia's integration into global economic and political structures?

As a result, it was decided to add a special "7 + 1" session on political and economic issues—pointedly leaving Russia out of the title. This was to demonstrate to the Russian President that the G7 members were committed to cooperation, but that there were still significant differences between them and Russia that could not be ignored. Initially, the host of the summit, Japanese Prime Minister Miyazawa, wanted to limit the political discussion to Russia's domestic situation and its relations with post-Soviet countries, but the White House insisted on expanding the agenda to include "issues in various regions of the world where Russia is a key player along with us." Clinton moderated the political part of the session, and the economic part was moderated by European Commission President Jacques Delors, sending a clear signal to the leaders that there would be no pressure on them to give more money to Russia (except for the agreed-upon SPRD program).

Clinton opened with a word Yeltsin loved—"partners." "*The US and Russia have achieved a partnership in our bilateral relations. I think it is now time that the G7 countries and Russia achieve a foreign policy partnership based on a common desire to use our power and influence for a more stable and peaceful world.*" The Middle East, Somalia, Iraq, Libya, Angola, Cambodia, the Balkans,

[57] CDL #101270. Status of G7 Multilateral Support Package for Russia as of June 30, 1993. Fact Sheets on Russian Issues.

[58] CDL #101338. Telcon with President Yeltsin of the Russian Federation. June 28, 1993.

North Korea, flashpoints in the former Soviet Union, nuclear nonproliferation, the role of the UN Security Council, and peacekeeping operations—after that Yeltsin could hardly doubt he was now treated as a peer on global issues. At the same meeting, the Russian President received an invitation to the next summit in Naples, after which it was easy to dissuade him from pressing for economic aid. After all, full members of the "Big Club" do not ask for help from each other but, on the contrary, discuss how to help others.

At the meeting between the two Presidents the day after the summit, it was noted that the first Vancouver package was under way while the second still awaited Congressional action, then moved to other topics that were very important to Yeltsin. The Russian President was assured that Congress would repeal the package of Cold War legacy laws discriminating against Russia during the fall session and that COCOM would be abolished. Russia would be given a seat in the new organization on an equal footing with other countries, and the United States, Britain, and France supported Russia's January 1992 proposal by Yeltsin for a moratorium on nuclear testing. Unfortunately, the Russian President received no promises to repeal the Jackson-Vanik amendment. He was told that because the US President could annually waive the clause—already granting Russia MFN status—"*Graduating Russia from Jackson-Vanik would not provide any tangible economic benefit.*" Moreover, Clinton handed over another list of "opt-outs," saying that this was an obstacle to discussing repeal in Congress and that "*You and I don't need to discuss it every time.*"

The summit in Tokyo was the last one where the topic of financial aid to Russia was discussed. It seems that after becoming convinced that "friend Bill" wished to help but could not, Yeltsin ceased pressing his requests. This was immediately reflected in the administration's financial plans: for fiscal year 1995, aid to the former USSR was slashed by 60%.[59] Russia's share dropped to over 40% against 65% in 1994.[60]

In June 1994, Dan Speckhard, who had replaced Talbott as policy coordinator for CIS countries at the State Department, sent the National Security Council the final report of the Economic Working Group, which defined the administration's policy goals for economic assistance to these countries. Among the report's most important findings was the need to dilute Russia's

[59] US Assistance to the Former Soviet Union 1991–2001: A History of Administration and Congressional Action. CRS Report to Congress. RL30148. Updated January 15, 2002, p. 57.

economic dominance in the post-Soviet space by expanding access of companies from this region to the developed countries' markets.[61]

In May 1996, on the eve of the presidential election in Russia, the outcome of which no one could predict, many companies began to delay tax payments to the budget, and the federal government could not pay pensions and salaries to government employees on time. At this point, Yeltsin reluctantly sought a loan for Russia, and the reply showed that his political instincts had not failed him—no further US assistance would be forthcoming. "*I think that the $2.1 billion that the IMF has already disbursed to Russia this year is a solid sign of the international community's determination to support your reform program. As you know that objectivity has been a guiding principle of US policy since I came into office, and you can count on my government to continue to work closely with the IMF.*"[62]

The transformational decline of the Russian economy ended in 1996. In the five years from 1992 to 1996, the cumulative size of US financial assistance to Russia (excluding grain loans) totaled just under $4 billion.[63]

Losing the Path

Russia Is Out of Focus

For seven weeks after Tokyo, Clinton virtually "forgot" Russia—no calls with Yeltsin and no urgent agenda items. America's domestic problems attracted much more attention from journalists, and no one asked questions about Russia; even the agreement on creating an international space station did not attract much attention. The Russia bailout package passed the Senate with great difficulty, and no one inside the White House was willing to spend their negotiating resources on solving poorly understood problems. The arrival of Russian Prime Minister Viktor Chernomyrdin—making his first US visit since taking office—jolted Washington into recalling "Boris's friend." In addition to introducing himself, he co-chaired the inaugural meeting of the Gore-Chernomyrdin Commission, which would eventually evolve into a genuinely

[60] WCPL&M. Meeting on Assistance Issues. Memorandum for Tom Simons and Tom Dine from Nick Burns. March 31, 1994.

[61] WCPL&M. Economic Integration in the NIS. Memorandum for Nick Burns and Jim Collins from Dan Speckhard. June 6, 1994.

[62] CDL #101238. Letter to President Yeltsin from Bill Clinton. June 9, 1996.

[63] CRS US Bilateral Assistance to Russia: 1992–2002. CRS Report prepared for Members and Committees of Congress. January 16, 2003, p.13.

working body that brought together officials and businessmen to find solutions acceptable to both sides on the most intricate issues, from the sale of Russian enriched uranium to the United States, and Russian arms sales to Iran, to mutual exchange programs.

The Russian Prime Minister made a generally good impression, although his peculiar views on economic policy occasionally raised a smile. Particularly amusing was his discussion with Summers, who tried to explain that the laws of economics work like the laws of physics and, therefore, meeting the conditions outlined in the IMF program would necessarily lead to success. Chernomyrdin had little understanding of Summers' role in determining US economic policy and his influence on IMF decisions. To him, Summers was merely a deputy finance minister; "*the egg doesn't teach the hen,*" he quipped. The counterarguments—that Russia was a great power, that its economic policy was shaped by the wishes of the electorate and parliament, and that other countries should not impose their own conditions on how Russia would reform its economy—failed to persuade Summers but cooled his fervor. "*Of course,*" he said, "*Russia has the right to determine its economic policy. Still, America and its G7 partners have the right to decide whether or not to give money to the Russian government, depending on the decisions of the Russian government.*" Vice President Gore summarized the discussion: "*A tie.*"[64]

After the Russian Prime Minister's visit, Clinton called the Kremlin[65] and praised the new commission's results—two agreements were signed on joint work on the international space station and a joint commission on energy and space. Unfortunately for Yeltsin, the visit did not result in the signing of a contract under the HEU/LEU agreement,[66] which he had been counting on since it would have allowed him to load the Russian nuclear complex with work. But America could not be blamed for this—the main obstacle was the position of Ukrainian President Leonid Kravchuk, who, having agreed with Yeltsin on the terms of the transfer to Russia of Soviet nuclear weapons on his country's territory and the transfer to Russia of virtually the entire Soviet Black Sea Fleet in exchange for debt repayment, wanted to take the

---

[64] Strobe Talbott. The Russia Hand. Random House/New York, 2002, p. 85.

[65] CDL #101340. Telcon with President Yeltsin of the Russian Federation. September 7, 1993.

[66] The intergovernmental agreement between Russia and the United States concluded on February 18, 1993. It was designed for 20 years, providing for irreversible processing at Russian enterprises of at least 500 tons of Russian weapons-grade (highly enriched) uranium (equivalent to about 20,000 nuclear warheads) into low-enriched uranium, which after further processing at American enterprises was used as fuel for American nuclear power plants in the United States. Over the 20 years of the implementation of this agreement, TENEX received about $17 billion, of which $13 billion was transferred to the federal budget of Russia (Annual Report of TENEX for 2010, p.58).

opportunity to bargain and get something from the US beyond the $175 million he had been promised.[67]

In general, the conversation between the two Presidents was brief. Clinton was interested in the prospect of withdrawing Russian troops from the Baltic states—he was scheduled to hold talks with the three countries' Presidents at the end of September—and wanted at least some promises from his Russian partner. Yeltsin, having asked his "friend Bill" about the prospect of repealing laws inherited from the Cold War, did not react in any way to his promises to pressure the Senate to pass the law on the aid pact promised after Vancouver—the Russian President's head was occupied with something else entirely.

Victory or Defeat?

After the political confrontation that had intensified in the spring, the situation had calmed down, but it was the calm before the storm. The President and the Supreme Soviet launched parallel processes drafting the text of the Constitution, which widened the gap between the parties' desires with each passing week. The Supreme Council passed populist laws involving enormous expenditure, even though the budgetary possibilities were shrinking by the day. Inexperienced in macroeconomic policy, the Prime Minister quickly found common ground with Viktor Gerashchenko, the head of the Central bank, who was an advocate of support for the industrial producers, resulting in a program of the so-called centralized loans. The government determined the distribution of the loans, which were financed by the Bank of Russia, by sector, and by enterprise, which subsidized the interest payments from the budget when the interest rate was raised at the request of the IMF. Since decisions to extend credit were not based on the borrower's ability to pay, it was not surprising that by the end of the year, almost 30% of loans were not repaid.[68] The Ministry of Finance's desperate attempts to stay within the monetary and fiscal program parameters agreed with the IMF, restrained the most unorthodox decisions, but could not change the destructive nature of economic policy. After a slight slowdown in inflation in the spring, when it fell

[67] Leonid Kravchuk got his way: Russia agreed to supply $160 million worth of fuel to Ukrainian nuclear power plants free of charge, and Ukraine's share in US international assistance programs to CIS countries (NIS account) for 1995 and subsequent years was doubled in 1996–1999. Ukraine became the largest recipient of such programs, receiving 65% more than Russia. US Assistance to the Former Soviet Union 1991–2001: A History of Administration and Congressional Action. CRS Report RL30148. January 15, 2002.

[68] Annual Report. Central Bank of the Russian Federation. 1993, p. 49.

to 10% per month, which seemed to many to be a sign of approaching stabilization, price growth began to accelerate in the summer, exceeding 25% per month by fall. The IMF mission that visited Moscow came to an unambiguous conclusion: the program is broken, there can be no talk of a second tranche of the loan, and new serious negotiations are needed.

The already uneasy relations between the Ministry of Finance and the Bank of Russia finally soured at the end of July, when the Central Bank took a basically correct but extremely poorly prepared step: a new type of cash banknote was put into circulation in Russia, which allowed Russia to separate its monetary system from other CIS countries that used the Soviet/Russian ruble as a means of payment. The Bank of Russia prepared this decision in complete secrecy; no one in the government, including the Prime Minister, knew about it, and the announced terms of cash exchange for the population were so vaguely worded as to make the government suspect a confiscatory monetary reform. Panic gripped the country for several days.

The battle for power was escalating: Yeltsin wanted to adopt a new Constitution and hold elections for a new parliament as soon as possible, while Khasbulatov, who actually controlled the Supreme Soviet, demanded that the Soviets retain their power in the new Constitution and that the elections be held as late as possible, realizing that his popularity and support in society was far inferior to that of the President. Negotiation and compromise had never been Yeltsin's strong suit, and in mid-September, his nerves were frayed, and he decided to "cut the Gordian knot."

On September 21, the President announced the suspension of the Supreme Soviet, the termination of the powers of the deputies of the Congress of People's Deputies, and scheduled elections for December 12 for the new legislative bodies, the State Duma and the Federation Council, defining their powers and the procedure for electing them. Khasbulatov's obvious retaliatory move was to invalidate the presidential decree, dismiss Yeltsin from office, and swear in Vice President Rutskoi as President. Two Presidents and two governments appear in Russia.

For 10 days, the parties tried to reach a compromise. Then, in early October, the situation got out of the politicians' control: first, demonstrators supporting the Supreme Soviet clashed with police, and then an armed rebellion broke out in Moscow—Khasbulatov's supporters stormed Moscow City Hall and started invading the television center in Ostankino. On October 4, by order of Yeltsin, the storming of the Supreme Soviet building began, which was broadcast live by CNN. The forces of the sides were unequal; the Supreme Soviet deputies and their supporters, who had barricaded themselves in the building, surrendered shortly after tanks fired a few shots at the building, starting a fire.

Yeltsin won the battle, retained power, and faced an unobvious choice. On the one hand, he eliminated the destructive the Deputies' Congress and the Supreme Soviet and ensured free parliamentary elections. Thus, regardless of who won the elections, Russia had a legitimate parliament. On the other hand, Yeltsin did not dare to go for simultaneous presidential elections, postponing them to 1996, which was in accordance with the law. In principle, after that, Russia could live under the existing Constitution—all its sections except "Bodies of State Power" did not interfere much with the country's transformation—and nothing required an urgent referendum to approve the Constitution, especially since its text was not finalized. However, postponing the adoption of the new Constitution could, in principle, slow down the process of constitutional reform and institution building. Although the President enjoyed the highest level of popular support among politicians, it was rapidly declining amid reforms that were not successful. Extrapolating this situation for two or three years made the scenario of a new round of political confrontation very likely. In turn, no one could guarantee the success of the referendum. In the scenario when the Constitution is disapproved, the legitimacy of the elected parliament would be higher than the legitimacy of the President who was elected in another country and in another political situation. That could lead to a new political crisis, and the President found himself in a weak position.

Yeltsin's decision was contradictory. On the one hand, he listened to the recommendation of the Russian Ambassador to France, Yuri Ryzhov, whose opinion he had always valued. He set the referendum date to approve the Constitution at the same time as the election of parliamentary deputies. On the other hand, during the parliamentary elections, he decided to "stand above the fray" and not create his own party, which could have united all supporters of reforms. This was Yeltsin's significant political mistake, which he repeated in December 1995 during the elections to the second State Duma. The consequences of the mistake were felt in 1999, when, after Yeltsin decided not to run for President in 2000, it became clear that he had no "political heir" and had to look for an "heir" from among the few bureaucrats who had worked with him. His choice fell on Vladimir Putin. But that is another story.

Lacking an apparent leader whose authority everyone could recognize, the supporters of reforms put up four parties for the elections,[69] of which only one, Vybor Rossii, unambiguously supported the course of the President and the government. But this party was headed by Gaidar, who had no strong

[69] Yegor Gaidar headed "Vybor Rossii," Sergey Shakhrai headed PRES, Anatoly Sobchak headed RDDR, and Grigory Yavlinsky headed Yabloko.

electoral charisma and could not communicate with voters. Most importantly, Russian voters associated him with every hardship of economic reform.

On December 12, 1993, Russian voters approved a constitution drafted by the President's team, making Russia a presidential republic, and elected members of the two houses of parliament. The pro-reform parties together garnered 34.18% of the vote. Still, these votes were dispersed—the Liberal Democratic Party of Vladimir Zhirinovsky, which went to the polls under populist-nationalist slogans, took first place among the parties. Vybor Rossii came second in the elections on party lists, and although the party won the most seats in the lower house of parliament in the single-party constituency elections, the election results were perceived by most analysts as a defeat for the reformers. Even more so because 100 seats in the Duma (out of 444) went to representatives of the Communists and agrarians close to them in ideological positions.

5

It Never Happened, and Once Again It Did

A Little Caution Wouldn't Hurt

Although Yeltsin clearly dominated Russian politics and managed to defeat his opponents regularly, Clinton was not convinced that this could last forever. On the one hand, personal relations between the two leaders were very warm and candid. On the other hand, it was difficult to understand the logic of the Russian political process and its driving forces and impossible to guarantee that Russia would keep moving toward integration with the wider world. This idea frequently cropped up in Clinton's conversations with his entourage and with the leaders of other countries; it was used as an excuse to make aid conditional on Russia's meeting various benchmarks: when discussing long-term prospects for cooperation with Russia, one could constantly hear the caveat that everything was clear under Yeltsin, after him things were bound to be worse.

Two weeks before Yeltsin signed the decree dissolving parliament triggering constitutional change, Clinton asked Kohl, "*How do you think Yeltsin is doing with all this political controversy in Russia?*" And the answer could not have pleased him: "*It is very difficult, but in a way it's irrational. Things might go smoothly or very bad. On the other hand it could be his chances are less than 50%*

This is one of the famous phrases said by Chernomyrdin, the prime minister in Yeltsin's time, known by his aphoristic style.

S. Aleksashenko, *Post-Cold War Russia and the Missed Opportunity for Global Stability*, https://doi.org/10.1007/978-3-032-01380-4_5

or it could also be said his chances are 50-50... Anybody that will come after him will not be as auspicious as they are now."[1]

The day after Yeltsin's decree, the two leaders spoke again by telephone, and they agreed immediately on which side to back. Clinton said he had already prepared his statement to support the Russian President and "*basically stating that I asked him to honor democracy, and he pledged he would.*" Kohl endorsed issuing the statement and offered to review its wording. He believed the West has no choice: "*Of all the people that play a role there, I trust him the most, and I am convinced that if he is no longer in power, if he's removed, it will be much worse.*"[2]

In January 1994, Clinton, before meeting in Moscow with Yeltsin, asked Ukrainian President Leonid Kravchuk how he assessed the political situation in Russia, what he thought about Zhirinovsky's success, and the possibility of changing Russia's foreign policy. Kravchuk offered a candid assessment: the danger was not in Zhirinovsky, but in the fact that together with his "political neighbors," he had a majority in the Duma: "*But there are two forces very close to him, the communists and the peasants and in those two parties there is a majority. The only guarantee is the adoption of the constitution. But this is possible only while Yeltsin is in office. But there is no eternal president and we worry about expansion. There are extremist forces in Russia and Ukraine. My vision is to support Russia; otherwise, the situation in Russia will become more tense. Yeltsin and Chernomyrdin understand. Now there is no serious worry or danger but the situation is not stable. Russians were brought up in greatness. They dream of empire, especially the officers of the army.*"[3] Imperial ambitions surely resonated with Clinton—he had warned of the danger just the day before, when meeting with the Presidents of the Visegrad Four countries.[4]

A few days later, Chancellor Kohl warned that the Russians were "*losing touch with the President*" and losing faith in its involvement in the changes taking place in the country. Clinton went further: "*The average person in Russia doesn't feel connected to the government or understand how it will come out for them. Even some of the better educated Russians feel uninvolved and disconnected.*

[1] CDL #101325. Memorandum of Telephone Conversation—Chancellor Helmut Kohl of Germany. September 7, 1993.

[2] CDL #101326. Memorandum of Telephone Conversation—Chancellor Helmut Kohl of Germany. September 21, 1993.

[3] *CDL* #101366. Memorandum of Conversation—President Leonid Kravchuk of Ukraine, January 12, 1994.

[4] *CDL* #101395. Memorandum of Conversation—President Lech Walesa of Poland, President Arpad Goencz of Hungary, President Michal Kovac of Slovakia, and President Vaclav Havel of the Czech Republic. January 12, 1994.

They believe Yeltsin is on the right side of history but don't feel connected to it." Helmut Kohl replied, "*I told him this during our last meeting and he had this air to him too. One gets the feeling he is disconnected, not that he wants that, not that it is part of his character, but there is this huge apparatus, this huge machinery around him that cuts him out.*"[5]

Yeltsin, willingly or not, scaled back his political activity: on the one hand, the victory (approval of the Constitution) had been achieved; on the other hand, after a stormy battle, there was simple human fatigue, especially since it was not clear what the next goal was. But politics, like nature, abhors a vacuum. Without information about the Russian President's plans, Western diplomats and politicians shifted the focus of their interest to other actors, often giving them excessive importance. Inevitably, the formal winner of the election, Vladimir Zhirinovsky, media-savvy and unburdened by decorum, seized the spotlight. He was perceived as an important player in Russian politics, and in some scenarios, he could become the next President of Russia. It would take a few months for it to become clear that he lacked lofty political ambitions and was willing to exchange the votes of his faction in the Duma for various benefits from the government.

Talbott, whose remit demanded constant contact with Russian officials, found Kozyrev exasperating, calling him a "*moron,*"[6] declared he was "*part of a problem rather than part of the solution,*" and characterized his position as "a *psychodrama*."[7] In addition to Zhirinovsky, Talbott saw a threat in the hardline, at times even militantly nationalistic stance now taken by the former Russian ambassador to Washington, Vladimir Lukin, who had become a Duma member.

Republicans accused Clinton of foreign policy indecision, blasted his soft line on Russia, and urged a tougher stance after the Russian parliamentary elections.[8]

All this created an unfavorable climate for the Presidents' next meeting in Moscow in January 1994. On the one hand, the visit succeeded because it finalized trilateral negotiations with Ukraine on the withdrawal of nuclear

---

[5] *CDL* #101394. Memorandum of Telephone Conversation—Chancellor Helmut Kohl of Germany. January 18, 1994.

[6] US DoS. Case F-2017-13,804. Doc No C06835969. Letter "Eyes Only" to the Secretary from Strobe Talbott. March 13, 1994.

[7] CDL #57236. Your Meeting with FM Kozyrev. Letter to the Secretary from Strobe Talbott. [Between first and tenth SA] January 1994.

[8] US DoS. Case F-2017-13,804. Doc No C06835973. Letter to the Secretary from Strobe Talbott. February 14, 1994.

weapons from its territory. On the other hand, the two leaders held no serious bilateral discussion—perhaps by mutual design.

On the morning of January 13, the Russian President tried to talk about financial aid. He said the Tokyo aid package was being implemented very slowly. Russia was facing massive unemployment, businesses needed money for investment, and negotiations on restructuring foreign debt were ongoing. Clinton and his team knew perfectly well that aid to Russia was minimal: "*We're not so heavily invested in support for reform that we couldn't turn on a dime and deal with overnight revision of the Russian government to the Soviet type. We don't want to dwell publicly to do that, but I'm sure it's true.*"[9] Clinton's reply was clear and cool: "*We've committed all of the Vancouver assistance package and distributed most of it. So the things that have been in our personal control we have moved quickly. On the second package, much is tied to the G7. I too am frustrated and committed to moving it along faster.*"[10] To soften the blow, Clinton added that the Jackson-Vanik amendment could soon be repealed, "*I have strong hopes we can get this done this year.*" Yeltsin muttered "*Good,*" and his interlocutor hurriedly changed the subject.[11]

On the same day, near the end of the big dinner, when Russian Defense Minister Pavel Grachev was talking about his agreement with NATO Secretary General Wörner to make a presentation of Russian military doctrine to the defense ministers of the alliance's member countries, Yeltsin suddenly announced that he agreed with Clinton about NATO's role in ensuring global security and that Russia should be the first of the post-socialist countries of Central and Eastern Europe to become a member of this organization. The statement appeared improvised, as the Russian President followed up by saying: "*I have to be honest, so far Russia is not ready to join NATO… Besides, we need to understand how China would feel about it,*" he added, and asked if the CIA could analyze the consequences of Russia's joining NATO and share its findings with Russia. Clinton did not respond to the latter request, but about Russia's NATO membership, he hinted that it was quite possible: "*We are all working together toward the time when we will all consider an attack on one of us, an attack on every one of us.*"[12] But it was already the end of the dinner, and there was no strength to continue discussing the topic….

---

[9] Letter to the Secretary from Strobe Talbott. March 29, 1994. US DoS. Case F-2017-13,804. Doc No C06835958.

[10] CDL #58577. One-on-one meeting with President Yeltsin of Russia. January 13, 1994.

[11] Ibid.

[12] CDL #58577. President's Dinner with President Yeltsin. Cable from Ambassador Pickering. January 14, 1994.

Even before dinner, Gaidar had informed Summers that he would leave the government, and Boris Fedorov would probably not remain there. This news shocked Summers, who knew this would sharply reduce the chances of continuing anti-inflation policy. He insisted that the President discuss this with Yeltsin and, at most, demanded that they remain in the government or at least make it clear that these resignations would naturally adjust the position of the IMF and the G7. These arguments failed to sway Yeltsin, who had already decided; he said that there were problems related to these people inside the country.[13]

It was difficult to understand all the nuances of Russian politics. The passionate Gaidar argued that Russia was sliding toward fascism. Georgy Arbatov, who had been an advisor to Soviet and Russian leaders in disarmament negotiations with the United States for more than 20 years, said that it was necessary to forget Yeltsin and start working with the Communists. He was countered by Alexander Yakovlev, who argued that the Communists were only lurking and ready to return to terror if they came to power and that there was no alternative to Yeltsin, who had a deep-seated aversion to Communism. Let those people sort themselves out and decide what they want. In the meantime, "*Russian politics are a mess, and they'll continue to be so for a very long time… While we must always be ready to deal with a truly, dramatically catastrophic turn for the worse, the more realistic challenge facing us is responding to the murkiness and volatility of events over there.*"[14]

Not Again, Huh?

The results of the referendum approving the new Constitution pleased Yeltsin, and the results of the Duma elections did not upset him too much: many independent deputies, whose political leanings were unclear, were elected, and the President expected that with their support, he would be able to form a majority that would support him, although, frankly, the chances of this were not high, 50-50. At least that's how he described the situation in mid-January to Clinton, who came to Moscow.[15] The Russian President believed that the elected deputies would take a constructive stance and not clash with the President and the government. He believed the Duma would be

[13] CDL #58577. One-on-one meeting with President Yeltsin of Russia. January 15, 1994.

[14] US DoS. Case F-2017-13,804. Doc No C06835958. Letter to the Secretary from Strobe Talbott. March 29, 1994.

[15] CDL #58577. The cable of the US Ambassador in Moscow T Pickering. January 14, 1994

counterbalanced by the Federation Council, in which "80% of deputies are democrats," and which would be headed by Vladimir Shumeiko, an associate of the President.

The hopes of the President, who, after the fall crisis, had relaxed into apathy, were not destined to come true. His candidate for the Duma's speaker, Vladimir Lukin, didn't get enough votes. Instead, the Communist Ivan Rybkin, who had supported Ruslan Khasbulatov during the October crisis and was among the last to be taken out of the White House at gunpoint, got this chair.[16] Viktor Chernomyrdin, who was to be confirmed as prime minister, had to negotiate with the parliamentary factions on his own to gain support, and one of his negotiating resources was the composition of the government. Capturing the mood of the President, who believed that the election results reflected voter dissatisfaction with economic reform, Chernomyrdin proposed to Yeltsin that Gaidar, Fedorov, and Chubais be fired and got his agreement.[17] Only the intervention of the head of the presidential administration Sergei Filatov, and Clinton's repeated insistence that he weigh the consequences of this decision led to Anatoly Chubais remaining in his post.

The government's economic bloc was radically weakened: Chubais' powers were limited to privatization issues, Alexander Shokhin lost his post of deputy prime minister to become minister of economy, and Sergei Dubinin, who had overseen the Finance Ministry after Fedorov's departure, remained acting minister until his dismissal in October 1994. The consequence was a rapid loosening of monetary and fiscal policy: Prime Minister Chernomyrdin felt it was his duty to fulfill all the spending commitments he had made in the Duma approval process. Economists know monetary or fiscal moves eventually drive inflation and the ruble's rate, but there was no one around the Prime Minister who was ready to explain this to him. The Prime Minister reacted only to the decline in inflation in the spring of 1994, which resulted from Boris Fedorov's tough policy in the second half of the previous year and believed that "*This time everything would be different.*" Even more so because by early April, the IMF had agreed on the government's program without any complaints and provided the second tranche of the loan that Russia had been waiting for since the previous summer.

In February 1994, Yeltsin faced unfriendly, from his point of view, actions of the State Duma: the deputies adopted a decree on amnesty, which exempted all participants of the October armed rebellion from responsibility. The President tried to prevent this by demanding that the Prosecutor General not

[16] Yuri Ivanov. *"Prostoj rossijskij spiker, kotoryj vsekh perekhitril."* (Ordinary Russian speaker who outsmarted everyone.) Kommersant. April 23, 1994. https://www.kommersant.ru/doc/76951

[17] Sergey Filatov. Sovershenno nesekretno. (*Absolutely unclassified.*) Moscow, Vagrius, 2000, p. 364.

implement this decision. But Alexei Kazannik, whom Yeltsin appointed to the post in early October, said he intended to abide by the law. According to the recollections of presidential aides, the beginning of a "protracted crisis streak" happened: Yeltsin made few public appearances, and his activity dropped sharply. The Kremlin's push for a Treaty of Public Accord, whose participants were to approve the President's constitutional reform program and the government's economic policy, collapsed when Communists and Agrarians, still demanding changes, refused to sign.

Everything that was happening was closely monitored and assessed by experts in Washington, and their voices sounded alarming: "*Yeltsin is staying out of the fray on day-to-day, even week-to-week matters… Yeltsin is peevish, losing his grip, throwing tantrums…*[18] *Russian politics are a mess, and they'll continue to be so for a very long time. It is very easy for card-carrying supporters of Russian reform to get as discouraged as the Russian reformers themselves are.*"[19]

> The proximate cause of the pessimism here is the departure of Gaidar and Fyodorov from the government… At immediate issue … is economic policy: credit and subsidy levels, inflation rates, what the repudiation of 'market romanticism' and the endorsement of 'non-monetary measures' will mean in practice … worries about the possible 'Sovietization' … of the Russian economy is fueling concern over a perceived similar trend in Russian foreign and security policy … the danger of 'a return to confrontation in US–Russian relations; a return to the division of Eurasia into blocs; a return, in short, to some version of the Cold War' … is more prominently on people's minds now than at any point since the collapse of the August 1991 coup.[20]

We're Eight!

Learning to Be Together

Communication between the US and Russian Presidents in the spring of 1994 became routine: the Presidents called each other or (as their aides prefer) exchanged letters to discuss narrow topics (NATO bombing in the former Yugoslavia, preparations for the UN Security Council meeting on the

[18] US DoS. Case F-2017-13804. Doc No C06835939. Letter to W. Christopher from S. Talbott. March 11, 1994.
[19] US DoS. Case F-2017-13804. Doc No C06835958. Letter to W. Christopher from S. Talbott. March 29, 1994.
[20] US DoS. Case F-2017-13804. Doc No C06835982. Letter to G. Mamedov from S. Talbott. January 29, 1994.

situation on the Korean Peninsula). Conversation on broader issues was postponed until a face-to-face meeting scheduled for July, when the G7 would meet in Naples and where Yeltsin has been invited as the eighth, full-fledged participant in the political discussion.

The two Presidents' personal warmth had improved bilateral relations, smoothing many rough edges. "*Not only is there no bad blood, but Boris Nikolayevich believes his political survival is closely associated with his partnership with the US and with Bill Clinton personally. He's not going to let anyone bring about a cooling of that relationship,"*—said Russian Deputy Foreign Minister Grigory Mamedov in a conversation with Talbott.

In turn, the American President was also willing to soften negotiating positions and seek a compromise: "*On the Russians in the Middle East, the President and Vice President … both expressed the view that we should keep trying to make sure that the Russians are included in the diplomacy. The President said he wants us to go the 'extra mile' in being accommodating to the Russians on the Middle East, partly 'to keep them from going off the reservation.'"*[21] This stance by the President did not always suit his entourage: "*There are limits to what we consider acceptable Russian diplomatic behavior; there are limits to our willingness to humor the Russians and go out of our way to make them, feel included.*"[22]

At the working level, a convoluted process tried to frame bilateral principles amid diverging interests. Russia, generally supporting pressure on the leaders of the countries in the former Yugoslavia to prevent the intensification of the armed conflict, was more sympathetic to Serbia and prioritized the idea of round tables and negotiations. The US, having received the support of the UN Security Council, preferred NATO-led force. Russia was slowly giving in but insistently asked to be "closely consulted" at every step.[23] Yeltsin was confident that the two Presidents agreed that "*any use of force in Bosnia must be preceded by US and Russian consultations.*"[24]

In early April, the Serbian army launched an offensive in the Goražde area, and NATO aircraft bombed the Serbs. The Kremlin viewed this as a breach of agreements, further souring relations. The White House claimed that either the UN Secretary General had given his consent to the use of force (although

[21] US DoS. Case F-2017-13804. Doc No C06835939. Letter to W. Christopher from S. Talbott. March 11, 1994.

[22] US DoS. Case F-2017-13804. Doc No C06835969. Letter to W. Christopher from S. Talbott. March 13, 1994.

[23] US DoS. Case F-2017-13804. Doc No C06694524. Yeltsin Foreign Policy Assistant on Bosnia. Cable to the Secretary of State from Ambassador Pickering. February 25, 1994.

[24] US DoS. Case F-2017-13804. Doc No C06837937. Letter to President Clinton from Yeltsin. April 16, 1994.

this was not within his authority; the Security Council should have made such a decision) or the situation had developed so quickly that the decision was made by the NATO commander even without consulting Washington.[25]

A few days after the events in Goražde, Talbott met with Mamedov, who frankly admitted that it would be enough for the Kremlin to receive a warning about the use of force in Bosnia. This would allow them to talk about Russia's involvement in the settlement process and participation in the search for solutions. As it was, he said, the Russians "*ended up with a double portion of egg on its face*": on the one hand, there were accusations from the opposition, and on the other, Serbs did not believe that Russia was not warned. However, these arguments had no effect on the US diplomat, who persisted in repeating that the US would not do anything that would allow Russia to put a stick in its wheels. At the end of the conversation, Mamedov pleaded: "*Trust us just a little bit more. Test us next time. We won't make you sorry*," but Talbott was adamant, he told Christopher: "*Needless to say, I didn't commit us on this.*"[26]

At the end of June, the Russian President sent Clinton a long letter outlining his vision of international problems that could be the subject of discussion by the Political Eight in Naples. Moreover, speaking of the need for "*economic cooperation according to the seven plus one formula,*" he hints at Russia's claim to full participation in the Big Club. Yeltsin implicitly acknowledged the futility of seeking new G7 aid, limiting himself to the vague call "*to support Russian reforms.*"

In the letter, Yeltsin spoke of the need for the G8 to focus on "*reforming the structures that ensure stability in the Euro-Atlantic region,*" putting the CSCE in the first place; reiterated Russia's desire to participate in negotiations to establish a new export control regime to replace COCOM; and mentioned Bosnia, North Korea, and the Middle East. In the end, the Russian President rather clumsily remarked that Russia, as the newcomer, pre-emptively claimed a veto over every decision: "*You understand, of course, that without US–Russia agreement, consensus within the G8 will not be achievable.*"[27]

---

[25] US DoS. Case F-2017-13804. Doc No C06835952. Letter to W. Christopher from S. Talbott. April 14, 1994.

[26] US DoS. Case F-2017-13804. Doc No C06835952. Letter to W Christopher from S Talbott. April 14, 1994. In September, Talbott and Mamedov met in Moscow, and the US diplomat described US plans for Haiti, including the decision in principle to intervene militarily. Mamedov earnestly requests that Clinton call Yeltsin just before the ultimatum to the members of the military junta and before US troops land on the island. See US DoS. Case F-2017-13804. Doc No C06835921. "No surprises" and "partners consult" are still the mottos of the day. Letter to W Christopher from S Talbott. September 11, 1994.

[27] US DoS. Case F-2017-13804. Doc No C06838126. Letter to President Clinton from Yeltsin. June 28, 1994.

When Comrades Disagree

In 1994, a mid-term election year, every administration flaw came under intense scrutiny. In late February, the Senate confirmed Talbott to the second most important position in the State Department, undersecretary of state, which dramatically expanded his powers but did not eliminate his shortcomings. He proposed a radical power shake-up inside State, briefly reducing its effectiveness. On the other hand, the promotion further complicated his relations with other agencies and led to growing tensions between the State Department and the NSC, about which Talbott honestly wrote to his boss: "*I see it as one of my major responsibilities to try to encourage smoother relations among DoD, NSC and State… This is already tricky, and it's going to become more so. There is, alas, already a certain degree of mutual apprehension, bordering on mistrust, in the air.*"[28]

Talbott sensed that actual US financing for Russian reforms was meagre, but his unwillingness to engage in a professional discussion and the lack of people in the State Department or the White House capable of assessing the state of the Russian economy and offering adequate tools had strained relations with the ambitious Summers: "*I fault myself for allowing a bit of an NSC-Treasury axis to develop over the last several months, to the detriment not only of State's equities but also of the policy itself. Treasury, quite simply, has taken an overly theological view of Russian economic reform. They define 'reform' and 'stabilization' too narrowly in terms of the indicators like inflation, deficit as a percentage of GDP, etc. They've got to mix a bit more politics into their thinking, and prescriptions, on Russian economics.*"[29]

As a result, press and Congress were increasingly baffled by White House foreign policy principles, and the administration was being increasingly criticized. Critics claimed the President was self-absorbed and unwilling to be tough: "*All the outsiders seemed to agree that the President himself is disengaged from foreign policy; there's apparently a widespread sense that he's not at the center of the thinking about the new world. Second, there's the problem of our willingness and ability to use force; the perception that Bill Clinton as commander-in-chief is*

[28] US DoS. Case F-2017-13804. Doc No C06835979. Letter to W. Christopher from S. Talbott. March 11, 1994.

[29] US DoS. Case F-2017-13804. Doc No C06835973. Letter to W. Christopher from S. Talbott. February 13, 1994.

a ditherer or a bluffer (you can just hear the Republicans warming up on this theme—'the sax is an uncertain trumpet)'."[30]

In response, Clinton's team boosted the clout of its congressional liaisons and campaign strategists. They, in turn, need to consider and respond to changing public sentiments and, as a result, consolidate control over the President's decision-making, including in matters of foreign policy.

The State Department drew increasing criticism, and its standing in the President's inner circle weakened: "*As an Administration and as a Department, we've got a problem with the vision thing. It has become a part of the conventional wisdom that … we're reactive, intellectually timid; that we have a bunch of policies and objectives, but they don't hang together as part of a single Grand Design, at least not one deserving of capitalization.*"[31]

The failures of pro-presidential parties in the Russian parliamentary elections, the acquisition of the Duma speaker's post by a representative of left-wing parties, and the growing number of nationalist statements by politicians were perceived as a defeat for Yeltsin, a reversal of reforms, and, consequently, as a failure of policy toward Russia. Yet, these doubts also crept into Clinton's "Russian team": "*The question on most Americans' minds is: Are we heading back into a new Cold War? The essence of our position is: No. Or at least, Not necessarily.*"[32]

Really?!

The Russian President traveled to the G7 summit in Naples in high spirits. Although the downturn persisted, inflation plunged from 18% in January to 6% in June, and the weakening of the reformist wing of the government did not have the catastrophic impact many had expected. This was recognized by the IMF's decision to grant Russia the first tranche of the STF systemic loan. But most importantly, Yeltsin's dream of fully integrating Russia into Western

[30] Reacting to this framing of the issue, Talbott offered his boss a simple explanation: we (the US) have too successful a foreign policy. Hence, the President's daily involvement is unnecessary (especially since he does not like regular meetings, preferring to "focus like a laser" on specific tasks). As far as Russia is concerned, Talbott's position seemed quite naive: although much of the problems in Russia are related to the slow transformation of the economy, he suggested that his boss should abstract from economic problems when publicly discussing issues related to that country. See US DoS. Case F-2017-13804. Doc No C06835973. Letter to W. Christopher from S. Talbott. February 13, 1994.

[31] US DoS. Case F-2017-13804. Doc No C06835979. Letter to W. Christopher from S. Talbott. March 11, 1994.

[32] US DoS. Case F-2017-13804. Doc No C06835973. Letter to W. Christopher from S. Talbott. February 13, 1994.

structures was coming true right before our eyes: on June 22, Kozyrev signed an agreement with NATO on Russia's entry into the Partnership for Peace; on June 24, Yeltsin signed a Partnership Agreement with the European Union, which was supposed to be an important step toward integrating the Russian economy into the European system; and here was the "cherry on the cake"—the doors of the Big Club were opening for the Russian President.

The Russian government perceived the agreement with the European Union as the most valuable, which is not surprising—Europe was Russia's leading trading partner. The agreement was believed to remove trade barriers between the partners, and Russia would receive the most favored nation status. However...

The first frustration was that the agreement would take effect only after every EU member-state parliament ratified it. This process lasted two and a half years, so the agreement was not entered into force until May 1999, when it was ratified by all 15 members' parliaments. To make some of its norms work earlier, a temporary agreement on partnership and cooperation was signed in February 1996. However, the main achievement of the Russian negotiators—the recognition of Russia as a country in transition—did not end the anti-dumping restrictions imposed on Russian producers under the rules applied to centrally managed economies. Russian government experts estimated that European anti-dumping procedures cost Russia about $250 million a year.

Since coal, steel products, and nuclear fuel were excluded from the trade part of the agreement, ferrous metallurgy was the only sector of the Russian economy that experienced positive changes.

The Russian government had hoped that, immediately after the agreement came into force, negotiations would begin on the creation of a free trade area between Russia and the EU and on recognizing Russia as a market economy, but they were first postponed until late 1998 and then this plan began to be talked about as a distant future—the European Union's Collective Strategy on Russia, adopted in June 1999, spoke of exploring "in addition to WTO accession, the possibilities of ensuring the necessary conditions for the establishment of a free trade area Russia and the EU in the future."[33]

[33] EU Collective Strategy on Russia (1999). https://mgimo.ru/files2/y11_2013/243404/4.3.collective_eu_strategy.htm?utm_source=google.com&utm_medium=organic&utm_campaign=google.com&utm_referrer=google.com

Meanwhile, Clinton, who persistently promoted the idea of Russia's full participation in the political dialog with the G7 countries, considered it a good deal. On the one hand, it made it possible to avoid another round of discussions on financial aid to Russia, which could not lead to a result that Yeltsin was happy with. On the other hand, it was "*relatively low-cost, high impact way of anchoring Yeltsin, therefore Russia, in the West... Russia's inclusion in the club might help serve as an antidote to its pariah complex—at least in the mind, and behavior, of its President.*"[34] The main goal that the US President intended to achieve was to obtain Yeltsin's promise of a complete withdrawal of Russian troops from the three Baltic states by the end of the summer.

Against this background, there were no serious preparations for the meeting of the Presidents. Even the fact that the $2.5 billion aid package to Russia that had been adopted in late September 1993 and proposed by the President after the Vancouver meeting had yet to be implemented did not arouse emotion either among the National Security Council staffers Bill Burns and Leon Fuerth, who spoke at the White House briefing, or among the journalists who asked them questions: "*That money has largely been unspent ... we don't want to spend money in the absence of programs... we have spent time ... trying to design programs which can then be, we hope, effectively funded... The President has given us very clear priorities on where he wants us to spend money, but it is best to be patient when you design programs to make sure they're going to be adequately designed.*"[35] That Russia was able to receive $30 billion of the $43 billion promised a year previously was hailed as "*a very good achievement.*"[36] Ukraine was becoming the central focus of the economic discussion in Naples, and Yeltsin had to consider Russia's contribution.

No one wanted to derail the agreed agenda of the summit, which was supposed to showcase a new phase in Russia–West relations. Like the other participants in the discussion, the Russian President was sufficiently accommodating. He gratefully accepted the positive assessments of Russia's participation in the Advisory Group on the former Yugoslavia, supported France's efforts to resolve the conflict in Rwanda, and did not object to the active US policy toward Haiti, up to and including the use of armed force to reinstate ousted President Aristide.

The most contentious discussions concerned Russia's policy towards neighboring post-Soviet countries. Since 1989, numerous interethnic conflicts have erupted in the Soviet Union: between neighboring republics (Azerbaijan and

[34] Strobe Talbott. The Russia Hand. Random House/New York, 2002, p.124.

[35] CDL #99886. Background briefing by senior administration official. June 21, 1994.

[36] CDL #606612. Background briefing by senior administration official. July 1, 1994.

Armenia in Nagorno-Karabakh), between a union republic and a constituent autonomy (the Georgian-Abkhazian war), within a single autonomous entity (between Ossetians and Ingush in the Ossetian-Ingush Autonomous Republic, which was part of the RSFSR), between a union republic and a part of its territory whose population differed sharply in national composition (the Transnistrian conflict in Moldova). These conflicts took the Kremlin by surprise: until now, they had been pre-emptively suppressed by the KGB, and when they spilled out into the open, no one knew how to respond.

Left unchecked, the conflicts escalated into armed clashes, and by the time of the collapse of the Soviet Union, many of them were in a heated stage. The Russian government led by Yeltsin, having signed an agreement recognizing Soviet borders as state borders, in practice felt no obligation to honor them and, in various forms, supported separatist sentiments in neighboring countries up to the direct involvement of the Russian military in the conflict in Transnistria. To stop the bloodshed in Moldova (1992) and Georgia (1994), the use of the Russian military as a peacekeeping force on the lines of contact was accepted by the opposing sides.[37]

The West perceived Russia's inconsistent policy toward these conflicts as evidence of resurgent imperial ambitions—Russia wanted to use the separatists as a lever of pressure on neighboring countries, but none of the G7 countries was ready to participate in peacekeeping operations related to these conflicts, as the risks of individual clashes escalating into a real war were too high. Each time, it was necessary to craft diplomatic language that satisfied all parties and to find ways to place Russian peacekeeping forces under international control.

The face-to-face meeting between the two Presidents was brief—an agreement had already been reached for another summit in September. Yeltsin received a promise of US support for an increase in the amount of IMF loans Russia could apply for—since this did not impose any budgetary costs on America, Clinton readily agreed. The US President secured his goal—Yeltsin promised to complete the withdrawal of Russian troops from the Baltic states by the end of August after being assured that his position on the

[37] In Georgia, the functions of peacekeepers were formally entrusted to the CIS Collective Peacekeeping Force, which was fully staffed by Russian military personnel.

"infringement of the rights of the Russian-speaking population" would be communicated by American politicians to the leaders of the Baltic states.[38]

The most serious discussion between the Presidents concerned export control issues after COCOM's demise and ongoing talks to create its successor regime. For the Russian President, who had already realized that Jackson-Vanik would not be quickly repealed, Russia's participation in the negotiations for a new organization was an important symbol; Clinton was charged with persuading Russia to limit arms sales to Iran. Diplomatically speaking, the parties had brought their positions closer together, but a final agreement was still needed.

Things Are Changing Fast

A Crisis that Helped

After successful international visits, which, Yeltsin said, had greatly enhanced Russia's standing, the Russian President returned to Moscow encouraged. By this time, however, the undesirable results of the Chernomyrdin government's loose fiscal and monetary policies were already becoming visible in the Russian economy. Although statistics showed a continued decline in inflation, this was primarily due to seasonal factors, such as the rapid decline in prices for new crops such as fruits and vegetables.

In July–August, the rate of price growth was 4–5% per month, which was in line with the goals of the program agreed with the IMF. But already in early July, the Fund's mission, visiting Moscow, heard extremely pessimistic assessments: inflation began accelerating, and there was no chance that it would fall below 10% per month by the end of the year.[39] The situation was aggravated by the fact that while the Ministry of Finance was trying to limit the growth of the budget deficit, which was financed by loans from the Central Bank, and was sequestering budget expenditures, the Bank of Russia supported the initiatives of the "red directors" and promoted the presidential decree on granting large loans to state-owned enterprises, which had actually become

[38] Another condition put forward by Yeltsin and accepted by Clinton was a visit to Moscow by the Estonian President, who defiantly refused contact with the Russian President. This condition was not public, and Yeltsin's theatrical negative answer to a direct question at a press conference about whether an agreement had been reached on a date for completing the withdrawal of Russian troops sounded like a thunderclap—leaks from the US delegation said otherwise.

[39] Russian Federation—Article IV Consultation Mission—Back-to-Office Report. July 20, 1994. IMF Archive. #138424. EUZAI Consultation Files. RM 2002-0048-001.

bankrupt, for restructuring. The government guaranteed the loans, although the budget law did not provide for this. John Odling-Smee, director of the IMF's European Department II, which dealt with Russia, visited Moscow and spoke of the defeat of the Ministry of Finance, which had lost control over the growth of the government's actual borrowing.[40]

As is typical in high-inflation economies, budget subsidies to enterprises and the provision of loans at favorable rates failed to revive economic growth. Moreover, in the first half of 1994, the economy's decline accelerated compared to the previous year. It was a big surprise, including for IMF experts, who listed several factors. For the first time, the Fund's documents said that one of the reasons for the downturn in the economy was the uncompetitiveness of Russian goods, often manifested in a complete lack of demand. Nevertheless, the Fund's experts could not take the next step and recognize that this caused a fall in budget revenues and, accordingly, a growing budget deficit and/or increase arrears of budgetary payments. To solve this problem Russia needed support for the budget, not support for the balance of payments; still, this was not incorporated into the Fund's charter and way of practice.[41]

Moreover, in mid-September, the next mission of the Fund came to Moscow to discuss economic policy for the following year. The Russian government received confirmation in private that the limits of lending to Russia would be significantly increased (the result of the talks between the Presidents in Naples); the emphasis in the IMF's proposals was on the traditional instrument—the use of a fixed exchange rate and a stabilization fund following the example of Poland. The tough position of the Ministry of Finance—"*we do not need a Polish stabilization fund; we need budget support*"—which was supported by the Central Bank,[42] forced the IMF management to pay greater attention to Russia's requests and agree with the arguments presented. The information that the IMF was ready to sharply increase the size of the loan which Russia can claim if it were to adopt the ambitious program became a powerful lever in the hands of reformers in the government, and they managed to convince the Prime Minister of the need to take a unique chance and

[40] Visit to Moldova, Russia, Georgia, Ukraine, and Belarus. Office Memorandum from John Odling-Smee to the Acting Managing Director and the Deputy Managing Director. August 3, 1994. IMF Archive. #138424. EUZAI Consultation Files. RM 2002-0048-001.

[41] Russian Federation—Staff Report for the 1994 Article IV Consultation. To Members of the IMF Executive Board. SM/94/231. August 26, 1994. IMF Archives.

[42] Russian Federation—Back-to-Office Report from Ernesto Hernandez-Cata. Office Memorandum to the Managing Director and the Deputy Managing Director. September 20, 1994. IMF Archive. Back to office reports/Russia, May 25, 1993–April 3, 1996.

turn the situation around. The Ministry of Finance began intensive work on planning the next year's budget, which would not include Central Bank loans.

In late September, Yeltsin met with the US President in Washington and made one last attempt to persuade "friend Bill" to provide serious financial assistance to Russia—he literally begged for the forgiveness of part of the Soviet debt: "*Taken globally, we owe $80 billion and we are owed $140 billion. We haven't been able to collect because it's from Cuba, Libya and Iraq. And none of the CIS countries have paid one kopek. Could you forgive the difference between $140 and $80 billion, or to $60 billion? It's only morally fair since we took over the debts of the old USSR,*" but was met with a cold reaction from Clinton: "*We'll have to take that up. Secretary Bentsen has talked about further debt forgiveness.*"[43] However, there was no continuation; the issue hung in the air, and the Russian President again encountered a wall of silence.

Meanwhile, the situation in the Russian financial market continued to deteriorate. The result of soft monetary policy, as often happens, was a devaluation of the national currency: banks used available funds to buy currency, the sale of which after two or three weeks brought significantly higher income than lending to the real sector. And these operations, unlike lending to companies, were practically risk-free: August–September in Russia was the season of traditionally high demand for currency on the part of importers, who started preparing for the New Year holidays, which inevitably led to the growth of the dollar exchange rate.

Traditionally, Central Banks in emerging economies have tried to resist pressure on the national currency by selling their foreign exchange reserves. However, such a policy requires careful analysis and understanding of the limits of what is possible; otherwise, the Central Bank, having spent a significant part of foreign exchange reserves and exhausted the resources of resistance, will agree to a sharp fall in the national currency's exchange rate. This is what happened in Russia.

In the first half of 1994, the Bank of Russia calmly looked at the weakening of the ruble, which was slower than the growth of prices, i.e. in real terms, the ruble was slowly strengthening. The IMF was sympathetic to this policy: the missions that came to Moscow spoke of it as a successful control of the macroeconomic situation by the Russian government. The increase in demand for currency at the end of summer was explained, on the one hand, by the seasonal factor and, on the other hand, by the fact that at that time, the banks got at their disposal the money that the Central Bank had given to

[43] US DoS. Case F-2017-13804. Doc No C06838269. Second Clinton/Yeltsin One-on-One. September 28, 1994.

state-owned companies at the beginning of summer. However, as the price growth rate slowed in the summer, the Bank of Russia decided to slow down the rate of ruble devaluation and began to intervene in the market. In July–August, the Central Bank's foreign exchange reserves fell by more than two-thirds, but this did not lead to a decrease in demand for foreign currency because, at the same time, the Bank of Russia continued to issue loans to enterprises at low interest rates. Matters came to a head on October 11. By that time, the Bank of Russia had only $300 million in liquid reserves,[44] and after another surge in demand, it was decided to stop currency interventions—the exchange rate rose by more than 38%. Although the ruble recouped its losses three days later, what happened delivered a major shock in the Kremlin. Yeltsin fired the Central bank governor Gerashchenko and acting Finance Minister Sergey Dubinin and created a special State Commission to investigate the causes of the sharp destabilization of the financial market.

Vladimir Panskov, Kremlin-controlled, a former USSR deputy finance minister implicated in numerous corruption scandals, was soon appointed finance minister. He immediately blocked all reform projects in the ministry but left intact the basic principle of the 1995 budget—the rejection of loans from the Bank of Russia. From that moment, Russia began a full-fledged stabilization program that lasted for the next five years. Ahead was the budget crisis of the first half of 1996, when on the eve of the presidential elections, many large companies stopped paying taxes, not being confident in the victory of Yeltsin and the sustainability of his political course. This crisis was softened by 20 tranches of IMF loans totaling about $9 billion, loans from Germany and France for more than $2 billion[45] and a sharp increase in short-term public debt, which became one of the main reasons for the financial crisis in the summer of 1998. This crisis was overcome at the cost of default, a sharp devaluation of the ruble, and the bankruptcy of the country's largest private banks.

The 1998 crisis forced the Russian government to radically change their monetary and fiscal policy approach, which has since become exemplary. This led to clearing the budget of unfulfilled expenditure promises, the repayment of budget debts, and the stabilization of the financial market. Together, this provided the basis for the beginning of a period of rapid economic growth:

[44] At the beginning of the year, the Bank of Russia's liquid reserves exceeded $4.5 billion.

[45] These loans were granted to Russia after Yeltsin's personal appeals to Helmut Kohl and François Mitterrand. The Russian President did not even appeal to Clinton, realizing the futility of this step.

the transformational recession in the Russian economy ended in 1996, and the ruble devaluation in August 1998 increased the price competitiveness of domestic goods; by the end of 1998, Russian industry was growing at 10%; from 1999 to mid-2008 (before the global financial crisis), the Russian economy grew at an average annual rate of 7%.

In the early 2000s, Russia was able to reap all the benefits of economic transformation and enter an era of prosperity (albeit at a rather low level). However, on the way to this, Russia did not receive serious support from the West. Of course, deferrals were granted in the payment of foreign debt, which alleviated the budgetary situation, but even with the deferrals, creditor countries received interest payments comparable to the loans that Russia received from international financial organizations. IMF and World Bank loans in 1992–1995 amounted to $13.3 billion—less than Russia spent on servicing Soviet foreign debt (interest payments and repayments). The irony of history is that the loans provided to Russia by the World Bank and IMF were quantitatively the same as the amount of aid to European countries under the Marshall Plan—the only difference being that inflation devalued the dollar more than six times and the country in need of support received loans, not grants.

Russia did not receive substantial amounts of gratuitous financial aid, did not become a member of the WTO, and access of Russian goods to the markets of the European Union and the United States continued to be restricted by anti-dumping decisions. The plans to support the conversion of enterprises producing military products remained plans. The main flow of foreign direct investment into Russia resulted in the creation of domestic market-oriented production facilities; only a few projects led to Russian companies' integration into global value chains. The share of raw materials and primary processed products in Russian exports was between 70% and 80% (depending on the world price environment). At the same time, armaments remained the main export commodity of the manufacturing industry.

The bottom of the Russian economy's decline was reached in 1998, when (considering all claims to the adequacy of statistical estimates at the stage of transition from fixed prices to free prices, in the period of hyperinflation and structural reorganization of the economy) Russia's GDP amounted to 55% of the 1991 level, and the level of industrial production—48%. It was only in 2007 that Russia's GDP exceeded the Soviet maximum; Russian industry passed this point in 2021.

In Search of Goals

On August 21, Talbott, at the end of his vacation, sent a 34-page letter to Christopher.[46] The main idea of the letter was that Clinton's foreign policy needed serious re-examination; it had no clear strategic goals, the decisions went unexplained and seemed improvised, and failed to convince the public or elites that they served US interests.

> One of the most basic requirements that the American people look for in a President is the ability to convey a sense of having clearly in focus a fairly simple set of principles for dealing with a complicated world. Granted, that was a lot easier in the Cold War.

A sad conclusion could be drawn from this—*It's often said that elections are rarely won on foreign policy, but they can be lost on foreign policy especially by Democrats. It is an enduring and potent truism of American politics that Democrats are less surefooted on the field of battle than Republicans. Johnson lost his presidency in Vietnam; Carter suffered a politically devastating setback at Desert One…*

The main problem was that the international landscape had shifted radically over the previous few years, the almost half-century-long confrontation between the two ideological systems was over, and what principles should underlie foreign policy under the new conditions remained unclear both to outsiders and, worse, to the Administration itself. Talbott argued this helped cost Bush the election; two years on, the Clinton team still offered no answers.

> He [President Bush] knew that the collapse of the Soviet Union required thinking, and talking, about US foreign policy interests in a new way. But he couldn't quite figure out how… Now we're halfway through what we hope will be the first of two Clinton terms, and we're in trouble, too, in large measure because we haven't yet succeeded where George Bush failed … with the end of the Cold War, we have the makings of a single international community in a sense, and to a degree, that did not exist before…

In the letter, Talbott questioned the wisdom of US forays into regional conflict-resolution.

> What reason is there for us to have anything to do with these wretched little countries and their problems? How do these far-flung trouble spots cohere in a

[46] US DoS. Case F-2017-13804. Doc No C06835924. Letter from Talbott to Christopher. August 21, 1994.

> way that establishes some larger American purpose, and that will thereby earn the support of the American people? What is the nature of US interests and when will expend blood and treasure to defend them?
>
> But the biggest problem is that in none of the current cases [Haiti, Bosnia, Rwanda, Somalia] it easy, or perhaps even possible, to make the traditional national-interest argument for our involvement ... Americans either have died (in Somalia) or may be asked to die (in Haiti and Bosnia). That makes our set-backs more concrete than our successes...
>
> These conflicts are troublesome enough each on its own; they're more so in their multiplicity. On every continent there seems to be some two-bit dictator and thug ... who has defied the will of the international community in general and the US in particular. They are the nasty Lilliputians who have tied down Uncle Sam—and, more to the point, Bill Clinton.

Although in all such situations the US tries to build coalitions, which is an important achievement of the administration according to Talbott, the Americans are not inclined to listen to their partners and take their interests into account, preferring to push their own ideas. "*In the case of Bosnia, we have, from time to time, strained our relations with the British, the French, and the Russians, raising questions about whether either the Western Alliance or the new partnership with Russia is worth saving (in each case, of course, the answer is yes, but we have to keep making the case).*"

But it is not by chance that Clinton called Talbott a good journalist, but not a politician[47]—having adequately diagnosed the problem, the author of the letter did not offer a solution, did not offer answers to the questions posed. It seemed to him sufficient that the President and the Secretary of State "*should lay out a systematic, boldly innovative 'theory of the case' for dealing with post-Cold War challenges, a vision for American foreign policy based on US a redefinition of interests and security in an increasingly interdependent world.*" In short, continue to deal with problems as they arose.

The lack of clear priorities in foreign policy, according to Talbott, was both a cause and a consequence of the weakness of the President's foreign policy team.

> The rules - and the objectives - of the game have changed in ways we don't entirely understand... In foreign policy, improvisation is unsettling to the performer and the audience alike. It's especially a liability for this President, who's relatively untested – and therefore not entirely trusted – in this area...

[47] Strobe Talbott. The Russia Hand. Random House/New York, 2002, p.133.

> Sitting in meetings around the Department or over at the White House, I often find that the air is heavy with self-doubt. Our own uncertainty communicates itself outside to the public, and that fans the concern that we don't know what we're doing; that we're missing a sense of direction and steadiness of purpose. That criticism, of course, then feeds back into our own lack of self-confidence. So the vicious cycle spins faster.

In addition to the general weakness of the team, Talbott stressed State's fading clout and its failures in planning and strategy. "*Both NSC and State are at fault. There's no question that the NSC is becoming too operational, to the detriment of its proper function, which is serving the President directly and coordinating (as opposed to micromanaging) the work of the various departments and agencies. But there's also no question that we, State, have underperformed in long-range planning and imaginative foreign policy formulation.*"

Talbott emphasized that the President was a staunch supporter of reform in the former Soviet Union, and that "*despite the amount of partisanship in the air during the present open season on our foreign policy, there is widespread support for our NIS and PFP policies.*" For Talbott, these points were so indisputable that his analysis of relations with Russia was incomplete. "*Nonproliferation is the arms control issue of the coming decade. It's also an issue on which we will succeed only if we have to keep Russian reform on track. Russia's capacity to be part of the problem remains vast … but so is Russia's capacity to be part of the solution… On the Middle East [there is a role] (albeit marginal, cosmetic, and largely inherited) for the Russians.*"

Talbott's calm about Russia stood out as the Presidents prepared to meet again in late September.

Two weeks earlier, Talbott and Nicholas Burns visited Moscow to set the summit agenda with Yeltsin's foreign affairs aide, Dmitry Ryurikov. At that meeting, Talbott radiated optimism, assuring that European security and the OSCE would headline the agenda, adding that Washington was studying Russia's proposals in detail. "*We need support for Russian integration into World and European issues. We began with slogans and now we are moving to institutionalization and the development of new activities. These would be the ideal headlines [in newspapers] for the summit. We rarely get them, but it would be the best possible portrayal of the US–Russian relationship.*" Talbott said the completed withdrawal of Russian troops from the Baltics had dramatically improved Congress's view of Russia—the Russian leader had shown that he keeps his word and can be trusted. In this regard, "*Our purpose was clearly full integration of Russia into the group of industrialized democracies.*"[48]

[48] US DoS. Case F-2017-13804. Doc No C06695297. Ryurikov Meeting. Cable from S Talbott to the Department of State. September 12, 1994

Yet, Clinton still lacked a clear post-Cold War framework for US–Russian relations. Since the spring of 1994, his aides had tried repeatedly to persuade him to deliver a Russia policy speech,[49] yet they only wanted him "*to put icing on the cake that someone else had baked*," explaining his moves as mere consolidation of earlier successes, which he categorically did not want to do.

Ten days before meeting Yeltsin, the President convened a lengthy strategy session with aides. All agreed that the super-power confrontation was over, and its attendant threats had largely vanished. The President wanted to explain the nature of the new era "in a nutshell" so that he could be understood by the electorate; but no one could come up with a suitable slogan. Clinton was dissatisfied. "*At the core of his discontent*," he said, was "*the big mess in Russia, which has got everyone afraid that things are going to fall apart. We can whine and analyze all we want, but until people can say it in a few words we're sunk.*"[50] Yet, no one ventured to extend real help to Russia—precisely what Yeltsin needed most.

"*Yeltsin comes to Washington with one concern above all others: Is President Clinton still committed to helping Yeltsin and the reformers build a strong, unified, democratic Russia that enjoys respect and exercises influence in the world?*"—This was the main purpose of the visit, as outlined by Georgy Mamedov, who met with Talbott on the eve of the Presidents' meeting. Mamedov warned that voices in Yeltsin's circle claiming America sought to pressure a weakened Russia were gaining influence. They had access to the Russian President's ear and broadcast their suspicions to him every day. Mamedov emphasized that Yeltsin wanted to avoid discussing issues that would reveal contradictions in positions; he wanted to hold the summit repeating positive theses: "*We work together, based on common interests; together we can do a lot.*"[51]

The Eternal Russian Misfortune

Georgiy Mamedov's warnings were not only related to the emergence of opponents of partnership with the United States in the Russian President's entourage; they were largely due to Yeltsin's poor physical and psychological condition. The Russian leader's addiction to alcohol was no longer a secret, and conversations about it among foreign politicians and diplomats became part of the "new normal." At times Yeltsin allowed himself to "relax" during

[49] Note for Victoria Nuland from Nick Burns. May 18, 1994. Burns files, May 1994 [2] Gearing up for the Yeltsin Summit. Memorandum for Anthony Lake from John Beyrle. September 7, 1994. Burns files, September 1994 [2].

[50] Strobe Talbott. The Russia Hand. Random House/New York, 2002, p. 134.

[51] US DoS. Case F-2017-13804. Doc No C06835916. Handling Yeltsin. Letter to Secretary Christopher and Tony Lake from S. Talbott. September 27, 1994.

official lunches or dinners, which was skillfully exploited by his negotiating partners. "*Yeltsin really drank a lot of wine at the lunch, and was clearly reeling around. At the meeting afterwards he did make some useful policy concessions, which we dutifully recorded while his officials looked rather glum,*"[52] recalls Lake. This time it was much worse.

In late August 1994, Yeltsin flew to Berlin to attend an event to mark the completion of the withdrawal of Russian troops from Germany, where he had a breakdown and the world watched as the barely standing Russian President tried to conduct a military band and then started singing "Kalinka." Upon his return to Moscow, Yeltsin's seven aides wrote him a letter, trying to "reason" with the President politely and carefully, explaining that such behavior was seriously damaging Russia's image. The letter had the opposite effect: Yeltsin cut off contact with the signatories and left Kostikov, Pikhoya, Ryurikov, and the newly hired Georgy Satarov behind when he travelled to America.

After landing in Washington, the Russian President's guards reported that he was not feeling well and asked that the ritual meeting at the gangway be cancelled, after which Yeltsin struggled to get off the plane and left for the Blair House residence provided to him. That night, a Secret Service agent had difficulty stopping the half-dressed Russian President at the exit. He was incoherently trying to say something, and the only distinct words were "Pizza! Pizza!"

After such a night, the Russian President struggled to regain his working rhythm. Yeltsin boasted of economic successes—low inflation, rapid privatization, store shelves filled with goods, and even exotic kiwi fruit. On the political front inside the country, he was also not worried about much—he managed to establish constructive interaction with the parliament, the opposition failed to hold mass demonstrations on the anniversary of the dispersal of the Supreme Soviet. In response, Clinton complained that Americans did not feel that the economic situation was improving and that the Democrats were likely to lose the mid-term elections. Then declared: "*Well, shall we get started?*"

Yeltsin, defying Mamedov's prediction, seized the initiative. "*We can speak publicly about disagreeable things. I have an issue to raise… I have the impression that the US approach to Russia is inadequate… There are some officials in the White House and Congress who believe that Russia has lost its superpower status. Of course, not you personally, Bill … but some of your promises have not been kept due to red tape in the bureaucracy. For example, who is throwing sand in our*

[52] Anthony Lake. https://millercenter.org/the-presidency/presidential-oral-histories/anthony-lake-oral-history-2002

peacekeeping efforts in Ossetia, Nagorno-Karabakh, Georgia and Tajikistan? We are not in agreement on all foreign policy issues. What of the promises made? For example, Jackson-Vanik. Things are left hanging in mid-air. There is no progress on COCOM … People need to see progress, or there will be a cooler partnership… Russia is not consulted on some issues but Russia is a great power…".[53]

Unaspiringly, that opening set the tone for the rest of the talks. The Presidents exchanged claims and responded to counterclaims. They made mutual concessions, but, overall, the dialogue hardly resembled a friendly discussion; rather, it served as a reminder that the winds of the Cold War were still blowing through the corridors in Moscow and Washington.

Clinton saved "the cherry on top" for the last minutes of the conversation—he decided to announce, NATO expansion had been decided.

> One last thing: on NATO: please note, I have never said we shouldn't consider Russia for membership or a special relationship with NATO. So when we talk about NATO expanding, we're emphasizing inclusion, not exclusion. My objective is to work with you and others to maximize the chances of a truly united, undivided, integrated Europe. There will be an expansion of NATO, but there is no timetable yet… The issue is about psychological security and a sense of importance to these countries. They are afraid of being in a gray area or a purgatory. So we're going to move forward on this… As I see it, NATO expansion is not anti-Russian; it's not intended to be exclusive of Russia and there's no imminent timetable.

It was a hard blow. "*I understand, and I thank you for what you've said,*" Yeltsin replied slowly, unprepared for the conversation's abrupt end and already thinking about the coming press conference. He continued: "*If you're asked about this at the press conference, I'd suggest you just say that while the US is for the expansion of NATO, the process will be gradual and lengthy. If you're asked if you'd exclude Russia from NATO, your answer should be no.*"[54]

Clinton did not tell Yeltsin the whole truth. At least a month and a half before the Presidents met, practical discussions had begun in his administration and within the NATO leadership about which countries could become members of the alliance and when. "*We are now at a point where informal consultations should begin on criteria and timing for NATO expansion.*"[55]

---

[53] Memcon. Meeting with President Yeltsin. September 27, 1994. FOIA 2015-782-M-1 CDL #57568.

[54] Memcon. Second Clinton/Yeltsin One-on-One. September 28, 1994. FOIA 2018-1215-M CDL #101758.

[55] US DoS. Case M-2017-11687. Doc No C06549364. Secretary's Meeting with NATO A/SYG Balanzino. August 18, 1994. Brussels. Secretary Christopher's cable. August 19, 1994.

6

It's Not Clear Why, But It's Necessary

Undoubtedly, NATO enlargement became the post-Cold-War decade's defining event, sowing the seeds of a new Euro-Atlantic confrontation. The decision surprised observers: neither Clinton nor his opponent, Bush, had mentioned enlargement during the campaign. In the first six months after his election, Clinton mentioned NATO in public speeches several times, mainly concerning events in Bosnia. The topic of the alliance's expansion was not raised in Congress when approving the President's nominees for senior positions in the State or Defense Departments. Few policymakers could explain why a politico-military alliance was still needed after the adversary and its threat had vanished. Asked about NATO's future during his Senate confirmation, the incoming defense secretary candidly said that it was "*a very, very important and critical question to which I have no immediate answer.*"[1]

NATO was created at the initiative of the United States in 1949 as a mechanism to protect the countries of Western Europe from possible invasion by the Soviet Army. The secondary objective of the alliance was to prevent the restoration of German military power, which was feared by neighboring countries, and this threat was neutralized by 1955 when Germany was allowed to create its own army and was admitted to NATO membership. The threat of a Soviet invasion finally disappeared by the late 1980s, symbolized by the fall of the Berlin Wall and German unification. Soviet/Russian troops remained in Eastern Europe until 1994 only because Russia lacked facilities to house them at home.

[1] Ronald D. Asmus. Opening NATO's Door. How the Alliance Remade Itself for a New Era. Columbia University Press, 1983, p. 21.

S. Aleksashenko, *Post-Cold War Russia and the Missed Opportunity for Global Stability*,
https://doi.org/10.1007/978-3-032-01380-4_6

The Wall Has Collapsed: Time to Disappear?

Traditionally, alliances dissolve when their founding threat vanishes; by 1989 the Soviet military danger was plainly fading. A month before the fall of the Berlin Wall, NATO Secretary-General Wörner, meeting with Bush, spoke frankly and urged finding a new purpose for the alliance. Wörner proposed that NATO be transformed into a political organization that would allow the United States to control the situation in Western Europe so that allied countries would take a common position. "*We need to identify NATO more as a political alliance dealing with political change… It is in the interest of the US to use NATO as a political platform to coordinate policy, not just on defense, but as an instrument for your leadership and influence… Many groups are now involved with Eastern Europe - the EC, the OECD, the World Bank, etc. NATO should not take their place in implementing policy, but we need one place for coordination of a common approach. The role of NATO here is equivalent to visible American leadership.*"[2]

Two years later, in late June 1991, Wörner met again with Bush.[3] The situation in Europe had changed radically: the Warsaw Pact and the Soviet threat had vanished, something unimaginable at their earlier meeting. Moreover, France, long semi-detached from the alliance, reacting to the changes in Europe was starting a game aimed at strengthening its position on the continent, for which, of course, it was necessary to weaken the positions of the United States and NATO. For this purpose, France was pulling the idea of a Western European Union out of the vaults and trying to breathe new life into it—it proposed creating the European Strategic and Defense Initiative (ESDI), a military alliance within the EU, in which, obviously, there should be no place for the United States. Acknowledging reality, Wörner called it a daunting task to draft the declaration for NATO's summit in early November: "*[in] the Rome Summit declaration … we need to state what the threat is. When I made my rounds on the Hill, I was asked repeatedly by Senators and Congressmen who have supported NATO in the past, "Who is your enemy? "We need to answer that question. Second, we need to finalize the transformation of the Alliance, in particular, point out what has changed in NATO. Third, we need to spell out our*

[2] GB M&T. Memorandum of Conversation. Meeting with Manfred Woerner, NATO Secretary General. October 11, 1989.

[3] GB M&T. Memorandum of Conversation. Meeting with Manfred Woerner, NATO Secretary General. May 25, 1991.

relations with other institutions such as the UN, CSCE, and WEU [Western European Union]."[4]

Or Maybe Not?

Four months later, at the next meeting, Wörner was no longer so adamant about NATO's fate. Taking a step back, he spoke of the need to preserve the alliance as a military structure that would confront possible threats to stability in Europe and the world. "*We need a new vision of NATO - not as a military alliance confronting the Soviet Union, but as a military alliance confronting instability and uncertainty, and as a political alliance of increasing importance for the establishment and realization of this new European and world order.*"Wörner then asked Bush to champion the idea of the alliance's cooperation with Central and Eastern European countries. "*I need your leadership in getting [Alliance members] to agree to a change in the quality of NATO's relationship with the states of Central and Eastern Europe,*" adding, in response to a direct question from the President, that the Baltic states, if they wish, could also join this project. Overall, the Secretary-General seemed to accept that NATO's best days were behind it, and he was ready to accept that in the future pan-European security issues would be discussed in another forum, the CSCE, and said he was ready to pass the baton—"*I want to see NATO give CSCE a new push.*"[5]

Clinton's arrival forced Wörner to start over: the new team lacked a clear view of NATO's future. In early March 1993, he arrived in Washington and spent a lot of energy and time trying to get Christopher to agree to hold a NATO summit in the summer.[6] Wörner, almost verbatim, repeated what he said a few months ago. "*The public continues to ask about the purpose of NATO*

[4] During that meeting, Bush bluntly asked if the Secretary General saw any role for NATO in resolving the Yugoslav crisis and received a blunt *Highly unlikely* response. "*We're not doing contingency planning. We're not thinking of intervening,*" the President said thoughtfully, and the Secretary-General immediately changed his position: "*If they use military force, we have to make it clear that there are limits to what the Yugoslav army can do.*"

[5] GB M&T. Memorandum of Conversation. Meeting with Manfred Woerner, NATO Secretary General. October 11, 1991.

[6] CDL #118876. The Secretary's Meeting with NATO SYG Manfred Woerner. March 3, 1993. Cable from the Department of State. March 6, 1993.

in post-Cold war Europe." It was impossible to answer these questions without America's involvement and a clear expression of its position. "*Summit would allow NATO to define clearly and convincingly its new roles and propose ... concrete initiatives... Summit would give the US a forum in which the President could ... give ... a clear view of his administration agenda. This [would be] visible exercise of US leadership.*" Wörner candidly admitted that NATO faced "competition" from the growing European projects, the European Security and Defense Identity (ESDI),[7] and the WEU, which gained momentum after the Cold War's end when European policymakers realized that NATO and the EU had different actors and interests. Moreover, when Christopher asked how Wörner saw the distribution of responsibilities between them, he replied that, in his opinion, in the future, the trend toward autonomy in foreign policy issues would increase in the EU, and soon NATO would have to *rest on two legs, the United States and the WEU.*

At the same time, Wörner made no secret of his wish to keep and expand NATO as a military-political alliance, explaining this by the position of the Eastern European countries. Cooperation with them within the framework of the North Atlantic Cooperation Council (NACC)[8] would be problematic "*as long as the internal situation in Russia is unstable and unpredictable."* In addition, Wörner asked, "Can we allow *a country to be part of the EU/WEU and yet not be a member of NATO?*" Alliance members, Wörner said, had not discussed the issue, but the United States should assess what effect EU enlargement would have on NATO. NACC member states, he emphasized, realized they will not become members of the alliance soon, but he continued, "*you [the US] should start considering possible timeframes, candidates and criteria for membership expansion."* In addition, there was already a rift among NACC members that would deepen—"*States like Hungary and Poland, where stable democracies are being built, object to equal treatment with Russia*"; moreover, Wörner assured Central and Eastern European countries that "*NATO, in fact, differentiates between NACC states, and cooperates with CEE states in ways it could not with Russia."*

[7] ESDI—the concept of transferring responsibility for the defense and security of the European Community member states to European countries with reliance on the military capabilities of the Western European Union but within NATO. This concept emerged in the late 1980s and was actively, but ineffectively, discussed while preparing the Maastricht agreements. In 1997, this concept was replaced by the Common Security and Defense Policy (CSDP), based on which the post of the EU's High Representative for Foreign Affairs and Security Policy was created.

[8] Northern Atlantic Cooperation Council—a body that existed from 1991 to 1997 as a platform for dialog between NATO and CEE countries; it ceased to exist in 1997 after the NATO-enlargement decision.

Developing his thoughts, Wörner put forward a thesis that would later become one of the central arguments in answering the question of why NATO should be expanded. "*NACC states are increasingly interested in moving closer to NATO because of anxiety about Russian instability and fear of their own domestic instability. By and large, most do not feel militarily threatened by Russia (except Ukraine and Baltic states) but all fear that conservative forces in their own countries could enlist Russia's support and destabilize their fledgling democracies.*"

There's a Fruitful Idea

On the eve of the meeting with the Secretary of State, Wörner had a brief meeting with Clinton and Lake, at which Wörner apparently summarized the same theses that resonated in the souls of his interlocutors—the idea of America's foreign policy aimed at supporting and promoting democracy in the world was contained in Clinton's campaign speech, delivered a month before the election.[9] A month and a half later, on April 20–21, a few days before the referendum in Russia, Clinton met in Washington with the Czech Republic and Poland Presidents Václav Havel and Lech Wałęsa. Both politicians' credibility as fighters against totalitarianism was extremely high, and for a newcomer to foreign policy issues, their positions were ones to be listened to. Havel and Wałęsa spoke with one voice—our countries need to join NATO—but their arguments differed; they took Clinton "in a pincer movement."

The Czech President was clear in his argumentation—that joining NATO would strengthen democracy and advance his country's integration into European structures. "*We now want to focus on entering NATO and the EC because we see ourselves as Europeans who embrace European values … membership in NATO will help promote peace in the Balkans and CIS … because it will serve as an example, luring these countries into the Western community … entry into NATO and the EC is central to expanding democracy not just to Central Europe, but also to the CIS.*"

The Polish President was more emotional, saying that NATO membership should protect against threats from Russia. "*It is possible that the reform process in Russia will reverse. This would spoil the progress that has been made in building peace in Europe. The Russian army may become factionalized and fight among*

[9] Clinton Indicts Bush's World Leadership. The Washington Post. October 1, 1992.

itself… If you succeed in ensuring that Europe no longer faces a threat from Russia, you will win a Nobel Prize… We need to stop Russian hegemony."[10]

According to Lake, Clinton embraced the idea of NATO enlargement and made it an important element of his policy,[11] a chance to make history! Although Clinton did not react in any way to his interlocutors' proposals during the meeting, according to Lake, at the end of the meeting, the President asked him, "*Tony, why can't we do this?*"[12] For months afterward, the topic of NATO enlargement was absent from his official speeches.

When reporters asked Clinton in June 1993 about his attitude toward NATO expansion, his response sounded extremely vague and unconvincing.

President*: "The clearest example I know to give you that NATO is not dead was provided by the leaders of all the Eastern European countries that used to be Communist … every one of those Presidents said that their number one priority was to get into NATO. They know it will provide a security umbrella for the people who are members. And I think we need to continue to be involved in it [alliance]. "*

Q*: "Who's the enemy?"*

President*: "Well, there will be different enemies. The enemy will be anybody that threatens the security and the peace of the member nations, the values that we hold important. There are all kinds of possible problems in the years ahead, from terrorism, from the proliferation of weapons of mass destruction, from yet unforeseen developments in countries around NATO. So I don't think it's time to dismantle NATO. I think it's very, very important."*[13]

At most, the President was persuaded that the alliance should be preserved. In September 1993, in a meeting with Italian Prime Minister Carlo Ciampi, Clinton said that there could be no talk of dismantling the alliance because it was the anchor that allowed the United States to hold Europe together. "*The US cannot hint at leaving Europe... A NATO that looks East means that the domestic electorate can be persuaded of the need to maintain NATO.*"[14]

The idea of alliance expansion was the subject of numerous discussions in the White House, the Pentagon, the State Department, NATO headquarters, and the governmental structures of the alliance member states. Still, no

[10] CDL #101110. Memorandum of Conversation. Meeting with President Lech Walesa of Poland. April 21, 1993.

[11] James M. Goldgeier. Not Whether But When. Brookings Institution Press, Washington DC, 1999, p. 20.

[12] Ronald D. Asmus. Opening NATO's Door. How the Alliance Remade Itself for a New Era. Columbia University Press, 1983, p. 24.

[13] The President's News Conference. June 17, 1993. PPP, 1993, book 1, p. 869.

[14] CDL #101347. Memorandum of Conversation. Meeting with Prime Minister Carlo Ciampi of Italy. September 17, 1993.

consensus could be reached on the purpose of the alliance's existence in the new conditions and why the countries of Eastern Europe should become its members.

The only external threat to Eastern European countries that supporters of the alliance's enlargement could offer was hypothetical aggression from Russia. However, nothing indicated aggressive intentions on the part of Moscow, which, on the contrary, demonstrated its readiness to develop military cooperation with the United States and NATO. The Russian threat was discussed in a strongly subjunctive mood, and the need to preserve the alliance was presented as "a *passive insurance policy in the event that Russia, in particular, would at some point in the future pose an active threat to the alliance or any of its members.*" [15] In effect, the President was being asked to sacrifice the centerpiece of his foreign policy, a new relationship with Russia, to confront a hypothetical threat. There was no disagreement or doubt among the experts who deeply understood the situation in Russia; they spoke with one voice that the entire Russian political elite perceived the idea of NATO enlargement as directed against Russia and that practical steps in this direction would inevitably change the nature of relations between the two countries. No one close to Clinton could weigh up the two ideas, comparing potential gains and losses. However, some people were ready at any moment to convince the President that the Russian threat was a reality.

Looking back, it seems apt to paraphrase Bulgakov's Woland: "*Fear your fears; they have a way of coming true*"—even if three decades later.

And Another One

The situation in Bosnia, where, after the collapse of Yugoslavia, an inter-ethnic and inter-confessional conflict began, and later turned into a multi-year war, became the flash point of competing interests between the United States and Russia. The international community's attempt to stop the armed conflict by using UN peacekeeping forces was unsuccessful. On the one hand, peacekeepers can only be effective when the opposing sides are committed to de-escalation. In Bosnia, the situation developed in the opposite direction, leading to an unacceptable risk for peacekeepers, and made it impossible to uphold peacekeeping principles to act as a buffer between the adversaries. On

[15] Robert E. Hunter. Toward NATO Enlargement: The Role of USNATO. In Open Door: NATO and Euro-Atlantic Security After the Cold War (edited by Danil S. Hamilton and Kristina Spohr). Washington, DC, Foreign Policy Institute/Henry A. Kissinger Center for Global Affairs, Johns Hopkins University SAIS, 2019, p. 300.

the other hand, the warring parties' overwhelming fire-power, especially after Serbia and Croatia became parties to the conflict, far exceeded that available to the international forces. The peacekeepers had no opportunity to implement the decision of the UN Security Council to establish a no-fly zone, for which the UN Secretary-General asked NATO for help; to implement the decision on the naval blockade of Serbia, the UN asked countries to contribute warships, yet set up no unified command.

There was no unanimity within NATO at this time as to whether and in what forms the alliance should be involved in peacekeeping operations in Bosnia. In late 1991, Bush declared that the situation in Bosnia did not affect US interests, and that the US military would not be involved in the conflict region. The Clinton administration took a twofold position: on the one hand, the decision not to affect the US military remained in force; on the other hand, it was suggested that the North Atlantic Alliance, where no decision can be made without US consent, should take up the issue. After the UN appealed to NATO for support, the alliance was unable to make a decision, as it was blocked by France, which wanted to take the leading role in Europe and proposed using the WEU.[16] Great Britain, which was not a member of the WEU, lobbied NATO to take the leading role and de facto took over the management of NATO forces. However, unified command of the military from different member countries of the alliance (each subordinate to their own military commanders) could not be created due to the France's position. Germany, not wanting to be reproached for excessive militarism, declared that it would refrain from involving its military in any offensive operations in Bosnia, which effectively limited its role to humanitarian projects only.

As a result, no real coordination emerged between civilian leaders led by UN Secretary-General Boutros Boutros-Ghali and David Owen[17] and the military: the European Commission had no leverage over the WEU, and there was no political component in the NATO governance structure, which made it impossible to make decisions, given the passive position of the United States. The conflict escalated, and the international community could do nothing. European leaders expressed growing fears about the possible spread of the military conflict to neighboring countries, and only NATO commanders claimed they stood ready to impose order by force. However, to do so, the alliance must include peacekeeping operations in its mandate.

[16] The French attempt quickly failed as it became clear that the WEU, due to the dormant nature of the organization, did not have a unified command and control system in place.

[17] Co-Chair of the International Commission on the former Yugoslavia on behalf of the European Union.

The Role of the Individual in History

The key catalyst for renewed NATO expansion talk was Yeltsin's statement—"*Expand wherever you want!*"—made in Warsaw at the end of August 1993 after a long, vodka-soaked private dinner, hosted by Polish President Lech Wałęsa. In the middle of the night, the Russian President summoned his foreign minister and handed him a handwritten text demanding that he include in the joint statement that Russia supports Poland's early accession to NATO. Although in the morning, the Russian delegation managed to convince the Polish President that this phrase had no practical content but would dramatically complicate the situation in the Kremlin, and Wałęsa agreed to a softer wording, the original text leaked to the press and became the official position of Russia.[18]

Russian President's statement sparked a burst of euphoria from NATO's Wörner[19]: *"NATO must seize the moment… There is currently an historic moment of opportunity regarding NATO's engagement in the East. If the moment is lost, who knows when it will occur again? NATO … cannot leave Eastern Europe out in the cold. Indeed, whatever Yeltsin intended - and many interpretations are possible - he has now given NATO a pretext to act."*

However, Moscow later clarified the Russian President's position: Russia certainly recognized the right of Eastern European countries to make independent decisions regarding their security, but in turn, NATO should not make decisions without paying attention to changing East-West relations, and security issues should be considered in a broader context; Russia wanted to be sure that NATO reforms would take into account Russia's concerns and that they would not lead to Russia's isolation in Europe.[20]

Clinton knew of the debate within his own circle. On September 7, in a telephone conversation with Helmut Kohl[21], he cautiously tried to gauge his vis-à-vis position: "*I'm interested in your opinion on the relationship of NATO to Eastern Europe*," and, after hearing the Chancellor's directly stated negative attitude toward the idea of *NATO* enlargement: "*I do have my doubts about the possibility of these countries joining NATO and becoming part of it,*" Clinton decided not to show his hand, "*My thoughts on this are very similar to yours.*"

[18] Andrei Kozyrev. The Firebird: the elusive fate of Russian democracy: a memoir. University of Pittsburgh Press, 2019, pp. 215–217.

[19] US DoS. Case M-2017-12017. Doc No C06555192. Woerner on Expanding NATO Membership. Hunter/Christopher Cable. September 3, 1993.

[20] CDL #100538. Possible Yeltsin Letter on NATO. Cable from Ambassador Pickering. September 3, 1993.

[21] CDL #57561. Telcon with Chancellor Helmut Kohl of Germany on September 7, 1993.

But 10 days later, during the President's meeting with Italian Prime Minister Ciampi,[22] Christopher laid out the US position: "*We are preparing for the NATO Summit. We are considering possible NATO expansion, including identifying criteria for membership. The alliance must thrust eastward.*" Ciampi argued the situation was fluid, that members must share values, and that NATO still lacked a future mandate. Yet Clinton pressed his point: "*NATO looking eastward will help explain the need for NATO to our domestic electorates.*" Guessing what was really worrying the Italian Prime Minister, Christopher says alliance expansion must take place in a way that does not isolate Russia. "*Yes,*" Ciampi exclaimed in relief, "*NATO expansion should not threaten Russia.*"

Compromise

Despite vocal opposition from European leading powers—Germany, France, and the UK—and even the Pentagon, which argued that NATO expansion would diminish NATO's military strength and undermine its constructive dialogue with Russia, in mid-October Christopher received a deputy-drafted proposal urging the January 1994 NATO summit to decide on enlargement while sidelining Russia: "*Of course, we cannot ignore its position, but we can ignore it: we will start consultations, sign an agreement, hint that the door to NATO is not closed. In short, it will sort itself out somehow.*"[23] Coincidentally—or perhaps not— the document was signed the day Talbott was away, and the motion was seconded by Christopher, who did not go into detail. On his return to Washington, news of what had happened led Talbott to write a long note to his boss urging reconsideration.[24]

Talbott noted that the administration faced three interrelated challenges—"*Our leadership of NATO's evolution, our support for reform in Russia, and our attempt to coax Ukraine into giving up its nuclear weapons.*" He continues, "*At the core of that test is the question of whether we put the three Visegrad countries (v3) on a fast track to membership, ahead of the other Central/East Europeans and certainly ahead of the NIS... The core is the question of whether we are prepared to accelerate the process of granting [NATO] membership to the Visegrad Troika.*" While no one in the administration was suggesting that an immediate offer of

[22] CDL #101347. Memorandum of Conversation. Meeting with Prime Minister Carlo Ciampi of Italy. September 17, 1993.

[23] CDL #118449. A Strategy for NATO's Transformation and Expansion. Memorandum for DC Meeting on NATO Summit. September 14, 1993.

[24] US DoS. Case M-2017-11814. Doc No C06550901. Note: To the Secretary from Strobe Talbott. October 19, 1993.

membership be made to new countries. "*The enunciation of criteria or guidelines for expanded membership, combined with talk about 'associate' status would immediately be interpreted as an implicit offer to accept the troika.... if we insist upon being evasive, we'll do damage to our policy towards NATO (and our overall foreign policy credibility), whereas if we answer the questions, we'll risk harming our policies to both Russia and Ukraine.*"

By this time Talbott had carefully reread Yeltsin's letter to Clinton, in which the Russian leader says that "*NATO is not being viewed as a bloc in opposition to us, but it is important to take into account how our public opinion might react to such a step [the NATO enlargement announcement]. Not only the opposition, but moderate circles as well, would no doubt perceive this as a sort of neo-isolation of our country in direct opposition to its logical admission into the Euro-Atlantic space.*"

And Talbott continues, "*on one thing the v3 and Russia agree: an expanded NATO's real mission will be a new version of containment, directed against some future manifestation of Russian expansionism. Thus, the v3's motives for wanting in are the mirror image of Russia's fear about being left out... I'm not saying that the v3's fear of Russia is groundless; we're all worried about the bad bear redux. Indeed, plenty ofRussians (including Yeltsin) are worried about it. We must make sure that we don't inadvertently contribute to precisely what we all want to avoid.*"[25]

Talbott's impassioned memo prompted Christopher to rethink his stance. In the forthcoming NATO Council statement, he agreed to leave only a general phrase that the alliance's expansion would be gradual and open to all and to support the project "Partnership for Peace."

The Partnership won US military support because cooperation with former adversaries was progressing; it opened the door to a gradual military framework linking NATO members with all ex-Warsaw Pact states—without driving a wedge between Poland and Russia. In addition, voices began to be heard more clearly regarding the increasing role of the CSCE as a political organization responsible for maintaining peace and stability in Europe. The emergence of a two-layered structure—the CSCE as a "governing" political body and NATO as a military instrument in the hands of politicians—also made it possible to balance the dominant influence of the United States in the military alliance and to strengthen the role and responsibility of European countries.

[25] US DoS. Case M-2006-01499. Doc No C17533698. Retranslation of Yeltsin's letter on NATO expansion. October 9, 1993.

Moscow took essentially the same position, neither denying the possibility of NATO expansion, but demanding it be open to all. "*Moscow hopes any expansion of ties with NATO (whether or not involving actual alliance membership) would be either offered to Russia first, or to be as open to Russia as to any other Eastern European state. Working through the OSCE/NACC, Russia seeks early development of a truly meaningful pan-European security structure, encompassing NATO and non-NATO states, which could effectively respond to the ethnic conflicts and nationalistic extremism which pose the biggest threat to European security in the foreseeable future.*"[26]

Mission Unaccomplished

In October 1993, Christopher flew to Moscow, where he was to convey the President's position to Yeltsin: at the upcoming alliance summit in January, it would be decided that cooperation with the former Eastern Bloc countries would take place within the framework of the Partnership, but the issue of NATO enlargement would not be removed from the agenda; participation in the Partnership would be seen as an opportunity to prepare for accession to the alliance. This was what Talbott told Kozyrev's deputy Mamedov, who met him at the airport in Moscow.

However, the President's position was not stated in his letter; Christopher would have to present it to the Russian President orally and face his furious response. The Secretary of State openly acknowledged that NATO expansion had been discussed. Still, there was no question of ignoring Russia's position or excluding it from the future security structure in Europe. Therefore, the Partnership would be announced at the NATO summit as an equal opportunity for all; no one would be excluded, and no one would get an advantage. The Russian President breathed a sigh of relief and exclaimed joyfully: *Genius! Great!* This decision allowed him to eliminate the attacks on his foreign policy at home, relieve the growing tension among Russian generals, and focus on non-conflict areas of US-Russian dialog.

Although Christopher added that the topic of alliance expansion was not going away altogether, he talked about it as a distant prospect: "*We will be looking at the question of membership as a long-term eventuality. There will be an evolution, based on the development of a habit of cooperation, but over time. And*

[26] CDL #118449. Russia, NATO and the two January Summits. Cable from Ambassador Pickering. September 29, 1993.

this too will be based on participation in the Partnership. Those who wish to can pursue the idea over time, but that will come later."[27]

Talbott said he was trying to complement his chief's position and told Kozyrev that the idea—"*Partnership today, expansion tomorrow*"—meant that the decision in principle to expand had been made; it just would not be announced in January. But this happened when the helicopter they were returning to Moscow in had taken off, and the Russian minister pretended to have fallen asleep. "*I actually closed my eyes to resist the temptation to open my mouth and tell both guests what I thought of their performance: they had just failed in their duty, which was to deliver their President's message to the* Russian *President.*"[28] Talbott was not sure that the Russian minister had heard his words,[29] but he did not make a second attempt, apparently expecting his deputy Mamedov to tell Kozyrev about it.

However, the actual US position became known not only to the Russian Foreign Ministry but also to the Russian intelligence services, which began to use the asymmetry of information in their own interests by whispering to the Russian President that the Partnership was just a smokescreen to cover up the decision to expand NATO.

The Movement Has Begun

"*Boris believed Bill's word*,"[30] as relayed by Christopher, and for several months, Yeltsin stopped discussions on the future of NATO. In turn, Clinton, confident that the Russian President knew NATO enlargement was a matter of principle, began to discuss the move publicly, gradually making his position more definite. These discussions started in January, during the NATO summit, and immediately after Clinton visited Prague. On the one hand, it was no secret that the White House supported enlarging the alliance. On the other hand, the Liberal Democratic Party's first-place finish in the Russian elections, led by Vladimir Zhirinovsky, who aggressively stoked imperial

[27] CDL #100538. Secretary Christopher's Meeting with President Yeltsin, 10/22/93, Moscow. Cable from Secretary Christopher. October 25, 1993.

[28] Andrei Kozyrev. The Firebird: the elusive fate of Russian democracy: a memoir. University of Pittsburgh Press, 2019, pp. 220–221.

[29] Strobe Talbott. The Russia Hand. Random House/New York, 2002, p. 101.

[30] Kozyrev later wrote in his memoirs that he consciously *closed his eyes to keep his mouth shut* because he realized that Christopher's diplomatic mission failed to deliver Clinton's position. Of course, the Russian minister had no desire to do the dirty work himself. Andrei Kozyrev. The Firebird: the elusive fate of Russian democracy: a memoir. University of Pittsburgh Press, 2019, pp. 221–222.

sentiment, provoked a surge of dire predictions about an imminent nationalist shift in Russia.

> *I'm not against expanding NATO. I just think that if you look at the consensus of the NATO members at this time, there's not a consensus to expand NATO at this time, and we don't want to give the impression that we're creating another dividing line in Europe after we've worked for decades to get rid of the one that existed before. What we want is a secure Europe and a stable Europe. And I think that the proposal that I put forward would permit the expansion of NATO, and I fully expect that it will lead to that at some point.*[31]

> *This Partnership will advance a process of evolution for NATO's formal enlargement. It looks to the day when NATO will take on new members who assume the alliance's full responsibilities…*
>
> *The Partnership For Peace will not alter NATO's fundamental mission of defending NATO territory from attack. We cannot afford to abandon that mission while the dream of empire still burns in the minds of some who look longingly toward a brutal past.*[32]
>
> *While the Partnership is not NATO membership, neither is it a permanent holding room. It changes the entire NATO dialog so that now the question is no longer whether NATO will take on new members but when and how.*[33]

The US President flew to Moscow a few days after the NATO summit ended, but the topic of the Partnership and, even more so, the expansion of the alliance was not on the agenda of the talks.[34] Only at the end of dinner on the first day of his visit did the Russian President mention the alliance, saying, "*Russia should be the first country to join NATO... But, truth be told, Russia is not ready yet...*" As Yeltsin continued to speak, Clinton did not react to this idea.[35]

Proponents of alliance expansion on the Clinton team realized the goal was achievable. Opponents were fragmented and mounted no serious push-back in Congress or the media. The most serious opponents—Chancellor Kohl,

[31] Exchange with Reporters Prior to Discussions with Prime Minister Ruud Lubbers of The Netherlands January 4, 1994. PPP, 1994, book 1, p. 6.

[32] Remarks to Future Leaders of Europe in Brussels January 9, 1994. PPP, 1994, book 1, p. 11.

[33] The President's News Conference with Visegrad Leaders in Prague January 12, 1994. PPP, 1994, book 1, p. 40.

[34] The most important content of the US President's visit to Moscow was the completion of long and complex trilateral negotiations with Ukraine, which resulted in that country giving up nuclear weapons and securing its nuclear-free status.

[35] CDL #58577. President's Dinner with President Yeltsin. Cable from Ambassador Pickering. January 14, 1994.

Ambassador Pickering, and the Pentagon—failed to coordinate their actions and had different arguments, allowing them to be neutralized one by one. Talbott, who was supposed to prioritize protecting relations with Russia, realized "which way the wind is blowing" (what decision the President was hatching) and quickly softened his opposition.

Germany's neutralization would rely on Eastern European leaders, who quickly found common ground with the US ambassador to the United Nations Madeleine Albright, who visited Eastern Europe in mid-January 1994 to discuss future relations with NATO. "*For the V4, the main danger is chaos in Russia; for the others, spillover from Yugoslavia… Whether the fear is Russia or spillover, it is not so much concern of armed invasion but of the chaos created by instability.*"[36] Since hints of a Russian threat found little traction in Washington, one had to paint scenarios of political chaos and unrest in Central and Eastern European countries that could spill over to Russia and destabilize it. Why could chaos have arisen in their countries? Economic transformation was slow; accession to the European Union and integration into the European economy were not expected, which meant that democratically oriented politicians might lose the upcoming elections and would inevitably be replaced by Communist supporters seeking revenge.

How Do You Neutralize a Friend of the President?

It soon became clear that Talbott's potential influence on Clinton's position on this issue posed no serious threat to advancing the idea of alliance expansion. On the one hand, Talbott had never opposed expanding the alliance, saying only that now was not the right time. On the other hand, the weaknesses of the President's college friend played a role—he was unable to formulate and agree with other actors on a clear new goal of US policy toward Russia and the mechanisms for achieving it; all his comments boiled down to a straightforward thesis: Russia's concerns must be considered. It was very easy to devalue this position—it was simply a matter of including in the text of the document a couple of sentences about the need to build a special relationship with Russia, which had no substance behind them.

In addition, if Talbott were handed a broader portfolio, the attention he could devote to Russia would inevitably diminish. Christopher, who wanted informal access to the President, became an "ally" in executing this simple

[36] CDL #57563. PFP and Central and Eastern Europe. Memorandum from Madeleine Albright for the President, the Vice President, the Secretary of State, and the National Security Advisor. January 26, 1994.

maneuver. In late 1993, Christopher initiated the promotion of Talbott, proposing his candidacy for his deputy post. However, when in late January, on the eve of his Senate confirmation, Talbott sent Christopher another memo in which he expressed his surprise that there was no interagency group in the administration to coordinate all aspects of the Partnership, NATO enlargement, and related European issues, the Secretary of State wrote in the margin that he would assign the job to his other deputy.[37]

Kozyrev's Tough Questions[38]

It takes two to tango. Probably in late 1993-early 1994, Russian diplomacy had a chance to play an important role by offering its vision of building a new security architecture in Europe that would make it possible to put aside the accumulated experience of confrontation between Russia and NATO and start life anew. That opportunity was missed; instead, the opposite happened: an attempt to start a conversation on this topic was unsuccessful.

In early January 1994, a week before Clinton's visit to Europe, Kozyrev published an article entitled "Partnership for a United Europe" in the German newspaper *Frankfurter Allgemeine Zeitung*, in which he outlined the general principles of how he envisioned a new security structure for Europe. Choosing a more unfortunate time and place for such a publication would have been hard. In a few days, the US President would fly to Prague to announce the creation of the Partnership for Peace. His team was busy making final preparations for the visit, and there was no time or desire to be distracted by unrelated ideas. In addition, the choice of Germany as the country where the (possibly) conceptual article was to be published was intentional—this country was not in Clinton's trip plan; still its political elites and public opinion were crucial in defining European position on the NATO expansion issue.

Any impromptu is good if it is well prepared. Kozyrev's article, in this sense, was a bad impromptu. No, its main points should not have caused serious discussions. Inclusiveness for all, joint peacekeeping operations, partnership with NATO, economic integration, respect for sovereignty and territorial values, and non-proliferation of nuclear weapons—these were in the vocabulary of American and European diplomats. But the key idea—strengthening the CSCE and turning this organization into a key element of European

[37] US DoS. Case F-2017-13804. Doc No C06835976. Strobe to Chris. January 26, 1994.

[38] CDL #100538. Yeltsin's May 11–13 Visit to Germany: Kozyrev's Comments on PFP. Cable from the US Ambassador in Bonn Richard Holbrooke to the Department of State. May 26, 1994.

security—came as a complete surprise to Talbott, from whom the President was expecting an analysis of Kozyrev's "new ideas."

If we ignore the fact that more space was devoted to psychoanalyzing the Russian minister than to analyzing his proposals, Talbott's position boiled down to one thesis: Kozyrev's idea should not even be discussed since it implied giving Russia a "voice" in European security issues and withdrawing NATO from Washington's rigid leadership.

> *Kozyrev … calls for placing NATO, the WEU, and the CIS under the coordinating authority of the NACC and the CSCE. It also would include a system of bilateral security guarantees, international funding for Russian peacekeeping efforts and incentives to limit nuclear proliferation… Essentially what Kozyrev is trying to do with his plan is dilute the primacy of NATO (to which Russia does not belong), create a new governing structure that includes the 52-member CSCE and NACC (in which Russia prominently does belong), and thereby underscore the moral and political equality of CIS and NATO… Kozyrev's plan is clearly designed to give Russia a bigger piece of the action in European peacekeeping and to create a mantle of international legitimacy plus Western funding for CIS peacekeeping, but it would also severely hamstring NATO's ability to act…*
>
> *In what Moscow would see as a perfect world, Kozyrev - and indeed many of Russia's foreign policy elite - would much prefer for Russia to be the architect and engineer, along with the US, of a completely new European security order. It sticks in their craw that NATO appears poised to dictate the terms of the new order and Russia has no choice but to accept a late invitation to a table that has been pre-set by Washington for 45 years. At the bottom, even our most enlightened colleagues in Russia have not fully adjusted to the loss of their status as a supposedly co-equal superpower.*[39]

In late April 1994, Russian Foreign Minister Andrei Kozyrev, meeting with his German vis-à-vis, Klaus Kinkel, took a tougher stance,[40] bombarding him with a hail of straightforward questions and critical assessments of NATO's expansion plans. In response to his main question—"*What will the alliance do after the dissolution of the Warsaw Pact?*"—he heard a list of four tasks: defense against external threats (although not very relevant, the German minister immediately said), peacekeeping missions, peacekeeping operations in

[39] US DoS. Case F-2017-13804. Doc No C06689721. Kozyrev's "European Security Plan." Memorandum from Strobe Talbott to Tony Lake. January 12, 1994.

[40] German diplomats attending the meeting emphasized that Kozyrev's position seemed far more critical than the comments of Russian Defense Minister Grachev. *CDL #100538 "Yeltsin's May 11–13 Visit to Germany: Kozyrev's Comments on PFP." Cable from the US Embassy in Bonn, May 26, 1994.*

specific cases (such as Yugoslavia), and the creation of the core of the European security architecture, which will eventually include the CEE countries.

Kozyrev pressed on, saying that what he had heard did not help him in any way to answer similar questions he received in Russia. If NATO wanted to engage in peacemaking and peacekeeping, it must be remembered that the alliance had no structures that can make the necessary decisions. Only the UN Security Council or regional organizations established under Chap. 8 of the UN Charter, the CSCE in Europe, had such powers. Thus, it was necessary to either change NATO's charter or subordinate the alliance to the CSCE. Furthermore, the decision to participate in UN peacekeeping operations was made individually by each country, and, for example, in the case of Yugoslavia, the United States and Germany had decided not to do so. The German minister did not object and agreed that only the UN was mandated to use force.

In discussing the function of defense against external aggression, Kinkel cited the example of the Czech Republic, Poland, and Slovakia, which had been outspoken about their concerns about Russia and stated their desire for greater security. The alliance's position was that discussions on the admission of these countries to the organization were going on regardless of whether their concerns are justified or not. If the fears were unjustified, the Russian minister responded that you could not base a serious policy on them, which would lead to mistakes. Suppose that by applying to join NATO, Poland wanted to get under the umbrella of the old security system based on the confrontation between the two military blocs. In that situation, NATO and Russia would remain adversaries, and Russia would have no choice but to build up its military power. However, if the discussions concerned a new, non-bloc security system in Europe, Russia should get an answer to the question of when it might be able to join the alliance. And was NATO ready for this? Kinkel replied that it was not at present.

At this point, the Russian minister decided to "escalate" and questioned not only the need for NATO expansion but also the creation of the Partnership for Peace, saying that he saw no point for Russia to participate in it because if NATO expanded, its interests would conflict with those of the alliance. Kinkel could not take it anymore and asked Kozyrev: "*Does everything you said mean that Russia wants NATO disbanded?*" "*No,*" the Russian minister replied. Russia would like to hold a conference on the situation in Europe after the end of the Cold War. Does NATO have an enemy from which it must defend itself? The question was not about dissolving NATO but about defining its future role. If NATO's objectives were positive, Russia could join the Partnership.

This was the end of the conversation. The German minister concluded the conversation by assuring that the Russian government should know that Germany was aware of the sensitivity of the problem and was doing everything possible to prevent new tensions. Germany knew that a new security system in Europe could not be created without Russia.[41]

To Be!

Until mid-summer 1994, there was no progress in Washington discussing possible NATO expansion. Creating a "Partnership for Peace" suited the Pentagon, which was gradually establishing contacts with the Russian military, noting that the Russian army was much more suited to the requirements of the countries joining the alliance than those of Eastern Europe. NATO's military was increasingly bogged down in Bosnia, where the escalating conflict amid organizational confusion required constant attention at the highest levels. Clinton, on the rare occasions when journalists asked him about the prospects for alliance expansion, repeated, with slight variations, phrases uttered in Moscow in January after talks with Yeltsin.

> *Partnership For Peace is a real thing now. It is real now. We invited all the republics of the former Soviet Union, all the Warsaw Pact nations, and the other non-NATO members of Europe to be part of the Partnership For Peace. All were invited. All were told that this can also lead to eventual membership in NATO, but that our objective is to create an undivided and united Europe, united around political freedom, economic freedom, military cooperation, and respect for one another's borders, for the first time in the history of the nation state. It has never happened before.*[42]

The situation changed in July when Clinton flew to Europe and visited Warsaw before the G7 meeting, where he comes under pressure/obfuscation from Wałęsa and Polish journalists and, without making any promises on timing, said that Poland will become a NATO member.

"*I have to make sure there is an agreement among the NATO members about what exactly the standards should be and the timetable. And they haven't all agreed. But I do want to make it clear that, in my view, NATO will be expanded, and that it should be expanded … a timetable should be developed, but I can't do*

[41] *CDL #100538 "Yeltsin's May 11–13 Visit to Germany: Kozyrev's Comments on PFP." Cable from the US Embassy in Bonn, May 26, 1994.*

[42] The President's News Conference with President Yeltsin of Russia in Moscow January 14, 1994. PPP 1994, book 1, p. 57.

that alone…"[43] *"I think that in the ordinary course of time, NATO will expand, Poland will be eligible."*[44]

But a week later, Clinton suddenly recovered the timing of a possible expansion of the alliance. "*Chancellor Kohl and I have discussed this a bit and in our personal meetings. The NATO members themselves will have to get together and begin to discuss what the timeline ought to be and what the criteria for membership ought to be.*"[45] These words did not get past the journalists, and on the same day, they pounced on Lake and Joachim Bitterlich, Kohl's security advisor, who gave a joint briefing.[46] Bitterlich said that he and Lake had begun discussing the issue some time ago and that "*We are grateful to the American President opening political debate with the Chancellor about this item… Because there is this feeling of lack of security. Look for example, Poland after elections in Ukraine and in Belarus.*"

Scared: But of What, Exactly?

It is unclear what alarmed the German official about the election results in the two countries.

In late March and early April 1994, Ukraine held its first parliamentary elections since independence; all deputies to the Verkhovna Rada were elected in single-member districts, and elections in each district were deemed valid with turnout above 50%. Two rounds elected three-quarters of the Rada deputies, while the remaining seats needed a third and even fourth ballot. Although the Communists held the largest bloc, their faction in the Rada never had more than 20% of the vote. The parliament contained more than 10 factions.

On July 10, incumbent Ukrainian Prime Minister Leonid Kuchma defeated incumbent President Leonid Kravchuk in the second round of the presidential election with 52% of the vote. This peaceful transfer of power was among the first in the post-Soviet space. He remains Ukraine's only two-term president.

[43] Interview With Tomasz Lis of Polish Television July 1, 1994. PPP 1994, book 1, p. 1187.

[44] Interview With the Polish Media July 1, 1994. PPP 1994, book 1, p. 1192.

[45] The President's News Conference with European Union Leaders in Berlin, Germany, July 12, 1994. PPP 1994, book 1, p. 1246.

[46] CDL #606609. Press briefing by National Security Advisor Tony Lake. July 12, 1994.

On the same day, July 10, 1994, Belarus held a second round of presidential elections in which the charismatic populist Alexander Lukashenko took over 80% of the vote, defeating incumbent Prime Minister Vyacheslav Kebich.

Russia Is Wary

At the very end of the briefing, after Lake said it was time to wrap up, Bitterlich chose to answer a question about the possibility of Russia joining NATO. "*While enlarging NATO, we have to take into account Russia and its interests...but I don't think we will bring in the Russians* [into the alliance]."[47]

NATO enlargement talks were under way inside the White House, with State largely in the dark about their progress. At the end of August, Talbott wrote another note to Christopher, telling him that he struggled to persuade Lake to set up an interagency group led by a deputy secretary of state. Christopher did not react, apparently judging "*it's the wrong hat for the wrong person*," but he did support Talbott's proposal to recall Ambassador to Germany Richard Holbrooke—an aide close to Talbott—and assign him the Europe portfolio.[48] Ironically, by late 1994 Holbrooke became one of the principal champions of NATO enlargement.

Yeltsin's visit to the United States was scheduled for late September, and Moscow was closely monitoring actions and statements in Washington. This was what Talbott told Christopher upon his return from Russia, where he had been to prepare for the visit. Russia's new Ambassador to the United States, Yuli Vorontsov, had already sent a telegram warning that the United States was about to "*change its NATO policy*" and next year "*open the doors to the Poles, Hungarians and Czechs.*" "*We may have re-started the NATO-expansion juggernaut without really intending to and without sufficient consideration of the consequences... We as an administration are vulnerable to the charge that we're letting Russia have a veto of some kind over NATO expansion. I am not eager to rekindle that debate... But I'm even less eager to see us slip, willy-nilly, into the opposite problem: an insufficiently well-thought-out NATO policy that jeopardizes the single most important and positive strategic trend in Europe, which is a reformist Russian foreign policy,*" Talbott wrote to Christopher. He soberly assessed what America had gained from good relations with Russia, "*If our NATO decision last year had gone the other way - that is, if we'd opted for*

[47] Press briefing by National Security Advisor Tony Lake. July 12, 1994. CDL #606609.

[48] US DoS. Case F-2017-13804. Doc No 06835943. Strobe to Chris. August 27, 1994.

fast-track admission for the V-4 countries - we might have had a very different Russia to contend with this year; we might not have gotten the trilateral deal with Ukraine, Russian cooperation in the Contact Group, and Baltic troop withdrawals (to say nothing of Russian acquiescence on Haiti in the Security Council)."[49]

Concurrent with the private memo, Talbott sent a formal memorandum to the Secretary of State in which he explicitly addressed how the administration's objectives fit together.[50]

This Administration is committed to both European integration and NATO expansion… The key elements of that approach were the following:

- *… Even though the Warsaw Pact has been disbanded and the USSR dissolved, NATO should be retained, and kept at the ready, in case a new threat should arise to the East.*
- *At the same time, NATO should be made relevant to the task of managing new, post-Cold War conflicts within Europe. We are trying, albeit with great difficulty, to do precisely that in the former Yugoslavia, where NATO has been used to enforce the will of the United Nations Security Council.*
- *Finally, NATO should also be a mechanism for integrating into the West the emerging democracies of the East.*

This last objective is crucial - and also complicated. NATO can serve the cause of integration in two ways: 1) by encouraging, through NACC and PFP, "habits of cooperation" and fostering a sense of common security across the old Iron Curtain; and 2) by accepting new members from the ranks of the former Warsaw Pact.

There is a potential tension between these two aspects of NATO's evolution. NACC/PFP is an inclusive institution (come one, come all), which is already up and running; NATO expansion, by contrast, is necessarily going to be an exclusive process (not everyone who wants to join will be able to do so, at least not at the same time or, in several cases, any time soon); it will also be a gradual process, and it has yet to begin - which arouses impatience on the part of those who expect to be among the first entrants and anxiety among those who don't.

Turning to the recommendations, Talbott put preservation of the Partnership first, arguing that NATO enlargement was premature and need not be rushed. He even admitted that the proponents of NATO enlargement had no arguments in favor of such a decision apart from the potential threat from Russian. As a result, he proposed building a new European security

[49] US DoS. Case F-2017-13804. Doc No 06835921. Strobe to Chris. September 11, 1994.

[50] US DoS. Case F-2017-13804. Doc No C06835918. The Future of European Security. Memorandum to the Secretary from Strobe Talbott. September 12, 1994.

architecture based on consolidating the capabilities of various organizations dealing with security issues in Europe. This brought him very close to Andrei Kozyrev's position, which he had previously discarded a few months earlier.

1. *Let's be careful not to shift energy away from PFP, or give others an excuse to do so... If we appear to have lost interest and confidence in the campaign on behalf of PFP and thrown ourselves instead into the NATO-expansion debate, it will confirm suspicions that PFP was just a diversionary tactic, a gimmick or a consolation prize of some kind...*
2. *Let's develop a more nuanced rationale for NATO expansion, one that supports the vision of integration rather than seeming like an insurance policy against the failure of integration. A year ago, we said ... that if Russia "went bad," we'd hasten the entry of the CEE states to protect them from newly aggressive Russian behavior. That remains a valid theme in our doctrine and in our contingency planning ("prepare for the worst while trying to bring about the best"). But it must not stand alone as a reason to expand NATO....*
3. *We must not think about NATO in a vacuum; we've got to look at it in the context of the other institutions and groupings that are to some extent cooperating, and to some extent vying, with each other for influence over the nature and shape of the new Europe. The NATO-expansion discussion to date has been too narrowly focused. We must address more broadly and systematically the interrelated functions of NATO, NACC, PFP, CSCE, EU/WEU, the UN and, yes, the CIS in the emergence of tomorrow's Europe.*

If this sounds to you like a sensible starting point, I propose to work with Peter Tarnoff and the NSC in setting up an interagency group on the future of European security.

But that Stopped No One

The last sentence in Talbott's memorandum showed how detached he was from White House discussions, where the course was already set.[51] Talbott sent his memorandum on Monday, and the previous Friday, Vice President Gore had said, addressing the Berlin conference, *"Several countries have already*

[51] The interagency group was established, but it was headed by Richard Holbrooke, who was a fierce advocate of an immediate decision to expand the alliance. At the first meeting of the members of this group, Holbrooke asked each of them how and when the alliance should grow. After hearing the unanimous position of the Pentagon representatives (including Deputy Secretary of Defense Ash Carter and the future commander of NATO forces in Europe, General Wessely Clark), "Never," he stated that there was a president who had already approved the relevant political decision and that the members of the group should ensure the preparation of the necessary plan of action. When Clark questioned the existence of a political decision by the President, Holbrooke sternly stated, *"Anyone who asks that shows dis-*

indicated their desire to become full members of the alliance. We will begin our discussions on this issue in the time remaining before the end of the year."[52] Four days later, National Security Council Director for Europe Alexander Vershbow released a memorandum to the administration for discussion[53]; the first line read, "*The goal is to achieve NATO expansion.*" Vershbow detailed the practical problems needing to be solved to make the announcement of the alliance's enlargement as smooth as possible.

Key elements for success: blurring the context, hiding the topic of NATO enlargement within the broader discussion on security in Europe, promoting the thesis that the enlargement of the alliance would increase security for all countries, as for those who would not be included in this process, other opportunities for participation in the new security architecture would be created, and not linking the topic of NATO enlargement to the development of the situation in Russia, which would make it possible to hide the true reason for the decision.

Vershbow stressed that the decision to expand the alliance would inevitably be perceived negatively in Russia (and Ukraine[54]), and therefore, special efforts would have to be made to neutralize Moscow's resistance. Among the measures he proposed were increasing activity within the Partnership so that it would be perceived as a serious initiative in which participation would be mandatory for future alliance members; developing a separate document formalizing Russia–NATO relations (although the substance and format of this document remained unclear); emphasizing Russia's symbolic and real involvement in decision-making at the "power players' table"; and deepening the US "strategic partnership" with Russia as compensation for the involvement of CEE countries in the West's orbit of influence.

loyalty to the country and the President" (James M Goldgeier. Not Whether But When. Brookings Institution Press, Washington DC, 1999, pp. 73–74).

[52] Department of State Dispatch, September 12, 1994, vol5, pp. 597–598.

[53] CDL #118731. NATO expansion: Concept and Strategy. September 17, 1994.

[54] For the White House, Ukraine's position on NATO enlargement also posed a serious challenge since, although the country had signed a treaty renouncing nuclear weapons, they had not yet been physically removed from its territory. Vershbow bluntly pointed out, "*The enlargement would leave it sandwiched between an Alliance it could probably never join and Russia… Ukraine will not be happy with the role of buffer between an expanding NATO and Russia and may question its decision to become a non-nuclear power.*" The solution for Ukraine was found in the signing of the Budapest Memorandum, under which Russia, the United States, and the UK pledged to respect Ukraine's territorial integrity and not to use arms and economic coercive measures against the country. The Budapest Memorandum was signed on December 5, 1994, but, as the events of 2014–2022 showed, it failed to protect Ukraine from aggression by one of the signatories.

The announcement of the decision to expand the alliance was set for December 1 during a meeting of NATO foreign ministers in Brussels, so anyone who could prevent it must be neutralized.

To keep Talbott out of the way, he was loaded with various assignments that required numerous foreign trips. As a result, the key official in charge of Russia policy was out of Washington most of the time from late September, when Yeltsin's visit to the United States ended, until the OSCE summit in Budapest in early December 1994.[55] The Pentagon's resistance to the very idea of expanding the alliance was overcome, thanks to Richard Holbrooke's bureaucratic talents. First, he turned the discussion with the military into the subjunctive mood—what might an action plan for alliance expansion look like if such a political decision were made? And when General Clark put a huge stack of documents on the table in front of the participants of the meeting, explaining that these were 1200 standards adopted in the alliance, which should be implemented in each country before its membership in the organization, Holbrooke said this was exactly what the group needed and urged the generals to draft the required action sequence together. Thereafter, willingly or unwillingly, the Pentagon became a constructive participant in furthering the process.

In mid-October, Lake placed on the President's desk a memorandum on NATO enlargement,[56] indicating in an accompanying note that it had been prepared to fulfill Clinton's public promise to begin discussing the issue with the allies by the end of the year.

The memorandum was written very compactly, without unfolding theses, leaving no room for discussing alternatives. The declared goal of creating an integrated and inclusive security system in Europe beyond NATO enlargement looked very appealing but lacked details and specifics. It made inclusion of key CEE countries in the first phase of the expansion of the alliance inevitable, leaving the possibility of Ukraine and the Baltic states joining so that, God forbid, "*they are not assigned to the gray zone or Russia's sphere of influence.*"

> *NATO expansion should take place in coordination with the enlargement of the EU, but should not be delayed to match the EU's likely* [longer] *timetable.*
>
> *To make clear expansion is not seen as directed against any country, process must be developed in parallel with long-term strategy vis-a-vis Russia that includes intensified partnership with NATO and development of other institutions (CSCE, G8)… This could take the form of a Treaty (an "alliance with the Alliance"). It should*

[55] James M. Goldgeier. Not Whether But When. Brookings Institution Press, Washington DC, 1999, p. 86.

[56] CDL #57563. NATO Expansion. Memorandum for President from Anthony Lake, October 13, 1994.

include a mechanism for consulting with Russia on NATO or NATO-led military operations as in ex-Yugoslavia, but without giving Russians a veto over NATO decisions… "Insurance policy"/" strategic hedge" rationale (ie neo-containment of Russia) will be kept in the background only, rarely articulated. On the contrary, possibility of membership in the long term for a democratic Russia should not be ruled out explicitly, as the President and Yeltsin agreed.

Were the objectives clear? Were the objectives defined? Promises must be kept! What would not be easy?—In the remaining month and a half it would be necessary to 1) convince the key NATO partners, Germany and France, who did not see the need to expand the alliance, warning of the inevitable aggravation of relations with Russia; even the UK feared that Washington may be moving too fast and too loud,[57] that the enlargement discussion should be "Russia-friendly"[58]; 2) explain to the Eastern European leaders the logic of the two-stage process in which participation in the Partnership was a preparatory stage for joining the organization; in addition, it was necessary to alleviate possible resentment that not all countries would be admitted at the same time; 3) of course, it was necessary to discuss everything with Russia in order to fulfill the President's promise of moving gradually and without surprises; 4) prepare proposals for strengthening the role of the CSCE, which the President would have to announce in Budapest; yes … it was also necessary to persuade the President to fly to Budapest, which he really did not want to do[59]—for several months, his aides had been putting on his desk a plan of foreign visits that included this trip, which had been promised to Yeltsin in April, but the President crossed it out every time.

A Clash of Giants

At 8.23 am on December 5, the US President's plane landed at Budapest airport, and 35 min later, Clinton entered the Hungarian capital's Convention Center to attend the summit of the Conference on Security and Cooperation in Europe. After another hour, he took to the podium to deliver a prepared speech. "*It was all yin and no yang- sure to please the Central Europeans and*

[57] US DoS. Case F-2017-13804. Doc No C06694673. The Deputy Secretary's October 19 Meeting with FCO Minister of State David Davis. Cable from the US Embassy in London.

[58] US DoS. Case F-2017-13804. Doc No C06694674. The Deputy Secretary's October 20 Meeting with FCO Political Director Neville-Jones. Cable from the US Embassy in London.

[59] US DoS. Case F-2017-13804. Doc No C06835906. Eyes only to the Secretary, from Strobe Talbott. October 20, 1994.

enthusiasts for enlargement, but equally sure to drive the Russians nuts, one Russian in particular": "We must not allow the Iron Curtain to be replaced by a veil of indifference . . . We must not consign new democracies to a gray zone... NATO will not automatically exclude any nation from joining. At the same time, no country outside will be allowed to veto expansion."[60]

If Talbott's assessment was right, the timing to pressure Yeltsin could not have been worse. Yeltsin arrived in Budapest, already tense and upset. He believed that "friend Bill" had deceived him.

Deception: Version[61]

On December 1, the day after the NATO foreign ministers' meeting, Kozyrev was to sign an individual program for Russia's participation in the Partnership for Peace.

Moscow knew the alliance was locked in heated debate over its future. When US diplomats said that the specific wording of the NATO communiqué would not be made public until the last minute because the discussion between the ministers was ongoing, on the one hand, this was not unexpected, but on the other hand, it made everyone wary. To be safe, the Russian Ambassador to NATO, Vitaly Churkin, was instructed to warn the participants in the NATO ministerial meeting against any surprises regarding NATO enlargement, which he did. Upon hearing this, Christopher assured Kozyrev that the American Ambassador to NATO, Robert Hunter, would give Churkin a "draft" communiqué as soon as there was agreement on all its points. Kozyrev wanted to be able to analyze the document and discuss it with Yeltsin before it was published.[62] Late in the afternoon, a call came from the American embassy—discussions were continuing, the document had not yet been agreed, and they would call again later.

In the morning, while waiting for the call, Kozyrev and Churkin decided to stretch out and play tennis, and soon embassy staff burst onto the court shouting, "*Call! ... From Moscow!*" Yeltsin's aide had called, saying that the ITAR-TASS agency had picked up the ministerial communiqué published in Brussels a few minutes earlier, adding that the Russian President had already

[60] Strobe Talbott. The Russia Hand. Random House/New York, 2002, p. 141.

[61] This account of the events in Brussels is based on the Kozyrev's memoirs (Andrei Kozyrev. The Firebird: the elusive fate of Russian democracy: a memoir. University of Pittsburgh Press, 2019, pp. 279–282).

[62] Robert Hunter, in response to my request to confirm or deny the fact of Christopher's promise to pass the text of the communiqué to the Russian Minister before its publication, said that he did not remember Christopher making such a request and that he (Hunter) had called Churkin in the evening. However, he added that he was not prepared to dispute these facts (personal correspondence with Robert Hunter).

asked several times about what was happening at NATO headquarters. Asking for 15 min to prepare for his conversation with Yeltsin, Kozyrev grabbed the printed news bulletins and was shocked to learn that NATO had announced its intention to make basic decisions on enlargement technology within a year—"*to determine how NATO will expand, what principles should guide the process, and what the consequences of membership will be... We will present the results of our discussions to interested partners before our next meeting in Brussels. We will discuss progress at our spring meeting in the* Netherlands."[63]

Churkin cornered the French ambassador in the corridor and demanded—how could this have happened? The French diplomat looked astonished and replied calmly: "*Christopher assured the participants in the meeting that you, the Russians, were fully informed and satisfied! Otherwise, the American proposal would not have passed.*"

The Kremlin rang; Yeltsin's aide noted that intelligence chief Yevgeny Primakov had just entered the office. A minute later, Yeltsin's voice rang out, thinly veiling his contempt: "*Now, Andrei Vladimirovich, what are your beloved Americans doing? The 'sources' you have always been so skeptical of knew better: Washington is pushing a new plan for speedy NATO expansion! I had a report on that already yesterday. And you called after the press report came out! Where is your friend Christopher? He had promised to give you advance warning if there were any new elements in the communiqué, hadn't he?... They want to start negotiations with new members - Poles, Hungarians, Czechs!... Don't be in a hurry to sign anything.*"[64]

"*What happened to my friend Bill? How could he do this to me?*" queried the Russian President.[65]

Forty minutes later Kozyrev strode into the conference room where his colleagues from NATO countries were gathered, approached Christopher, and, demanding the text of the NATO communiqué, announced that he would not sign the program of cooperation between Russia and NATO.

German Foreign Minister Klaus Kinkel turned to Holbrooke and loudly asked: "*Are you satisfied, Dick?*"[66]

[63] Communiqué NATO M-NAC-2(94)116 Issued at the Ministerial Meeting of the North Atlantic Council. NATO Headquarters, Brussels December 1, 1994. https://www.nato.int/docu/comm/49-95/c941201a.htm.

[64] Andrei Kozyrev. The Firebird: the elusive fate of Russian democracy: a memoir. University of Pittsburgh Press, 2019, p. 281.

[65] Strobe Talbott. The Russia Hand. Random House/New York, 2002, p. 140.

[66] Robert E. Hunter. "Toward NATO Enlargement: The Role of USNATO" in "Open Door: NATO and Euro-Atlantic Security After the Cold War" (Edited by Daniel S. Hamilton and Kristina Spohr). Washington, DC, Foreign Policy Institute/Henry A. Kissinger Center for Global Affairs, Johns Hopkins University SAIS, 2019, p. 319.

He Said What He Thought

On the eve of November 30, Yeltsin sent a brief letter to the US President. One can see a "yellow card," in soccer parlance: "*I shall frankly say that against the background of our promising joint efforts, one completely fails to understand the reasons behind a new revitalizing of the discussion on speeding up the broadening of NATO. We have agreed with you that there will be no surprises, that first we should pass through this phase of partnership, whereas issues of further evolution should not be decided without due account to the opinion and interests of Russia. Adoption of an expedited time-table to start negotiations with the candidates in the middle of the next year will be interpreted, and not only in Russia, as the beginning of a new split of Europe.*"[67]

The next day, Clinton replied, saying the ministers had misunderstood the grasp of the document, that the Russian President's alarm was exaggerated, and he expressed his bewilderment at Kozyrev's behavior and his motives. The American President claimed that the decisions in Brussels were made in full accordance with the agreements of the two Presidents—"*no surprises, the highest priority of preserving and strengthening the Russian-American partnership and thorough, inclusive, transparent discussions.*" He confirmed that Kozyrev had asked Christopher for clarification of the document being prepared and said he "*believes that Christopher explained to Andrei in Brussels the evolutionary nature of our approach to* NATO *enlargement.*"[68]

Although tension was obvious between the two leaders, the US President saw no point in discussing it[69]—Clinton's tightly planned schedule had left the two politicians no opportunity to talk eye to eye before the meeting,[70] and Yeltsin picked up the gauntlet and chose to air the dispute publicly.

> *Europe, not yet able to shake off the legacy of the Cold War, risks plunging into a cold world... NATO was created during the Cold War. Today, the alliance is trying to find its place in Europe, and it is not doing so efficiently. It is important that this search does not create new fault lines but promotes European unity. Why sow seeds of distrust? After all, we are no longer adversaries, we are partners... It is a dangerous*

67 US DoS. Case F-2017-13804. Doc No C06837138. Letter from Yeltsin to President Clinton. November 30, 1994.

68 CDL #118450. Message from President Clinton to President Yeltsin. December 2, 1994.

69 It should be noted that on the day of the Budapest meeting, Talbott was in Haiti, where he had been thoughtfully sent to hold another meeting. Strobe Talbott. The Russia Hand. Random House/New York, 2002, p. 142.

70 Clinton's visit to Budapest lasted 7 hours, including the trip to and from the airport. During that time, he and Yeltsin could talk for no more than 30 s, exchanging words and shaking hands in front of television cameras while signing the nuclear arms reduction agreement.

delusion to believe that the fate of the continents and the world community can somehow be managed from a single capital.[71]

Yeltsin's statements went beyond what Clinton and his team could comprehend. *"The President was really pissed off and his anger grew when we returned to Washington to see how the evening news treated it... He felt that Yeltsin showed him up by criticizing not only our NATO policy in such strong and unexpected terms but also his criticism of the US role in the world. He felt like a pawn… He was offended by the manner in which he was treated and by the Kozyrev incident last week… The President did not want to be used as a pawn by Yeltsin any more."*[72]

What Was It?

In hindsight, no single cause fully explained Yeltsin's sharp statement. Perhaps Thomas Pickering's assessment was correct, i.e., that a whole set of objective and subjective factors played a role.[73] In the first place, he cited Kozyrev's show-man instincts and his need to fend off domestic critics of his allegedly too pro-Western policy, which was voiced inside the country. The next factors, according to the Ambassador, were the general rejection of NATO-enlargement policy within the Russian political elite and the obvious gap between the words and promises of Clinton, who spoke of slow movement without surprises, in contrast to remarks, comments, articles in the press, which came from his closest circle, and which allowed for the conclusion that the decision to expand the alliance in the near future has already been made, and even identifying those countries that would be the first on this path.[74]

In addition to these factors, we must add one more, which Thomas Pickering could not appreciate at the time—in a week, Russia would start the Chechen war, and undoubtedly, preparing for the decision, the Russian President was in a state of heightened irritability and anxiety.

At that moment, something cracked in the Bill–Boris relationship. Although they would meet a lot over the next five years and demonstrate close

---

[71] Address by President of the Russian Federation Yeltsin in Budapest to the Plenary Conference on Security and Cooperation in Europe (CSCE). https://yeltsin.ru/archive/audio/9035/.

[72] US DoS. Case F 2017–13804. Doc No C0683850. Letter to Yeltsin on Budapest and other items. Note for Strobe Talbott from Nick Burns. December 6, 1994.

[73] US DoS. Case F-2017-13804. Doc No C06838441. RUSSIA AND NATO. Cable from Pickering to the Secretary of State. December 6, 1994.

[74] An informal agreement that Poland, Hungary, and the Czech Republic would be the first Eastern European countries for which NATO's doors would be opened was already formed in Washington in the summer of 1994, and it can be assumed that this was no secret to Russian intelligence.

relations in every way possible, the "Budapest splinter" never disappeared and was constantly making itself felt. According to Yeltsin's foreign affairs aide Dmitry Ryurikov, with whom Talbott met in the Kremlin 10 days after Budapest,[75] the Russian President realized his partner did not believe or trust him. "*We heard people in the US – not the administration, but others – saying we have to expand NATO as a hedge against developments in Russia. This really upset Yeltsin. The notion of uncertainty regarding us as a partner upset him. This didn't fit his concept of partnership. It's a strange business venture … when you have two partners, but at some stage one says, "This guy is not reliable; I've got to take precautions in case he fails." This is why we reacted.*"[76]

Talbott believed the Kremlin had its reasons for this stance: "*The Russians believe that NATO expansion and the $25 billion increase in the defense budget are just two of many signs that we're abandoning partnership, engagement and integration and adopting instead a strategy of preemptive containment. In fact, quite a few Americans, including some of our own colleagues, believe we should do something of that sort.*"[77]

Cooling Down and Going Their Separate Paths

Of course not; in December 1994, both sides desired a quick fix. The Clinton team reassessed Russia's concerns, recognized the validity of the Kremlin's concerns,[78] and within two weeks, Vice President Al Gore flew to Moscow to discuss once again how NATO enlargement would contribute positively to a stronger security system in Europe.[79] "*We didn't have enough content in the compensatory CSCE enhancement … we had a second track, but there was no train on it … we should recognize - and the Russians should recognize - that they've never been very clear about what they want out of CSCE.*"[80]

---

[75] "*He [Ryurikov] twice cited Yevgeny Primakov, the head of SVRR, as having provided key analysis that influenced Yeltsin's original expectations and post-Brussels anger*"—wrote Talbott in his cable.

[76] US DoS. Case F-2017-13804. Doc No C06694734. December 15 Talbott–Ryurikov meeting on NATO, Chechnya. Cable from Talbott to the Secretary of State. December 16, 1994.

[77] US DoS. Case F-2017-13804. Doc No C06835880. Memorandum to the Secretary from Strobe Talbott. Dealing with Russia. December 11, 1994.

[78] "*Part of Yeltsin's real concern … There is a direct concern about the psychological impact on the Russian people*," said Clinton, meeting with Chancellor Kohl. *CDL* #57651. Memorandum of Conversation. Meeting with Chancellor Helmut Kohl of Germany. December 5, 1994

[79] CDL #118450. Memorandum for the President. Message to the Russian President Yeltsin on NATO expansion. December 7, 1994.

[80] US DoS. Case F-2017-13804. Doc No C06835880. Memorandum to the Secretary from Strobe Talbott. Dealing with Russia.

Yeltsin also made a conciliatory step, admitting that his vision of possible threats was somewhat exaggerated. A call from Kohl, long skilled at soothing Yeltsin, proved decisive. "*I told him it was important to keep in close and constant contact with you, and that no one in the West, certainly not you, had any interest in creating a new chasm between them and the West. He should not listen to those around him who are making him distrustful. They have influenced him to be distrustful of our purposes. My impression is that people around him are not keeping him aware of the reality of the situation. There are quite a few who aren't interested in keeping him informed or in working toward goodwill.*"[81] Kohl assured Yeltsin that NATO's first expansion would not come until the late-1990s and would track EU enlargement.

During his talks with Gore, Yeltsin stated that Russia "*did not endorse NATO enlargement. Nor did claim a veto over it… NATO is still perceived in Russia as a military alliance system that is either directed at them, or it is maintained and plans to expand pending the failure of Russian democracy.*"[82] Nevertheless, the Russian President agreed that there was a misunderstanding in his reading of the Brussels communiqué due to its failure to mention the CSCE, the EU, the Partnership, and other institutions. As a result, Yeltsin and Clinton exchanged letters in which they confirmed that "*No negotiations on the admission of new states to NATO are envisaged in 1995*, that a new relationship between Russia and NATO should be agreed upon, and that *Work will be done within NATO on both possible expansion and necessary evolution of the alliance.*"[83]

Clinton visited Moscow in May 1995 and wept at the sight of WWII veterans marching on Red Square. During this visit, the Presidents agreed that any action on NATO expansion would be postponed until after the Russian presidential election scheduled for mid-1996. In late 1995, an agreement would be reached on the participation of the Russian military in NATO's peacekeeping operation in Yugoslavia, under US operational control. In May 1997, a month and a half before it was announced that negotiations would begin for the three Eastern European countries (Czechia, Poland, and Hungary) to join the alliance, the NATO-Russia Founding Act would be signed.

All these gains mattered, yet counter-currents were already gathering that would soon shelve any talk of a US–Russian alliance. Whenever a rift appeared,

[81] *CDL* #57651. Telcon with Chancellor Helmut Kohl of Germany of December 13, 1994.

[82] US DoS. Case F-2012-25789. Doc No C05314191. Department of State Cable. December 21 NAC: Guidance for Discussion of the Vice President's Visit to Russia.

[83] CDL #118450. Letter from Yeltsin to President Clinton. December 29, 1994, and NSA. President Clinton Letter to President Yeltsin. January 6, 1995.

hardliners calling for a break surfaced at once. Though few, their words stick, widen the gap, and set the tone.

Immediately after Budapest, the Russian military urged Yeltsin to delay army reform—you don't change horses in mid-stream—and to draft plans to counter a potential enemy concentrating its forces near Russia's borders.[84] In mid-January 1995, Christopher told NATO staff to add potential foreign-troop and nuclear arms placement on their territory to the negotiation agenda with prospective members.[85]

In Moscow, a hard-line bloc led by intelligence chief Primakov and Security Council Secretary Lobov coalesced around the President. A week before Kozyrev was to fly to sign Russia's individual program within the Partnership, they nearly derailed the move. First, at a Security Council session, Lobov claimed the Council had not approved the Foreign Ministry's NATO stance; the next day Yeltsin unexpectedly visited the ministry and publicly rebuked Kozyrev.

"Why are you, Andrei Vladimirovich, conducting negotiations on the conditions under which we could accept NATO membership or NATO enlargement? Who authorized that? I did not... That is a precipitous step and it is in the wrong direction... Our opponents in NATO take your overtures simply as a sign of weakness in our position and an offer to bargain over the price for enlargement... There is unambiguous information on that matter from reliable sources[86] *very close to those people you are talking to in Washington... I want everybody here to remember that Russia - the President of Russia - is against NATO, against its enlargement, and we are not going to negotiate any terms or conditions of our agreement since we just don't agree.*"[87] Only Kozyrev's reminder of Yeltsin's promise to sign an Individual Partnership Program cooled the outburst.

In December 1995, Russia held parliamentary elections, and Kozyrev was re-elected to the State Duma. Updated law barred ministers from the Duma, leaving Yeltsin to decide Kozyrev's fate. They met the day after Christmas, and according to Kozyrev's recollections, Yeltsin was ill and tired; during the conversation, he repeatedly questioned the correctness of decisions on rapprochement with the West; even Kozyrev's words that Russia's admission to the G7

[84] US DoS. Case F-2017-13804. Doc No C06694734. December 15 Talbott–Ryurikov meeting on NATO, Chechnya. Cable from Talbott to the Secretary of State. December 16, 1994.

[85] US DoS. Case M-2017-03979. Doc No C06323567. Secretary Christopher Cable. US Draft Outline of NATO presentation on Expansion for January 12 SPC/R. January 12, 1995.

[86] Kozyrev later learned that the Russian President met with Yevgeny Primakov 30 min before Yeltsin left for the Foreign Ministry.

[87] Andrei Kozyrev. The Firebird: the elusive fate of Russian democracy: a memoir. University of Pittsburgh Press, 2019, pp. 299–300.

would be announced in six months did not arouse his enthusiasm. Two weeks later, the Russian President called and told Kozyrev that it would be better if he became a member of the Duma. Yevgeny Primakov was appointed Foreign Minister.

On the other side of the ocean, in Washington, advocates of pressing ahead insisted, "*Russia's objections* [vis-à-vis NATO expansion] *are well known and loudly voiced. But there is no indication that this is a core issue between the two countries. This is theater of a very minor sort. It will not determine the future of Russia,*"[88] and quickly outflanked compromise-seekers, especially since the latter could not (or did not want to) propose any constructive steps even for the realization of the ideas voiced. Plans to give the OSCE real weight and fuse it with NATO establishing a new system of European security remained only on paper. The idea to give real powers to the WEU, making it a security instrument for the European Union, was immediately blocked by Great Britain.

Yeltsin treated diplomacy as leader-to-leader and liked to settle hard issues in a private handshake, without aides. Often, this led to the fact that when working out the agreements reached by the leaders, it was necessary to find solutions to problems that remained out of the leaders' sight. In such situations, US negotiators routinely squeezed their Russian counterparts, citing presidential deadlines that could not be moved. "'*Table and stick' we'd called it: go straight to your bottom line and stick with it; wait until the other side bends. We'd been able to look the Russians in the eye and tell them that we were going forward with or without them.*"[89] American officials were well versed in the tactics of working with Yeltsin, which Clinton used with success—it "was *much easier to negotiate*" with the Russian President when he was inebriated or when it was possible to send his aides out of the negotiating room, for example, to bring some necessary document or object.[90] It was naïve to assume such tactics strengthened the Boris–Bill relationship.

[88] Richard Holbrooke at the Council of Foreign Relations, December 9, 1996. https://ciaotest.cc.columbia.edu/conf/hor01/.

[89] Strobe Talbott. The Russia Hand. Random House/New York, 2002, p. 382.

[90] For example, Strobe Talbott. The Russia Hand. Random House/New York, 2002, pp. 163, 183.

7

A Rebellious Republic

The main reason for the collapse of the USSR was the inability of the existing governance structures to solve the rapidly growing economic problems. No active participants in the political reform process until the fall of 1991 aimed to liquidate the Soviet Union, except for the three Baltic republics, whose public memory retained memories of pre-Soviet life and the Soviet occupation of 1940 and 1945, and a small mountainous republic in the North Caucasus, Chechen-Ingushetia. In these regions, Gorbachev's political reforms and encouragement of freedom of speech gave impetus to the development of a powerful anti-colonial movement, the main slogan of which was the freedom to secede from the unified country.

The Chechen-Ingush Republic was created after adopting the USSR constitution in 1936, and the territories were united by two close peoples, Chechens and Ingush. Still, their history of incorporation into the Russian Empire was different. The Ingush, who had no state of their own and lived in territorial communities, gradually joined Russia in the 1770s, mainly after signing agreements on accepting Russian citizenship. One of the main reasons for this was that the Ingush lived on the plains and needed protection of their lands. Chechens,[1] on the other hand, lived mainly in the mountains, divided into numerous gorges, which, on the one hand, strengthened the *quasi-tribal*[2] way of life and, on the other hand, made the problem of defending their

[1] This included many peoples of the areas that are now Dagestan, Cherkessia, and Kabarda.

[2] Chechen society is based on teips. Teip (clan) is a group of people self-identified through descent from a common ancestor or geographic location. The population of Chechnya is close to 1,600,000; there are about 150 teips.

S. Aleksashenko, *Post-Cold War Russia and the Missed Opportunity for Global Stability*,
https://doi.org/10.1007/978-3-032-01380-4_7

territory less urgent—few people sought to conquer unfamiliar, inaccessible mountains. The Russian Empire decided to take this step in the 1830s, which was the last phase of the Caucasian war, which lasted almost 50 years (1817–1864) and is considered in Russian historiography as a continuation of the Russo-Turkish wars. Chechens, led by Imam Shamil, resisted stubbornly for 30 years, but eventually, in 1859, Shamil was captured, and the Chechens ceased their resistance.

After the final establishment of Soviet power in 1924, Chechnya and Ingushetia received the status of autonomous regions being included in the North Caucasus Krai, which united the vast territory of today's Rostov Oblast, Krasnodar Krai, and Stavropol Krai and all North Caucasus republics. In 1934, Chechnya and Ingushetia were united into a single Chechen-Ingush Autonomous Republic, and in 1978, this entity was granted the status of a "Socialist state" within the RSFSR. When the Constitution of the RSFSR was amended in April 1992, the words "Soviet socialist" were deleted, and Chechen-Ingushetia became a state within the RSFSR.

In November 1990, the First Chechen National Congress was held in Grozny, the capital of Chechnya-Ingushetia, which proclaimed itself "the supreme forum of the people's power of the Chechen Republic" and established its governing body (the Executive Committee of the Chechen National Congress), headed by Major General Dzhokhar Dudayev. Dudayev was the only Chechen to be promoted to the rank of general in the Soviet Union. From 1987, he had commanded a division of strategic bombers stationed in the Estonian city of Tartu. In case of war with NATO, this division was to be the first to strike the enemy's territory. In January 1991, when mass protests broke out in Vilnius, the capital of Lithuania, and the Kremlin decided to use army units, including tanks, to suppress them, Dudayev announced that he would not allow Soviet aircraft into Lithuanian airspace. A few days later, Dudayev, having learned of a possible assassination attempt on Yeltsin, who was in the Estonian capital of Tallinn, warned the Russian leader about it and gave him his car, in which Yeltsin left for St Petersburg.

In May 1991, Dudayev resigned from the Soviet Army and returned to his homeland,[3] taking control of the established organization's activities, which had shown little progress by that time. Almost immediately after Dudayev's return to Chechnya, the Executive Committee of the Chechen National Congress adopted a resolution on the illegitimacy of the republic's Supreme

[3] In fact, Dudayev lived in Chechnya for only a few months after his birth before his entire family was deported to Kazakhstan. In February 1944, Chechen-Ingushetia was liquidated on Stalin's orders, and between 500,000 and 650,000 Chechens and Ingush were deported to Central Asia.

Soviet, and dual power was effectively established in Chechnya. Taking advantage of the weakening of Soviet state structures after the putsch of August 1991, the Executive Committee of the Chechen People's National Congress declared the Supreme Soviet deposed and became the sole authority in Chechnya. In mid-September, a decision was made to hold presidential elections, and Dzhokhar Dudayev won a landslide victory in late October. In late November 1991, a referendum was held in Ingushetia, which decided on the creation of the Ingush Republic. In early December, Chechnya and Ingushetia officially became autonomous from each other in the Constitution of the Russian Federation.

These events rapidly changed the political situation in the region. Still, Moscow paid little attention to them—the tectonic process of the collapse of the USSR was a much more significant event. At times, Dudayev was referred to as "Yeltsin in the mountains," which forced Moscow officials sent to Grozny (the capital of Chechnya) into tempering their assessments. As a result, neither Gorbachev nor Yeltsin grasped developments in the mountainous republic, and much less could they agree on a common position since the struggle for the main prize, power in Moscow, made it impossible to compromise. In mid-October, Yeltsin issued a formidable proclamation demanding that the illegal armed formations be disbanded, surrender their weapons, and vacate the premises where the state organs were housed. On November 7, the Russian leader declared a state of emergency in Chechnya; however, Gorbachev, who retained control of internal troops, refused to support his opponent and provide him with army units.

By early 1992 Chechnya lay almost entirely outside Moscow's control, and a peculiar political regime was formed there, combining elements of nationalism, anarchism, and criminality. The Russian-speaking population, which constituted about 20% of the total number of inhabitants, was forced out of the republic by threats. Massive attacks on army units took place, resulting in the seizure of weapons by Chechen freedom fighters—eventually, in May 1992, the Russian Defense Ministry signed an agreement with Dudayev's government, according to which the latter received half of all weapons on the republic's territory, including tanks, aircrafts, and helicopters. Drug-smuggling corridors emerged in Chechnya, and the workshops forging rubles and US dollars appeared. After gaining Central-Bank access and exploiting the payment system's antiquated technology, fraudsters devised a scheme of counterfeit payment orders that siphoned off billions of rubles.

This development did not suit Dudayev well, and in July 1992, he wrote a letter to Yeltsin in which he offered to exchange Chechen political independence for financial support from the federal center. Chechnya had never possessed significant economic potential, and after the expulsion of the Russian-speaking population, which formed the basis of the engineering staff, many factories shut down. A modest oil sector survived, yet export barriers kept its revenues meager. The Russian President sent this proposal to Gaidar, the acting Prime Minister, but his offer vanished into obscurity.[4]

During 1992–1994, several attempts were made to launch the negotiation process, but all of them failed—neither Moscow nor Grozny had a clear vision of the desired structure of relations between Russia and Chechnya, and there was no unity within the Yeltsin and Dudayev teams. In Moscow, the supporters of a forceful solution and the supporters of seizing power by exploiting the intra-Chechen split opposed each other. Yet both teams foresaw Chechnya simply as another Russian region. But since the struggle in Grozny was between supporters of full independence and broad autonomy, it was impossible to find a crossroads. Dudayev approached Yeltsin several times with a proposal for a personal meeting, but the Russian President never agreed to it. The reasons for this are still unclear. Some believe that the reason for this was one of the interviews in which Dudayev called Yeltsin "*an unworthy leader and an alcoholic*"[5]; others say that Dudayev demanded that he be called "President of the Chechen Republic," thus wishing to be recognized as such. Moscow, which did not recognize the 1991 elections,[6]refused, agreeing only to call him "General Dudayev."

Chechnya's worsening economy eroded Dudayev's popularity further as state and social structures crumbled. Those in Yeltsin's inner circle who favored a forceful solution believed that this created good preconditions for the emergence of a political alternative to Dudayev in Chechnya and to seize power. Many Chechens lived in Moscow and offered the Kremlin their services in the hope of becoming republic leaders after Dudayev's overthrow. In mid-October 1994, they received 40 crewed tanks, enabling Chechen "militia" groups with anti-Dudayev slogans to enter Grozny and quickly occupy the city, including Dudayev's residence. Planners expected internal troops to enter the city immediately afterward to establish control, but this did not happen, and the "militias" left the city late at night.

The next attempt to realize the scenario of an intra-Chechen split proved disastrous for the Kremlin. Again, the tanks managed to enter Grozny unhindered, after which the "militias" proclaimed that they had taken power into their own hands. However, as darkness fell, detachments of Dudayev's

---

[4]Ehpoha El'cina. Ocherki politicheskoj istorii. (*The Yeltsin's Era. Essays on political history*). Moscow, Vagrius, 2001, pp. 588–589.

[5]Timothy Colton. Yeltsin: A Life. New York, Basic Books; 2008, p. 362.

[6]Sergey Filatov. Sovershenno nesekretno. (*Absolutely unclassified.*) Moscow, Vagrius, 2000, p. 267.

supporters began destroying the tanks with rocket-propelled grenades. Several dozen tank crews, who had been recruited for this operation by the FSK,[7] were captured, and the Chechen television footage went around the world. Apart from the fact that the Kremlin had to admit that the operation was authorized by it implicitly, the failure of the operation had the opposite political result—Russian troops on Grozny's streets rallied the Chechen populace behind Dudayev.

Although it should have been clear to everyone that the Russian security forces lacked coherence and were unable to develop and implement an adequate plan for a forceful operation, in late November, Yeltsin finally chose the hawkish path, ordering preparations for a military invasion of the rebel republic with massive use of the Russian army. He decided despite Defense Minister Grachev's warning that the army was unready and would need at least six months to prepare. At the end of November, the Russian President temporarily threw out of his entourage anyone who might have tried to persuade him to change his decision.[8] The Chechen problem was becoming the main topic of domestic politics.

On December 6, having already received the order to launch the invasion, Defense Minister Grachev flew to Chechnya, where he met with Dzhokhar Dudayev. The two men knew each other well, having fought together in Afghanistan, and held friendly face-to-face talks. Grachev's attempt to persuade Dudayev to abandon armed confrontation failed. "*Then war*," said the Russian minister. "*Yes, war!*"—Dudayev replied. The generals shook hands and parted ways.

Late in the evening of December 11, Yeltsin signed a secret decree starting the Chechen war, which would last almost 15 years until April 2009.[9]

---

[7] Federal Counterintelligence Service (Federal'naya Sluzhba Kontrrazvedki), later renamed FSB.

[8] Ehpoha El'cina. Ocherki politicheskoj istorii. he Yeltsin's Era. Essays on political history.) Moscow, Vagrius, 2001, pp. 598–599.

[9] Ilya Kramnik. *Vtoraya chechenskaya vojna oficial'no zavershena*. (The second Chechen war is officially over.) https://ria.ru/20090416/168270914.html.

8

The Perfect Storm

The perfect storm is a popular term. The combination at one point and at one time of several, sometimes unrelated factors leads to unexpected, catastrophic consequences, although the effect of each factor separately would be very limited. Such a situation has been forming in Russia in connection with Russian-American relations since the end of 1994. No, it did not lead to an immediate catastrophe that would occur almost 30 years later, but the simultaneous combination of several factors at this point in early 1996 reversed the trend in relations between the two countries; first, the movement toward alliance relations stopped, and then numerous disagreements began to surface, each time emphasizing the differences between Russia and America and intensifying the rift between the countries. These factors affected the main blocks of social and state life—the economy and domestic and foreign policy.

A Phoenix Economy

In 1995, the Russian economy began to sense the approaching end of the agonizing stabilization period.

On the one hand, structural transformation was coming to an end. Those companies that could not survive the fall in state demand for their products or withstand the competition with imports ceased to exist, and thus the reduction of their production indicators stopped dragging down the statistical data. The decline in industrial production and GDP in 1995 amounted to 4.5% and 4%, respectively, against 17% and 15%, on average, for 1992–1994.

S. Aleksashenko, *Post-Cold War Russia and the Missed Opportunity for Global Stability*,
https://doi.org/10.1007/978-3-032-01380-4_8

Adopting the 1995 budget, in which the government refused to use monetary financing for the deficit, dramatically changed the situation in the financial markets. The end of the era of free money forced banks to choose their lines of business more carefully. In February, the Bank of Russia began intensive purchases of foreign currency on the market. As of February 1, Russia's foreign currency reserves were $4.6 billion; by May 1, they had grown to $8.2 billion. Endless purchases of foreign currency, which brought guaranteed income, turned out to be not just pointless but, on the contrary, began to bring losses. From May, the ruble began to strengthen, and by early July, its exchange rate had risen by more than 11%, while the country's foreign exchange reserves continued to grow, reaching $12.4 billion by mid-year.[1] On July 8, the government and the Bank of Russia announced the introduction of a "currency corridor" that fixed the maximum level of ruble devaluation for the next three months[2]. Although this commitment was not guaranteed, the tightening of monetary policy and the opportune moment for the announcement of the currency corridor—due to seasonal factors from early spring to mid-summer, the supply of currency on the Russian currency market traditionally exceeds the demand for it—led to the fact that the strengthening of the ruble continued until mid-August, which had a strong psychological impact on the financial markets and on the population in general. In addition, the ruble appreciation played the role of a powerful anti-inflationary anchor: while in January 1995, monthly inflation was 18%, in the last four months of the year, it fell to an average of 4%.

As the economy continued to decline and the reduction of budget expenditures was much slower than desired, the budget deficit in 1995 remained at a dangerously high level of 5.5% of GDP, but the structure of its financing changed dramatically. In 1994, when the deficit was 10.4% of GDP, almost three-quarters of it was financed by Central Bank loans and borrowing in the domestic financial market accounted for less than 10% of deficit financing. In 1995, 90% of the funding for the federal budget deficit came from borrowing from the domestic financial market and privatization. That year, for the first time, Russia received significant loans from international financial organizations: the IMF strongly supported the efforts of the Russian government and already, in April, signed an agreement on a new program that gave Russia access to a $6 billion loan, which was received over the next 12 months; the World Bank during the year approved nine loan projects totaling about $2 billion. However, this money was not even enough to pay off old debts: by the

[1] By the end of the year, foreign exchange reserves exceeded $17 billion.

[2] The currency corridor was later extended until the end of 1995 and then until the end of 1997.

end of the year, the IMF and World Bank disbursed less than $6 billion, while Russia paid $6.7 billion to its creditors.[3]

The tightening of monetary policy made domestic government bonds an attractive target for Russian investors and foreign players. In addition to high interest rates (200% per annum at the beginning of the year, just over 50% in May, and between 100% and 120% per annum in the fall), investors saw the exchange rate stabilize, and thus the foreign exchange yields secured became markedly higher than any alternative instruments in emerging markets. Although Russian law prohibited foreigners from buying government bonds, experienced players quickly found a way around this restriction: the main buyer of the government bonds was Credit Suisse's Moscow subsidiary, which began operations in September 1993. The parent bank welcomed funds from international investors to invest in Russian bonds and transferred them to the Credit Suisse in Moscow as a loan. By the end of 1995, this bank owned more than 10% of the total volume of Russian government bonds.

In 1997, the Russian economy began to grow, although GDP inched up just 1.4%, yet that uptick marked a turning point in Russia's economic transformation. Although there would still be a crisis ahead in 1998 when GDP would again collapse by more than 5%, the economy hit bottom and then, from 1999 until the 2008 crisis, averaged about 7% growth a year.[4]

In the eyes of Russian politicians and Russian society, the economy's turnaround occurred with scant Western support. Russia was shut out of G7 talks and denied OECD membership—an institution that distils policy lessons for advanced economies. Even associate status would have let banks cut the risk premium on Russian borrowers.[5]

Russia never secured favorable market access to Europe or the United States.

On June 11, 1993, Yeltsin solemnly handed GATT Director General Arthur Dunkel a letter requesting him to start the procedure for Russia's admission to the organization. Although the application was considered at the GATT session five days later, no one would rush Russia's admission: the member countries were engaged in persistent negotiations within the framework of

[3] This was about one-third of what Russia had to pay for its debt obligations. The Paris and London Clubs of creditors granted a deferment for the remaining amount.

[4] The crisis of 1998, being extremely powerful and painful for the Russian financial sector, laid a solid foundation for such growth: on the one hand, the default on domestic and foreign debt allowed the government to normalize its budget policy and begin to finance budgetary obligations fully; on the other hand, the almost threefold appreciation of the dollar created a powerful barrier to imports, creating a space of opportunity for Russian industry working for the consumer market. For more details on the Russian economy's growth factors in 1999–2008, see "Counterrevolution," pp. 27–38.

[5] Banking regulators set this level of risk, which is 20%–50% higher for non-OECD countries than for member countries.

the Uruguay Round talks, culminating in the agreement that created the WTO. Russia's WTO working group first met in July 1995—two years after the application. The last round of negotiations took place in November 2011. On August 22, 2012, the Russian Federation officially became the 156th member of the World Trade Organization. All these years, Russian exports met a raft of barriers—higher duties and anti-dumping probes targeting value-added metal and chemical products.

Washington and Brussels created no insurance or promotion schemes for investment in Russia. Potential investors were ready to assume economic risks but not political risks, which Western countries could have neutralized by creating special insurance instruments.

In short, Russia remained largely outside the global economy. Of course, the degree of isolation was significantly lower than before the collapse of the USSR: having stopped wasting resources on military needs, the Russian economy was able to become an important supplier of primary resources to the world market, which ensured the ability to pay for imports of necessary consumer and investment goods. But at that time, the Russian economy almost completely lost access to foreign markets for finished goods—Eastern Europe was rapidly moving into the EU's orbit. Firms from former CMEA states did not sever production links with Russian partners after governments removed their backing. Still, the development of trade relations with the EU countries was supported by politicians from both sides and received various financial support. Deprived of imported components, Russian products rapidly declined in quality or vanished, because domestic substitutes were technologically impossible. Russia's limited potential to export finished goods shrank to arms and nuclear engineering, fields that faced stiff US opposition.

In 1972, the Soviet Union and the Federal Republic of Germany signed a historic deal to build the West Siberia-Europe gas pipeline, which became known as "gas-for-pipes" because Germany was the supplier of large-diameter pipes and compressor units for the pipeline. The nature of the economic ties between Russia and the West that had developed by the mid-1990s could be described by the same term, with the adjustment that oil and metals became a complement to gas, and pipes were added to consumer goods. Though imperfect, the commodity-for-manufactures model proved stubbornly stable. The West had no desire to change it, and Russia had no opportunity.

From the late 1990s, FDI rose to a steady flow—aimed at serving Russia's home market, not at plugging firms into global value chains. The commodity bias made the economy oddly resilient: oil price crashes in 1998, 2009, 2015, and 2020 triggered recessions, yet growth resumed as soon as prices stabilized. The economy repeatedly rose from each slump like a phoenix.

Divorce from the Democrats

In 1995, the balance of political forces in Russia changed dramatically due to the impact of the war in Chechnya, which had begun at the end of the previous year, and the State Duma elections at the end of the year. By the 1996 presidential vote, Russia faced a much-strengthened security apparatus, which Yeltsin decided to rely on to resolve the conflict in Chechnya. It also had consolidated left-wing forces that had gained an absolute majority in the lower house of the Russian parliament and opposed many reform initiatives of the President and the government. There were also fragmented democratic forces that had lost the support of Yeltsin, and were unable to unite before the parliamentary elections, and, in fact, lost the ability to influence the political process.

War

The military operation in Chechnya did not go well for the Russian army immediately. Although Defense Minister Grachev had boasted he could seize Grozny in three days with a single parachute regiment, the generals had no time to draft an operational plan or ready their troops; the decision had been made on impulse, with no careful deliberation. As early as late November, the Kremlin believed that the anti-Dudayev opposition, with minimal support from federal forces, could turn around the situation in Chechnya. Three days later, on November 29, a meeting of the Security Council was held, at which it was decided to launch an army operation that would involve tens of thousands of troops. Before the meeting, Yeltsin met with his national security aide, Baturin, who detailed his vision of the situation and possible courses of action, clearly leaning toward a political solution. After silently listening to Baturin, Yeltsin summarized the conversation: "*I have appointed a Security Council on Chechnya. You don't* need to *be there.*"[6] At the meeting, only Defense Minister Grachev spoke out against immediately introducing troops into Chechnya.[7]

> *Before the vote on this issue, I made a report in which I said that after the troops were brought into Chechnya, the militants would offer serious armed resistance, and therefore, it would be inexpedient to launch a military campaign in Chechnya with-*

[6] Ehpoha El'cina. Ocherki politicheskoj istorii (*The Yeltsin*'s Era. *Essays on political history*). Moscow, Vagrius, 2001, p. 599.

[7] Other sources say that the only vote against was cast by Justice Minister Kalmykov, who was sent to resign shortly afterward. B Minaev. Yeltsin. Moscow, 2010, p. 514.

out any preliminary preparations, and even in winter - in the most unfavorable weather conditions for combat operations. In the course of the vote against the hasty deployment of troops, my vote was the only one. Yeltsin abstained. The other members of the Security Council voted in favor of starting the military operation as soon as possible. At the same meeting of the Security Council, President Yeltsin gave me an order - to prepare a plan for the introduction of troops into Chechnya and, in two weeks, to report on its readiness.[8]

Before the decision of the Security Council, many high-ranking military officers— Chief of the General Staff Kolesnikov, Chief of the Ground Forces General Semyonov, Chief of the Border Guard Service Nikolayev—sharply spoke out against the immediate start of the operation, sometimes doing so publicly.[9] But after the decision was made in the Kremlin, they had to carry out the order or resign—dozens of generals were sent to the borders of Chechnya, who were given the status of military advisors without the slightest coordination of their work. A week after the order from the Kremlin, Pavel Grachev dismissed General Mityukhin, who disagreed with the minister's position on the pace and methods of the military operation. Grachev offered General Vorobyov to lead the operation, who refused and resigned. Grachev was saved by Deputy Chief of the General Staff Kvashnin, who personally offered his candidacy for the place of commander.[10]

However, Kvashnin's desire alone was insufficient to achieve the task. Dudayev and his commanders understood engaging in open combat with the Russian army was a disastrous tactic. The Russian army moved slowly toward Grozny without an overall plan of operation and updated maps, encountering hostility from the population, ambushes, and night attacks by Chechen fighters.

On December 26, a regular meeting of the Security Council took place, at which a decision was made to storm the Chechen capital. Kvashnin's order to storm Grozny on New Year's Eve showed that the failed attempt to seize the city in late November had taught the Russian generals nothing. The tanks and armored vehicles that entered the city unhindered became a good target for the militants, who had prepared more than 50 strongholds in familiar locations. Kvashnin's plan envisioned an incomplete encirclement of the city, with

[8] "*We don't need to learn from those who want to conquer us!*" Interview with Pavel Grachev. Nezavisimaya Gazeta. Nezavisimoe Voennoe Obozrenie. March 20, 2009. https://nvo.ng.ru/forces/2009-03-20/1_Grachev.html.

[9] Boris Minaev. Yeltsin. Moscow, 2010, pp. 514–515.

[10] "*We don't need to learn from those who want to conquer us!*" Interview with Pavel Grachev. Nezavisimaya Gazeta. Nezavisimoe Voennoe Obozrenie. March 20, 2009. https://nvo.ng.ru/forces/2009-03-20/1_Grachev.html.

the ring of Russian troops not closed in the south. This "window" was left for civilians to leave the city by design. Still, in practice, the militants skillfully used it for the opposite purpose, organizing the entry of additional forces into the city and supplying it with ammunition. During the first day of the assault, the Russian army lost about 350 people and more than 70 tanks and armored vehicles and was forced to withdraw from the city center.

On January 4, Yeltsin held a meeting in a small circle, with only Prime Minister Chernomyrdin, Security Council Secretary Lobov, Defense and Interior Ministers Grachev and Yerin, Border Service Chief Nikolayev, and National Security Aide Baturin present. The Russian President, who had not met with anyone in the previous three days and was carefully studying the documents that came to him, asked direct and tough questions about how the assault on Grozny had been planned, why the army and internal troops had not been coordinated, and why tanks had been used in the city, even though three days before the assault the defense minister had said that this was an illiterate decision. Having received no clear answers, Yeltsin ordered the cessation of bombing and artillery shelling and demanded that the military prepare for a new assault.

The subsequent reshuffling of generals and the appointment of General Rokhlin as the person responsible for the capture of Grozny led to a change in Russian troops' tactics. By early March, methodical artillery pressure and step-by-step advances let Russian forces seize the shattered city.

However, the capture of the Chechen capital, unlike the capture of Berlin in 1945, did not mean the end of the war—the militant groups withdrew into the mountains, which significantly hampered the actions of the Russian military. The Russian military had to disperse its forces and fight in mountainous areas, for which the Russian military was even less prepared than for the storming of Grozny.

Western politicians found themselves in a difficult position. On the one hand, they were aware of what the Chechen fighters were all about. "*With regard to Chechnya, no one knows the background of the situation. I am surprised that people in the West hail the Chechens as democratic heroes. To put it bluntly, they are gangsters. Our experts say that a large part of the Mafia in Berlin is made up of Chechens. So this is not the nice group in white hats that the press sometimes describes,*" said Kohl meeting with Clinton.[11] On the other hand, the inadequacy of information provided by the Russian military and the horrific footage of the bombing of a large city led the Western media to almost unanimously

[11] CDL #57651. Memorandum of Conversation. Expanded Meeting with Chancellor Helmut Kohl of Germany. February 9, 1995.

stand up for the weaker side, demanding that politicians react to what is happening.

At the end of January 1995, Japan officially announced its refusal to grant any new relief to Russia regarding the servicing and repayment of its foreign debt,[12] and Kohl suggested that the US President take a unified position and tell Yeltsin that Russia would not receive any aid unless the law and human rights were respected in the country. Clinton put on pause making a final decision on a trip to Moscow in May, despite the fact that for Yeltsin, this visit, timed to coincide with the 50th anniversary of the victory in World War II, to which leaders of the world's leading countries had been invited, was to be the most important evidence of recognition of Russia's role both in World War II and in the modern world. Kohl admitted that he was tired of calling and telling the Russian President that Russia's image was diminishing before his eyes. The German leader had a growing confidence that the military in Yeltsin's entourage had framed their President, and many decisions were being made without consulting him. "*I urged Yeltsin on the phone to stop the bombardment. At the end of the conversation, after talking to some people, he said the bombing would stop that day. I urged him to publish that fact and he did. But after 24 hours, the bombing resumed. I am 100% certain that Yeltsin didn't lie. Someone else did this, perhaps to topple him.*"[13]

Clinton was trying to find language that would both satisfy US public opinion and avoid weakening Yeltsin at home.

"Chechnya is part of the Russian Federation, and we support the territorial integrity of Russia, just as we support the territorial integrity of all its neighbors. But the violence must end. I call again on all the parties to stop spilling blood and start making peace. Every day the fighting in Chechnya continues is a day of wasted lives and wasted resources and wasted opportunity."[14] But this was not enough, and the President was asked directly—*"Do you support economic sanctions because of the situation in Chechnya?"—"I don't think = we just started, and we haven't had a chance to have a conversation yet. We'll have a press conference later, and we'll all answer questions then."*[15]

On June 14, 1995, as Yeltsin was preparing to travel to Halifax for the next G7 meeting, Chechen fighters decided to carry out a daring operation and

[12] US DoS. Case F-2017-13,804. Doc No C06694639. Deputy Secretary Talbott Discusses Russia with MOFA European Affairs Director General. Cable from the US Embassy in Tokyo. January 30, 1995.

[13] *CDL* #101409. Memorandum of Conversation—Chancellor Helmut Kohl of Germany.

[14] Remarks in Cleveland, Ohio, at the White House Conference on Trade and Investment in Central and Eastern Europe January 13, 1995. PPP 1995, book 1, p. 43.

[15] Exchange with Reporters Prior to Discussions with Chancellor Helmut Kohl of Germany February 9, 1995. PPP book 1, p. 180.

seize Mineralnye Vody airport, a key airport in the North Caucasus. More than 160 people in three trucks stolen from Russian military units drove about 300 kilometers through the territory of Chechnya's neighboring Dagestan and Stavropol Krai and were stopped by a police checkpoint in the town of Budyonnovsk when the airport was still 130 kilometers away. This forced the militants to engage in a firefight and change their plan: they seized a hospital, taking more than 1400 hostages.

The Russian President did not cancel his trip to Canada—it had been agreed at the previous G7 meeting in Naples that Halifax would be the first time he could participate in a political discussion as an equal partner, a coveted goal for the Russian leader. Yeltsin assigned Prime Minister Chernomyrdin to negotiate with the militants, who demanded the withdrawal of Russian troops from Chechnya and the start of direct talks. At the same time, Yeltsin ordered the heads of security agencies to take a "tough stance" in case of casualties among the hostages.[16]

Security forces adopted a hard line immediately: on the night of June 16–17, an order was given to begin storming the hospital building, although there was no elaborate plan to seize the building and, according to estimates, 90% of the terrorists and 70% of the hostages could be killed in the course of the operation.[17] The assault was unsuccessful, with 30 people killed and more than 70 wounded. Chernomyrdin, lacking legal authority over law enforcement (*siloviki* nowadays), opened talks with the militant leader Shamil Basayev, which were broadcast on Russian television, and negotiated a ceasefire and the release of the hostages in exchange for allowing the militants to leave freely for Chechnya.

Immediately thereafter, negotiations between Chechen and Russian delegations' OSCE-brokered talks in Grozny produced a three-day moratorium on fighting. Although both sides occasionally violated the moratorium, the negotiations continued, and it was hoped that the conflict could be resolved without further casualties. However, in early October 1995, a major terrorist attack occurred in Grozny, leaving the commander of the Russian military group, General Romanov, severely injured. Immediately thereafter, hostilities resumed.

The Chechen war reshaped Russia—and outside attitudes toward it. Yeltsin and his circle no longer saw legal (violation of human rights, ban on the use of the army inside the country) or moral norms (barbaric bombing and mop-up operations in Chechnya) as restraints, which led to a sharp deterioration in

[16] Boris Minaev. Yeltsin. Moscow, Molodaya Gvardiya, 2010, p. 530.

[17] Alexei Filatov. Budyonovskyi rubezh. (*Budyonovsky frontier.*) Moscow, Knizhny Mir, 2020, pp. 60–61.

relations with human rights activists, who had been an essential part of the democratic movement and one of the pillars of the course for the transformation of the country. The war greatly boosted the security services, which Yeltsin now needed—and they used the leverage to reclaim power, both formal and informal. The role of Alexander Korzhakov, head of the Presidential Security Service, was sharply strengthened. After the events in Budyonovsk, he promoted his protégé Mikhail Barsukov to the post of FSB chief. The appointment proved pivotal for Russia's subsequent course. Until then, Yeltsin tried to maintain political control over Russia's leading security service by appointing people who had not previously worked in the KGB structures to head it. Barsukov was brought into the Soviet KGB structure straight out of high school. Although his service was in the Kremlin's security units, he was certainly a carrier of the cultural code of Soviet security officers. All subsequent heads of the FSB came from the USSR KGB.

The brutal military operations in Chechnya, the seemingly arbitrary brutality of Russian troops, and numerous civilian casualties led to the formation of a new view of Russia in the outside world. G7 leaders faced sharp media criticism that demanded an end to support for a country whose government was not ready to respect human rights.

Defeat

The war split Russian society, triggering fierce criticism of the Kremlin. Reasons abounded: murky strategy, inept operations, brutality toward civilians, and a failed information campaign. Yeltsin and his team were most seriously criticized by their reformist allies, the democratic movement and human rights activists, which gradually led to the breakup of an already fragile political alliance on the eve of the State Duma elections scheduled for December 1995.

Yeltsin saw the Duma vote as a dress rehearsal for his own contest six months later. Yet the picture was anything but clear. On the one hand, the President wanted to obtain a loyal and stable majority in the Duma. On the other hand, a performance by any party that was too successful in the elections made its leader a potential rival to Yeltsin in the June 1996 elections. Yeltsin feared Prime Minister Chernomyrdin most in this regard. Of course, he was absolutely loyal to the President, but inexplicably, he managed to gain political points exactly where Yeltsin lost them. He could get away with it when it came to the economy, which was not in the President's circle of interests. But it was hard to forgive Chernomyrdin for the success of his peacekeeping efforts in Budyonovsk, where Yeltsin's subordinate security forces once again demonstrated their ineptitude.

The strategy Yeltsin's team adopted was overly intricate—and clumsily executed: it was decided that the Kremlin would simultaneously support two pro-presidential parties: one headed by Chernomyrdin, which would be positioned to the right of center, and the other headed by Duma Speaker Ivan Rybkin, which would take a center left position. The lack of a good reason for this decision became immediately apparent: neither leader of the future party had any experience in party life. Chernomyrdin's rough charisma and colorful phrasing drew voters; Rybkin had neither. However, perhaps the biggest mistake was that Yeltsin announced the decision to go to the elections endorsing two parties. After that, there was no doubt about the puppet characters of both.

The December 1995 elections were arguably the freest in Russia's history—43 parties nominated their lists,[18] but only four of them managed to pass the 5% threshold, garnering a total of 51% of the vote. Among the winners, only the Yabloko party held democratic positions, but it never supported Yeltsin, constantly criticizing him and the Chernomyrdin government on a wide range of issues. The democratic forces could not agree on a single electoral bloc, and five parties, led by politicians who had worked with Yeltsin in different years, took part in the election. Collectively, they garnered almost nine percent of the vote, but none could break the five-percent threshold.

Chernomyrdin's bloc took just over 10%, finishing behind both the Communists (22%) and Zhirinovsky's party; Rybkin's party showed a resounding failure, gaining only 1.1 percent of the vote. After the first sessions of the new lower house of parliament, it became clear that the leftist forces, led by the Communists, controlled more than half of the votes.

Yeltsin's reaction to the election results surprised many—he dismissed the leader of his reformist wing, Anatoly Chubais, from the government, blaming him not only for the fact that many enterprises in the country had delayed wage payments, but also for causing the defeat of the ruling party in the elections. "*Chubais is to blame for the fact that only about 10% of voters voted for the NDR in the parliamentary elections. If it were not for the mistakes he made in conducting economic policy, the number of those who voted would have been at least 20%.*"[19]

[18] According to the law in force, one-half of the 450 deputies were elected by party lists and the other half by single-mandate constituencies.

[19] "*Krylatye frazy Borisa El'cina.*" Winged phrases of Boris Yeltsin.) Kommersant, 24.04.2007. https://www.kommersant.ru/doc/761764.

Change at the Helm

Although Kozyrev won the Duma election in his district, he was hardly happy about this victory. Yeltsin decided that the time had come to change the man who occupied the main office in the Russian Foreign Ministry sending Yevgeny Primakov there.

Primakov and Kozyrev truly belonged to different generations—the new minister could have been Kozyrev's father. Born in 1929, Yevgeny Primakov had had an interesting career in the Soviet Union: starting as a researcher at an academic Institute of the World Economy and Foreign Relations (IMEMO) he immediately went to work in the foreign editorial office of Gosteleradio, broadcasting to Arab countries, where he rose to editor-in-chief. Returning to IMEMO, Primakov was forced to resign at once after clashing with supervisors from the Communist Party Central Committee. His posting as *Pravda*'s Middle-East correspondent opened the region to him and became his focus for the next quarter-century. As his network of contacts widened, Primakov gained access to Arab leaders and began carrying out confidential assignments for the Communist Party and Soviet intelligence. Returning to Moscow, Primakov became deputy director of IMEMO and joined the circle of intellectuals who provide support for the international department of the Communist Party Central Committee. Working for Pravda, Primakov published many articles backing the official anti-Israeli line, yet on returning to Moscow he sent the Kremlin analytical notes on the situation in the Middle East, proposing a policy rethink toward Israel, including establishing diplomatic relations. Primakov's reason for changing the position of the USSR was due to the new Egyptian President Anwar Sadat's rapprochement with the United States. This proposal was supported by Soviet leader Leonid Brezhnev, and in summer 1971 the Politburo instructed Primakov to open a secret channel to Israel's leadership.

After Gorbachev came to power in 1985, Primakov's position was strengthened: he became director of IMEMO and one of the new Soviet leader's confidants. In 1988, Primakov lost his bid for the important bureaucratic chair of the International Department of the Communist Party, but this strengthened his ties with Gorbachev, who, a year after the first competitive elections in the Soviet Union, offered Primakov the chairmanship of one of the chambers of the USSR Supreme Soviet. This job was out of character for Primakov, but he could not refuse Gorbachev. But less than a year later, he left this position, and in September 1991, after the failure of the August putsch, Primakov became head of the Soviet Foreign Intelligence Service. After the collapse of the USSR,

Yeltsin, who removed almost everyone from Gorbachev's entourage, kept Primakov in charge of Russian intelligence, perhaps because he had played no part in the late-1980s campaign against Yeltsin. It could be every participant in Yeltsin's December 1991 meeting with intelligence chiefs endorsed Primakov when the President asked whom he should appoint.[20]

The entire Soviet foreign policy was based on confrontation with the United States, which was customary for Primakov, who had witnessed that rivalry firsthand in both the Middle East and Moscow. In this respect, the KGB, which until the collapse of the USSR was also engaged in foreign intelligence, was at the forefront of this confrontation, actively fighting "world imperialism" on all fronts. However, as times changed rapidly, Russian intelligence needed a new concept and a change of priorities. Primakov, being against conflict and prone to compromise, proposed prioritizing the dangerous phenomena of the modern world: weapons of mass destruction, terrorism, drugs, and organized crime—relegating the "main enemy"—the United States and NATO—to the background, keeping them under watch without advertising it. This approach suited the intelligence officers: on the one hand, it allowed them to retain all the established information sources and communication channels, and on the other hand, it gave them the opportunity to play an independent role in the Kremlin in shaping first the information space on foreign policy issues and later in developing practical recommendations.

The formation of Primakov's restrained position on rapprochement with the United States was facilitated by opponents of such rapprochement on both sides. It is unlikely that the intelligence chief harbored warm feelings after the CIA officers, having agreed to exchange information on programs for the development of weapons of mass destruction in third countries after receiving information on North Korea from their Russian colleagues, refused to provide the promised information on Pakistan, as Deputy Director of the CIA Robert Gates proudly told at the time.[21] On the other hand, Kozyrev was overburdened with multiple tasks and had no time (and sometimes no desire) to engage in discussions of all aspects of Russian foreign policy, believing that he had a mandate from the President. Meanwhile, Kremlin opponents of his pro-Western line could always find "consolation" in conversations with the leadership of Russian intelligence, which took pleasure in irritating the Foreign Ministry.

---

[20] Leonid Mlechin. Evgenij Primakov. As bol'shoj politiki. (*Yevgeny Primakov. Ace of Big Politics.*) Moscow, Molodaya Gvardiya, 2022, pp. 113–114.

[21] Miller Center. George H.W. Bush Presidency. Brent Robert Gates Oral History.

The new minister's philosophy was to protect Russia's national interests, which were not identical to, and sometimes directly opposed to, those of the United States. He was a pragmatist, ready to negotiate but not ready to concede, prepared to treat Russia as an ad hoc partner, not a formal ally.

American officials were well aware of Primakov's stance. In August 1993, at a dinner hosted by Yeltsin when CIA Director James Woolsey was visiting Moscow, Primakov openly voiced his suspicions about American policy in Ukraine, saying that the United States sought to drag Ukraine into its camp, which would "*allow it to encircle Russia and its former brotherly republics.*"[22] In December 1994, when Kozyrev flew to Brussels to sign a program of cooperation with NATO, Primakov deliberately planted doubts in Yeltsin's mind, leading him to believe that Clinton was deceiving the Russian President about NATO-expansion plans. When in May 1995, during negotiations in Moscow, Clinton, noting Yeltsin's after-dinner ease, persuaded him to agree that Kozyrev would sign the Partnership for Peace program on behalf of Russia two weeks later, Primakov and Lobov, secretary of the Russian Security Council, tried until the last moment to prevent this step.[23]

Of course, in Russia, where the President's prerogative was to formulate the main directions of foreign policy, the foreign minister cannot contradict them; however, Yevgeny Primakov did not advocate abrupt steps. He realized that major changes could result from many small, not always conspicuous, decisions. To make a "U-turn over the Atlantic," it was necessary to wait for the right moment. That moment would come on March 24, 1999, when by then the head of the Russian government, Yevgeny Primakov, flying on an official visit to the United States, turned his plane over the ocean and returned to Moscow to protest the start of the bombing of Yugoslavia. Clinton saw no reason to delay it until after the Russian Prime Minister's visit.

Capricious Partner

Yeltsin's political vulnerability had preoccupied White House since the first months of Clinton's term. Every time something happened in Russia, analysts sketched the worst-case scenarios, predicting a radical change in Russian policy both in terms of domestic reforms and foreign policy. In that regard, Clinton's stance differed little from his predecessors'.

[22] Strobe Talbott. The Russia Hand. Random House/New York, 2002, p. 80.

[23] p. 165.

In June 1992, on the eve of Yeltsin's arrival in Washington, James Baker wrote to Bush: "*While Yeltsin remains the preeminent Russian politician, his efforts to establish a functional, democratic political process have so far had only limited success. Conservative forces, led by Vice President Rutskoi and the military-industrial complex, are becoming more vocal and positioning themselves to offer an alternative to Yeltsin's democratic course.*"[24]

In May 1995, when Clinton planned to travel to Moscow, Lake submitted a memorandum outlining the main objectives of the visit. The document begins by stating that there was no consensus in the Russian leadership on relations with the United States and that Russia's future did not look clear-cut.

"Yeltsin has refused to abandon the central features of his American policy and has repeatedly reaffirmed the importance to Russia of its "partnership" with the United States. He continues to champion the logic of political and economic integration and to reject the counsel of those who would have Russia turn its back on the West in favor of a go-it-alone strategy. That said, Russia will remain a fractious "partner" for the United States as it continues to search for the right balance in the conduct of its foreign policy between integration and isolation, engagement, and withdrawal.

Three and a half years after the Soviet collapse, Russia's second great experiment with revolution in this century remains very much a work in progress. It is an open question whether the forces in Russia supporting democratic development and the transition to a market economy will triumph over more primitive, inward-looking elements, which would impose a more authoritarian political order, curtail civil liberties, and re-nationalize the economy."[25]

[24] GBPL&M. Your Meetings with Yeltsin. [no date] Memorandum for the President from James A. Baker, III.

[25] *CDL* #101272. Moscow Summit. Memorandum for the President from Anthony Lake. May 1995.

9

Did We Have Any Alternatives?

There's Always Someone Against

Although the end of the Cold War and the collapse of the Soviet Union created a fundamentally new situation in the world—without military and political confrontation between two superpowers, two ideological and economic systems—the American political class apparently could not fully accept this fact and regarded Russia with apprehension, seeing it as the Soviet Union's successor. Fears that the weakened "Russian bear" might revert to its old ways ran deep. While policy toward Central and Eastern Europe coalesced quickly, essentially echoing the Marshall Plan (full integration into European economic and political structures, accession to the European Union and NATO), the answer to the question of what to do with Russia remained elusive.

Of course, it cannot be said that this issue was not on the agenda: to a lesser extent for the Bush administration and to a greater extent for the Clinton administration, Russia was one of the most important foreign policy topics, but every time serious decisions that could provide substantial support for Russian reforms were put on the table, these proposals had opponents who routinely mustered arguments to block them.

In 1991, when it became obvious to everyone that the Soviet economic system was collapsing and that the world economy was on the threshold of consolidation into a single system, the White House discussed the issue of transforming the international financial organizations created in 1944 by the Bretton Woods conference—the International Monetary Fund and the World Bank. The then Treasury Secretary Nicholas Brady refused, and Scowcroft—who chose not to press him—later called this a missed opportunity: "*We*

S. Aleksashenko, *Post-Cold War Russia and the Missed Opportunity for Global Stability*,
https://doi.org/10.1007/978-3-032-01380-4_9

should have pushed, by '91, hard for a new - maybe not a new Bretton Woods conference, but to take a look at the IMF and the World Bank and see what restructuring was needed to bring them into a new economic environment. Very different from the Bretton Woods environment in which they were set up... I remember pressuring Nick Brady... He didn't want to do it and I just didn't push it."[1]

The same Scowcroft, almost to the end of Bush's administration, did not believe in the sincerity of the democratic motivations of Yeltsin, whom he had disliked since their first meeting,[2] and categorically opposed serious aid to Russia, explaining that the Russians would not listen to anyone and would steal everything: "*We had the same reservations about Yeltsin [as about Gorbachev] - and the feeling that money was not going to be used for any worthwhile purposes. The Russians did not take the advice either of our own technical experts or the IMF, or the World Bank. Therefore, we didn't think it was worthwhile.*"[3]

The Jackson-Vanik Amendment, introduced in 1974 into the US Trade Act, established a discriminatory trade regime against the Soviet Union and several Eastern European countries due to the prohibition of travel, primarily of Jews, from these countries. After Gorbachev came to power in Moscow and proclaimed perestroika, the situation began to change rapidly, and the restrictions on Jews leaving the USSR began to loosen. In 1986, 787 people received permission to leave the USSR for the United States; in 1987, their number increased to 3694 people; in 1988, it exceeded 20,000. In August 1989, the US National Security Council faced an unexpected problem: the consulate in the Soviet Union was unable to cope with the flow of emigrants; their number was estimated at 90,000 people in 1989 and 150,000 in 1990.[4] All the evidence showed that restrictions had ended, so the Jackson-Vanik amendment could have been repealed, but... Permits to leave the USSR had to be requested and their issuance was not automatic; therefore, Gorbachev was told, a law had to be passed to repeal the amendment. It was passed in May 1991, but the amendment continued to exist, and Yeltsin inherited this problem along with many others. Yeltsin raised the issue at every summit; Washington pledged to push it, yet neither the Bush nor Clinton administrations made a real effort: mild appeals to Congress met with resistance from Jewish organizations that

[1] Miller Center. George H.W. Bush Presidency. Brent Scowcroft Oral History Part II.

[2] Dimitri Simes. After the Collapse: Russia Seeks Its Place as a Great Power. Simon & Schuster, 1999. pp. 46–47.

[3] Miller Center. George H.W. Bush Presidency. Brent Scowcroft Oral History Part II.

[4] GBPL&M. Meeting on Soviet Emigration, PCC Paper for Deputies Committee Meeting on Soviet Emigration, August 29, 1989.

found several cases of travel permit denials in Russia, resistance from lobbyists who demanded that Russia lift its ban on imports of chicken meat from the United States, or the administration decided to put pressure on Russia because of its intensified relations with India, Iran, Iraq, or in response to its overly tough stance on Yugoslavia. In addition to the fact that the Jackson-Vanik amendment restrained trade and economic ties between the two countries (the US share in Russian exports did not exceed 4%, while Russia's share in US exports was about 1%), its retention carried significant symbolic weight: the opposition in Russia often reproached Yeltsin for constantly making concessions to America but failing to get his partners to repeal a clearly inadequate piece of legislation.

In July 1990, the NATO summit in London stated that the Warsaw Pact Organization had ceased to exist and announced that the alliance no longer viewed Moscow as an enemy and extended a hand of friendship to its former adversaries by deciding to create a unique cooperation program. This decision materialized in the fall of 1991 when Baker and German Foreign Minister Genscher proposed to institutionalize this program within the framework of the North Atlantic Cooperation Council (NACC), the creation of which took place at the NATO summit in Rome. The 16 NATO member states, the Soviet Union (after its collapse, all post-Soviet countries), Central and Eastern European countries, and the three Baltic states became members, and the NACC began its substantive work. A work plan was adopted that outlined a program of consultations and joint activities on security and related issues covering political, military, economic, scientific, and environmental topics. Specific topics for cooperation included defense planning, conceptual approaches to arms control, civil-military coordination of air traffic control, defense industry conversion, and the participation of all countries in NATO's Third Dimension scientific and environmental programs. Washington's shift toward NATO enlargement in January 1994 ended the NACC's substantive work; the newly created Partnership for Peace was to take over most of its functions. However, for both Central and Eastern European countries and the United States, NATO enlargement was an unquestionable priority, and the process was actively pursued. The Partnership did not receive strategic elements, and its development was instead a reaction to Russian pressure—for the rest of the former members of the Warsaw Pact Organization, it became little more than a holding area.

By promising Yeltsin in October 1994 to intensify work on a new European security architecture that would, among other things, integrate the CSCE and NATO, the Clinton team believed that it had received the Russian President's consent to move toward NATO enlargement. All brakes were then removed on the road to the Brussels meeting, where the policy of moving the alliance eastward was supposed to be announced. At the same time, the promise of integrating European security structures was put under the table. When in October 1994, US Ambassador to the CSCE John Kornblum and Deputy US Ambassador to Moscow Jim Collins sent joint proposals to Washington on how to expand the CSCE's functions that Clinton might put forward in Budapest,[5] National Security Council Director for Russia Nick Burns indicated his categorical rejection of these ideas and, in order to keep them from surfacing before the Brussels meeting, sent them for interagency coordination. Although the proposals were aimed at significantly enhancing the role of the CSCE (authority to prevent and resolve conflicts on the territory of the participating countries, mandatory consideration of all conflict situations before bringing them to the UN for discussion, creation of a working body at the level of deputy ministers that could make decisions between summits), they did not contain a direct reference to NATO and did not affect relations between the two bodies.[6]

Yeltsin's demarche in Budapest in December 1994 forced the United States to go back on its promise to make the CSCE a key element of the European security system, but when the Russian President agreed that the first wave of NATO expansion would take place in the middle of his second term, the incentive to knit the CSCE with NATO evaporated. The only Kornblum/Collins idea that was being realized was turning the CSCE into the OSCE.

The Plan Was on the Table

On March 2, 1993, Talbott, selected by Clinton to be the top man in Russia but not yet confirmed in his position, received a memorandum from US Ambassador to the European Union James Dobbins, with whom he had met a few days earlier. During the meeting, the ambassador shared his views on the principles on which US policy toward supporting Russia could be based, and Talbott asked him to put them on paper. The logic of Dobbins' letter grew out of the logic of the Marshall Plan: linking economics and security, the need to

[5] Although the United States supported the idea of biennial meetings at the CSCE Paris Summit in 1990, Clinton's inner circle did everything possible to prevent the President from traveling to Budapest. Three visits to Europe were placed on his 1994 calendar, and the Summit of the Americas in Miami was scheduled to be held immediately adjacent to the Budapest meeting, complicating overall logistics. Beginning in March 1994, the President was asked several times to decide whether to attend the CSCE summit, but he procrastinated until the last moment: the decision to go was made in early November after Clinton received letters from Yeltsin and Helmut Kohl insisting that he come to Budapest.

[6] WCPL&M. Note to Sandy Vershbow, Dan Fried, John Beyrle from Nick Burns. October 20, 1994.

consider the former Soviet Union and Central and Eastern European countries as a single entity, and combining the efforts of the United States and the European Community within a single framework:

So far, neither the United States nor Europe has put forward any concept of how a democratizing Russia should fit within structures for Western cooperation. In the absence of such a concept, Western economic assistance to Russia, whatever success it may have in promoting reform, is not contributing to a transformation of political relationships between Russia and its European neighbors of the sort of the Marshall Plan set in train between Germany and its former adversaries 40 years ago.

Western policies since the overthrow of Communism, and the disappearance of the Soviet Union, have, in fact, tended in the opposite direction. The EC's focus on Eastern Europe, and the American emphasis on bilateralism in its relations with Russia have the effect, however unintentional, of isolating Russia from broader developments in Europe, and in Western collaborative institutions.

The United States has a natural inclination to develop a strategic partnership with Russia primarily along familiar bilateral lines. Our European allies, for their part, have an even more irresistible impulse to define Europe in a way which excludes Russia. The WEU decision to create a consultative forum on security issues which includes all of Eastern Europe and the Baltic States, but excludes Russia, is only the most graphic and, from a Russian standpoint, the most provocative manifestation of this tendency.

As a result of these US and European tendencies, we are drifting toward an implicit division of labor in which the United States seeks to coopt Russia through bilateral defense collaboration, while Western Europe gradually enlarges its defense perimeter to the Russian border. An arrangement whereby Western Europe provides security to Russia's neighbors while the United States establishes a strategic partnership with Russia is a formula for disaster. The United States cannot alone offer a democratizing Russia a place in the world responsive to its legitimate desires to be considered modern, Western, and European. Europe alone cannot defend Russia's neighbors. Unless these two objectives, each laudable, are integrated in a broader set of policies, Europe will in the end be burdened with defense commitments it cannot fulfill, and America will be burdened with Russian expectations which it cannot meet.

The idea of a Euro-Atlantic Community provides a conceptual framework for Russian integration into broader Western structures. The North Atlantic Cooperation Council provides an institutional basis for multilateral defense cooperation. The central role of NATO should remain the containment of Russia. This function can now be fulfilled, however not through confrontation, but through cooperation. The inclusion of Russia, and other NACC partners, in NATO managed peacekeeping operations, and the use of the NACC for meaningful consultations on Yugoslavia would be useful first step toward reorienting NATO toward this new or redefined role. Over time, NATO'S role with respect to a democratizing Russia could become analogous to NATO's role vis-a-vis Germany in the 1950's.

In the economic area we also need to use aid and trade in ways which bring Russia into a broader community.

Western assistance to all of the emerging democracies of Europe is presently provided almost exclusively on a bilateral basis. We, the EC, and the various IFI's deal with each recipient separately. We give these countries little incentive to cooperate among themselves. Western coordination of aid to Eastern Europe on the one hand, and to the CIS on the other, takes place in entirely different forums, under different chairmanship, in different cities, with different US representatives, further reinforcing dividing lines among the new democracies.

This is not how America reconstructed Western Europe 40 years ago. After World War II, the United States chose to deal with the mutually antagonistic countries of Europe multilaterally, not bilaterally. We channeled US aid regionally. We invited these countries into the collective decision making process on aid and trade. We promoted new political and economic arrangements among these states which overcame ancient hostilities at least as keen as those between Russia and its neighbors, arrangements which ultimately led to the integration of Western Europe in the European Community, and the integration of Germany in NATO.

Today, we should again be using our assistance not just to promote economic development, but to transform political relationships among all the countries of Eastern Europe and the former Soviet Union. We should be moving as rapidly as possible to multilateral aid and trade flows. We should be encouraging the development of regional arrangements among these states in transition, looking to stimulate the modern equivalents of the Coal and Steel Community, the European Payments Union, the Common Market, EURATOM, and the EEC.

Of course, the Poles don't want to be lumped together with the Russians, or the Czechs with the Slovaks. Forty years ago, the French did not want to be lumped together with the Germans. But the United States made the decision then that a stable Western Europe could not be created without the integration of a prosperous democratic Germany. The position of Russia today is not entirely analogous to that of Germany in 1945. Russia is defeated, but it is neither divided nor occupied. Russia is even more indigestible than Germany. It is too big, and too exotic to ever become a member of the European Community. This is why we need to promote the concept of a still larger community, a community in which the presence of the United States counterbalances that of Russia.

If we are to promote the integration, rather than the disintegration of the formerly Communist half of Europe, we should begin by breaking down the distinction between the separate mechanisms for coordination of Western assistance to Eastern Europe on the one hand, and the CIS on the other.

The United States, Western Europe and Japan should start to condition elements of our aid upon cooperation among the recipient countries regarding its use. Projects with regional impact should receive preferential consideration.

The United States should consider establishing a new Agency, parallel with AID. This new agency, perhaps with a 10 year mandate and 'sunset clause' should concentrate exclusively upon the task of converting the developed industrial societies of Eastern Europe and the former Soviet Union into free market democracies - a very different task from the traditional Third World mission of AID.

Finally, the United States should support Helmut Kohl's proposal, now almost a year old, to create a new international institution, similar to that which managed the Marshall Plan, to coordinate Western aid, and Eastern transformation. Donors and recipients should belong to such an organization.[7]

Two days later, Talbott wrote back, thanking Dobbins for many good ideas: "*I totally agree with your basic point that we've got to have a more inclusive, unifying, embracing approach, both operationally and strategically.*" However, he immediately refuted the fundamental principle that the countries of the entire socialist bloc should be treated as one, without even bothering to make an argument: "*I suspect you probably understand the political reasons for it.*"[8]

In the summer of 1993, James Dobbins' tenure would end, and he would return to Washington. In March 1994, Talbott, by then the second-in-command at the State Department, would recommend to Christopher that Dobbins be assigned to peacekeeping operations.[9]

In politics, inaction itself is a decision, and accumulated non-decisions eventually formed a strategy of refusal to systematically support the former enemy and refusal to use a tool that had had a positive result half a century earlier. The Marshall Plan for Russia was abandoned.

It's Just Impossible Not to Help

Looking at how the views of US politicians and officials regarding aid to Russia have been shaped, one might get the impression that the US political system was too gridlocked to make significant aid decisions for other countries. The isolationist sentiments that never disappeared only intensified after the end of the Cold War. The US economy went through a recession in 1990–1992 and slowly emerged in the following three years, which strained the budget and deprived the administration of the freedom to maneuver with

[7] US DoS. Case F-2017-13804. Doc No C06689987. Memorandum dated March 2, 1993. From James F. Dobbins to Strobe Talbott.

[8] US DoS. Case F-2017-13804. Doc No C06689984. Memorandum from Strobe Talbott to James F. Dobbins. March 4, 1993.

[9] US DoS. Case F-2017-13804. Doc No C06835955. Letter to Christopher. March 31, 1994.

spending. The traditional confrontation between the two political parties and the need to obtain congressional approval for any aid programs to other countries played a prominent role during the presidency of Bush when, in 1991–1992, the Democrats firmly controlled both houses of Congress, and after the defeat of the Democrats in the midterm elections of 1994, when control of both houses went to the Republicans.

At any moment, Congress could decide to cut spending, including those aimed at helping Russia, and the promised support was melting away. In December 1993, during one of the first meetings of the Gore-Chernomyrdin Commission, the US pledged to provide $125 million to Gazprom to modernize its gas pipelines, which would increase the company's export capacity and reduce environmental damage. When Congress considered the budget, this amount was reduced to $90 million. In the summer of 1995, Congress cut $16 billion in budget expenditures, including $250 million cut from Russia-aid programs. Faced with a choice between Gazprom aid and market-institution programs that mainly benefited US consultants, the White House was guided by the maxim "*self comes first.*" The program for Gazprom was reduced to $70 million, i.e., by 45% of the original amount.[10]

Undoubtedly, the influence of the above factors was very significant. However, not everything is so clear-cut…

Brady Bonds

In the late 1980s, most Latin American countries were on the verge of default. Lack of control over budget deficits and slow economic growth led to increased government borrowing. The main lenders were banks, which risked collapse if debtor nations defaulted. Extraordinary measures were therefore needed to ease budget burdens while averting a wave of bank failures.

In March 1989, US Treasury Secretary Nicholas Brady announced a plan to reduce the debts of heavily indebted developing countries. The plan offered debt relief by writing off part of the debt, reducing coupon payments, and exchanging old debt for new government bonds denominated in foreign currency with low rates and long maturities. In practice, US and Japanese guarantees let debtor states purchase matched-maturity zero-coupon US Treasuries, which were lodged in a collateral account at the Federal Reserve. Coupon payments were guaranteed by the proceeds from the countries' purchases of quality securities from the IMF loans received.

[10] CDL #101836. Cutting Russian Assistance Strategically. Memorandum for Anthony Lake from Sheila Heslin and Carlos Pascual. August 14, 1995.

Although participating banks took losses on the write-downs, they could free part of their loan-loss reserves and replace non-performing assets with Brady bonds, which investors now regarded as tradable assets.

A total of 17 countries participated in the Brady Bonds program,[11] restructuring over $150 billion in debt. Except for Ecuador, which defaulted once on a coupon payment, all bonds were serviced and repaid on or before maturity.

Poland

The external debt crisis in Poland happened 10 years earlier than in the Soviet Union—the country signed its first debt restructuring agreement with the Paris Club as early as 1981, followed by three agreements with creditor banks in 1981–1984.[12] By the beginning of 1990, the country's foreign debt was $48 billion, 77% of GDP at the exchange rate adopted at the beginning of the stabilization program. Polish politicians openly sought partial debt forgiveness, and every visiting cabinet minister pressed the case in creditor capitals. Poland soon won US backing; Washington pressed the other Paris-Club creditors, and by March 1991 Poland obtained the relief it sought.

The Paris-Club deal wrote off 50% of Poland's official debt which represented nearly 70% of its total external liabilities. A few days later, the creditor banks made a similar move. David Mulford, under-secretary for international finance, acknowledged the decision's political motive: "*We see this as a historic event similar to the reduction in debt in Germany in 1953, which we hope will put Poland on the path of sustained economic recovery and will make it one of the leading economies of Eastern Europe, provided they stick to their reform program.*"[13]

At the beginning of the negotiations, Poland asked for 80% debt forgiveness, the United States agreed to 60% debt forgiveness, and France did not agree to more than 40%, citing that even the poorest African countries usually received a third of their debt forgiveness. Germany would concede only token relief, while Japan rejected any write-off and instead offered low-interest loans. After persistent overnight negotiations, the United States got the other

[11] Sometimes, statistics on the Brady Bonds program includes Russia, which, in the summer of 1998, agreed with investors to replace part of its ruble bonds with foreign currency bonds with extended maturities. While outwardly similar, the Russian restructuring was very different from the classical one: it did not require IMF credit support or guarantees from other countries. It did not involve the purchase of US government bonds to secure the repayment of the securities issued.

[12] Poland: The Persistent Debt Dilemma. An Intelligence Assessment. CIA. EUR84-10188, September 1984. https://www.cia.gov/readingroom/docs/CIA-RDP.85S00316R000200150004-0.pdf.

[13] "Poland Is Granted Large Cut in Debt." The New York Times. March 16, 1991.

creditors to accept half of the debt forgiveness, with interest payments reduced by 80% in the first three years to $660 million instead of $3.3 billion.

Russia assumed responsibility for all the Soviet Union's debts, which amounted to about $110 billion—equal to roughly 150% of GDP in 1992 and 50% in 1993, according to IMF estimates. The creditor countries refused to discuss the cancellation of Soviet debts, limiting themselves to granting annual deferrals. Russia's annual foreign debt service payments in 1992–1994 amounted to about $5 billion per year.

According to IMF estimates, Russia's GDP exceeded Poland's in 1993–1994 by a factor of 2.5 to 3.

Mexico

In February 1990, Mexico was the first country to restructure its public debt using Brady Bonds, then the largest issue at $54 billion. Although the fiscal position improved, growth remained sluggish as markets adjusted. Meanwhile, Mexico completed negotiations with the United States and Canada to create the North American Free Trade Agreement (NAFTA), which became operational on January 1, 1994.

1994 was President Carlos Salinas de Gortari's final year in office; he, eager to helm the nascent WTO, had to avert an economic crisis. Traditionally, an outgoing president launched a broad, socially oriented spending program, financed by issuing short-term peso-denominated bonds. The US investors were eager to buy these bonds because the Bank of Mexico kept the peso exchange rate within a narrow band, guaranteeing high foreign exchange investment returns. To keep the peso rate, the Central Bank regularly bought dollars, which it immediately sold to importers—the abolition of most customs tariffs led to a sharp increase in consumer imports. The Central Bank issued short-term dollar bonds to disguise falling reserves.

High inflation drove a real appreciation of the peso, stoking devaluation fears—even as Salinas and the Bank of Mexico repeatedly vowed it would not happen. To support the President's spending program, the Bank of Mexico intensively bought government bonds on the secondary market, which increased the money overhang in the economy.

As the elections approached, some investors decided to lock in profits by selling government bonds or refusing to buy new ones after the redemption of previous issues. The received pesos were converted into dollars, and the foreign exchange reserves of the Bank of Mexico were rapidly melting. Still, President Salinas refused to devalue and forbade the Central Bank to raise the interest rate. On December 1, 1994, Ernesto Zedillo became the country's President, whose economic team quickly realized the severity of the problems. On December 20, the Bank of Mexico announced a 15% devaluation of the peso while maintaining its currency corridor. This provoked panic and capital flight—investors sold peso-denominated assets and refused to buy the Bank of Mexico's foreign currency bonds. Mexico was on the verge of default, and on December 22, the Central Bank announced a new 15% devaluation. Domestic prices jumped 24% in December.

As usual, turmoil spilled over: Chile, Brazil, and several Asian economies were soon hit by capital flight.

In early January 1995, Clinton held a meeting[14] with Federal Reserve Chairman Alan Greenspan, Treasury Secretary Robert Rubin, whom the Senate has just confirmed,[15] and his deputy, Larry Summers. The latter put the needed aid at $25 billion and added: "*Mr President, if you send that money to Mexico and it doesn't come back before 1996, you won't be coming back after 1996.* The President asked *Do you think there's a substantial risk that if we don't do this there will be really grave consequences, if Mexico fails, that will have serious consequences for the United States and for other countries?*" and, receiving an affirmative answer, asked a second question, "*Do you think there is a reasonable chance that if we act we can prevent that?*" After telling the meeting participants that the odds were very good, the President called congressional leaders, urging them to support a program to help the neighboring country.

Remembering their recent electoral victory, Republicans balked, offering assorted objections: that they should not support a country that supports the Castro regime in Cuba or that they should seize the moment and force the Mexicans to change a union law that gives them too much power. Help came from an unexpected quarter when Senator Bob Bennett of Utah remarked: "*Look, Congress isn't going to get there. You all have the authority through something called the President's Exchange Stabilization Fund.*" The Fund was created

[14] Larry Summers on his Work in the Clinton and Obama Administrations. Conversations with Bill Kristol. November 23, 2015. https://conversationswithbillkristol.org/transcript/larry-summers-transcript.

[15] In November 1994 midterm elections, the Democratic Party was soundly defeated, with Republicans gaining control of both houses of Congress for the first time since 1952. Unsurprisingly, any appointments proposed by the President thereafter were met with great difficulty.

in 1934 under the Gold Reserve Act, when Treasury assumed the Fed's gold stock. The President was given the power to determine the price of gold under the gold standard, which Roosevelt took advantage of on the second day by announcing a 40% reduction in the dollar's value in gold. The Fund aimed to prevent too strong fluctuations of the dollar exchange rate, first in gold and, after abandoning the gold standard, in other currencies.

The law contained no explicit authority to lend abroad, but its wording gave the Secretary of the Treasury, with the President's approval, quite broad authority to use the Fund's resources if the loan was large. After fierce Republican outcry, the President's team compromised by agreeing to report to Congress semi-annually on the use of the Fund.

Clinton accepted using $20 billion from the Stabilization Fund to provide loans and guarantees to Mexico; in addition, Summers assembled a pool of $32 billion in aid that included the IMF, the Bank for International Settlements, and several countries. At the IMF, the decision to lend to Mexico was made on the fly, the board members had little time to review the materials provided, and the United States provided no details to the rest of the G7.

Mexico suffered severely: sharp contraction, surging inflation, a banking crisis, and a steep fall in living standards. Yet the chief goal was met—the Mexican crisis never spilled into the United States, and the US Treasury earned more than half a billion dollars on a loan to Mexico, which was repaid on time.

> The IMF estimates that in 1994–95 Russia's GDP was four times Mexico's at market rate and nine-times at PPP (purchasing power parity). The maximum IMF loan received by Russia in 1992–1996 was $6.75 billion.

Asian Crisis

In the final two decades of the twentieth century, the world financial system was reshaped by two powerful forces. On the one hand, the world economy entered a period of globalization when many developing countries became attractive to large international companies seeking to reduce their costs. Surging FDI into Latin America and Southeast Asia accelerated growth, bolstered by expanding domestic firms. Accelerating growth led to rising fiscal and personal incomes, which required even greater investment growth. Low household incomes left scant savings, rendering domestic banks fragile. To finance investment, countries needed to attract capital from developed markets, which could only be done through higher interest rates. Governments, banks, and companies became active borrowers, financial systems rapidly became more complex, and banking supervisors did not have time to transform.

On the other hand, after the collapse of the Bretton Woods system, based on the dollar's peg to gold and stable exchange rates of other currencies against the dollar, the world monetary system has been slowly moving toward floating exchange rates. Developed countries repeatedly tried to agree on the principles of maintaining mutual exchange rates and on the limited and coordinated use of devaluations and currency interventions, but these attempts were unsuccessful. The objective inconsistency of economic cycles, different economic dynamics, and the impossibility of pursuing a unified monetary and fiscal policy led to differences in inflation rates, differences in interest rates, and, as a result, significant capital flows, which intensified as currency restrictions were abandoned.

The creation of the European Exchange Rate System for the countries of the European Community in 1979 and the G7 Agreements of 1985 and 1987 (Plaza Accord and Louvre Accord) were the last attempts of the developed countries to fix the principles of exchange rate policy. However, as early as late 1992, the UK announced a move to a floating exchange rate for the pound after financial market pressure had devalued it by 15% against the Deutsche Mark and 25% against the US dollar in three months. Following this, the United States, Japan, Canada, and Switzerland switched to floating rates. At the same time, most members of the European Community decided to go the other way and began the transition to a single European currency.

What is right for Jupiter is not right for the bull. While developed countries moved toward floating exchange rates, most developing economies pursued adjustable, fixed, or managed exchange rate policies. Such policies were not objectionable to the IMF because they allowed the use of exchange rate policies to provide an anti-inflationary anchor during stabilization programs. In addition, tight fiscal and monetary policies were considered to create sufficient preconditions to prevent devaluation. Most Southeast Asian countries, which became attractive for foreign capital, held the same view, especially since the stability and predictability of exchange rate dynamics was an additional lure for foreign investors, allowing them to receive guaranteed high returns.

Life is always more complicated than a textbook. The foreign-capital wave in Southeast Asia spurred investment, but growth lagged. In addition to investment, the capital inflow also stimulated private consumption growth—banks were actively lending to the population. At the same time, neither banks nor financial regulators paid attention to the growing currency risk:

banks' money sources were loans in foreign currency, and the overwhelming part of the loans provided were denominated in national currencies. In such a situation, devaluation leads to instant losses for banks, but everyone was sure that there would be no devaluation because governments and Central Banks constantly spoke about their intentions to keep control over the exchange rate of the national currency.

Those with capital at stake learn—and act—more quickly. Investors who lent to the fast-growing economies of developing countries learned quickly. They closely monitored statistics and critically assessed any negative trends, ready to start recovering their investments at any moment. In May 1997, Czech Prime Minister Václav Klaus introduced a package of laws to tighten financial policy in parliament to combat rising inflation and trade deficits. By that time, 12 banks had gone bankrupt due to the poor quality of banking supervision in the country, and there were numerous cases of fraud on the stock market, which increased public discontent and made investors doubt the success of market reforms. Capital began to flee the country: investors sold assets and converted the proceeds into hard currencies.

Credit should be given to the Czech government, who reacted quickly and decisively: the Central Bank sharply limited lending and raised its interest rate while devaluing the koruna by 8% and promising to continue to keep its exchange rate within a wide band. The Bundesbank's outstretched hand helped to extinguish the fire in the Czech Republic quickly. Still, financial players, wary of what had happened, looked for the following weak link: Thailand, whose central bank had been selling foreign exchange reserves to support the baht for more than half a year.

In early July, when more than a quarter of foreign exchange reserves were lost, the Thai government went for devaluation, but the 20% fall of the baht only spurred capital flight, as happened in Mexico in December 1994. The private debt of companies and individuals, denominated in dollars, by that time, exceeded 20% of GDP, and mass bankruptcies of borrowers began, followed by the collapse of banks, which further encouraged devaluation. In mid-August, when the national currency lost half of its value, the IMF decided to provide a loan of $4.5 billion, which was supported by loans from Japan and six other Asian countries amounting to about $13 billion. However, Thai government could get no more than $3 billion immediately and the rest of the money only after many conditions were met. The baht continued to fall, and the crisis gradually spread to neighboring countries.

The Philippines, Malaysia, Indonesia, Korea, Taiwan, and Hong Kong were hit. Some economies, such as Hong Kong and Taiwan, weathered the turmoil confidently. Others, like the Philippines and Malaysia, coped on their own by imposing severe restrictions on capital flows and bank lending. Some needed serious financial support: Indonesia's bailout package amounted to $23 billion, while Korea's bailout required almost $60 billion.

In total, Thailand, Indonesia, and Korea received an aid package of $100 billion, of which just over a third was provided by the IMF and about half by other countries. Japan's contribution was just under $30 billion, and the US lent $3 billion to Indonesia and $5 billion to Korea.

According to IMF estimates, in 1997, the combined GDP of Thailand, Indonesia, and Korea, which received support to overcome the crisis, was about twice that of Russia using current exchange rates and one and a half times that of Russia using purchasing power parity.

Jordan

When Iraq invaded Kuwait in 1990, Jordan, which had good relations with the United States, suddenly decided to support Saddam Hussein, which was an unpleasant surprise for Western countries. Moreover, after the liberation of Kuwait, Jordan maintained warm relations with Iraq, continuing to trade with the neighboring country despite UN sanctions. However, hopes of receiving financial assistance from Iraq to solve economic problems, primarily the problem of foreign debt, did not materialize, and King Hussein decided to return to the US camp.

In June 1994, King Hussein declared Jordan's willingness to make peace with Israel even if Syria refused to join him. Clinton set the price for Amman's shift, pledging to seek congressional approval to cancel Jordan's US debt, $700 million.[16] In October of that year, Jordan and Israel reached a peace agreement, and within three years of that, the debt was canceled.[17] In addition, the United States actively supported Jordan's request for an IMF loan, and for nine years, the country received new loans from the Fund every year, which doubled the cost of servicing and repaying earlier loans. The United States also decided to allow duty-free access to the US market of goods produced in Jordan's special industrial zones, provided Israel's share in its component value was at least 8%.

In February 1999, King Hussein died, having changed his mind two weeks before about the heir, appointing his son Abdullah. To support the new monarch's position, Clinton asked Congress for additional aid to Jordan in the

[16] "Clinton Promises to Seek Forgiveness of Jordan Debt". The Washington Post. 1994. June 23.

[17] "US "forgives" last of Jordan's debts". United Press International. 1997. September 25.

amount of $300 million. By 2003, Jordan had moved to third place on the list of US financial aid recipients, totaling $950 million (compared to $7 million in 1996).

In the annual Special 301 Review, the US Trade Representative acknowledged multiple IP-rights concerns, yet dropped Jordan from its watch-list, paving the way for Jordan to finalize WTO accession negotiations in early 2000.[18] Three months afterward, the United States signed a duty-free trade agreement with Jordan. Jordanian exports to America, only $9 million in 1998, exceeded $1 billion in 2004.[19]

According to IMF estimates, Russia's GDP exceeded Jordan's in 1997–2000 by 40–45 times compared to the current exchange rate of the national currency and purchasing power parity.

[18] Malkawi, Bashar H. Jordan's Accession to the WTO: Retrospective and Prospective. The Estey Center Journal of International Law and Trade Policy. 2010. vol. 11. No 1. pp. 12–45.

[19] William J. Burns. The Back Channel: A Memoir of American Diplomacy and the Case for Its Renewal. Random House, 2019. pp. 129–130.

10

Remember History

Prepare Your Sleds in Summer

If we assess Russia's economic and political transformation after 1990 as of 2000 or 2005, it cannot be judged either a great success or a failure. Russia has built a solid foundation for a market economy, ranking in the top half of roughly 30 other transition countries in Southern, Central, and Eastern Europe and the former USSR. That foundation's strength was proved after Russia's invasion of Ukraine, when the economy withstood numerous sanctions, rapidly finding work-arounds. At the same time, Russia could not boast comparable progress in political and democratic institution-building.

Could the transformation in Russia have been more successful? Probably, yes. The Soviet economy lagged too far behind in terms of the quality of its output, which made it uncompetitive in the new conditions; the Russian elite spent too long negotiating their path—both internally and with former Soviet neighbors; attempts to implement a stabilization program were too inconsistent; the construction of such vital institutions as an independent court, federal relations, and local self-government was too slow.

These factors suffice to explain why Russia lagged the front-runners of post-communist reform. But fast-forward to 2005–2025 and Russia faces the Georgian war in 2008, the annexation of Crimea and the outbreak of military conflict in eastern Ukraine in 2014, and a full-scale invasion of Ukraine in February 2022. During these 20 years, the quality of Russian political institutions slowly, and later rapidly, deteriorated, and Russia turned into a country with an authoritarian regime. From a country whose leader was the first to call the US President after the 9/11 attacks, Russia has turned into a country that

S. Aleksashenko, *Post-Cold War Russia and the Missed Opportunity for Global Stability*,
https://doi.org/10.1007/978-3-032-01380-4_10

for three and a half years has waged a brutal war against a neighbor, threatened critics with nuclear weapons, flouted treaties and UN sanctions, and is now viewed as the principal threat to global peace.

The rapid severing of Russia-West ties showed just how tenuous they had been. Thirty years after the collapse of the Soviet Union, Europe is once again the site of a war that has every chance of escalating into a world war. By the time of Russia's invasion of Ukraine, the level of mutual trust had sunk so low that the very mechanisms that might have averted war were paralyzed. Russia did not become part of the Western world; on the contrary, it was once again its adversary. An adversary with no coherent ideology—uninterested in ideological struggle yet ready for hybrid warfare, separated from open conflict by only a thin partition. In this regard, we can confidently assert that the Russian transformation has failed.

It takes two to tango. The saying reminds us that success—and failure requires both partners.

It would be a clear mistake to attribute the failure of Russian transformation solely to internal reasons. It was evident that Russia undertook an extraordinarily complex transformation with only minimal Western economic or political support, mainly debt-service deferrals and modest IFI loans—small relative to Russia's scale and needs. Western markets stayed mostly closed: the United States recognized Russia as a market economy only in 2002, and WTO talks dragged on another decade. Global corporations came to Russia, but this did not lead to the integration of Russian companies into global economic chains. Many Western companies saw Russia as a territory with substantial natural resources, and Western leaders actively supported the desire to participate in their extraction. Other companies eyed Russia's 150 million consumers and set up local plants to supply food and everyday goods. In neither case did the Russian economy become more competitive.

Russia's entry into Western political clubs stalled almost immediately. Although already in 1995, the Russian President was invited as a full participant in the political part of the G7 meeting, in the same year, the NATO enlargement strategy began to be implemented, which restored the dividing line between "us" and "them" in Europe. Meanwhile, NATO's expansion goals were left vague, and the promised integration with European structures never materialized. It was no secret to anyone in Washington that "*All major players in Russia, all across the political spectrum, are either deeply opposed to, or at least deeply worried about, NATO expansion*,"[1] but this did not make them slow down and try to find less confrontational solutions.

Yet the tango—success or failure—always takes two. Yes, one can find enough arguments in favor of the fact that Russia itself did not know what it wanted its relations with Western countries to be. Russia's aspirations were excessive according to Clinton and Gore—"*The Russians have a compulsion to be part of every club… They want to join the Paris club, and NATO, and have a special relation with the US*."[2] It was hard to argue with Al Gore, who saw "*the threat to freedom and democracy from a growing security apparatus*" when he visited Moscow in December 1994. Russian officials could be accused of having wanted to torpedo the process of rapprochement between the two countries, which showed in refusals to meet or in scrapping agreements that had taken weeks to craft.

However, none of this makes much practical sense. The past cannot be brought back, and history knows no subjunctive mood. However the war in Ukraine ends, one plain result will be openly hostile relations between Russia and the West—unlikely to improve while Vladimir Putin remains in power. It is not that talks are impossible; if he retains power, any deal with Russia is a deal with Putin. The low chances of a new détente are because the Russian leader's credibility in the West is nil—he has repeatedly broken agreements, misled interlocutors, and supplied fabricated "facts."

But as the Russian proverb goes "prepare the sled in summer and the cart in winter." The collapse of the Soviet Union in December 1991 came as a surprise to most of the world's politicians, as both opponents in the struggle for power in Moscow, Gorbachev and Yeltsin, demonstrated their willingness for dialog, to find a compromise on the future structure and powers of the Union, and broadcast to the outside world their conviction that in one form or another, the Soviet Union would survive. One could guess what the renewed state might look like but not predict when it would vanish. This was the basis for all decisions about the Soviet Union, whether it was the position on foreign debt negotiations or humanitarian aid.

Russia's situation today is fundamentally different: everyone recognizes that Putin will leave one day, yet no one knows how or when. This means preparations must start now—it may come at the least expected moment. The parallel recalls 1943 in World War II: Allied victory seemed inevitable, yet its timing

[1] US DoS. Case F-2017-13,804. Doc No C06698878. Note to the Secretary from Strobe Talbott. April 13, 1995.

[2] CDL #100490. Memorandum of Conversation. Working Lunch with Prime Minister John Major of the United Kingdom. April 4, 1995.

and shape remained unclear. At that moment, the anti-Hitler coalition allies discussed Germany's future for the first time.

Of course, no one can guarantee that Putin's successors will swiftly admit his errors and pivot Russia's foreign policy toward the West. Most likely, a period of high turbulence and uncertainty awaits Russia, which may last several months or even years.

Putin's system leaves little space for strong parties or independent politicians to claim power once he is gone. Under the constitution the sitting prime minister succeeds first, yet that may be a long-standing insider with elite ties—or a newcomer elevated only weeks before.[3] The main actors and drivers of the political process will be the Russian elites, who must redefine their interests and goals, identify allies, and build new alliances.

Inevitably, some elites will argue for renewing ties with the West and restoring Russia's pro-European orientation. But attempts to establish a dialog with the West will be met with its unwillingness to perceive Russia as an equal partner and its desire to punish Russia for its aggressive war. After the end of World War I, this position led to the Versailles Peace Treaty; after the end of World War II, the Morgenthau Plan appeared. Suppose the West, after Putin's departure from the political scene, takes a similar position and puts forward a set of tough preliminary demands to Russia. In that case, it will undermine the position of the pro-Western part of the Russian elites and sharply reduce the chances of a turnaround in Russian foreign policy. The task of Western politicians today is to formulate a "roadmap" for Russia's transformation, which will contain a set of political and financial requirements that Russia will have to fulfill step by step. But at the same time, the roadmap should contain the West's counter obligations to gradually lift sanctions on Russia and return it to international institutions. The existence of such a roadmap will undoubtedly strengthen the arguments of the pro-European part of the Russian elites and allow them to exert a stronger influence on the trajectory of the transition period.

[3] Three of the five prime ministers who held this position under Vladimir Putin made such leaps: Mikhail Fradkov was Russia's ambassador to the European Union, Viktor Zubkov was head of Rosfinmonitoring, and Mikhail Mishustin was head of the tax service.

The Lesson of History Is That It Teaches Nothing

History does not repeat itself. The transformation of Russia after Putin's departure will differ in many aspects from the events of the first half of the 1990s.

Russia now has a market economy that is hardly efficient—growth averaged just 1.2% in 2013–24 versus the world's 2.8%—yet remains resilient thanks to natural-resource exports. Many international companies have experience operating in Russia, and although many left the country after the start of the Russian aggression, the understanding of how to work in Russia and how much you can earn in Russia still endures in corporate memory. Today, none of the companies that left are ready to discuss the conditions for returning to Russia: the main deterrent is remarkably high political risks and sometimes a direct ban in the form of sanctions restrictions. Yet once political risk abates, Western companies will almost certainly eye the Russian market again.

Some of them will exercise options to buy back their assets, which they were forced to sell after the beginning of the Russian aggression; some of them will decide to sue the Russian officials in international courts, expecting compensation for losses incurred; some of them will choose to forget about the assets lost in Russia, but will not be able to refuse attractive contracts for the supply of goods to Russia, as, for example, Siemens, whose Russian factories the Bolsheviks nationalized in 1918, did in 1920.

Russia will not have to face a severe economic downturn comparable in scale to the first half of the 1990s. Therefore, we should not expect rising unemployment and a sharp weakening of the budget due to the loss of tax revenues.

Since the 1998 financial crisis, the Russian officials have pursued an exceptionally restrained fiscal policy, tightly controlling the size of the budget deficit and public debt, which amounts to less than 20% of GDP and whose maturity is highly stretched over time. Thus, the topic of providing Russia with some form of financial assistance, which was key in the 1990s, will not be on the agenda.

It is hard to imagine a situation in which Russia would need humanitarian aid: Russian agriculture has been growing steadily since 1999, and although a quarter of the country's food is imported, production of most basic foodstuffs (except milk and beef) exceeds domestic consumption, making Russia one of the largest food exporters in the world. Nor is massive technical aid likely: a new generation of bureaucrats already understands market principles and modern regulatory tools. The roadmap's main task and the West's goal should be integrating Russia as closely as possible into its political and economic structures. That is precisely what the West failed to achieve in the early 1990s.

History does not repeat itself, but those who have not learned its lessons pay a high price. The successful integration of Germany and Japan into the Western world after World War II and the failure of a similar attempt against Russia after the end of the Cold War allow us to analyze and highlight the key elements of policy in the late 1940s and early 1950s that ensured success, to see how different the approach was in the 1990s when similar problems arose.

Lesson 1: Stick or Carrot?

It is well known that people are motivated to make decisions and to act based on positive or negative incentives. Politicians are also human beings and are, therefore, no exception, but they often follow the maxim "avoid rocking the boat." Big decisions require potent threats.

After the end of World War II in Europe, the United States, Britain, and France were given control of West Germany and the responsibility of returning it to normalcy. To begin with, Germans needed to not starve to death, to have access to potable water, to not freeze from the cold, and to receive limited medical care. The war-torn German economy could not operate at full capacity and provide the budget with sufficient financial resources. The situation in Britain and France was not much better, and the entire burden of finding the necessary resources to keep people alive in Western Europe fell on the United States. In 1945–1947, before the Marshall Plan, the United States spent more than $13 billion, but the situation did not change fundamentally; the economy was still in a state of ruin, and it did not want to grow.

Many American politicians saw the war's end as an opportunity to return to their pre-war isolationist life, leaving Europe to solve its problems. Seeing vast sums of money being spent without making a positive difference, the American voter began to turn away from the Democratic Party, to which President Truman belonged. In the November 1946 midterm elections, the Democrats were soundly defeated, and the Republicans gained control of both houses of Congress. In February, both chambers voted for the President's proposed budget cuts of more than 20%, demanding a drastic reduction in defense spending, which requires the withdrawal of US troops from Europe and a significant reduction in aid to European countries. One of the points of compromise reached afterward would be that US spending on aid to European countries would be capped at $13 billion for the next four years.

The failure of the occupation administration to restore normalcy led to disillusionment with democracy and free-market ideals, which had been articulated in the United States as the goals of European policy. It caused European citizens to look around for an alternative, which, in the eyes of many, was the Soviet Union. Lacking information about life inside the USSR and the problems of its postwar reconstruction, not knowing how vital the lend-lease program was for maintaining the stability of the Soviet economy and building the military strength of the Red Army during the war, Europeans viewed the Soviet Union as the power that had withstood Hitler and prevailed. In the 1945–1946 elections, Communist parties in Western Europe, which promoted a Soviet alternative to rotten bourgeois democracy and a chaotic market, received strong voter support. In Italy, the Communists received 19%, Finland 24%, and France 26% of the vote. Together with the Socialists, the left electorate reached 39% in Italy and 47% in France. Given a little more time, the leftist forces could have gained control of governments.

The combination of these threats (to which should be added the Soviet Union's increased pressure on Turkey and Greece, as discussed below) pushed the State Department to develop a plan to rebuild Europe, which would involve Germany. Decisions on the proportions of American money to be distributed among countries would be left to European politicians.

Although Germany was defeated and lying in ruins in 1945, the fear of a potential new war that this country could unleash in the future was firmly in the minds of European politicians. In March 1947, France and Great Britain signed the Dunkirk Treaty of Alliance and Mutual Assistance in case of a possible attack by Germany or the Soviet Union. In March 1948, the Benelux countries joined this alliance, and it received the name of the Brussels Treaty Organization, which was gradually supplanted by another name—the Western Union.[4]

The split of Europe into two camps was becoming increasingly visible, and the coup d'état in Czechoslovakia in February 1948 may have been the point of no return—it provoked the United States to begin negotiations for a broader military alliance that could include North America. These negotiations resulted in the signing of the North Atlantic Treaty on April 4, 1949, by the member countries of the Western Alliance and the United States, Canada, Portugal, Italy, Norway, Denmark, and Iceland.

The euphoria of victory in the Cold War and the disappearance of a fundamental adversary after the collapse of the Soviet Union created the illusion of the end of history, of system-driven rivalry and its attendant fears. Unsure of

[4] 1954, the Brussels Treaty Organization was transformed into the Western European Union.

Russia's democratic prospects, US policymakers feared an aggressive "Russian bear" more than a failed transition. The instability of the democratic institutions under construction in Russia, political conflicts between former allies in the struggle for power in Moscow, Yeltsin's refusal to establish his own political party, and his break with the democratic movement fueled predictions about the rise to power of Rutskoi (1992), Zhirinovsky (1993), the Communists (1995), and prophecies about the inevitable restoration of the ghost of the Soviet Union and the resumption of military and political confrontation. In such a situation, financial support to Russia seemed too risky.

In contrast, the scenario of a failed Russian transformation received little serious consideration, primarily since the logic of Russia's transformation differed little from that of Eastern Europe, leading to the conclusion that Russia was moving in the right direction. The possibility that painful reforms might drive Russian voters away from democratic parties was not seen as a direct threat to American interests. It was offset by the belief that rising living standards would inevitably ensure the victory of democracy in Russia. The rapid restoration of anti-Western, anti-American sentiment in the Russian military and political elite under the influence of NATO's assertive expansion and disdain for arguments that questioned the expediency of this process was also not seen as a threat—the belief that Bill and Boris's relationship and Bill's ability to persuade Boris to make a decision favorable to the United States were considered ample reassurance.

Subsequent events have shown that this balance of fears was inadequate—in Russia, the threats that American politicians dismissed as pesky flies were realized.

Lesson 2: Clarity of Purpose

May 8–9, 1945. The Second World War in Europe ended.

On March 12, 1947, US President Harry Truman delivered a speech to Congress in which he formulated the basic provisions of American foreign policy, known as the Truman Doctrine. The United States was not satisfied with the fact that the Soviet Union was interpreting the Yalta agreements rather broadly and freely and was creating authoritarian regimes under its control in the countries of Eastern Europe. In addition, in Turkey and Greece, which under the Yalta agreements were to be included in Britain's sphere of influence, the Soviet Union supported armed guerrilla warfare aimed at overthrowing legitimate governments. The Truman Doctrine provided for the implementation of a policy of containment of the Soviet Union and initiated the active use of economic and military support in achieving the goals of US foreign policy: speaking in Congress, the President announced financial assistance to Greece and Turkey, and the dispatch of military and civilian personnel at the request of the governments of these countries "*to assist in meeting the challenges of reconstruction.*"

Three months later, on June 5, George Marshall gave a speech at Harvard University in which he outlined the reasons that prompted the administration to launch an extensive program of support for the reconstruction of postwar Europe and the goals of this program, later called the Marshall Plan:

> *The breakdown of the business structure of Europe during the war was complete. Recovery has been seriously retarded by the fact that 2 years after the close of hostilities a peace settlement with Germany and Austria has not been agreed upon. But even given a more prompt solution of these difficult problems the rehabilitation of the economic structure of Europe quite evidently will require a much longer time and greater effort than had been foreseen…*
>
> *The truth of the matter is that Europe's requirements for the next 3 or 4 years of foreign food and other essential products - principally from America - are so much greater than her present ability to pay that she must have substantial additional help or face economic, social, and political deterioration of a very grave character. The remedy lies in breaking the vicious circle and restoring the confidence of the European people in the economic future of their own countries and of Europe as a whole…*
>
> *It is logical that the United States should do whatever it is able to do to assist in the return of normal economic health in the world, without which there can be no political stability and no assured peace. Our policy … purpose should be the revival of a working economy in the world so as to permit the emergence of political and social conditions in which free institutions can exist.*[5]

Less than a year later, on April 3, 1948, the US Congress passed, and President Truman signed, the Economic Cooperation Act,[6] which spelled out the goals of US policy in support of Western Europe: 1) "to promote industrial and agricultural production in member countries; 2) to promote the restoration or maintenance of stability in European currencies, budgets, and finances; and 3) to facilitate and stimulate the growth of international trade of member countries with each other and with other countries by appropriate measures, including reduction of barriers which may hamper such trade."

The words Marshall used to describe the situation in Europe two years after the end of the war could well apply to the situation in the Russian economy

[5] The Marshall Plan Speech. https://www.marshallfoundation.org/the-marshall-plan/speech.

[6] Economic Cooperation Act of 1948. https://www.marshallfoundation.org/wp-content/uploads/2014/06/Foreign_Assistance_Act_of_1948.pdf.

after the collapse of the Soviet Union. The goals that Marshall outlined could have been used to describe the goals of US policy to support Russian reforms. They could have been, but they were not. Bush did not utter these words; these words were not uttered by Bill, who was repeatedly asked by his advisors throughout 1994 to give a speech that would have defined the goals and instruments of US policy toward Russia.[7]

No one ever uttered these words, nor explained US policy toward Russia.

Lesson 3: Size Matters

On April 3, 1948, President Truman signed the Economic Recovery Act, which allocated $13.3 billion to the Marshall Plan over four years. This amount exceeded one-third of US federal budget expenditures in 1947 and was equivalent to 5% of US GDP that year. The factual US aid to European countries was almost twice as much: in addition to Marshall Plan spending, the United States spent an additional $10.5 billion over the same time on programs to strengthen the security of NATO member countries.[8]

US federal spending averaged just over $1.2 trillion in 1992–1995, and America's GDP averaged just under $7 trillion in 1993–1994.

In 1992–1995, the United States donated $5.4 billion in aid to 12 countries of the former Soviet Union,[9] of which just over 28% was humanitarian aid; the rest was provided through various technical assistance programs. In addition, over the years, Russia received from the US $1.3 billion in Nunn-Lugar Initiative assistance for its nuclear disarmament program. The US technical assistance programs did not support the Russian budget financially; the bulk of it went to pay for the services of US consultants, whose low efficiency angered even US politicians. Technical assistance in the Marshall Plan amounted to $31 million over four years, i.e., less than 0.25% of the total expenditures.

In addition to grant aid, in 1992–1995, the United States provided 12 post-Soviet countries with $6.16 billion in loans, more than half of all dedicated resources. The share of loans in the Marshall Plan amounted to 11.2%.

---

[7] WCPL&M. PR and the Legislative Strategy for the New Independent States (NIS). Memorandum for Anthony Lake from Tara Sorenshine and Bill Danvers. April 7, 1994.

[8] Harry Bayard Price. The Marshall Plan and Its Meaning. Cornell University Press, 1955, p. 162.

[9] Assistance to the three Baltic states was provided under separate programs. In 1992–1994, the United States did not separately account for post-Soviet countries; Russia roughly accounted for 60 percent of aid provided in those years.

All aid programs to post-Soviet countries over four years totaled US $13.3 billion—exactly as much as the Marshall Plan cost (ironically!). Of course, one dollar in 1948–1950 is not the same as one in 1994, and there is probably no adequate conversion formula for all cases. If consumer price inflation is considered, the cost of aid to the post-Soviet countries was six times less than that of the Marshall Plan. If we recalculate these amounts as a share of GDP, the difference is 25 times; if we compare them as a share of budget expenditures, the difference is 33 times.

In 1980–1990, the average annual US military expenditures amounted to 6.1% of GDP; in 1992–1995, their average level fell to 4.4% of GDP. That is, the cumulative "peace dividend" for the US budget amounted to $476 billion in these four years.

During the post-Putin transformation, Russia will not need financial assistance from other countries. However, this does not mean that the topic of the size of aid can be forgotten. The post-Putin transformation will be aided by removing sanctions restrictions and speeding up decision-making regarding Russia's return to participation in international organizations and forums. Practice shows that sanctions can be imposed very quickly and lifted very slowly. The history of the Jackson-Vanik amendment is a vivid example of this. When the transformation in Russia begins, it will suddenly appear that there are no rules and procedures for lifting sanctions; there will undoubtedly be many arguments that sanctions should be lifted very slowly and in small increments. To many, such a position will seem justified and expedient, but in hindsight, it would be a mistake.

"Think bigger! Think bigger!"—Clinton demanded of his aides on March 18, 1993, as he prepared for his first meeting with Yeltsin in Vancouver. At that moment, the US President had a package of aid to Russia totaling $1 billion on his desk. Five days later, the President's team was able to increase it to $1.6 billion, and the President was satisfied.[10]

Lesson 4: One-Stop Shop or Know Your Customer

"It would be neither fitting nor efficacious for this Government to undertake to draw up unilaterally a program designed to place Europe on its feet economically. This is the business of the Europeans. The initiative, I think, must come from Europe. The role of this country should consist of friendly aid in the drafting of a European program and of later support of such a program so far as it may be

[10] Strobe Talbott. The Russia Hand. New York: Random House, 2002, pp. 53, 58.

practical for us to do so. The program should be a joint one, agreed to by a number of, if not all European nations," said Marshall, speaking at Harvard in June 1947.

On July 12 of that year, the foreign ministers of 16 European countries met in Paris to agree on a unified plan for the continent's economic recovery and then to send a consolidated request for US assistance. Twenty-two countries, including the Soviet Union, were invited to participate in the conference, but, by Stalin's decision, no Eastern European country took part. Under pressure from the United States, which had initiated the conference but did not participate, West Germany and Austria were equal participants in the discussion—by this time, few in Washington had doubts that Europe's economic recovery was possible without Germany. The German economy was closely intertwined with the economies of other countries on the continent. Before the war, European countries accounted for 60% of German imports and three-quarters of exports. After the war, exporting goods from Germany became impossible—all German goods were confiscated at the border because the importing countries held unpaid German debt.

On September 25, British Foreign Secretary Bevin handed Secretary of State Marshall the 690-page final report of the Paris Conference, which asked for $19.3 billion in aid. The report was loose, vague in places, and drifted into a discussion of minor details, but it contained the essential point—Europeans' willingness to act together and an agreement that "*the German economy should become part of the European economy, contributing to a general improvement in living standards.*"[11]

On April 3, 1948, President Truman signed the Postwar Reconstruction Act, which approved the Marshall Plan and created a unique agency, the Economic Cooperation Administration (ECA), to administer the plan. The ECA reported to the State Department and the Commerce Department but had full decision-making authority over the use of appropriated funds. The ECA, which received, discussed, approved, or rejected applications from national agencies, had offices in all countries that became recipients of US aid. The Marshall Plan did not provide for the allocation of money to governments; it financed the import of American goods needed to feed the population, provide enterprises with necessary raw materials or components, and implement urgent investment projects.

Drawing up aid programs for Russia (and other CIS countries) was fundamentally different. Because many believed that any cash aid to Russia would simply vanish, Russia did not receive any resources for distribution. It was practically excluded from the process of deciding what money would be spent

[11] Benn Steil. The Marshall Plan. At the Dawn of the Cold War. Simon & Schuster. 2018. P. 174.

and for what purposes within the framework of technical assistance. Moreover, Washington made decisions about adopting programs, their objectives, funding levels, and implementation timelines without giving any authority to those working in Russia.

A dozen and a half US government agencies devised their own assistance programs, which were partly based on requests from Russian officials, but mostly born in the minds of American experts, who came to Russia to decide what the country lacked. Since virtually all technical assistance programs involved hiring American consultants or contractors, whose services were paid for at very high rates, the experts from Moscow favored designing programs that guaranteed them roles. The fact that these programs would not benefit Russia was of little concern to anyone. At Clinton's behest, the bulk of the programs were directed to the non-state sector, and the Russian officials could not expect any helpful effect from them. When aid programs were directed to state structures, the recipients quickly realized their low effectiveness and quickly lost interest in continuing them: people who knew little about the country, its economy, and legislation came to Russia for a few weeks, or at best, months, took up extensive time from local officials, and sent back their report from Washington a few months later containing outdated recommendations—life in Russia was changing rapidly. Then the next time, within the framework of the same program, other experts might come, and everything would start all over again.

This arrangement quickly revealed its flaws.[12] Each agency set its own strategy and objectives for assistance programs. Still, no one was responsible for ensuring that agency programs were coordinated with one another and avoided duplication. Projects started slowly—it took about a year after congressional appropriation before contractors began work. Legislative decisions to allocate aid contained many conditions, precedents, or constraints that required Russia to take preliminary actions that could delay or stop the program altogether. Congress could decide to cut spending or reallocate it at any moment between areas or recipients, which inevitably slowed down all processes. Spending decisions required many interagency approvals, which rarely happen quickly in Washington.

The creation of the position of CIS aid coordinator helped only marginally—by the summer of 1994, it was possible to approve country-specific aid strategies—but his authority did not allow him to intervene in the content of programs, but only to reallocate resources between programs. By the end of

[12] The Former Soviet Union and US Foreign Aid: Implementing the Assistance Program, 1992–1994. January 18, 1995. CRS report 95–170.

1994, it was clear Thomas Simons, who had been appointed to this position, could not materially improve the aid architecture. On the one hand, this was due to his personal qualities; on the other hand, the coordinator's standing was relatively low; the heads of the agencies that implemented aid programs quite easily bypassed him and sought to change decisions contrary to his position. In April 1995, the coordinator received the status of special advisor to the President, and Richard Morningstar was appointed to this position, but there were no fundamental changes. In any case, by then, aid flows were already shrinking fast.

If and when a roadmap for Russia emerges and begins to be implemented, the key success factor will be the ability of both sides to fulfill their commitments on time and in full. Russia is likely to be able to ensure this. If the country's new leaders undertake such a project, they presumably understand the potential gains from a change in relations with the West and will seek to realize them. On the other hand, it is unlikely that Russia's organized bureaucracy will stop following the orders of the country's top officials.

However, whether the West can meet its commitments is far from certain. The The West has little experience lifting sanctions on specific countries: South Africa in 1994, four years after political liberalization began and after Nelson Mandela won the presidential election, and Iran in 2015 after the nuclear agreement. However, three years after the Iran agreement, the United States withdrew the pact and reinstated sanctions on Iran.

The likelihood that the West will become mired in EU-style arguments—about whether it is too early to ease pressure on Russia, whether Russia has done too little, and what safeguards are needed against another "Putin"—is high. And if that possibility is realized, there is a risk that the window of opportunity may slam shut altogether.

Lesson 5: Window of Opportunity

This term is widely used in politics when discussing major reforms. What seemed impossible yesterday becomes possible today, and conversely, what was very easy yesterday suddenly starts to stall today. Each time, we later identify the factors that made today's achievements possible—or the mis-steps that turned yesterday's easy tasks into today's impossibilities. But this understanding and realization come later.

We can only hypothesize how history might have unfolded had socialist-communist coalitions taken power in postwar Italy or France. This did not seem impossible in 1946–1947 when Europe was freezing in winter and surviving solely on aid from America.

We can only hypothesize about how history would have turned out had North Korea, backed by China and with the tacit approval of the Soviet Union, not started the Korean War, which gave huge military orders to the Japanese economy and paved the way for a military alliance between the two countries.

We can only hypothesize about how history would have turned out if, in May 1990, the Politburo had not ordered Ivan Polozkov to withdraw his candidacy in the third round of voting to elect the Chairman of the Supreme Soviet of the RSFSR. He had a high chance of beating Yeltsin—the Congress of People's Deputies composition was quite conservative. However, Alexander Vlasov, chosen by the Politburo to replace Polozkov, lost, and Yeltsin became the legal leader of Russia. This opened the way for a power struggle with Gorbachev, which Yeltsin won largely thanks to the putsch in August 1991.

In late October 1991, Yeltsin won—without resistance—unlimited authority from the Congress of People's Deputies to run economic policy. The President's decrees became tantamount to laws, and the deputies agreed that the President would simultaneously head the government. In another month and a half, the Soviet Union would disappear, and the window of opportunity for reforms would open wide. Would it be wide and opened for a long time?

At that very moment, Chairman of the Supreme Soviet Ruslan Khasbulatov and Vice President Alexander Rutskoi felt deprived of power and began to fight Yeltsin. Already in the spring of 1992, they were able to block many of the government's reform proposals.

No one knows the future. No one can predict what will follow Vladimir Putin's departure from power. We can only guess which political forces will fight for control in the country, how this struggle will end, and what course Russia will take after the turbulent transition period is over. And how long it will last?

One can recall that after Stalin, it took Khrushchev three years to consolidate power and subdue the party and state top brass of the Soviet Union. Two and a half years separated Brezhnev's death from Gorbachev's ascent to the Kremlin, and another two years passed before "perestroika" and "glasnost" became watchwords of reform.

In the United States, it has become almost the norm that the party of the President who wins the elections for the first time simultaneously gains control over both houses of Congress but loses it in the following intermediate elections. Also, biennial House elections intensify partisan conflict and, from the spring of each mid-term year, make even modest bills hard to pass from the spring of the mid-term year—about 15 months into a presidency.

In a good scenario of the future, when Russia after Putin turns towards the restoration of democratic principles of state building (it is not the purpose of this book to examine bad scenarios, in which Russia falls into even more severe authoritarianism or dictatorship), the end of the transition period is likely to be the first parliamentary elections, which will be held after the revision of electoral legislation and changes in the practices of political life.

Legislation might be revised quickly; bans on forming and funding parties could be lifted within months; repressive laws depriving several million Russians of the right to be elected could be scrapped as well. An amnesty can be granted to political prisoners, and rules granting political forces national-TV access can be drafted. But it will take at least two years for the new political forces to prepare for the elections—to build organizations, secure funding, and reach voters. Thus the transition will likely last two to three years, a window during which new leaders can still make hard choices with few constraints.

Probably, we should not expect that the first free elections in post-Putin Russia will result in an absolute majority in the State Duma, which will allow nominating a candidate for the post of the head of the government, and, consequently, Russia will face the need to form a coalition. If the coalition is stable, we can talk about the end of the turbulent period: the balanced government will determine its political line and will consistently pursue it. If the coalition proves unstable, turbulence will persist—but of a different kind: coalition fragility will breed policy instability, with ad hoc majorities deciding most issues, as it happened in 1992–1995.

Lesson 6: Rigidity of Requirements

Anyone familiar with the past century will recall that postwar Germany and Japan were governed by Allied occupation authorities. Have you forgotten that the basic laws based on which postwar Japan was built were prepared or at least passed through the rigid filter of MacArthur and his team? Have you forgotten that although the decision to create West Germany was taken in 1949, the Allied administrations had considerable control over the political life of the country until 1955, when the General Treaty signed three years earlier came into force? Only then Germany, having been given full freedom to conduct its domestic and foreign policy, including the creation of its army, gave the three countries a complete free hand in stationing their troops on its territory and pledged not to enter into international agreements prejudicial to their interests.

Of course, this cannot be forgotten, and the role of the occupation administrations in Germany and Japan, whose rigid demands were at times prohibitive, cannot be minimized. But the United States made no less stringent demands on its allies.

When Latin American countries in 1940 faced the closure of their exports to Europe, which after the German occupation could not pay for imported goods, the United States provided them with financial aid. Still, it conditioned its use solely on imports from the United States.

By the beginning of the World War II, Great Britain's gold and dollars reserve of dollars totaled $4.5 billion (remember, this was the era of the gold standard when the country had to repay the negative balance in bilateral trade in gold). Officials believed that this would be enough for three years of war, but events quickly dashed these hopes. Import requirements were higher, but the Roosevelt administration required that the French and British governments, when placing orders for military products in the United States, invest in expanding the capacity of American companies, which allowed, in addition, to circumvent the restrictions imposed by the law of neutrality. By February 1940, France and Britain had spent more on investment than on arms purchases (also because US arms production was very low and companies did not want to increase capacity at their own expense).[13]

By the end of 1940, Britain had not only used up almost all its reserves, but it had signed contracts with US companies to buy and invest about $10 billion without any way to pay for them. The US Treasury became aware of the problem as early as May 1940, but there was no good solution. The Neutrality Act, reaffirmed in September 1939, did not allow loans or financial aid to Great Britain; it was necessary either to abandon this country to its fate or to accept that contracts would continue to be concluded with the full understanding that there was nothing to pay for them. Of course, officials tried to come up with various ways to scoop the barrel to the bottom. They offered a lot of things! Pay in advance for importing whisky from Great Britain for 10 years. Sell all the wool stock held in Australia and South Africa so that the money received could be deposited in an account in the British Treasury. Britain was forced to sell a stake in the Viscose Corporation, and the sale of the tin and rubber companies in Malaysia was stopped only after it became clear to American officials that, together with the dividends from these companies, they would have to assume full responsibility for the management of Malaysia.[14]

---

[13] Hancock W.K., Cowing M.M. British War Economy. London, 1949, p. 118.

[14] Ibid, pp. 232–234.

In May 1940, when France was close to surrender, and the fall of Great Britain, according to the US ambassador to that country Joseph Kennedy, was inevitable, President Roosevelt proposed to Prime Minister Churchill leasing military bases in the Caribbean islands. Churchill insisted that this was only possible in exchange for something substantial, e.g., destroyers. Roosevelt refused, but in late August, when Churchill frightened the US President by saying that if Britain fell, the islands, along with the bases, would be controlled by Germany, and this would pose a direct threat to America, he decided to give Britain 50 old destroyers in exchange for the lease of the bases for 99 years.

In the spring of 1941, American securities worth $1.5 billion held by British citizens and companies were transferred by government decision and sold to pay obligations to American companies.

On March 11, 1941, President Roosevelt signed the law creating the lend-lease program. By this point, Britain's foreign exchange reserve was $12 million.[15]

In December 1948, Paul Hoffmann, head of the Economic Cooperation Administration, the body that oversaw the use of Marshall Plan funds, met with Stafford Cripps, British Chancellor of the Exchequer and Chairman of the Organization for European Economic Cooperation, a body of US aid recipients that was working out the distribution of funds among the countries. Hoffmann demanded that Cripps agree to halve customs tariffs on trade between European countries by February so that President Truman's administration could tell Congress, when it debated the budget for the next fiscal year, that Europe was moving in a coordinated direction. Hoffmann refused to finalize the negotiations until he got what he wanted. At three o'clock in the morning, Cripps surrendered.[16]

Lesson 7: Historical Memory

The Burden of Duty

History does not repeat itself, but it often poses the same questions to policymakers and experts, the workable and unworkable answers to which can be

[15] William Adams Brown, Jr. and Redvers Opie. American Foreign Assistance. The Brookings Institution, 1953, p. 30.

[16] Benn Steil. The Marshall Plan. At the Dawn of the Cold War. Simon & Schuster. 2018. P. 306.

found in the past. Since the mid-1980s, Georgetown University's Institute for the Study of Diplomacy (ISD) has used the case study method to analyze and teach international relations. The ISD library has more than 250 cases from US diplomatic history. However, because the first of these cases dates from the 1950s, it is difficult for us to assess how deeply US diplomats studied European history in the first half of the twentieth century.

According to the Treaty of Versailles, which summarized the results of World War I and was signed in June 1919, Germany and its allies were obliged to pay substantial contributions to the victorious countries. The Reparations Commission completed its work in May 1921, when an agreement was signed in London, according to which Germany was to unconditionally pay 50 billion gold marks ($12.5 billion US dollars, a little less than 19 thousand tons of gold). Germany's payments were to be $500 million a year plus the value of 26% of German exports which was equal to 50% of the revenues or 20% of the Weimar Republic's budget expenditures, which was an "intolerable burden" on the public finances.[17]

In the first half of 1921, the US dollar one US dollar bought 90 German marks. In November 1923, its value rose to 4210.5 billion marks; the German hyperinflation of 1923 has been described in detail in economic literature and in fiction. Of course, it cannot be explained only by the reparation payments, but it is beyond doubt that they contributed significantly to the destruction of the German financial system.

In October 1923, the victorious countries recognized that further pressure on Germany could lead to unpredictable social and political consequences, and the reparations agreement was replaced by the Dawes Plan, which provided for external loans to Germany, from which the country was able to pay the bulk of the reparations. From 1918 until the end of 1932, when the Lausanne conference decided to end reparations payments, Germany paid a total of just under $21 billion, having received after the adoption of the Dawes Plan loans totaling, according to various estimates, from $27 to $38 billion. Mantoux estimated that Germany spent between 2% and 2.5% of GNP on reparations after adopting the Dawes Plan. On January 30, 1933, Adolf Hitler became German Chancellor. 2405 days later, World War II began.

After the collapse of the Soviet Union, Russia assumed obligations on its foreign debt, which amounted to about $110 billion. Although creditors granted regular deferrals of principal and a significant portion of interest

[17] Niall Ferguson. The Balance of Payments Question: Versailles and After (Publications of the German Historical Institute). The Treaty of Versailles: A Reassessment after 75 Years. Edited by Manfred F. Boemeke, Gerald D. Feldman, Elisabeth Glaser. Cambridge University Press, 1998, p. 425.

payments, Russia had to make substantial payments in favor of the creditors. In 1992, payments on foreign debt amounted to at least 40% of revenues and at least 30% of expenditures of the republican budget[18]; in 1993, these payments amounted to 20% and 14%, respectively.

One Is Not a Warrior in the Field

Soon after the Marshall Plan was launched, a significant obstacle to Western Europe's economic recovery was discovered: a general shortage of dollars. The currencies of the war-torn countries were non-convertible, and economic recovery required the restoration of trade between the countries. However, international payments were in dollars, and exports to America were at a minimum.

Proceeding from the set goals—development of international trade and restoration of convertibility of national currencies—the United States supported the project of creation of a system of clearing settlements between countries, which was called the European Payments Union (EPU). Within the framework of the EPU, prices for goods produced in European countries were fixed in a special unit of account, which had a gold content. The Bank for International Settlements kept records of mutual deliveries between the countries and summarized bilateral trade at the end of each month. But even after that, the member countries were not required to repay the resulting balance in dollars or gold—each country had its limit, which was financed from the capital of the EPU, formed at the expense of the US contribution. Suppose a country cannot normalize its trade balance. In that case, it can apply for loans from the IMF or initiate negotiations on the devaluation of the national currency to overcome the structural deficit.

As the European economy recovered and trade between countries expanded, central banks began lending to each other in national currencies, reducing the need for dollars and further encouraging economic cooperation. The EPU ceased to exist in 1958 when all Western European countries restored the convertibility of their currencies.

The economies of the Soviet bloc countries were highly integrated. The long-standing existence of two isolated economic systems and the

[18] The authors' estimates are based on data from the Ministry of Finance of Russia and the Bank of Russia and various authors' publications. There are no quarterly reports on Russia's budget execution and foreign debt payments in 1992, and the multiplicity of exchange rates in the first half of 1992 and the rapid devaluation of the ruble in the second half of that year make any estimates very approximate. The 1993 estimate is based on the hypothesis of uniform external debt payments during the year.

technological lag between the East and the West led to the fact that by the time the Iron Curtain fell, a substantial part of the products of Eastern Europe and the Soviet Union could not compete in world markets. The problem was exacerbated by the fact that the currencies of the former socialist countries were non-convertible, and settlements between them were made in an artificial currency called the "transferable ruble," the exchange rate pegged to the dollar. (Very similar to the EPU, isn't it?)

At the G7 meetings in 1990 and 1991, Kohl tried to draw the attention of his colleagues to the problem of a sharp decline in the Soviet economy's demand for the products of Eastern European countries, which worsened their economic situation and proposed the creation of a unique mechanism to support inter-country trade, but the only one who supported him was EU Commission's Vice President Frans Andriessen.[19] However, the leaders of Eastern European countries were not eager to maintain economic ties with their former patron and sought to distance themselves from him as much as possible.

The situation repeated itself in 1992 when the Soviet Union collapsed: the economies of the former Soviet republics were much more tightly integrated, and the complicated processes of economic transformation were sometimes overlaid by political factors, such as the displacement from Central Asia of the Russian-speaking population, which constituted a significant part of industrial employment. The leaders of the post-Soviet countries were reluctant to coordinate the economic policies of their governments, which caused different speeds and depths of transformation. The logical step in this situation was to introduce national currencies as soon as possible. Still, IMF experts were on the side of the Bank of Russia, which opposed this, fearing a more profound economic decline. However, having said "A," the IMF did not say "B" and did not propose to create a version of the EPU, not to mention credit support for inter-country trade in the post-Soviet space.

As a result, until the end of June 1993, there were 12 independent states in the former Soviet Union that used a single currency and whose central banks were independent of each other in conducting monetary policy. The Bank of Russia estimates that in the second half of 1992, the 11 post-Soviet countries purchased goods from Russia through ruble emission to the amount of about 4% of Russia's annual GDP, and in the first half of 1993—another 3% of Russia's GDP. This accounted for about 20% of the increase in the Bank of Russia's domestic assets during this time, i.e., 20% of its inflation Russia imported from the CIS countries.

[19] GB M&T. First Plenary Session, London Economic Summit. July 16, 1991.

Aid or Credit?

Total US aid to the Soviet Union and CIS countries in 1991–1995 amounted to $14.8 billion, of which almost 40% came from grain- and food-loan guarantees. The guarantees were never called, and their real impact was only the interest-rate differential, which is difficult to estimate since, at that time, the recipient countries could hardly count on attracting loans on market terms. On the other hand, these loans served as an important tool to support the competitiveness of American farmers in the global food market, guaranteeing them sales of their products. $2.4 billion (16.3% of the total) came from Eximbank loans for US equipment and technology plus OPIC investments. The remaining 45% of aid programs were grants, almost half of which was Nunn-Lugar money. The bulk of the grants, $5.4 billion (36.5% of the total support to Russia), went to technical assistance programs and were spent to pay US consultants.

A Russian proverb says that you should not look a gift horse in the mouth. And, of course, we cannot say that there was no US support or that it was imperceptible. In 1991–1993, US grain loans and humanitarian, food, and medical aid (which accounted for slightly more than 10% of the support programs) were crucial in averting famine across the post-Soviet space. However, at the same time, comparing the support programs for the CIS countries with the way the US supported the countries of Western Europe under the Marshall Plan, one can see fundamental differences in the assistance, which largely accounted for the difference in the outcome.

, gratuitous, irrevocable, and free aid. With these funds, European countries could buy raw materials, components, and equipment in the United States, which they needed to establish normal production processes and pay for their transportation across the ocean. Some of the grants were conditional and were used to support the work of the EPU, which stimulated intra-European trade.

US grants did not give firms free American goods; they still paid full price in local currency. European governments could use those *counterpart funds* at their own discretion, coordinating projects with the Economic Cooperation Administration. Germany channeled funds into investment—chiefly energy and transport infrastructure. France emphasized the modernization of heavy industries, mainly steel production, and support for infrastructure projects. For the Netherlands, repairing dams and other waterworks was critical, so most counterpart funds went there. For the UK, the priority was to rebuild the financial sector due to the continuation of the colonial empire, which required maintaining the stability of the pound sterling and the soundness of the banks and reducing public debt.

Do It Yourself!

The Marshall Plan Act created a unique US government agency responsible for analyzing the state of the European economies and government requests for the use of US aid and for accounting and control of allocated funds. The April 3, 1948, law created the ECA; within two weeks it had 30 staff, three weeks later 135, and by late July 741. Overall, the ECA headquarters in Washington employed 770 people, the Paris office coordinated the country offices employing 290 people, and more than 1100 others worked in European countries.[20]

At the G7 meeting, a proposal was discussed to create a coordinating body that would include representatives of the sponsor countries to analyze the situation in the post-Soviet space and make recommendations to the leaders of the nations. This idea was categorically rejected by the Treasury Secretary Brady[21], and at subsequent G7 meetings, it was no longer discussed.

In April 1992, Bush, announcing a $24 billion package of support for Russian reforms, said that international financial organizations—the IMF and the World Bank—would coordinate aid to Russia. This decision, which no one could argue with, caught IMF and World Bank leaders off guard—no one had consulted them. Moreover, Russia was not a member of these organizations, and any financial support could only be provided to full members. The Fund and the Bank had no experts in the economics of the Soviet Union, and the newly created departments were staffed with people who knew nothing about their subject matter.

There is a clear division of responsibilities between the IMF and the World Bank: the Fund is responsible for macroeconomic (monetary and budgetary) policy issues, while the Bank deals with structural reforms related to individual sectors or territories. In a "normal" situation, when a recipient country is engaged in one or the other task, the coordination between the two organizations should not be very tight. Still, in the first months and years of Russian reforms, when the situation in the country and in the economy was changing rapidly, differences in business culture and principles of planning credit programs created a lot of friction.

But the most serious disadvantage of this organization of support for Russian reforms was that even the top officials of the Fund and the Bank could not reach the White House in their communications: the limit of their

[20] Herbert A. Simon Birth of an Organization: The Economic Cooperation Administration. Public Administration Review. 1953. vol 13. No 4 (Autumn), pp. 227–236.

[21] GB M&T. Memorandum of Conversation. Second Plenary, London Economic Summit. July 16, 1991.

reach was the Deputy Secretary of the US Treasury, so when the US administration discussed policy toward Russia, the position and opinion of these organizations largely sidelined. The Fund and the Bank were seen as technical executors on a not very wide range of issues, but at the same time, in the eyes of the general public, they were held responsible for the success or failure of Russian reforms.

In general, the IMF's Second European Department, which dealt with all 15 countries that emerged from the ruins of the Soviet Union, employed 120–130 people, half of whom specialized in Russia. They were supported by 3–4 experts from functional departments of the Fund, bringing the Fund's "Russia team" to roughly 150 staff.

Why Today?

To repeat the Russian proverb: "Prepare your sleds in summer." Today, it is impossible to imagine an open or even secret discussion with the participation of representatives of Russian elites about how Russia will live after Putin—the fear of becoming a "traitor" in the eyes of the authoritarian leader is so great that the only desire is to live, to live to see him go.

But eventually Putin will exit political life and lose all sway over Russian decisions. No one knows when this will happen, but it will happen for sure, and this is a fundamental difference from the situation in 1991, when, until the very last moment, it seemed that the Soviet Union could be preserved in one form or another.

It is possible that even after Putin's departure, Russia will want to continue its hybrid war with the West, as the Cold War continued after Stalin's death, Khrushchev's ouster, Brezhnev's death, and Gorbachev's arrival. But undoubtedly, at some point, there will be people at the helm of power in Moscow for whom the scenario of normalizing relations with the West will be acceptable or even desirable—the long-term losses to Russia from the continuation of Putin's policy are too obvious, and their severity will only grow with time.

At this moment, history will offer the West another chance to emerge from the dangerous political-military confrontation in Europe, a chance to turn Russia from an adversary into an ally. At that moment, Western policymakers will face questions that will strongly resemble those their predecessors agonized over in the early 1990s: How much credence can be given to the words coming out of Moscow? Do the new leaders have a firm grip on power, or can conservatives remove them at any moment? Does Russia's military power still pose a threat to the life of the entire planet, and will the softening of Western policy toward Russia be used by the "Russian bear" to lick its wounds and prepare for new aggression? Undoubtedly, these questions will be fair and reasonable, but they cannot be brushed aside. Any hint of engaging Moscow will draw criticism from many quarters, and any steps toward Moscow will require considerable political courage.

Such courage was shown after the end of World War II in relation to the question of Germany's and Japan's future. Today, we know very well how justified that risk was, how effective economic aid to the two countries was from all points of view, and how important a role in stabilizing the world was played by including the two countries in the military and political structures of the West.

Such courage was absent in the early 1990s toward Russia, when leaders took the path of least resistance, recognizing that all risks were justified and deeming large-scale aid to a former adversary undesirable. The naïve belief that a weakened Russia would never recover and that the experience of German resentment in the 1930s could not be repeated 80 years later allowed short-term interests to prevail. Still, it led to the gravest strategic challenges facing the next generation of Western policymakers.

Today, it seems to everyone that the discussion of the problem of "the return of Russia" should be postponed until after Putin is gone, after Russia repents and demonstrates to the world that it has changed. History shows political windows open unexpectedly and close sooner than one would hope. Russia's post-Putin transformation will take an uncharted, winding path, on which the Russian politicians who will tackle this task will face many complex problems, and of course, they will need help and support. For me, the main motivation for writing this book was to encourage Western politicians and experts to develop a roadmap that would outline the path of Russia's return to the civilized world.

This roadmap should not be made a secret; on the contrary, it should be publicly discussed and presented. The emergence of such a document will show Russian elites and society the opportunities for the country, what it will cost, and how quickly it will be necessary to transform the political system. During his 25 years in office, Vladimir Putin has been unable to present his vision of Russia's future, unable to explain in what direction the country will develop and how the quality of life of Russian citizens will change. He will unlikely be able to present this in his remaining years in power. As he ages, he will have no desire to discuss what will come after him: such discussions will remind him that his life term is ending, and he must prepare for the inevitable.

What should the roadmap contain? On the part of Russia, first of all, the beginning of a political dialog with Ukraine on overcoming the consequences of the war of aggression; the abolition of repressive laws that criminalize not only political activity but also freedom of speech; the return of the electoral system to the situation of the late 1990s; and the creation of a round table with the participation of the main political forces, including Russian politicians in forced emigration, whose task will be to destroy Putin's political system and hold free elections in 18–36 months.

It takes two to tango, and the roadmap should contain actions that the Western countries are committed to take: the gradual lifting of sanctions, the creation of a free trade zone between the European Union and Russia (EurAsEC), and the transformation of NATO into a political alliance of three participants (the United States, Europe, Russia) with the conclusion of a mutual defense treaty, the dissolution of the military structure of the alliance, and the creation of the armed forces of the European Union. These ideas may sound radical—even unrealistic—yet, as the saying goes, "Be realistic; demand the impossible."

Sad as it may sound, the most likely scenario for the last years of Putin's power is a continuation of the policy of tightening the screws and searching for enemies. At some moments, this policy will be pursued more intensively, prompting talk of the formation of a harsh dictatorial regime; at other moments, the iron grip will loosen, prompting talk of a mini-thaw and a transit of power. However, in any case, we should not expect an internal discussion about how we should organize Russia after Putin before he leaves. The Kremlin's propaganda machine will flood the information space with official narratives, whose disconnect from real life will gradually become more and more evident. But because the Kremlin's power machine will carefully burn out any dissent in Russia and attempt to erect an iron curtain of information, society and elites will be deprived of the opportunity to discuss the problems facing the country and agree on how they can be solved.

The Kremlin itself will create a monopoly position for the West's roadmap—of course, we should not expect this plan to be widely discussed inside Russia, but it will gradually become known to everyone who thinks about the future. Not everyone will agree, but without alternative concepts, it will be impossible to pretend it does not exist. In an ideal forecast, a new generation of Russian politicians will adopt this roadmap to form their own plan of action. Of course, some elements of the roadmap will be discarded, the realization of others will be shifted in time, and discussion will develop around others. However, in any case, the roadmap will become the basis for negotiations with the West, which will have a chance to participate actively in Russia's transformation.

It is a chance not to be missed.

Bibliography

1. Dean Acheson. Present at Creation. Norton & Company, New York, 1969.
2. Pierre Allan and Dieter Klei. Afganskiy kapkan. Pravda o sovetskom vtorzhenii. (RUS *The Afghan Trap. The Truth about the Soviet Invasion*). Moscow, Mezdunarodnye otnosheniya, 1999.
3. Graham Allison and Grigory Yavlinsky. Window of Opportunity. The Grand Bargain for Democracy in the Soviet Union. Pantheon Books, New York, 1991.
4. Ronald D. Asmus. Opening NATO's Door. How the Alliance Remade Itself for a New Era. Columbia University Press, 1983.
5. John Beal. John Foster Dulles, 1888–1959. Harper and Row, New York, 1959.
6. Michae R. Beschloss and Strobe Talbott. At the Highest Level. The inside Story of the End of the Cold War. Little, Brown and Company. 1994
7. Michael Beschloss. The Conquerors: Roosevelt, Truman and the Destruction of Hitler's Germany, 1941–1945. New York: Simon & Schuster, 2002.
8. John Morton Blum, ed, From the Morgenthau Diaries (Boston: Houghton Mifflin, 1959).
9. William Adams Brown, Jr. and Redvers Opie. American Foreign Assistance. The Brookings Institution. Washington DC, The Brookings Institution, 1953.
10. William J. Burns. The Back Channel: A Memoir of American Diplomacy and the Case for Its Renewal. Random House, 2019.
11. Chernyaev. Sovmestnyi iskhod. (RUS *Joint Exodus)*. Moscow, Rospan, 2008.
12. Jerome Cohen. Japan's Postwar Economy. Indiana University Press, 1958.
13. Timothy Colton. Yeltsin: A Life. New York, Basic Books; 2008.
14. Milovan Djilas. Conversations with Stalin. Posev, Frankfurt. 1972.
15. Ehpoha El'cina. Ocherki politicheskoj istorii. (RUS *The Yeltsin's Era. Essays on political history*). Moscow, Vagrius, 2001.

S. Aleksashenko, *Post-Cold War Russia and the Missed Opportunity for Global Stability*,
https://doi.org/10.1007/978-3-032-01380-4

16. John Emerson. The Japanese Thread. Holt, Rinehart, and Winston, New York, 1978.
17. Alexei Filatov. Budyonovskij rubezh. (RUS *Budyonovsky frontier*). Moscow, Knizhny Mir, 2020.
18. Sergey Filatov. Sovershenno nesekretno. (RUS *Absolutely unclassified)*. Moscow, Vagrius, 2000.
19. Richard Finn. Winners in Peace. University of California Press, 1992.
20. Yegor Gaidar. Dni porazhenij i pobed. (RUS *Days of defeats and victories*). Moscow, Vagrius, 1996.
21. John Gimbel. The American Occupation of Germany. Politics and the Military, 1945-1949. Stanford University Press, 1968.
22. James M. Goldgeier. Not Whether But When. Brookings Institution Press, Washington DC, 1999.
23. James M. Goldgeiger and Michael McFaul. Power and Purpose: US Policy toward Russia after the Cold War. Washington, DC. Brookings Institution Press, 2003.
24. David Halberstam. The Reckoning. William Morrow and Company, Inc. New York, 1986.
25. Daniel S. Hamilton and Kristina Spohr (eds.). Open Door: NATO and Euro-Atlantic Security After the Cold War. Washington, DC, Foreign Policy Institute/ Henry A. Kissinger Center for Global Affairs, Johns Hopkins University SAIS, 2019.
26. W.K. Hancock and M.M. Cowing. British War Economy. London, 1949.
27. Daniel Harrington. Berlin on the Brink. The Blockade, the Airlift, and the Early Cold War. University Press of Kentucky, 2012.
28. A History of Corporate Governance around the World: Family Business Groups to Professional Managers. NBER, 2005.
29. Warren Hunsberger. Japan. New Industrial Giant. American-Asian Educational Exchange, 1972.
30. Marvin Kalb. The Nixon Memo. University of Chicago Press, Chicago, 1994.
31. Ian Kershaw. To Hell and Back: Europe, 1914–1949. New York, Viking, 2015.
32. Andrei Kozyrev. The Firebird: the elusive fate of Russian democracy. A memoir. University of Pittsburgh Press, 2019.
33. Milton Leitenberg and Raymond A. Zilinskas. The Soviet Biological Weapons Program: A History. Harvard University Press, 2012.
34. Douglas MacArthur. Reminiscences. McGraw-Hill, 1964.
35. Boris Minaev. Yeltsin. (RUS) Moscow, 2010.
36. Leonid Mlechin. Evgenij Primakov. As bol'shoj politiki. (RUS *Yevgeny Primakov. Ace of Big Politics*). Moscow, Molodaya Gvardiya.
37. Harry Bayard Price. The Marshall Plan and Its Meaning. Cornell University Press, 1955.
38. George Shultz. Turmoil and Triumph: My Years as Secretary of State. Scribner's, 1993.

39. Dimitri Simes. After the Collapse: Russia Seeks Its Place as a Great Power. Simon & Schuster, 1999.
40. Benn Steil. The Marshall Plan. At the Dawn of the Cold War. Simon & Schuster, 2018.
41. Strobe Talbott. The Russia Hand. Random House/New York, 2002.
42. Tatsuro Uchino. Japan's Postwar Economy: An Insider's View of its History and Future. Kodansha International, Tokyo/New York, 1983.

9783032013798